School Libraries in a
Time of Change

D1597138

School Libraries in a Time of Change

How to Survive and Thrive

Kathleen W. Craver

LIBRARIES
UNLIMITED®

An Imprint of ABC-CLIO, LLC

Santa Barbara, California • Denver, Colorado

Library of Congress Cataloging-in-Publication Data

Names: Craver, Kathleen W., author.
Title: School libraries in a time of change : how to survive and thrive / Kathleen W. Craver.
Description: Santa Barbara, California : Libraries Unlimited, 2019. | Includes bibliographical references and index.
Identifiers: LCCN 2019008318 (print) | LCCN 2019010964 (ebook) | ISBN 9781440873096 (ebook) | ISBN 9781440873089 (paperback : acid-free paper)
Subjects: LCSH: School libraries—United States—Administration. | School libraries—United States—Forecasting. | School libraries—Information technology—United States.
Classification: LCC Z675.S3 (ebook) | LCC Z675.S3 C7584 2019 (print) | DDC 025.1/978—dc23
LC record available at https://lccn.loc.gov/2019008318

ISBN: 978-1-4408-7308-9 (paperback)
        978-1-4408-7309-6 (ebook)

23 22 21 20 19   1 2 3 4 5

This book is also available as an eBook.

Libraries Unlimited
An Imprint of ABC-CLIO, LLC

ABC-CLIO, LLC
147 Castilian Drive
Santa Barbara, California 93117
www.abc-clio.com

This book is printed on acid-free paper ∞

Manufactured in the United States of America

Contents

Acknowledgments   vii

Introduction: A Pace a Pace   ix

1   Reading the Tech Tea Leaves   1

2   Technology Trends   13

3   Economic Trends   69

4   Employment Trends   93

5   Educational Trends   121

6   Social and Behavioral Trends   153

7   Instructional Trends   181

8   Organization and Management Trends   201

9   A Summons for Survival   221

Index   229

Acknowledgments

I wish to thank my husband, Charlie, whose encouragement and editorial assistance helped this book become a reality. I gratefully acknowledge the advice and support that my editor, Sharon Coatney, gave me throughout this exciting project. I would finally like to express my appreciation to production editor, Nicole Azze; senior project manager, Jitendra Kumar; and copy editor, Lisa McCoy, for their highly professional assistance.

Introduction: A Pace a Pace

Librarians have sometimes been referred to as two-legged encyclopedias of superficial information. While many of us do seem to have an inordinate fondness for trivia, it's probably because so many of us practice our profession as generalists in public and school libraries. The questions we've been peppered with over the years can easily be scaled from trivial to essential, with numerous ones categorized as downright wacky. I am willing to bet, however, that a little frisson of fear went down the spines of many of us on February 16, 2011, when we watched former all-time *Jeopardy!* champion, Ken Jennings beaten by an IBM form of artificial intelligence embodied in the appellation Watson (Markoff). Mr. Jennings really did not have a chance, and neither would any of us. Watson had access to 200 million pages of content and contained four terabytes of memory (Kaplan 31).

Five years past with all of us busy learning and adapting to new technologies and, because it was not televised with all the hoopla it deserved, we were unaware of the next technological leap. On February 16, 2016, Lee Sedol, the top Go player in the world, was defeated by Google's AlphaGo, another form of artificial intelligence (Moyer). This win was definitely the one that should have made us sit up and take notice. Go is an ancient Chinese game where players place white or black stones, depending upon their chosen side, at the intersections of a 19×19 grid. The goal is to remove the freedom of your opponent's stones by surrounding them and have them taken from the board. The player with the most captured territory wins (McAfee and Brynjolfsson 1). Although Go is a game of strategy, professional players find it challenging to explain their moves because they are intuitive in nature. Unlike chess, which has published gambits that players can master, Go players cannot easily articulate their moves. Whereas Watson was loaded with millions of facts, AlphaGo was structured on a neural network modeling how the human brain works. Google engineers designed a system that enabled AlphaGo to learn on its own. It had to detect subtle patterns in large amounts of data and make connections to winning moves (McAfee and Brynjolfsson 3–4).

The questions that Watson's and AlphaGo's victories pose are valid ones. How will artificial intelligence (A.I.) affect school librarians? What routine tasks can be easily and more economically performed by A.I.? Will school librarians' positions become redundant?

Alvin Toffler published a ground-breaking book in 1970 titled, *Future Shock,* in which he described a syndrome of disorientation caused by rapid technological change. With a fair degree of accuracy, he predicted that various government and social institutions would not be able to keep pace (Toffler 343–344). Fueled by swift technological changes in their workplaces and other parts of society, he foresaw that people would become increasingly confused and distracted, creating a climate in which it would be challenging to make intelligent decisions about their personal and professional lives. While the pace of change in Toffler's time was considered fast and disorientating, contrast it with the following facts. In 1970, about 7,000 new items were placed on supermarket shelves. Over half hadn't existed before 1960. This number truly pales in comparison to the 22,252 products funded by Kickstarter in 2014 (Webb 21, 23). Change, even though its pace is a mathematical constant, has truly accelerated from rapid to quantum (Burstein 27). It's disconcerting, and when it moves at an increasingly faster clip, it challenges our competencies, standards, methods, and core values. It makes it difficult to achieve our goals in new surroundings (Hartzell 163). Ray Kurzweil, director of engineering at Google, places us squarely in an age of rapid change generated by "the explosive power of exponential growth, the twenty-first century will be the equivalent to 20,000 years of progress; organizations have to redefine themselves at a faster and faster pace" (Kurzweil).

START YOUR ENGINES

If there is any doubt as to Kurzweil's prediction, gaze back just a few years in time to confirm his prophecy. In 1995, mobile phones cost about $1,000 and approximately 13 percent of the population purchased one. Daily newspapers were an integral component of even the smallest American town. Totaled, America's newspapers produced $46 billion in yearly profits. Periodicals created an additional $19 billion. Radio stations also prospered. By 2000, more than 10,000 AM and FM stations garnered profits of $20 billion. In the same year, recorded music brought in $14.3 billion dollars and had an annual 7 percent growth rate since 1990. During that same period, film photography was a $10 billion industry, including camera buys, film purchases and developing charges (McAfee and Brynjolfsson 130–131).

It took only a short time from the arrival of the Internet in 1994 to affect these businesses and related occupations, as change eventually placed its obsolescence mark on them. By 2013, total U.S. newspaper and print advertising profits had decreased by 70 percent, and online ads had only earned $3.4 billion of the $40 billion lost in annual profits (McAfee and Brynjolfsson 132). By necessity, 13,400 newspaper newsroom positions were slashed as the newspaper business tried to cope with their plummeting circulation. Globally, sales of recorded music declined by 45 percent, from $27 billion to $15 billion between 1999 and 2014 (McAfee and Brynjolfsson 134). Instead, streaming music sales garnered $3.9 billion in 2016, up 69 percent, making it the majority of U.S. sales for the first time (Sisario, B2).

The telecommunications industry has also been affected, especially in the area of local and long-distance landlines. Long-distance voice calls generated $77 billion in 2000. Only thirteen years later, the companies were bringing in $16 billion in revenue (McAfee and Brynjolfsson 135). Currently, 51 percent of Americans are living in households with no landline connection, only a cell phone (Selyukh). As smartphone purchases increased, their memory storage grew exponentially, with almost no awareness on the part of the public. Beginning with eight gigabytes of memory, the upgrade two years later came loaded with eighteen gigabytes. It was followed by thirty-two, and then sixty-four gigabytes. Smartphones now contain eight times as much memory as they did three upgrades ago. None of the upgrades increased the cost of the smartphone significantly, which is probably why we were not really cognizant of the gigabyte jump. Author Jerry Kaplan of *Humans Need Not Apply* asks "if your car got eight times the gas mileage it did six years ago, on the order of, say, two hundred miles per gallon, you may have taken some notice" (Kaplan 26).

The comparison of books to web pages is even more indicative of our changing times. Approximately 130 million books have been published since recorded human history (McAfee and Brynjolfsson 231). In comparison, the indexed Web contains at least 4.45 billion pages ("World Wide Web Size"). Wikipedia is the world's sixth most popular site, as many of us know from our students instantly clicking on it after receiving a research assignment. In 2001, it held 617 articles, but by 2016 it soared to 35 million articles, 2.9 billion words in 291 languages ("How Many Words Are There in Wikipedia?").

Change is the only constant, and it is challenging us to see the patterns and trends because advances in technology have accelerated the pace. Most of the information we encounter that has ever existed is less than ten years old. In the progression of kilo to exabytes, an exabyte is 1,000,000,000,000,000,000 bytes. A smartphone photograph consumes about 3 megabytes or 3,000,000 bytes. Five exabytes of data have been created between the beginnings of human civilization and 2003. By the time you have read the previous paragraph, 2.8 million pieces of content were posted just on Facebook, and Instagram hosted 250,000 new photos (Webb 24, 295).

CRYSTAL BALLS, OUIJA BOARDS, AND TAROT CARDS

Prediction is a tentative algorithm. It has never fully obeyed any law of science. It has always been dependent on a set of technological, economic, employment, political, and social variables that can render its forecasts laughable in the present, and is sometimes hilarious in retrospect (Atwood). In 2004, two notable Harvard scholars opined that human perception was an essential need for operating a motor vehicle. In October 2010, Google consigned this assertion to the scrap heap of history by announcing that it had re-engineered several Toyota Priuses to be completely self-driving (Frey and Osborne 3). The concluding corollary to this example might be, so why do we bother to predict and forecast change? What is the accuracy of prediction, and is it a wasteful use of our precious time and efforts?

Many researchers have studied the science of prediction and concluded that it is a pseudo-science unworthy of all the formal research methods that apply to it. To challenge that assumption, from 1984 to 2004, Professor Philip Tetlock conducted a twenty-year study of the accuracy of expert judgement in scientific literature concerning changes in the economy, stock market, politics, wars, and other societal issues. His verdict was rendered with a tongue-in-cheek primate analogy: "that *many* experts were as accurate as a dart-throwing chimpanzee" (Tetlock and Gardner 4). The key word in that former quote is actually "many," for not *all* of the experts were wrong. Tetlock found that one group was able to forecast a little better than the chimp, and it did not correlate to their advanced degrees or access to confidential information or data sets. The deciding variable was "how they thought" (Tetlock and Gardner 68). An analysis of this thought method reveals two types of thinking that Tetlock compares to a hedgehog versus a fox. Attributed to an essay by historian Isiah Berlin and originally from a poem by the Greek poet Archilochus: "The fox knows many things but the hedgehog knows one big thing," Tetlock found that experts who succeeded in predicting better than a chimp exhibited the following characteristics: They sought information from as many sources as possible. When thinking, they mentally changed perspectives, punctuating their correspondence with qualifiers such as howevers, buts, and althoughs. They spoke about possibilities and probabilities rather than certainties. All of them were able to admit when their forecasts were erroneous and alter their thinking accordingly. So how in this Aesopian comparison did the hedgehogs and foxes fare? Well, foxes trounced hedgehogs by actually "hedging" their forecasts within the 60 to 70 percent range, whereas hedgehogs strongly predicted a future occurrence within a 90 to 100 percent range. Foxes also stole the lead on both calibration and resolution. They showed real vision, whereas the hedgehogs lacked it (Tetlock and Gardner 69).

The tools that the foxes have at their disposal are similar to the ones that school librarians have always possessed: unfettered access to online databases, print collections, and educational media featuring opposing points of view. Current controversies provide us with the evidence to course-correct our curricula, physical environment, programs, and services. With our formal training in information technology, no one at school is better equipped to cope with accelerating change than school librarians.

RUNNING IN PLACE

School librarians are ensnared in a technology-induced maze learning how netbooks and cloud computing work. Just as we've mastered one technological skill, we must cope with newly implemented bring your own device (BYOD) programs and assist with emergency repairs. We're setting up wikis and helping a math teacher flip all of her courses, while troubleshooting another teacher's interactive whiteboard glitch. With just one turn of the technological wheel, we have also added educating ourselves, faculty, and students about the use of mobile devices for student response systems, tagging, scrapbooking, microblogging, Snapchat, eBook devices, RSS (Really Simple Syndication) groups and readers, virtual conferencing, podcasting and music, streaming media, custom and micro-federation, and eLearning. In addition, we are responsible for providing information literacy instruction, designing resource-based units, honing critical thinking skills, complying with Common Core Standards, and enhancing STEM (science, technology, engineering, math) and STEAM (science, technology, engineering, math, the arts) learning (Scheeren xvii, 256–257).

ARE THE KIDS ALL RIGHT?

If the pace of change is fast for us, it is also for digital natives, our user population. Although they may be quicker than we are to pick up on the operational aspects of a new device, research indicates that they are clueless as to its challenging searching and distracting aspects. Nonetheless, acquisition of mobile devices continues to increase at a rapid rate. Thirty-eight percent of children under age two now use a mobile device to access media. The average age for a first cell phone user is 12.1 years. Fifty-six percent of children ages eight to twelve have a cell phone, and 88 percent of teenagers ages thirteen to seventeen do ("Kids Wireless Use Facts"). Although cell phones' addictive qualities are readily apparent to even the most casual observer, a Pew Research Center study reported that teenagers especially "could not live without one" (Rainie and Keeter). A 2015 study of young adults found that they were using their phones five hours per day at eighty-five separate times. Most of their interactions lasted less than thirty seconds, but they do accumulate. Smartphones have captured approximately one-third of teenagers' waking hours. When students were interviewed about their usage, they lacked any idea of the extent of their addiction. Most thought that they picked their phones only 50 percent of the reported time (Sullivan).

As our students involve themselves more heavily with their devices and social media, the dark side of the Web has begun to emerge from the shadows. Years ago, students who bullied one another did so by passing nasty notes that were frequently intercepted by a watchful teacher. If the student read the note, he or she may have been hurt, but the simple act of disposing of it usually minimized any long-term psychological harm. Cyberbullying is more pernicious and has actually resulted in the deaths of some students. The Centers for Disease Control (CDC) has recognized it as a youth health problem and collects data on it. Nationwide, 14.8 percent of students reported being bullied through some form of electronic media. LGBT youth are especially vulnerable, and 55.2 percent of them have experienced cyberbullying ("Youth Risk Behavior Surveillance Survey . . ." 30–44).

Hours spent alone online may also be contributing to an increase in student depression. In the last *Youth Risk Behavior Surveillance Survey*, 29.9 percent of students felt so sad or hopeless for two consecutive weeks that they ceased engaging in some of their usual activities. Although the percentage increase on this survey question was not statistically significant, in 2011 28.5 percent reported being depressed compared to 29.9 percent in 2013. Depression is one of the leading causes of suicide, and 17 percent of students reported having seriously considered it ("Youth Risk Behavior Surveillance Survey . . ." 47). Unfortunately, the rate of those who commit suicide also increased from 7 per 100,000 in 2011 to 9 per 100,000 in 2014 ("Suicidal Teens").

All of these factors influence how well students will perform in school, but the dominant variable is child poverty. Starting in the mid-1970s, our students have been more likely to be poorer than adults. For a family of four with two children, the poverty level in 2015 was defined as income of $24,036 or less. One student in five lives in poverty, which translates to 15.5 million impoverished students. Minority students are the most affected, with Hispanic and black children much more likely to live in poor families than white and Asian children. The U.S. government spends 10 percent of the national budget on children, a fraction of what other developed countries spend. When children suffer from hunger, the physical, mental, and emotional problems that accompany it result in lower reading and math scores ("Child Poverty in the U.S."). The increasing income inequality has also created an academic apartheid. A national study reported that the gap in high school students' average family income between the top and the bottom jumped by 50 percent between 1972 and 2002. Lower family income affects the ability to rent or own homes in areas where there are better schools and teachers (Duncan and Murnane 41).

THE 3 R's

With child poverty so pervasive, it is no surprise that functional illiteracy is a continuing problem for our country. Seven million Americans are illiterate, and 27 million cannot read well enough to complete a job application. Fifty million can only read at the fourth- or fifth-grade level (Hedges 44). A transcript analysis of past presidential debates reveals a steady decline in their educational levels. The Lincoln and Douglas debates of 1858 show that Lincoln spoke at the educational level of an eleventh grader and Douglas that of a twelfth grader. The Bush and Gore debates showed Bush at 6.8 and Gore at 7.6 (Hedges 46). An analysis of campaign speeches rather than debate transcripts of Clinton versus Trump found a similar pattern of a sixth-to eighth-grade educational level in grammar and vocabulary (Spice).

Can we as a nation reverse this downward trend in literacy and public discourse? "The writer Philip Roth claimed that 'the screen will kill the reader,' ushering what some commentators term a 'post-literate' age" (Doyle). Will our future students primarily obtain information from short videos and superficial websites? Questions similar to the previous ones are being posed by school librarians who have to make draconian decisions between acquiring print and nonprint sources because of budget cuts and space reconfigurations.

The educational challenges that teachers face require the full support of school librarians. While both professions need to cope with increasing administrative pressure from their respective state-mandated initiatives, teachers are on the firing line. The average teacher is in his or her late forties and has neither been trained nor prepared to deal with high-stakes testing, Common Core standards, ethnic diversity, the educational implications of school choice, vouchers, charter schools, site-based management, and block scheduling (Hartzell 163).

Even the traditional pedagogical model of "learn early, benefit for a lifetime" is evolving. When the majority of job skills remained constant, it was an understandable educational goal. In an environment of rapid change, however, students will need to be educated as lifelong learners, ready to return to school for short- or long-term retraining or formal education to keep their positions. It's already happening at AT&T. With its 280,000 employees, AT&T has adopted re-education as a labor mantra committing itself to retaining their employees, but with one caveat. Choose to become a "perpetual learner" or find work elsewhere. They are also introducing a mind-set among their employees that their jobs will probably change every four years. Required skill sets were charted not only for blue-collar workers but also for all management and administrative positions. Employees in the latter category had to draft their own "future profiles." If education gaps are identified, employees are expected to remedy the problem with appropriate re-education on their own time and sometimes dime. Every year, AT&T spends $250 million for employee education and $30 million for tuition assistance. It expects, however, that many employees will sometimes need to factor re-education at their own time and expense as a job requirement (Donovan and Benko 68–73).

WHITHER SCHOOL LIBRARIANS?

With change leapfrogging up the schoolhouse steps, every profession must question its current place and role in the employment matrix. Unfortunately, educators and legislators tasked with balancing ever-shrinking budgets have viewed school librarians as a gratuitous part of the education hierarchy, similar to music, physical education, and art teachers (Johnson 4). This view is reflected in The National Center for Educational Statistics' reported decline in the number of school librarians from 2005 to 2012. Sadly, they decreased more than any other school staff during that period (Scheeren 16). Schools throughout the country are cutting library programs, budgets, and staff support. In many cases they are replacing school librarians with educational technologists and using the funds to invest in corporation-designed curricula that promises improved test results (Johnson 4). These events are occurring despite sixty rigorous library science studies demonstrating that students in schools with qualified librarians learn more, receive better grades, and score higher on standardized tests than do students in schools without libraries ("School Library Impact Studies"). In a time of growing economic, educational, and social inequality, what can school librarians do to remain essential to their schools?

APPLICATIONS FOR HUMANS ARE DOWN

Throughout the nineties and into the current century, the gross domestic product growth rate can be likened to that of a slow loris. The belief in American exceptionalism has begun to wane, and there is more social mobility in some European countries than in the United States. Computerization is the driving force, making blue- and now white-collar jobs susceptible to redundancy and depressed wages. Between 2000 and 2010, the number of college-enrolled Americans increased by 29 percent. Within the same time frame, the number of college-educated janitors rose by 69 percent (Bruni 199). One study places 47 percent of total U.S. jobs at risk to computerization within the next twenty years (Frey 38). Since Facebook is a total online company, it should come as no surprise that they have automated most of their repair and software fixes. They now need only one technician for every 250,000 servers. Most IT companies have ratios of 1 to 250 or 1 to 500 (Davenport and Kirby 207). Income inequality is on citizens' minds because there are fewer jobs that pay well. For people without college degrees, the number of jobs is steadily dwindling. In today's economy, most high-paying jobs are going to a small slice of the population, that is, hedge fund managers, CEOs, investment bankers, and tech wizards (Davenport and Kirby 6).

DO WE STILL TEACH FOR THE TEST?

The instructional role of school librarians is being redefined by these tectonic changes in technology and its impact in the economic and employment sectors. Our students are being propelled into an information labyrinth worthy of Daedalus. For any research assignment, they are confronting subscriptions databases, blogs, gargantuan online university catalogs, video libraries, wikis, chatrooms, and millions of personal and questionable websites (Johnson 93). If you are a freshman at Columbia University, you have access to 1,500 online databases accessible from any Wi-Fi connection ("Fast Facts: Your Libraries at a Glance").

For years we incorporated critical thinking skills into our resource-based instruction that entailed a hierarchy of websites, with education and government usually given a higher selection value than organization and commercial sites. With the challenges of fake news on Facebook, Twitter, and other social media sites, however, students are being exposed to information that is not only false, but many times racist, anti-Semitic, sexist, and vicious in its goal to distort the truth (McAfee and Brynjolfsson 234). How are we going to teach information-seeking skills that can inoculate our students against a new type of information carcinogen that is stealthily infiltrating an information system that students automatically tend to trust and make their first searching point for research assignments?

SCHOOL LIBRARIANS AS FORECASTERS

School librarians are perfectly positioned to become future forecasters, not only for the educational institutions where they are employed but also for their school libraries. We have access to a world of information, are skilled searchers of Google and other search engines, and definitely have been trained to recognize valid and reliable information sources. We must be able to anticipate today's technological changes and foresee their educational and instructional impacts on the administration, faculty, and student population.

Although trends can be challenging to correctly identify, they are vitally important to recognize because they are the trail markers that will enable us to make necessary course corrections for ourselves and institutions and be a participant rather than a victim of the future (Webb 44). Amy Webb, in her outstanding book *The Signals Are Talking*, acknowledges that it is hard to distinguish between a trend and something that is trendy. Gamification is a trend, but everyone running around playing Pokémon Go was trendy. At the time, Pokémon Go seemed to be the app to download, and in July 2016, 5 to 10 million Android users did so, but slowly the game faded away, and we now think of it as a 2016 summertime fad (Metz). While innovative school librarians may have created a similar game to teach students how to identify areas of their school libraries, Pokémon Go wasn't a forerunner of a "sustained change within an industry, the public sector, or society, or in the way that we behave toward one another" (Webb 47).

While technological trends are the foreshocks of sustained change, they are vulnerable to specific variables that can hasten or slow their speed of acceptance. How is the economy functioning? Has the government just passed a bill authorizing the placement of sensors on all major highways to enable autonomous car lanes and designating new flight paths for commercial drones? What is the employment situation likely to be in the near future? People's job status can affect the rate at which trends develop. What societal and behavioral changes are taking place that seem to indicate how society will deal with new technologies? How many of us could have predicted that with the debut of the iPhone in 2007, people would be checking themselves into retreat centers to cure themselves of their addiction to it (Friedman 200)?

A TIMELINE FOR THE FUTURE

Predictions seemed easier years ago, because technology was not driving it at such a wicked pace. Relying upon the New Media Consortium's annual *Horizon Report* for a snapshot of the future was a sufficient guidepost because it relied upon more than seventy subject experts in numerous countries who were charged with evaluating not only the influence of specific technologies but also developing a timeline for their possible adoption. Reading it consistently can give school librarians a sense that change is more manageable as we track the pace of one of their forecasts moving into the mainstream of education (NMC Horizon).

Some scholars, however, believe that a fundamental shift is occurring that necessitates short-term rather than long-term monitoring. It will call for constant vigilance, testing new paradigms, and re-evaluation of our present programs and services. One- to five-year plans might not serve us as well as they have in the past. We will definitely need to shorten our deadlines for thriving in a time of rapid changes.

WAYS TO READ THE TEA LEAVES

This book is written to provide school librarians with an analysis and discussion of the future technological, economic, educational, employment, social, instructional, and organizational trends that are affecting our institutions. The second goal is to present a more structured approach using trend analysis to improve our thinking and decision-making skills. Nothing can truly prepare us for the future, nor can we predict it with 100 percent accuracy. With some guide posts, it may be possible to become a fox rather than a hedgehog when it comes to detecting major trends that we and our institutions must foresee to remain competitive locally, nationally, and globally. The final goal is to provide school librarians with current statistics and data that can be employed to formulate persuasive, justifiable arguments for (1) the purchase of new technologies, (2) instructional reforms, (3) the redesign of school library physical layouts, and (4) full implementation of resource-based learning.

Throughout most of the chapters, readers will observe references to the influence of advanced technologies and the subsequent need for improved student information-seeking and critical thinking skills. Both trends are so powerful in their potential to change school libraries that they will be emphasized in many aspects of the book. Each chapter closes with a set of questions that are designed to provoke thought and discussions for in-house library department retreats, school library district meetings, or sole practitioners.

School Libraries in a Time of Change: How to Survive and Thrive assumes that the majority of school libraries, because of local developments in the economic and employment sectors, will be in transitional phases with regard to utilizing many of the technology developments discussed in Chapter 1. An attempt to provide a nuanced overall portrait of technological change can give school librarians the means to position themselves as one of the most essential members of their respective schools.

SUGGESTED USES FOR THIS BOOK

The book serves as a resource for all stakeholders in the school, including instructional coordinators, educational technologists, and more specialized digital librarians. It is written to initiate conversations about the future not only of school libraries but also of the educational communities where they reside. The information can be used to build bridges and alliances among departments and to start sharing resources and space with complementary disciplines, including technology, learning skills, and literacy teachers. Its utility lies in providing librarians and other relevant members of the school community with current information about where these seven trends seem to be taking us and what we can do to respond wisely to them.

REFERENCES

Atwood, Margaret. December 27, 2015. "A Survival Story." *The World in 2016. Predictions, Predictions.* Available at: https://www.economist.com/international/2015/12/27/the-world-in-2016-predictions-predictions.

Bruni, Frank. 2015. *Where You Go Is Not Who You'll Be: An Antidote to the College Admissions Mania.* New York: Grand Central Publishing.

Burstein, David D. 2013. *Fast Future: How the Millennial Generation Is Shaping Our World.* Boston: Beacon Press.

"Child Poverty in the U.S." 2019. Children International. Available at: https://www.children.org/global-poverty/global-poverty-facts/facts-about-poverty-in-usa.

Davenport, Thomas H. and Julia Kirby. 2016. *Only Humans Need Apply: Winners and Losers in the Age of Smart Machines.* New York: Harper.

Donovan, John and Cathy Benko. October 2016. "AT&T's Talent Overhaul." *Harvard Business Review.* 94(10): 68–73.

Doyle, Christopher L. March 31, 2014. "K-12 Education in a Post-Literate Age." *Education Week.* Available at: https://www.edweek.org/ew/articles/2014/04/02/27doyle_ep.h33.html.

Duncan, Greg J. and Richard J. Murnane. 2014. *Restoring Opportunity: The Crisis of Inequality and the Challenge of American Education*. Boston: Harvard Education Press.

"Fast Facts: Your Libraries at a Glance." Accessed October 27, 2018. Columbia University. Available at: https://library.columbia.edu/about/facts/html.

Frey, Carl Benedikt and Michael A. Osborne. September 17, 2013. "The Future of Employment: How Susceptible Are Jobs to Computerisation?" Available at: http://www.oxfordmartin.ox.ac.uk/downloads/academic/The_Future_of_Employment.pdf.

Friedman, Thomas. 2017. *Thank You for Being Late: An Optimist's Guide to Thriving in an Age of Accelerations*. New York: Picador.

Hartzell, Gary N. 2003. *Building Influence for the School Librarian: Tenets, Targets, and Tactics*. 2nd ed. Santa Barbara, CA: Libraries Unlimited.

Hedges, Chris. 2010. *Empire of Illusion: The End of Literacy and the Triumph of Spectacle*. New York: Nation Books.

"How Many Words Are There in Wikipedia?" Accessed on October 26, 2018. Available at: https://www.quora.com/How-many-words-are-there-in-Wikipedia.

Johnson, Doug A. 2013. *The Indispensable Librarian: Surviving and Thriving in School Libraries in the Information Age*. 2nd ed. Santa Barbara, CA: Linworth.

Kaplan, Jerry. 2015. *Humans Need Not Apply*. New Haven, CT: Yale University Press.

"Kids Wireless Use Facts." Accessed October 24, 2018. CTIA Foundation. Available at: http://www.growingwireless.com/get-the-facts/quick-facts.

Kurzweil, Ray. March 7, 2001. "The Law of Accelerating Returns." Kurzweil Accelerating Intelligence Essays. Available at: http://www.kurzweilai.net/the-law-of-accelerating-returns.

Markoff, John. February 6, 2011. "Computer Wins on Jeopardy! Trivial, It's Not." *The New York Times*. Available at: https://www.nytimes.com/2011/02/17/science/17jeopardy-watson.html.

McAfee, Andrew and Erik Brynjolfsson. 2017. *Machine, Platform, Crowd: Harnessing Our Digital Future*. New York: W. W. Norton.

Metz, Rachel. July 12, 2016. "Here's Why Pokémon Go Is Taking Off." *MIT Technology Review*. Available at: https://www.technologyreview.com/s/601880/heres-why-pokemon-go-is-taking-off.

Moyer, Christopher. March 28, 2016. "How Google's AlphaGo Beat a Go World Champion." *The Atlantic*. Available at: https://www.theatlantic.com/technology/archive/2016/03/the-invisible-opponent/475611.

NMC Horizon. Accessed October 26, 2018. New Media Consortium (NMC). Available at: https://www.nmc.org/nmc-horizon.

Rainie, Lee and Scott Keeter. April 3, 2006. *Americans and Their Cell Phones*. Pew Research Center. Available at: http://www.pewinternet.org/2006/04/03/americans-and-their-cell-phones-2.

Scheeren, William O. 2015. *Technology Handbook for School Librarians: Theory and Practice*. Santa Barbara, CA: Libraries Unlimited.

"School Library Impact Studies." Accessed October 25, 2018. Library Research Service. Available at: https://www.lrs.org/data-tools/school-libraries/impact-studies.

Selyukh, Alina. May 4, 2017. "The Daredevils Without Landlines and Why Health Experts Are Tracking Them." National Public Radio. Available at: https://www.npr.org/sections/alltechconsidered/2015/12/03/458225197/the-daredevils-without-landlines-and-why-health-experts-are-tracking-them.

Sisario, Ben. March 31, 2018. "After Driving Streaming Music's Rise, Spotify Aims to Cash In." *The New York Times*. Available at: https://www.nytimes.com/2018/03/31/business/media/spotify-streaming-music.html.

Spice, Byron. March 16, 2016. "Most Presidential Candidates Speak at Grade 6–8 Level." Carnegie Mellon University. Available at: https://www.cmu.edu/news/stories /archives/2016/march/speechifying.html.

"Suicidal Teens." Accessed October 25, 2018. Child Trends Databank. Available at: https:// www.childtrends.org/indicators/suicidal-teens.

Sullivan, Andrew. September 18, 2016. "I Used to Be a Human Being." *The Intelligencer*. Available at: http://nymag.com/intelligencer/2016/09/andrew-sullivan-my-distraction -sickness-and-yours.html.

Tetlock, Philip E. and Dan Gardner. 2015. *Superforecasting: The Art and Science of Predicting*. New York: Crown.

Toffler, Alvin. 1970. *Future Shock*. New York: Bantam.

Webb, Amy. 2016. *The Signals Are Talking: Why Today's Fringe Is Tomorrow's Mainstream*. New York: Public Affairs.

"World Wide Web Size." Accessed October 25, 2018. Available at: http://www.world widewebsize.com.

"Youth Risk Behavior Survey Data. Summary Trends Report 2007–2017." Accessed October 26, 2018. Centers for Disease Control and Prevention. Available at: https:// www.cdc.gov/healthyyouth/data/yrbs/pdf/trendsreport.pdf.

1

Reading the Tech Tea Leaves

WHITHER THE FUTURE?

Friedrich Nietzsche believed that human beings internalize a belief that future events are beyond our control and are fated instead of a series of choices that we make ourselves (Webb 18). Fortunately, most U.S. institutions, companies, and organizations work to defeat this view by requiring yearly goals, perspectives, five-year plans, annual budgets, and data collection. In the past, many of the traditional tools that school librarians have used to gaze into the future have served us well. Yearly we peruse NMC's *Horizon Report*, review "top ten" listings for tech trends, attend American Library Association (ALA) meetings that address future issues, and continue to ably serve our user populations.

Change, however, is at hand. We are in an era that some scholars have compared to the Cambrian Age—450 billion years ago—when mankind and many other species achieved an exponential leap in development (Viswanathan). This transformative era is making it challenging to forecast change as newer technologies emerge at such a rapid pace. The washing machine, for example, was considered a "killer app" technology in the early 1900s. Yet it took nearly thirty years for more than 50 percent of Americans to purchase one (Webb 21). Indeed, forecasting has become a form of nowcasting as we try to maintain our equilibrium in a world on a permanent spin cycle.

Technology is also requiring more of our implicit trust. Our cars contain microchips that are absolutely essential to their successful operation, yet can be remotely hacked by any semi-talented dark-hat techie. Physicians are performing delicate surgeries upon us with the aid of robot-controlled scalpels (Webb 282). Obsolescence is occurring at a faster rate. Doug Johnson, in his excellent book, *The Indispensable Librarian*, reminds us that flash drives, eBooks, Facebook, and Nooks may soon seem as antiquated as floppy disks and acquisition stamps (Johnson 185). In a 2016 survey of 10,000 teens in forty-six states, the majority of them report that they now prefer Snapchat and Instagram to Facebook.

Many of our schools, however, are plunging into purchasing various technologies with scant evidence that they improve learning. Trusting these fast-appearing technologies is not a guarantee for either our professional or institutional futures. It is time to study the future more scientifically by employing criteria that can be applied not only to technological change but also to the economic, educational, social, instructional, and organizational trends that affect its adoption speed. Failure to study the future in a methodical manner will put our schools and our professional roles in them at risk.

The trends that we identify should also be evaluated not only for the change that they will bring to our profession but also their impact upon our core values as school librarians. These core values encompass ensuring confidentiality and privacy, diversity in our collections, literacy-based programs and services, equitable access, and intellectual freedom and expression. How can some trends enhance our work, and which ones might challenge it? What technology is looming on the horizon? How will students and faculties react to it? How might we employ some trends to our greatest advantage and recognize those that will be problematic to our user population goals of learning and achieving (Figueroa 33)? These are some of the questions that plague us but need to be addressed.

This chapter charts a method for forecasting the future. Its goal is to improve our understanding of the world as it is transforming. After reading it, school librarians will have a method for how to think like a futurist, to forecast emerging trends, and to make more accurate decisions about the future (Webb 9).

DO FORECASTERS WEAR SWAMI HATS?

The word *swami* means master, and one of the goals of a swami is to gain control over habit patterns (Bharati). Habits, as we all know, are our repetitive ways of performing a task and thinking. They are sometimes extremely challenging to change. We must, however, adopt the characteristics and qualities of a forecaster to methodically begin to think like one. Naisbitt, in his groundbreaking book *Megatrends*, warned against becoming a "gee whiz futurist." This is someone who believes that technological innovation travels in a straight line. In reality, it "weaves and bobs and lurches and sputters" (Naisbitt 41). His description is accurate. Anyone following the technical progress of artificial intelligence (A.I.) knows that one component of its successful growth resulted from the development of neural networking rather than continuing research with expert/knowledge systems. It is the former technical breakthrough that enabled AlphaGo to defeat the expert human Go player in 2016 (McAfee and Brynjolfsson).

So what characteristics and habits do forecasters need to adopt to improve their accuracy and comfort level besides thinking like a fox? Recall that the fox knows many things. According to author Tetlock, "superforecasters are in perpetual beta mode" (Tetlock and Gardner 190). Their philosophical outlook seems to reflect some of the qualities that have been traditionally associated with our esteemed profession: school librarianship. Superforecasters tend to be cautious, humble, and nondeterministic. They do not crave certainty. Their sense of reality is complex, and they are not fatalistic in thought. As for their thought processes, an analogist might easily make the comparison that a forecaster's thinking skills and abilities mirror those of a school librarian. Superforecasters tend to be actively open-minded. They favor testing beliefs like hypotheses. They are inquisitive, with a thirst for knowledge and enjoy puzzles and mental challenges. Superforecasters tend to be reflective, introspective, and self-critical. They have an ease with numbers and data. Their approach to forecasting is pragmatic, and they are not harnessed to any idea or agenda. They tend to be analytical and are capable of developing a more removed perspective that is considerate of diverse viewpoints. When facts change, they are able to alter their mind-sets. If they were to sit for the Myers-Briggs test of emotional intelligence, they would score high for intuitive thinking preferences. Superforecasters revisit their thought processes for cognitive and emotional predilections. The two most important qualities of their thinking concern a belief that it's possible to improve and a determination to achieve their goals (Tetlock 191–192).

Psychologist Jonathan Baron has classified a foxlike thinking pattern as active open-mindedness (AOM). See if you agree or disagree with his statements. "1. People should take into consideration evidence that goes against their beliefs. 2. It is more useful to pay attention to those who disagree with you than to pay attention to those who agree. 3. Changing your mind is a sign of weakness. 4. Intuition is the best guide in making decisions. 5. And it is important to persevere in your beliefs even when evidence is brought to bear against them" (Tetlock and Gardner 126). All of us can easily predict how superforecasters scored. They embodied the thesis and antithesis of the respective statements. Their beliefs are always subject to change and not set in stone.

DO WE NEED TAROT CARDS?

An accelerating future is only manageable if you commit to constantly studying emerging trends. Webb, in her book entitled, *The Signals Are Talking*, defines a trend as "driven by a basic human need, one that is catalyzed by new technology." Trends are contemporary and evolutionary in nature and continue to persist. They usually appear on the fringe and are dependent upon other variables such as economic and employment-related trends and then move to the mainstream. A trend has to meet three criteria. It must be probable, plausible, and possible (Webb 47–50). Larry Page, cofounder of Google, requires that it pass the toothbrush test: "Is it something you will use once or twice a day, and does it make your life better (Gelles)? Let's submit a new company entitled "Popup Picks the Community Reading Platform" to Webb's and Page's standards. The company was cited in a Top Tech Trends 2017 list by the Library and Information Technology Association (LITA) division of ALA. Popup Picks is a geolocated eBook platform that promises to eliminate the one copy/one user problem currently vexing every library with eBook collections. As we know, this legal and technical barrier is the quickest way to drive every library user into the arms of Amazon. What library user wants to be put on eHold for a bestseller or research title that they are either excited to read or need to read for a class? Popup Picks has developed an app that erases the IP authentication address problem. It locates readers by bringing them to the library via geolocation and downloads the title when users open the app. The company is already partnering with library consortia, book distributors, and a tech lab for further development ("Top Tech Trends . . .").

If you are a school librarian with a burgeoning eBook collection, Popup Picks should look probable, plausible, and possible to you. It should pique your curiosity. While it is not yet mainstream, it might even pass the "toothbrush test." Your students and faculty would definitely use it more than once or twice a day for recreational and assignment reading. And it would make their lives better by providing them with 24/7 convenience at no cost. Who knows, it might even turn them into perpetual readers and meet one of our enduring goals as school librarians.

CAN FORECASTING BE TAUGHT?

Both Webb and Tetlock claim that forecasting is a teachable skill. Futurists or forecasters learn to search for discernible patterns or pre-trends similar to scatter graph dots on the fringe. They observe them as they tend to converge and then move to the mainstream. Some of these patterns or trends such as Popup Picks may never reach fruition, but forecasters monitor them to see if they emerge into bona fide trends. For them, trends are mirrors into the future and a way to look over the rainbow's arc of time (Webb 17). If we apply some facile strategies to trend observance, we can become school library futurists and position ourselves as absolutely indispensable to our schools.

Now, if your heart is beating faster about the time factor, slow it down. For the future is evolving at a pace that is going to enable us to track trends and develop strategies. Webb encourages us to become "chronologically ambidextrous," developing abilities to gaze into the near and far future simultaneously (Webb 33). So after learning about Popup Picks, which is clearly in the near future, can you picture a robot in your library that contains responses for the most common reference questions that you've answered within the last ten years? Students can query it and receive help while you are providing individual term paper assistance to other students in an American history class. This short scenario might seem like pie-in-the sky to you, but eventually it may pass the probable, plausible, possible, and toothbrush tests. We need to prepare ourselves for this type of eventuality as much as we are investigating the possibility of purchasing Popup Picks as a means of facilitating access to our eBook collections.

A FUTURIST'S GUIDE TO PREDICTION

Fringe is a buzzword for a futurist because it's where trends are formed. It's also the area where school librarians have traditionally shied away from, because of its association with the terms *bleeding edge* versus *cutting edge*. None of us want to be the one to recommend something like the 1990 Apple Newton, considered one of the top ten computer flops of all time. Billed as an oversize tablet that could read handwriting, Apple Newton could not deliver on its claims, and by 1993 it gravitated into the tech trash pile (Williams). In a time of rapid change, however, the fringe is where school librarians need to reside, and they are perfectly positioned to bide there.

To examine the fringe of any technology, cast a wide net. Read periodicals such as *Wired*, *PC World*, the *Futurist*, and *Computer World* on a regular basis. Visit

ALA's website *Center for the Future of Libraries* and check out the blog, events, and new publications that are listed. Explore new developments at Harvard University's *The Library Innovation Lab* and *Experiments at the MIT Libraries* websites. View films like *Ex Machina, Robot & Frank, Minority Report, I, Robot, I Am Legend,* and others and don't dismiss their themes out of hand. Read science fiction for its fictional glimpses of possible future technologies and its provocative social commentary. Play with some of the more absurd fringe developments in your mind and mentally test their probabilities, plausibilities, and possibilities. Visit nearby academic libraries and ask their librarians what they foresee for their programs, spaces, and services. If their university has a Computer Science Department, find willing professors and graduate students who will speak with you and your department members about what they think lies ahead. Take a field trip to libraries that are featured in ALA publications or convention tours such as the James B. Hunt Jr. Library in Raleigh or Imaginon in Charlotte, North Carolina. The former library features a book-retrieval robot and virtual reality lab, and the latter is a collaborative library with the Children's Theater of Charlotte and is replete with state-of-the-art multimedia equipment. Convene an annual in-house retreat in combination with your Educational Technology Department and employ the latest editions of *NMC's Horizon Report*, MIT's Technology Review's *10 Breakthrough Technologies*, and LITA's *Top Tech Trends* as starting points for brainstorming possible fringe developments.

When you observe or see something that looks weird, don't dismiss it out of hand. Ask yourself if a present-day problem could be surmounted soon or could something be modified for future use? Seek answers to the following questions. Who has been researching in this area? Matthew Boyer, codirector of the Digital Media and Learning Labs at Clemson University in South Carolina, and Stephen Moysey, codirector of Clemson's Center for Geospatial Technologies, have been evaluating whether virtual reality will be the next content delivery platform for education (Figueroa 37). Look at their publications and read their conclusions. Are other companies or research institutes doing work in this area?

Is it a company that you recognize, like Facebook, Amazon, Microsoft, Google, or Apple? They are currently the dominant technology players, and if they are working in a field, it might be time to take notice. Who is funding a project? Occasionally, for example, from the Google home page, click About and then Our Products. Scroll through the list and click on any products that arouse your curiosity or are unfamiliar to you. When you see something extraordinary, ask yourself who might be directly affected by its development. Who might be motivated to oppose this kind of change because it would affect them economically, organizationally, or socially (Webb 117–118)? The fossil fuel industry, for example, is incentivized to maintain their current subsidies and will definitely oppose and lobby against any proposed legislative downward changes. Picture a seesaw with oil subsidies and education funding on either side. Which side do you envision moving upward and which one downward in the current political climate ("Fossil Fuel Subsidies Overview . . .")? Lastly, ask yourself if someone might envision a technological, economic, societal, or educational change as an impetus for improvement or betterment. School librarians everywhere, for example, are welcoming passage of the

Common Core Standards in many states and seeing the opportunity to integrate themselves more fully into the curricula of their schools by teaching information-seeking skills in compliance with the Common Core subject area standards (American Association of School Librarians).

Technology does not develop in a void. It is driven by and subject to external forces, including economic, educational, and social ones. Jawbone, for example, is a fitness app that tracks sleep patterns, but it also furnishes prompts to wearers of their device to get to bed earlier. It's a technological response to society's smartphone addiction at the expense of our need for more sleep ("Track Your Sleep . . ."). Continue to follow developments in the economic and employment sectors for fringe patterns. Are businesses in areas where you live robotizing? How will it affect employment patterns in the future?

The first stage in locating the fringe is one of the most enjoyable parts for school librarian futurists. It involves what most librarians have always loved to do and that is read. The second stage that Webb terms CIPHER is more challenging, however, because it entails active open-mindedness. It's a mind-set that is not easily mastered. CIPHER involves mentally submitting what you think might be new trends in technology, social behavior, or education to more rigid criteria. It stands for *contradictions, inflections, practices, hacks, extremes,* and *rarities* (Webb 36).

The first criterion, contradictions, occurs when two trends fail to parallel one another. Distracted driving, for example, is causing an increase in the number of road accidents, while simultaneously automobile technology featuring touchscreens, access to the Internet, and monitoring cameras is increasing. The latter automobile improvements should make driving safer and reduce accidents, but just the opposite is happening. The contradictions criterion may also be operating with school library eBook collections. Our libraries are increasing eBook collections, which should result in more accessible reading, but our students appear to be reading less. When evaluating a trend, we need to look for possible contradictions in how it might be received and employed.

Inflections is a time when a catalyzing event speeds up or slows down the introduction of a new technological, educational, or pedagogical trend. A fundraising event for your library, for example, might precipitate your acquisition of a 3D printer. The passage of Common Core Standards in your state may expedite changes in school librarians' instructional approach to information-seeking skills. As mentioned, inflections can also slow the progress of a trend. Natural disasters, such as the hurricanes that struck Houston and Florida, were definite speed bumps for their respective areas. Playing an inflection game of "What if?" when studying prospective trends can pay off for your library and school (Webb 151).

Practices is the third stage in the CIPHER model. It's the point at which a new trend threatens established orthodoxy. For years, for example, Broward County, Florida, schools relied upon teacher and parent recommendations for admission into their gifted programs. After testing students with a new nonverbal I.Q. exam, 80 percent more black and 130 percent more Hispanic children qualified for admission (Dynarski). This shocking increase not only violates an educational orthodoxy of reliance solely upon professional judgment, but it also introduces a more data-driven approach to decision-making in a school system. It represents a threat to the status quo for Broward County gifted program admission requirements.

The fourth stage of the CIPHER model is *hacks*. This part of the model may be an action that will be extremely beneficial to school libraries. It concerns improving on technology so that it becomes more useful (Webb 152). Sites such as GitHub contain programs, fixes, and workarounds that school librarians may be able to employ to supplement their own programs and services. Open-source coding aids white-hat hackers and may provide school libraries with some unexpected improvements by tweaking computer programs and improving their applicability. One of the best examples of positive hacking concerns Twitter. Chris Messina, a strong proponent for open-source code, created the hashtag for highlighting topics and following conversations. His successful hack paved the way for aggregating and sharing content across social media (Webb 152).

Extremes, the fifth step in the CIPHER model, is when people are really thinking out of the box and achieving something entirely unexpected with a technology. These are people who have devised new ways to construct, explore, visualize, make, or replicate something that currently exists. On October 29, 2015, a ten-year-old boy walked into a Wilmington, Delaware, public library and used the 3D printer to design a completely functional prosthetic hand for himself that allowed him to grasp a Pringles can and hurl it across the room (Cuellar). Three-dimensional printers had been in libraries for several years, but neither librarians nor other 3D printer users had ever envisioned this groundbreaking employment of it until that day.

The last CIPHER model step is to consider *rarities*. Something rare in society, be it an object, a new business practice, a community, or an educational policy, can be the outlying start of a trend because it addresses a basic human need or changes some aspect of society (Webb 152–153). No one, for example, spotted this rarity: In 2011 House Bill 2220 was declared law in Oregon. It caused no stir and passed with no testimony from the Democratic and Republican sides. It encompassed all school districts and stated that "assessments must clearly show the parent and student whether the student is achieving the course requirements" (Hammond). With the passage of House Bill 2220, would you have guessed that an entire state had just rejected homework as a graded assessment tool and now required demonstration of proficiency only on a formal test as evidence of course knowledge? Would you have guessed that passage of House Bill 2220 just ushered in the subject mastery movement? Overnight a trend began that has continued in many other parts of the country and has implications for school librarians because many teachers became obsessed with ensuring that their students passed various state proficiency exams. Library time for resource-based projects and reading motivation programs in many schools have been curtailed as a result of the development of a "teach to the test" mentality (Johnson 4).

DOES A TREND HAVE TRAIL POSTS?

After employing CIPHER and mentally posing questions of what may be a trend, it's also important to track it. Actively monitoring the development of something you've identified as a trend is vital because of the acceleration factor. Identifying where a trend is along its developmental path provides you and your school library with an advantage (Webb 197). Even though most schools are publicly funded, they still must deal with neighboring charter, private, online, and specialized schools within their systems for enrollment-size-linked tax dollars. Capitalizing on a trend can place your school library in a competitive position for additional resources. If you can show, for example, that there is a student trend toward using online reference collections rather than print ones, track the data and prepare to request a budget increase to purchase additional eReference titles. If you visit a library that's using a book robot to retrieve print books, watch for its appearance in other libraries. If it's only occurring in academic and special libraries, do you foresee a school district with multiple libraries employing one in the future? If so, how soon do you think it will occur? How would removal of parts of your collection to a remote storage facility affect the library's space configuration?

Webb states that a trend has a typical trajectory that adheres to an S-curve. It begins on the far fringe and frequently evolves slowly and incrementally. As the curve ascends, the new trend becomes operational and finally enters the mainstream (Webb 203). Most of us were school librarians when smartphones appeared and witnessed in a blink of an eye how they captured our students' attention like no other device. Think if we had been able to foresee this technological development rather than paddle furiously in its stream. What educational changes might we have planned for rather than reacting to concomitant social and behavioral trends among our students such as cyberbullying, mob justice, and trolling?

Unfortunately, most of us require a prototype of a new technology to recognize its potential in our field. Visualization without one is truly a challenge for many of us, but we need to sharpen our skills in a time of change. Although the education field does not operate on a profit-and-loss model with shareholders breathing down our necks, it will require more vigilance on our parts if we are to provide our students with the skills to thrive in a faster-changing world.

PASSING THE LAST TREND TEST

After researching the fringe and applying the CIPHER method to a trend that you have detected, Webb recommends submitting it to a final test termed *F.U.T.U.R.E.* The first letter represents the word *foundation*. We all work in hierarchical environments and need the approval of various people in key positions in our schools. Assuming you have a "seat at the educational table" or are the sole implementer of technology in your building, you will still need assurance that your principal, district school library supervisor, and possibly superintendent support you. Are all of you in agreement about the trend that you have observed? If so, now you have a strong basis for future action. *Unique* is the second word in the test. Does your proposal for dealing with a new trend offer a uniquely feasible and executable action plan? If you decide, for example, to commit to a bring your own device (BYOD) program, what is your plan for students who lack consistently functioning devices?

The next letter, "T," stands for the word *track*. Given your school's environment, what is your yardstick for measuring and evaluating your results? While the cost savings can be significant with a BYOD program, how do you think it will affect learning? Will it enhance it or add another distracting burden to teachers trying to focus students' attention? *Urgency* is the fourth acronymic letter, and in a time of change, it is as relevant to schools as to businesses on the cutting edge. A trend plan needs a sense of urgency because just like perennial faculty discussions about changing the schedule, it can easily be postponed for another school year. Once you have obtained approval for your project, you need to implement it with all due speed.

The penultimate letter in this useful acronym is *recalibrate*. Have you built into the new change a means to tweak and fine-tune it at various points? If you have initiated a BYOD program, for example, have you established a secure device lender location for students who forgot to bring a web-connectible device? Are faculty finding themselves engaging in time-wasting attempts at repairing devices or trying to make them lesson-compatible? Finally, is the trend *extensible*? Do you have the ability to adjust for future changes, or are you dependent upon an outside agency? Some technical support staff, for example, are not totally comfortable assisting with various PC versus Apple devices. Will your school have to hire additional personnel or contract with an outside company to solve various technical glitches (Webb 239)?

BEWARE OF TREND VERSUS TRENDY TRAPS

In a time of rapid change, it is easy to mistake something that's trendy for a trend, especially when our pattern-seeking brains are constantly in search of cognitive time-savers. One trend trap is termed the availability heuristic. It was researched extensively in 1973 by two Nobel Prize–winning psychologists, Daniel Kahneman and Amos Tversky, who were curious about the following questions: Why is it so challenging for us to reason statistically? Why do we have strong tendencies toward excessive overconfidence in our beliefs? Why do we consistently underestimate the role of chance in events? Kahneman and Tversky proposed that the availability heuristic acts upon us because our brains rely upon immediate examples or perhaps prototypes of what we've seen and then draw fallacious conclusions from it (Kahneman 13–14). It is what can trick our brains into thinking that something is a trend when the latest technology is really just trendy.

There is no better example of the availability heuristic operating with technology than the Uber for X syndrome noted by Webb in her book, *The Signals Are Talking.* The creation of the ride-sharing decacorn plus Uber (a company valued at more than $10 billion) was so financially successful that it also succeeded in setting a classic trend-versus-trendy trap for more than 526 companies that described their start-ups with the word "Uber" for whatever service they were selling. One university even proposed an Uber-like tutoring company. The phenomenon became so trendy that a humorist for a financial website wrote a poem about it.

The sad news about these start-ups is that they went down to financial and professional defeat because of their ignorance of the availability heuristic. Various start-up companies witnessed the explosive growth of Uber and immediately leapt to the conclusion that similar share-based companies would also succeed. Failing to study Uber extensively and submit their Uber for X idea to a set of rigorous trend criteria and pose the critical questions caused most of their downfalls. Is my

Uber-like company "a new manifestation of sustained change within an industry, the public sector, our society, or the way that we behave toward one another" is the big question these companies should have posed multiple times before, during, and even after launching their businesses (Webb 182–185). While some of their failures were caused by inadequate funding, most of them were not providing a service that people needed to use frequently enough, nor did they have the potential to improve their quality of life.

A second trend trap that lies in wait concerns "belief bias." This trend trap may be even more insidious to avoid than the availability heuristic because it goes to our internalization of truth and evidence. Belief bias can best be defined as our inability to recognize the flaws in our reasoning in favor of our personal beliefs. All of us are prone to evaluating evidence according to our personal preferences (Sa, West, and Stanovich 498). For example, if you truly believe that eBooks and eReaders are the wave of the future, it is more likely that you will ignore evidence in the form of low circulation statistics, minimal requests for eReaders for check-out, and a general absence of them among the students using the library. Challenging your personal beliefs calls for the consistent application of the same critical thinking skills that we require of our students. It means formulating a hypothesis and then trying to prove it wrong. Whenever you find yourself totally agreeing with something that you think is a new trend, begin asking additional questions and work to find all types of evidence, especially data that can support your belief in what you think is an emerging trend.

The last trap is one that is afflicting us all and will continue to ensnare us throughout our attempts to correctly interpret the tech tea leaves. Because technology is the primary driver in changing times, we are vulnerable to developing a "techno-fix mentality." All of us are potential victims of the availability heuristic and bias belief and the errors that these can produce in our reasoning. The most dangerous trend trap, however, is to think that new tech tools are solutions. Falling into this trap may cause us to do irreparable harm to our programs and services and, consequently, our students (Naisbitt 52). With new apps and bots appearing daily, it is so easy to imagine that technology will cure reading and attention span problems, provide our students with the exact kind and amount of information they need to complete an assignment, and even write it for them. Years of experience with technology should have taught us that it will never provide us with the electronic, educational Holy Grail that will make our students lifelong learners. If, however, we do not monitor the trends, it does have the potential to lead us and our schools down the proverbial rabbit hole.

Questions

1. Assume that virtual reality will become the next content delivery platform. How is the school and its library poised to successfully employ it in various disciplines?

2. Choose a technology that has been cited in a recent "top ten tech list." Apply the CIPHER method to it and analyze whether it may become a trend or is simply trendy.

3. Select a trend that seems to be entering the mainstream from any of the following sectors: technological, economic, employment, educational, social/behavioral, or organizational/managerial. Create a response plan for incorporating this change into the library's programs and services.

4. Hypothesize about a technology that has the potential to make the library a victim of one or more technology traps.

REFERENCES

American Association of School Librarians (AASL). 2011. "Learning Standards and Common Core Standards Crosswalk." Available at: http://www.ala.org/aasl/sites/ala.org .aasl/files/content/guidelinesandstandards/commoncorecrosswalk/pdf/Cross walkEnglishAllGrades.pdf.

"American Library Association Center for the Future of Libraries." 2014. Available at: http:// http://www.ala.org/tools/future.

Bharati, Jnaneshvara. Accessed February 7, 2018. "Traditional Yoga and Meditation of the Himalayan Masters." Available at: http://www.swamij.com/faq.htm#what_is_a _swami.

Cuellar, Dann. October 29, 2015. "Delaware Boy Creates Prosthetic Hand with Library 3D Printer." Available at: http://6abc.com/news/del-boy-creates-prosthetic-hand -with-library-3d-printer/1058543.

Dynarski, Susan. April 8, 2016. "Why Talented Black and Hispanic Students Can Go Undiscovered." *The New York Times*. Available at: https://www.nytimes.com/2016 /04/10/upshot/why-talented-black-and-hispanic-students-can-go-undiscovered .html.

Figueroa, Michael. March/April 2017. "Our Futures in Times of Change." *American Libraries*. 48(3/4): 32–36.

"Fossil Fuel Subsidies: Overview. Oil Change International." 2017. Available at: http:// priceofoil.org/fossil-fuel-subsidies.

Gelles, David. August 17, 2014. "In Silicon Valley, Mergers Must Meet the Toothbrush Test." *The New York Times*. Available at: https://dealbook.nytimes.com/2014/08/17 /in-silicon-valley-mergers-must-meet-the-toothbrush-test/?_r=0.

Hammond, Betsy. September 7, 2013. "Missing Homework, Late Assignments Matter Little as Oregon Schools Grade Exclusively on Academic Mastery." *The Oregonian*. Available at: http://www.oregonlive.com/education/index.ssf/2013/09/missing _homework_late_assignme.html.

Johnson, Doug A. 2013. *The Indispensable Librarian: Surviving and Thriving in School Libraries in the Information Age*. 2nd ed. Santa Barbara, CA: Linworth.

Kahneman, Daniel. 2013. *Thinking, Fast and Slow*. New York: Farrar, Straus and Giroux.

McAfee, Andrew and Erik Brynjolfsson. 2017. *Machine, Platform, Crowd: Harnessing Our Digital Future*. New York: W. W. Norton.

Naisbitt, John. 1982. *Megatrends: The New Directions Transforming Our Lives*. New York: Warner Books.

"Our Products/Google." 2018. Available at: https://www.google.com/intl/en/about/products.

Sa, Walter C., Richard. F. West, and Keith E. Stanovich. 1999. "The Domain Specificity and Generality of Belief Bias: Searching for Generalizable Critical Thinking Skills." *Journal of Educational Psychology*. 91(3): 497–510.

Tetlock, Philip E. and Dan Gardner. 2015. *Superforecasting: The Art and Science of Predicting*. New York: Crown.

"Top Tech Trends—2017 Annual." June 25, 2017. LITA. Available at: www.ala.org/lita/tt.

"Track Your Sleep with the Jawbone UP24." October 9, 2015. Available at: https://hibr.com
/track-your-sleep-with-the-jawbone-up24.

Viswanathan, Shrinth. September 10, 2017. "The Cambrian Explosion in Technology, and
How It's Affecting Us." *The Economic Times*. Available at: http://economictimes
.indiatimes.com/small-biz/security-tech/technology/the-cambrian-explosion-in
-technology-and-how-its-affecting-us/articleshow/57217991.cms.

Webb, Amy. 2016. *The Signals Are Talking: Why Today's Fringe Is Tomorrow's Mainstream*. New York: Public Affairs.

Williams, Justin. April 15, 2009. "The 10 Greatest Flops in Computer History." *The
Telegraph*. Available at: http://www.telegraph.co.uk/technology/5132085/The-10
-greatest-flops-in-computer-history.html.

2

Technology Trends

THERE OUGHTA BE LAWS FOR THIS

If you were to play a technology forecasting game called "trend versus trendy" and began with the preceding terms, how accurate do you think your guesses would be? Where do you think adaptive learning algorithms, gamification of content, cloud-based word processing, platform agnosticism, computer coding, and bots rank on the trend versus trendy scale? Are they trending up or trending down (Heick)?

Trying to read the technological tea leaves is a challenge, especially in a time of rapid change. Technology does not respond to testable hypotheses and experimentation, which in turn rely upon quantifiable data and mathematical models. The scientific method that produces the statistically significant degrees of accuracy and objectivity that we witness in fields like physics, chemistry, and biology does not exist with technology (Storer 78). We yearn for laws that have been tested in laboratories and replicated many times so that the decisions we are constantly required to make with technology acquisitions and their concomitant need for changing educational pedagogies are the correct ones. The lack of formal laws, however, similar to those tested in the mathematical and scientific arenas and found to be consistently stable, should not prevent us from performing one of the first rules of the scientific method and that is observation. We need to continually observe where technology is taking us and step back frequently, for there are some generalities that are applicable to technology. Although these technological preferences are not scientifically based laws, they will facilitate wiser decisions about technology's use in our classrooms and school libraries.

Currently, technology is moving in incremental steps that combine elements of computing power, processing chips, software, storage chips, networking, and sensors in a concatenated suite of offerings (Friedman 22). Using the analogy of the mathematical order of operations: divide, multiply, add, and subtract; compare it to computer power and processing, big data, platforms, clouds, and machine learning. Sometimes it helps our thought processes to widen the lens for technology forecasting. Retreat a few steps and search for general trends and patterns that seem to be driving the acceleration process. Although technology suffers from a lack of formal laws that we can base some of our suppositions on, one law has been acting as a dominant variable in the big picture that warrants our understanding.

MOORE'S LAW

For fifty-three years one law has withstood the onslaught of technology's fast-paced advancements. In 1965, George Moore, cofounder of Intel, observed that the number of electronic components that fit onto an integrated circuit were doubling approximately every eighteen months. It is this exponential speed that makes most of the breakthroughs with technology possible. It is also a major link in an inter-dependent, overlapping series of technological developments. Moore's Law, how-ever, is facing a challenge because of the size of the chip.

During the time that Moore's Law has been operational, many computer scien-tists forecasted that the computer chip would have a limit as to the number of tran-sistors that could fit on it, thus eventually nullifying Moore's Law ("Double, Double . . ."). The minute this occurs, the research and development of new tech-nologies will dramatically slow down. Each year, however, computer scientists push the envelope by designing bigger chips and smaller transistors and new techniques such as using stained silicon to coat the chip that may subsequently extend Moore's Law into the mid-2020s ("A New Way to Extend . . .").

Thomas Friedman, author of *Thank You for Being Late*, provides a mind-blowing example of the doubling effect of Moore's Law: "Intel's first-generation chip was produced in 1971. Intel's sixth-generation chip furnishes 3,500 times more perfor-mance, is 90,000 times more energy efficient, and is about 60,000 times lower in cost" (Friedman 35). Friedman compares it to the progress that a 1971 Volkswagen Beetle would have made and claims that its speed would be about 300,000 mph with two million miles per gallon, and the cost would be four cents (Friedman 35).

For most of us, these developments are difficult to comprehend, so it might help to envision Moore's Law as an enabler. Its doubling effect is making a linked series of developments that include big data, the cloud as a network, storage and applica-tions facilities, platforms, machine learning, increased bandwidth, sophisticated algorithms, and artificial intelligence (McAfee and Brynjolfsson 74–75). As Moore's Law continues to function, it will enable the three P's: everything with technology will be more powerful, more portable, and less pricey.

BIG DATA

One of the major players in this time of change is big data. Although it seems to be on everyone's educational radar, it follows the traditional technology pattern of incremental step development. The first institutions to deal with the problem of big data were, of course, libraries. As early as 1944 Fremont Rider, librarian at Wes-leyan University, observed that American university libraries were acquiring so many books and other print materials that their size was going to double every sixteen years. Librarians did take notice of this alarming trend, known as "Fremont Rider's Law," and began to successfully develop coordinated collection development and interlibrary loan programs and to use microforms as active use and storage media. The problem with data accumulation and no real efficient means to quantify, analyze, and store it continued to plague every organization throughout the remaining decades. In 1995, however, Microsoft's Windows program gave users the ability to create the first business report using multiple sources of data. One year later, Microsoft debuted Excel. With its spreadsheet functions able to perform mathematical projections into the future and compute at acceptable processing speeds, the term big data was coined ("Big Data—A Visual History"). Merriam-Webster's Dictionary defined it as "an accumulation of data that is too large and complex for processing by traditional database management tools." That definition, as we all know, is already out of date. For in 2006, a new open-source software program called Hadoop gave users with inexpensive standard servers the ability to crunch huge data sets ("Big Data—A Visual History").

Now, with the present power of even a desktop computer, gigantic sets of data can be manipulated, correlated, and stored for present and future analysis. Big data is currently being referred to as the "oil of the digital age" ("The World's Most Valuable Resource" 7). We are afloat in an enormous cataract in the amount and quality of all types of available information. Years ago, managing the flow of information from the Internet was described as trying to drink out of a fire hose. Today it would be more like attempting to drink from Niagara Falls. We ourselves are the generators of almost all of that big data.

It has become a growth industry employing computer scientists, mathematicians, statisticians, marketers, and psychologists who are busy sifting through it, correlating it, and analyzing the results. Huge companies like Siemens and GE are marketing themselves as data firms ("The World's Most Valuable Resource" 7). So what has changed? How and why has big data become one of the major links in this overlapping series of accelerating technology changes?

The use of smartphones, the Internet, and social media are creating a treasure trove of data that are unrivaled for their ability to reveal almost everything about us from our product likes and dislikes to our secret fears and hopes. On an average day, we generate 2.5 million trillion bytes of data. Picture a typical school day: A student Googles for information about the Visigoths to complete a research assignment. She checks Facebook and her school Gmail account. She signs on to Twitter and sends several tweets to her friend. Another student is feeling anxious about an upcoming exam and Googles "teenage test anxiety cures." A middle school student has a fight with her best friend and blocks her on Facebook. Another student fails to make the football team and Googles "how to lose weight" (Stephens-Davidowitz 15–16). Whether we are watching a Netflix film or just idling in traffic, every activity is issuing a digital trace and creating more data for potential use and abuse. Using big data, the current information technology titans, Apple, Microsoft, Google, Facebook, and Amazon, now have a "God's eye view of seeing what we buy, look at, research, and how we entertain ourselves" ("The World's Most Valuable Resource" 7).

IT COMES IN ALL SIZES AND SHAPES AND IS POWERFUL

For years, we've thought of data as numbers, but data are accessible as words, photos, song selections, speech, personal appearances, images, or video. The trillions of data generated worldwide are not only available for analysis but, more importantly, to design algorithms to research and determine our preferences, tendencies, and behaviors. Disciplines such as English and history that in the past loaned themselves only to primary sourced text-based analysis can be researched using big data. Google Trends and NGram Viewer, for example, provide students with the ability to perform "search term research" in the social sciences by entering various keywords into Google Trends. English and history students can use Google's NGram Viewer to search millions of books published between 1500 and 2008 by history- or literature-based terms and perform quantitative research in English and history (Craver 2014, 1–2).

A second library-related big data example concerns the use of an online library to determine if book selection data could be used to ascertain readers' or viewers' degrees of sadness or happiness. A team of University of California, Berkeley School of Information scientists criteria-selected thousands of the most frequently downloaded fiction books from Project Gutenberg and employed sentiment analysis, coding each title for a happiness or sadness arc. Their coded database of books fell within six categories ranging from "rags to riches (rise)" to "Oedipus (fall, then rise, then fall)." The questions that this big data study generated are pertinent to libraries as well as publishers. Although the number of titles was relatively small (just 1,387), it shows the potential for big data results to influence what we may or may not be able to read. Publishers have a thin bottom line and may come to rely upon their own big databases to issue or not issue contracts to future authors based upon their own larger sentiment analyses. Will we or should we rely on our own big data generated by online public access catalogs (OPACs) to determine future acquisitions based upon sentiment analyses? (Reagan 4, 91).

Two Wharton School of Business professors also relied upon sentiment analysis to code the mood of articles and their placement on the pages of newspapers to see which types of stories get shared more often. Can you guess whether positive or negative stories are shared more frequently? The answer is positive ones, and the more positive the content, the more likely it is to become viral. Although this finding contrasts with the old newspaper business adage, "If it bleeds, it leads," the use of big data opens the door for newspapers to massage the news sufficiently so that we can be deprived of the actual facts of events (Berger and Milkman 10).

The significance for these two findings involving big data is alarming. Just imagine if a newspaper, as many presently are, is experiencing financial difficulties. The editing of a story to spin it in a more positive fashion or placing it in a section of the paper to improve its chances of going viral might be serious considerations for any journalist trying to survive in a world of reduced newspaper circulation. The implications of these big data examples are serious. Once data are crunched and analyzed, the temptation to act upon the results is enormous for profit-motivated organizations (Stephens-Davidowitz 93).

CAN BIG DATA HELP US?

Big data also has the ability to provide our school systems and libraries with several benefits. The first is having access to systemic contemporary data. Just think back to previous U.S. censuses. By the time government computers had crunched the data, many of the conclusions that could be drawn from it were already unreliable because demographic shifts in population, immigration, or economic downswings had invalidated the outcomes. With software programs that allow simultaneous data collection and analysis, such as Socrative (a student-response system), teachers and school librarians can determine if the majority of the students have understood a concept before they have even left the class (West 2). It gives us the opportunity to literally make a "course correction" during or immediately after a class by reteaching the material, altering our pedagogical approach to it before the next class arrives, or moving more quickly through an area because class performance is so strong.

For years, most teachers and school librarians have been able to predict the students who were going to be challenged by a specific research assignment. Our predictions were based upon their previous grades in the course, their attitude toward the assignments, and their levels of difficulty. Because we could control the last variable, assignment level of difficulty, we assigned some students easier research questions or more difficult ones depending upon the previous criteria. Big data in schools is starting to provide us with predictive assessments that will enable us to forecast what students already know and where the gap is between that and what they are expected to know with much more accuracy. For national assessments and subsequent assessment-based funding, the predictive aspects of big data are formidable. School librarians and teachers will have pre-knowledge of what students already know and should be able to target lessons to bridge the learning gap. In many states, predictive assessment data are being used to identify potential dropouts and obtain additional assistance for them. School librarians are in a perfect position to help students identified as needing assistance by providing remedial, Lexile-based reading materials and creating resource units specifically targeting identified learning weaknesses (West 5).

Discovering learning deficiencies in real time and being able to predict more objectively which students will benefit from additional educational help or increased academic challenges are not the only benefits of big data. The last concerns our ability to monitor learning on a larger scale by tracking performance via dashboard software and visual displays. As schools identify grade-based proficiencies, big data–level software gives them the ability to develop a systemic picture in real time. Districts can identify schools and even classes where students are achieving at normal grade-based rates and where they are failing to thrive. Based on these data, budget allocations can be distributed more democratically and results monitored monthly or even more frequently (West 6–8).

Big data make possible experimentation that in the conventional world is costly. In the digitized world, the user population does not need to be solicited. One benefit of big data is termed A/B testing. With database numbers large enough, a line of code assigns each participant to a randomly designated group. There are no surveys to be completed, with typical minimal response rates negating the conclusions that can be drawn. The total number of respondents remains constant. A program can code the responses, perform the relevant correlations, and determine their statistical significance. Finding relational effects, the "Holy Grail" of education, rather than implied results, is increasingly possible (Stephens-Davidowitz 276). Here is an example of A/B testing that paid off handsomely for a school district. EduStar, an education tech-testing company, randomly assigns students to different lesson plans to determine their efficacy. Students take a short test afterwards to see which lesson plans worked better for assisting students to learn the material. One of their surprising results occurred with students learning fractions through a gamification program versus a standard computerized method. As we all know, educational games have been touted for many years as a means to motivate students to learn material that is tedious but essential to concept mastery. School districts have spent millions of dollars on software programs, often with misplaced confidence in company-promised achievement gains. So which type of program do you think produced higher achievement for students learning to divide fractions—the standardized computer drill or the one that incorporated a basketball theme? Well, in this case, the boring one won out. While students spent five more minutes with the game-formulated lesson, they learned less.

The second EduStar A/B experiment involved 1,457 middle schoolers to see if a math program teaching a particular skill should include warnings and examples of common mistakes that students tend to commit. The second program tested whether just teaching the skill would result in the students accomplishing their learning goals more effectively. The results showed that the latter method produced better results (Molnar).

EduStar is attempting to establish itself as the *Consumer Reports* of ed-tech. As companies continue to ply schools with computerized programs that promise gains in student achievement, it will be imperative that schools have access to government-funded organizations that require rigorous A/B testing of programs, apps, and bots before schools invest their precious funds and are post hoc confronted with poor results (Chatterji and Jones 17).

THE DARK SIDE OF BIG DATA

In the age of big data, the entire world is a laboratory. With neither our knowledge nor permission, Google and Facebook are executing thousands of A/B tests to determine who clicks on which ad, picture, video, or message. (Stephens-Davidowitz 211). A/B testing can definitely be used for diabolical purposes from determining which sites, images, search terms, or action decisions in games are more addictive than the other. Armed with this new knowledge, it becomes so much easier to increase a site's addictive qualities (Stephens-Davidowitz 220).

Analysis of data can be employed to focus our attention, and those of our students, on just a few items. While we and our students are relieved of facing the "paradox of choice" in an information deluge, companies are making those decisions for us based upon analyzed information preferences, thus directing us toward what is most popular rather than thought-provoking or relevant ("Winner Takes All" 12).

BIG DATA AND SCHOOL LIBRARIES

There is no doubt that school districts across the country are embracing the benefits of big data to assist their administrators with early diagnosis of student learning problems, improving remediation efforts with predictive analyses, and monitoring student progress in real time. School librarians will also need to demonstrate that they are "making an empirically measurable difference" with their students as well (Johnson xvii). Where, however, cometh the data? Big data exist for school librarians both within and outside their schools. Outside the library, big data are being generated every day in the form of state and city reading and writing tests results, school district graduation rates, and demographic and socioeconomic data. Inside the library, data are readily available from general to student-specific circulation rates, circulation by material format rates, library usage by students, faculty and classes, resource-based unit citation analysis, library programs, services, and expenditures (Lickteig and O'Garro). Nationally, school library impact and reading data are conveniently accessible from the Research and Statistics part of the American Association of School Librarians (AASL) website. Citing national data about the measurable value of school libraries is useful, but can sometimes be dismissed because it is considered dated or doesn't reflect the local school community demographics and so forth. Conducting a local study that replicates some of the previously published data is even more important. Throughout the country, principals live and die by their schools' test score results. Presenting the results of a study showing that students who check out and read more books from the school library achieve higher scores on state reading and writing assessments is the most positive and valuable justification for the continuation of the funding and staffing of school libraries. Big data should be able to provide school librarians with the approximate number of books a child needs to read to improve his or her test results on state tests.

Publicizing the findings is, of course, vital. While all of us can recite the normal outlets for publicly disseminating them, one communication outlet is often overlooked. Once the relational link between student library reading and test scores has been learned, school librarians need to inform parents of the number of books their children are reading. Are they reading a sufficient number to score above average on state assessments, or are they not reading enough? Including this information about their reading progress on student quarterly reports is not a demanding task once the data collection process is automated. Big data should be viewed as a boon to school librarians because it will endow them with the ability to replicate national studies at the level that administrators and parents can feel deeply connected to.

THE ALGORITHM RULES

Algorithms are not a trend, but how they are coming to rule our environment is a fast-moving one. They are an essential part of the technological equation in a time of change. Raised on a diet of big data, algorithms are now a part of our daily lives and have the potential to run them. Algorithmic rules are devised from patterns distilled from volumes of data. The more data are acquired, the more algorithms can be created and then actually begin to find their own patterns within the data ("The Algorithm Kingdom" 53). They are faster, cheaper, and usually less error prone than we are. Computer scientists describe algorithms as a sequence of decision trees where the solution for complex problems with a large set of variables can be broken down into a series of binary choices that we might phrase as "if this, then that" (Steiner 6). The baking of a cake comparison is often used to illustrate algorithmic thinking. If, for example, we wish to bake a chocolate cake, our recipe would contain precise, order-ranked instructions: 1. Sift two cups of flour. 2. Melt one chocolate bar, and so forth. If we desired to bake a vanilla cake, a different set of instructions or algorithms would be required (Hickman).

While algorithms may make fewer mistakes than humans, they are not foolproof. One of the most famous examples of dangerous algorithmic computing occurred on May 6, 2010. Called the "flash crash" because of the lighting-like speed with which it occurred, the Dow Jones Industrial average plummeted 1,000 points in just a few minutes because of a series of competing algorithms that were programmed to sell a stock when the price reached a designated amount. Fortunately, human beings stepped up and repaired the damage within 20 minutes (Hickman). The "flash crash" illustrates a classic algorithmic pattern of "if this, then that."

Other algorithms are set to evaluate or predict risk for organizations or companies and can render judgment accordingly. The former chairman of the Federal Reserve, Ben Bernanke, became a victim of this form of algorithm when he went to refinance his home in October 2014. An algorithm was set to automatically deny a refinance of a mortgage if the person requesting one had recently left his job. Even though Mr. Bernanke's speaking fee was reportedly $250,000, the program's algorithms were set to reject his application based on previously collected data that had found a correlation between people who left their jobs and their ability to pay their mortgages (Irwin).

As a database grows, it gives programmers the opportunity to look for subsets of data, such as indirect or hidden correlations, with sometimes deleterious results. Insurance companies, for example, have programmed algorithms to assess the degree of risk for selling insurance to people who have long commutes to work (Hickman). The boundaries of algorithms are pushing outwards every day and displacing people who are currently performing routine work, such as welders working in an automobile factory assembly line. The disruptive factor of algorithms is high, and school librarians need to monitor their potential for good and bad in their respective environments (Steiner).

People are going to be ambivalent about algorithms. On the one hand, they have composed symphonies on a par with Beethoven, diagnosed us more accurately than physicians, written sports pages of newspapers that are undetectable to readers, and navigated highways and urban streets in various states with far fewer accidents than humans (Steiner 7). Their impact upon education and our school libraries is going to be considerable.

Algorithms will be used to support student retention, identify students in need of remedial assistance, personalize learning, and motivate them. Bill Gates, former president of Microsoft, foresees the development of virtual tutors that can give feedback on assignments and even query learners for their understanding of subjects (*NMC Horizon Report 2017 Higher Education Edition* 46–47). School librarians will welcome these improvements in education and in their ability to develop library programs and services that complement them, but we also have another important role to play with algorithms.

Reams of behavioral data are being fed into algorithmic systems, and none of us so far have any say-so about it. What is somewhat more alarming is that our own data in the form of search histories, online buying patterns, and so forth are algorithmic fuel. The variables that companies, organizations, and institutions correlate and base algorithmic decisions on continue to remain invisible to us. Computer programs are going to determine how we are treated by machines, the ones that select the advertisements we see, set prices for items we purchase, and make our doctor appointments (O'Neil 71).

A recent Pew Research Center report found that 73 percent of Americans believe that their search results are both accurate and impartial (Purcell, Brenner, and Rainie). The majority of Americans are clueless that their favorite search engine, Google, is functioning with algorithms that bias what they are accessing. Presently, Google is concentrating solely upon constructing revenue-enhancing algorithms, but in the future, they could alter their algorithms to influence something as serious as voting behavior. In August 2015, two researchers presented some startling study results at the National Academy of Sciences. In a series of five experiments, their research requested 4,556 undecided voter participants in the United States and India to use a search engine with pre-biased search rankings to research political candidates. Their results showed that the biased search rankings resulted in shifting undecided voter preferences by 20 percent or more. The researchers also found that the shift could be even greater with some demographic groups and how the rankings can be masked so that voters are totally unaware of the manipulation (Epstein and Robertson).

Google is the owner of the most powerful search engine in the world, and its company code of conduct motto is "Don't be evil." Google and Mr. Eric Schmidt, president of Google's spinoff company, Alphabet, fund The New America Foundation (NAF) to the tune of $21 million. In August 2017, Google was ordered to pay the European Union $2.7 billion for antitrust violations. When a scholar at NAF posted a statement on NAF's website praising the EU's decision, Mr. Schmidt expressed his displeasure at the posting, and the researcher was summarily fired (Vogel). Now, Google is a company with political algorithms at its disposal that have the potential to dramatically alter elections, not only in America but throughout the world (O'Neil 185). Most tech observers believe that Google would not engage in biased algorithms to influence voter behavior, but the potential for abuse if they are pressured about monopolistic business practices seems to exist from the latter incident.

ALGORITHMS AND SCHOOL LIBRARIANS

School librarians are the proverbial canaries in the educational coal mine. We have always been quick to observe the effects of technological changes and how they are affecting the information-seeking skills of our students at all grade levels. As more of our students evidenced organizational confusion with the number of web sources they had collected, we taught them how to use electronic note-taking and information format capture systems such as Evernote and Google Drive to manage and facilitate the information flow. When primary sources became required to complete historical research assignments, we introduced them to the deep web and showed them how to keyword search with more accuracy.

But the two previously cited studies—one revealing that 73 percent of Americans believe that the information they find on the Internet is accurate and impartial, and the other showing how easy it is to manipulate voter preference by skewing page ranking results—should be sufficient evidence for our instructive mission regarding the pros and cons of algorithms. Students will need to be taught not only how they are derived but also how they are working behind the scenes to ascertain our information-seeking tendencies, buying habits, political preferences, and messages that we respond to. Cathy O'Neil, author of *Weapons of Math Destruction*, claims that we will need "algorithmic audits" to dissect how mathematical algorithms were constructed. Princeton, Carnegie Mellon, and MIT universities share her concerns and have launched WebTAP, a Web Transparency and Accountability Project to increase algorithm construction awareness (O'Neil 185). In the meantime, it will be up to us to provide instruction in their potential to serve or abuse us.

THE CLOUD

The concept of the cloud is nebulous for many of our users. So vague in concept, that 51 percent of survey participants by Citrix that included a majority of millennials thought that stormy weather could obstruct cloud computing. According to Business Insider, only 16 percent comprehended that the cloud is a network that permits users to store, access, and share data from anywhere (Friedman 82). The cloud hosts a convenient, shared pool of networks, servers, storage capability, applications, and services, and it can be easily accessed with good Internet connections through major providers such as IBM, Intel, Amazon, and Google (Scheeren 81). Looking at the big picture in a time of change, the development of the cloud permits big data and its attendant algorithms to thrive because of its large storage capabilities. For school librarians, the cloud has been a cost- and time-saving development. For school districts, it's been a win-win, with practically no downsides.

Gone are the days when we struggled with school computers that had maxed out of memory and storage. The cloud is delivering on its promise of providing a flexible, scalable, cost-beneficial infrastructure that does not require a major investment in hardware or software. It creates a form of remote standardization that pools similar applications for everyone such as Google Docs, Google Sheets, and so forth. It also reduces the need for as many onsite technical support personnel, thus freeing up precious funds for curriculum-driven expenditures. Its last technical benefit is the ability to support multiple client platforms, whether onsite or remotely connected (Scheeren 85).

There are only a few downsides to the cloud and, so far, they have been negligible. Schools need to confirm that they have sufficient security to protect their data, and a reliable connection is needed to the Internet. Schools may be the recipients of unwanted advertising, and they usually have to commit to one commercial entity (Scheeren 86). In a time of increasing state budget deficits and less funding for education, the cloud could not have arrived at a better time.

THE CLOUD AND SCHOOL LIBRARIANS

The cloud has created opportunities for school librarians to extend their services beyond their conventional walls and to offer more diverse students, such as home-schooled and GED candidates, improved access to the library. With only a browser and an Internet connection, our students can experience SaaS (software as a service), an array of educational tools from companies like Google and Microsoft that let them type their papers, add some spreadsheet data, share it with an assigned partner, and present it to the class the next day from anywhere. They do not even need access to printers.

School librarians in districts that offer online courses or virtual schools can establish online libraries that provide students in virtual classrooms with library-related coursework, LibGuides, assignment-related searching tips, recommended eBooks, and more. Links to any digital source can be posted for a specific course using Blackboard or Google's Classroom application (Dickson). Adding links to free, full-text libraries, such as Project Gutenberg and the International Children's Library, or subscription-based eBook collections available through TumbleBooks or Overdrive exponentially increases the school library's collection size (Hart). Collaboration, that dreaded type of assignment for students with after-school activities or responsibilities, is no longer a burden with the cloud. Using Google Docs or a similar company's system, students assigned to work as partners or in groups can collaborate and share their work online without having to be in physical contact.

The last benefit of cloud computing concerns labor distribution. For many years, school librarians have had to rely upon onsite technologists to make repairs to equipment and perform general maintenance. Many times, school librarians were the first line of troubleshooters until help could arrive. With the cloud, it may be possible to modify this position to include media production services and instruction since their services will not have as high a demand. As schools adjust to the seamlessness of the cloud, they may be able to gravitate to a BYOD program that frees up funding for other important expenditures (Scheeren 82–83).

STAND ON THE PLATFORM

As the power of the chip increases, it enables all entities to collect and analyze large quantities of data, which in turn enables various types of algorithms to determine correlations. The analyzed data need to be stored for additional collection and analysis, which requires the cloud. The cloud makes possible the next link in this overlapping and interesting chain. The name for it is platform. Many computer scientists and other observers of the current tech environment believe that we are going to become a platform-based economy similar to Amazon, Google, and Uber. In the computer science world, GitHub is one of the best known. Approximately 12 million programmers use it to find preproduced programs for their businesses, download one and modify it, or create a new one and share it on GitHub (Friedman 63, 64). GitHub fits to a tee McAfee and Brynjolfsson's, authors of *Machine, Platform, Crowd,* definition of one. Their concept of a platform is "a digital environment with near zero marginal cost of access, duplication, and distribution" (McAfee and Brynjolfsson 163). Platforms are designed to transport the demand for a product—for example, books, articles from a library subscription database, or note-taking tips—to the user. Good platforms share the following characteristics. Their interfaces and how the user interacts with them are of utmost importance. The interface must also be as appealing and intuitive to users as possible. We have all observed how our students are attracted to the Google basic search page as their first go-to source of information. Most of them have to be required to cite sources from subscription databases in an assignment because their interfaces are so cumbersome to use compared to Google's. The authors remind us of Einstein's admonition that "everything should be as simple as possible, but not simpler" (McAfee and Brynjolfsson 169–170). Well-designed platforms complement themselves when they are reinforced with feedback from users and tweaked internally from the data they are collecting. They are in constant improvement mode, either in front or behind the scenes. Strong platforms are also asymmetrical by employing a two-way reputational system. Uber passengers reading this page will instantly recognize the company's policy of mutual evaluation, even in the absence of any laws requiring it. While Uber employs it to build trust between the rider and driver, a platform that allows for various opportunities for two-way interchanges between users and platform host will benefit from the receipt of new ideas for content, programs, and services. The last characteristic of a strong platform is almost antithetical to one favoring asymmetry in design. A strong platform maintains control of the interface and the experience that users have when they interact with it. So even though users have the opportunity to propose modifications, give recommendations, and so forth, the platform itself is proprietary, and the code and algorithms behind it are not open-sourced (McAfee and Brynjolfsson 208–211).

SCHOOL LIBRARIES AS PLATFORMS

By now the similarities between the definition and characteristics of strong platforms and school cyber libraries are apparent. School libraries with robust websites featuring mobile access to their OPACs, supplementary links, and so forth already meet part of the definition of a platform. They are clearly emerging as a major trend for the conduct of business, and they are fast becoming a vehicle for transmitting education in our schools. The questions we need to pose of them concern their efficacy and adoption in our libraries. Can the library as a platform, for example, pass the Google toothbrush test? Will a seamless, easy-to-use, asymmetrical school library platform be something that our students, faculty, and administrators will use once or twice a day, and will it make their lives better (Gelles)?

Many librarians are answering these questions in the affirmative, and others will need to develop platform-based libraries if they are to thrive in rapidly changing times.

School libraries have always been the center of learning in conventional schools. With the development of platform-based libraries, we can create virtual libraries that are available 24/7 for students to use: after school, while enrolled in an online course, being home-schooled, or in an alternative educational setting. The technical expertise once required for virtual libraries' design and maintenance is no longer a barrier to their development. School librarians are using companies such as Google Sites and Weebly to design, host, and store their data in the cloud gratis (Scheeren 165).

With the emerging technology trends previously described, school OPACs no longer need to reside on local school servers with their smaller memories and need for expensive server replacement every three years. OPACs can now live in the cloud where updates, fixes, and new iterations are seamlessly incorporated into daily library routines. Because they are not dependent upon small servers, companies like Follett and Mandarin can offer more sophisticated software versions that resemble public library systems. Their features include Google-like search boxes and Amazon-like images of book jackets that our students really respond to. Take a virtual field trip to Hempfield Area High School Library's platform and look at their OPAC and how it's configured. The search box is similar to Google's, and their link to online databases is right below the OPAC access and on the same page. Their librarians are definitely aware that most users leave a website within ten to twenty seconds and that they need to provide their students with the most essential links within those initial ten seconds (Nielsen).

What is critical right now is imagining the school library platform in a time of change. How can school librarians capitalize on this emerging trend and position their virtual libraries as the primary go-to site? Many school libraries already possess attractive, well-used websites, but they lack the intuitiveness, asymmetry, and appeal of platforms like Google and Amazon. As we have witnessed, they are not the primary place that our students go to search for information.

According to John Palfrey, author of *BiblioTech*, a school library platform that enables school librarians to thrive during a time of change will require a common digital infrastructure (Palfrey 90). School librarians are going to need to collaborate and share resources to offer more and improved resources to their user populations if they are to compete with companies like Google and Amazon (Palfrey 90). In a decade of diminished funding for school libraries and pressure to discard print collections and replace them with eBook collections, sharing access to remote storage print collections is probably out of the question (Antolini). Sharing digital collections, however, is not beyond our abilities. Just as university libraries initiated coordinated collection development programs years ago to counteract Fremont Rider's Law operating to burst their libraries at the seams, school librarians will need to negotiate sharing of digital resources as a means of increasing their eBook collections and access to more online databases and educational websites. Storage in the cloud facilitates this process because the computer memory problems are nonexistent. Starting locally is the first rewarding step. The Washington, D.C., Public

Libraries, for example, provide free online tutoring for students ("Homework Help"). If your students live in Washington, D.C., all they have to do is obtain a library card. Many city and county public libraries offer similar homework help programs. Once all of your students have cards to their local public library, the second financially rewarding step is to place a link to their online databases on your school library's platform. Students immediately have access to all of their school's and public library's online databases from the school library's platform.

After acquiring local digital resources, cast the net even further and pay an online visit to your state library. Kansas State and New York State Libraries, for example, offer a host of subscription databases that students can use 24/7 for successfully completing research assignments. Again, obtaining an e-card is all they need to access them. By placing and publicizing their riches on the school library's platform, you have increased access to materials that could never be funded or physically housed at your site. Continue to think past local and state resources to some of the large free digital public library collections. Include digital libraries such as Project Gutenberg on the library's platform. Most English classes still require students to read classic texts such as *The Iliad, Jane Eyre,* or *Lord of the Flies.* While students usually purchase paperback copies to perform marginalia, they frequently forget to bring them to class. One link to Project Gutenberg on the library's platform, and they can keep up with their in-class–related text assignment by downloading the text to any web-connected device.

School library platforms serving elementary populations can link to The International Children's Digital Library that contains 4,619 children's books in 59 languages. As our school populations become more diverse, the ability of a student to hear a story read to them by a parent in her or his native language through the school library platform is a wonderful educational experience. Create a link to the Digital Public Library of America that contains more than 18,000,000 items in all material formats from America's libraries, museums, and archives. It's searchable by data, county, state, image, and exhibitions. It also features a link to Europeana that includes access to more than 23 million digitized books, paintings, films, objet d' arts, and archival records. Both huge resources contain primary sources that would be excellent for use with American and European history projects (Palfrey 102–105). Keep looking outwards and observe the work that The Council on Library and Information Sources is doing. Their full-text reports about emerging library trends concerning the future of publishing, collaboration, and networking are timely and excellent. Periodically click on the Library Innovation at Harvard University and check out their most recent projects. One of their products is called Stack Life, and it allows users to visualize and virtually browse Harvard University's stacks containing millions of volumes.

If you are in a school district without a union catalog, approach other like-minded librarians to initiate plans to make all of your holdings searchable, retrievable, and shareable. School libraries need to modify their space to accommodate group projects and students with computers and to create teaching areas. As these changes become more urgent, the pressure to remove books from the collection will become acute. If, however, your school district has developed a school library network with policies in place for interlibrary loans and materials delivery, school librarians can establish coordinated collection development programs and begin heavily weeding collections with the proviso of keeping one copy somewhere in the system for future use.

TALKING BACK AND RATING OUR PRODUCTS

The asymmetrical aspect of a school library's platform is increasingly important as our students are accustomed to rating everything from the films they watch via Netflix to a meal they have at Panera. They also have valuable feedback to give us regarding our programs and services. With the exception of teacher evaluations at the end of a course and membership on teen library advisory committees, our students do not have much, if any, input into the operation of their respective school libraries. If your OPAC does have a feedback feature, install Awesome Box from the Harvard University Library Innovation Lab. It's free and gives students a chance to rate library materials that they have recently read or viewed. Once you have installed it, find a way to premiere it at some all-school gathering. After you've received a sufficient number of ratings for various items, create a webography of students' "Awesome Picks."

Having a library Facebook page and Twitter handle is de rigueur for any school library platform, but inviting students to communicate with a librarian while they are on your library platform is even better. When you search public library platforms, notice the availability of chat boxes. They will enable you to provide individual reference and research-related assistance to students who for all kinds of reasons cannot visit conventional libraries for consultations. While having a Facebook account in some school districts is not a permissible means to transmit information to students, the availability of a library chat box will be a solution. If your company's OPAC lacks this feature, begin agitating for one.

School libraries cannot waste time developing contemporary library platforms because we face too much competition from outside companies that would like to leapfrog our programs and services. Although we know the dangers of information propriety, our users do not. Our school library platforms are free and open to all, and they need to reside in the heart of our schools and become the primary place where our students, faculty, and administrators turn for help navigating during changing times (Palfrey 107–108).

MACHINE LEARNING

Machine learning, just like other technology advancements, adheres to a classic, incremental-steps pattern. Forms of it have been operative going back centuries, but it's the twentieth century that enables us to make those connections that trend analysis requires. In 1952, for example, Arthur Samuel created a computer checkers program that could beat human players. More importantly, the more games the computer played, the better it got at developing additional moves and strategies. In 1967, an algorithm was written to map a route for traveling salesmen to ensure stops at all their planned destinations. Eleven years later, Stanford University students designed a cart that navigated around obstacles in a room (Marr). As we gaze back at these milestones with machine intelligence, would you have been able to foresee Watson finishing off Ken Jennings on *Jeopardy!* or Lee Sedol bowing to a computer that just defeated him in the complex game of Go? Would you have been able to envision a computer program that mapped out routes for a salesman evolving into the GPS systems that we use in our cars? Finally, could you have foreseen an autonomous cart morphing into a little gumball-machine-shaped Google car that may have whizzed by you on a local street?

Developments in machine learning have reached a point where it will become imperative to apply trend analysis to our decision-making process. Although many of the advancements in machine learning are taking place on the fringe or are not yet operable for our discipline, changes are occurring so rapidly that school librarians need to keep abreast of them. The average auto design cycle, for example, used to be about every five years, but now it's taking place every twenty-four to thirty-six months. While it took thirty-nine years for only 40 percent of the population to use conventional telephones and another fifteen years to achieve full adoption, smartphones gained a similar 40 percent adoption rate in just ten years (McGrath).

IS IT MACHINE LEARNING OR ARTIFICIAL INTELLIGENCE?

Computer scientists are still splitting hairs among themselves about the differences between machine learning and artificial intelligence. Several books and articles state that each one is a subset of the other and that distinctions exist between them. What is not disputed, however, is how machines learn. Thriving on big data sets, multiple layered algorithms, and faster processing speeds, computers are becoming smarter about how they learn (Bostrom 7). With machine learning, the software educates itself by crunching data, rather than having to be explicitly programmed. Facebook, for example, employs machine learning to identify us in photos and to determine which status updates and ads to push to us ("Imperial Ambitions"). As Internet connections speed up with improved bandwidth and networking software, layered algorithms, and the availability of the cloud for storage, huge "data lakes" can be analyzed for correlations and data patterns ("Machines Learning").

Nowadays, machine learning is ubiquitous. It classifies and sorts our smartphone photos, detects spam in our e-mail accounts, and for librarians provides us with read-a-likes in our OPACs. To accomplish all of these behind-the-scenes operations, machine learning employs application programming interfaces, or APIs. These are sets of programming commands that allow us to archive our office memos when we click the "save" button and so forth (Friedman 62). One of the leading machine learning APIs that will affect school libraries is AT&T's Speech API. It's a speech recognition and natural language understanding platform. Our students, for example, may soon be able to query search engines using their natural manner of speaking and grammar, while the API converts their natural speech into text. Google Prediction, for example, is an API that developers can use for computer operations such as sentiment analysis of data, document classification, and purchase prediction (Wagner).

ARE BOTS THE NEW APPS?

New developments are occurring with machine learning almost at the speed of Moore's Law, about every eighteen months. Bots are the latest on the tech scene, and the most recent buzz concerns their ability to replace APIs and apps. Bots have actually been part of our discipline since the early nineties when they had a different name. School librarians are probably more familiar with the prebot term web crawler, an automated software system that toiled its way through millions of Internet sites, parsing keywords that we entered into a search box, anticipating that it would retrieve relevant search results. For years they've been used for automated stock trades and in e-tail stores like the Apple App Store to manipulate an app's sales position to garner more positive reviews (Martin).

As fast as business-based bots emerged, so did their black-hatted cousins. All of us know about spambots that gobble up millions of websites and then impregnate them with tons of ads, along with bots that purchase most of the great seats at a concert to sell at exorbitant prices later. They seem to be the opposite and equal reaction part of the equation that happens whenever a positive technological breakthrough occurs. Their ability to infiltrate and inflict harm is why we need to enter those time-consuming "captcha letters" to verify that we are indeed human and not bots. Bots are on the march throughout the Web. By 2017, they represented 52 percent of all Internet traffic, and the bad ones (29 percent) edged out the good ones (23 percent) in Internet transactions (La France).

Bots have now morphed into forms of software that permit natural language queries, allowing us to interact with them in a more human-like fashion. Using an office bot, for example, allows us to verbally send a congratulatory message to a colleague upon the birth of a child. The bot not only sends our message but also forwards an acknowledgement to us. Behind this new software development is an API that sends the actual email to our colleague. The new layer or bot tier serves to protect the API that is the foundation for the request but also makes it more secure from potential hacking. APIs will still be needed, because many times it is simply quicker to click on the "Open file" command on our computers than it is to verbally request it (Sandoval).

The use of bots is another form of machine learning that is fast becoming ubiquitous in all areas of our lives. Amazon's Echo, Google's Home, and Apple's HomePod are forms of residence-based bots that allow verbal commands to turn our lights on and off, that allow our televisions to change channels, that can bark like watchdogs, and that can even read bedtime stories to children. Currently, 35 million Americans are using them, and by 2020, at least three-quarters of households are expected to have them (Carr 12). Giving commands to a bot like Echo and HomePod is still machine-like in our interaction. We are still issuing various directives to these bots and not engaging them in extended communication that we would consider more human. Bot technology, however, is changing rapidly because of big data in the form of millions of voice samples culled from the Internet. Bots can almost match humans in transcription accuracy so that even computerized translation systems are improving quickly. Their text-to-speech recognition systems are becoming more human-like and less robotic sounding. While bots cannot yet understand the meaning of language, they are amassing the vocabularies and sentence structures to carry on more extended conversations involving, for example, booking more complicated travel itineraries to advising customers about mortgages.

Amazon is so intent on further development with voice-activated bots that they are offering a $1 million prize for a bot that can "converse coherently and engagingly for twenty minutes" ("How Voice Technology Is . . ."). More than 100 million Chinese are using a Microsoft chatbot called Xiaoice. The majority of users "chat" with Xiaoice between 11 pm and 3 am frequently about the problems that they experienced during their days. As Xiaoice collects more voice data and learns from the communications with its users, it is becoming smarter. Where it used to give users encouragement and relate jokes, it has moved on to produce a collection of poems that have set off debates about the issue of "artificial poetry" ("The Algorithm Kingdom" 54).

SCHOOL LIBRARIES AND THE NEW BOTS

These fast-moving technological trends have the ability to transform our schools and libraries as never before. Talking will clearly compete with typing. Humans can converse at 150 words per minute, on average, but type only 40 (Siegele). Although Google Suggest is already making inroads into the need for students to formulate their own keyword search strategies, voice-activated bots may eliminate this information-seeking skill all together. Our students will be able to tell a search bot what they are searching for, and it will seamlessly translate their natural query into a search for relevant assignment-related information.

We should be able to dramatically improve our library services to visually impaired and learning-disabled students. Our library platforms with the use of bots can be utilized as a general help system, posing questions such as, "What is the nature of your assignment?" or "What books do you like to read?" Querying online databases with their more advanced search features will be performed easily with prompting questions from library bots.

The application of bots to schools are numerous and especially relevant to elementary school libraries. In language arts, for example, students will be able to verbally craft their own stories with verbal encouragement from bots as preparation for learning to read. In the area of writing, voice-to-word transcription is four to six times faster than handwriting. Talking is a much faster way to express thoughts than with computers. With elementary school children, handwriting is a labor-intensive activity, averaging four words per minute with second graders. Some researchers suggest that children's rich, fluent, and complex vocabulary and active imaginations would be enhanced by the use of bots. They will permit a form of dictation allowing students to verbally transmit assignments; interact with bot-like tutors; and read aloud for correct pronunciation, speed, and syntax (Craver 1994, 27–28).

As companies like Amazon, Apple, Microsoft, and Google are quick to offer up these labor-saving bots, so will education companies be eager to exploit school systems with ones that promise to enable our students to learn more rapidly, to score higher on assessments, and to be more motivated to learn. School librarians need to be prepared to research and demonstrate where there are flaws with machine learning or actual misrepresentations about what it can do to help students. With the huge amounts of text and voice data being collected, there is a significant danger of "algorithms exploiting known preferences rather than encouraging exploration" ("How to Devise . . ."). Big data are allowing companies to constantly push similar books, films, and news items in a way that is so transparent that students are not fully cognizant of the trade-offs. One of the most important aspects of our jobs will be to alert them to the danger of homogeneity in student reading, listening, and viewing habits by teaching and demonstrating the danger of a lack of opposing viewpoints and how it hinders understanding of and empathy with others.

ROBOTS

The definition of a robot is becoming hazier by the year. Most of us envision R2D2 from the film *Star Wars*, but robots exist in all forms and even include software. They can be mobile or stationary, but they do share a set of common characteristics. They are programmable devices that are capable of executing commands automatically and possess internal or external control devices that their designers can use to manipulate them. They are becoming ubiquitous in industry, with an estimated 2.5 million predicted to be in use by 2019. The International Federation of Robotics classifies them into three categories: (1) service robots that perform necessary tasks such as delivering inventory in an Amazon warehouse to packers on an assembly line; (2) personal service robots that furnish individuals with some type of domestic care such as lifting a heavy object; and (3) professional service robots that deliver drugs in a hospital or clean buildings ("Impact of Robots . . ." 1). School administrators, rightly concerned with the increased employment of robots in the workforce, are heartily embracing robotics programs to expose students to robotics technologies, computer coding as a literacy, improving job readiness, and enticement for additional course work in STEM fields (*NMC/CoSN Horizon Report 2017 K-12 Edition* 3–5).

Robots have the best potential for schools when they perform in a professional service capacity by facilitating learning programs or functioning as teacher aides Dubai in the United Arab Emirates, for example, intends to employ fifteen TeachAssist robots in its schools to help teachers seamlessly integrate digital media and coursework into their class presentations. Voice-activated, the robots contain their own libraries of all the course material, from texts to images, films, and so forth. They obey commands from teachers to project a document or image onto a whiteboard or open a necessary app for the class. TeachAssist robots will even conduct class assessments to measure learning and provide graded reports to the teachers and parents.

Robots are also being used to enhance learning and encourage interdisciplinary work. Students at Benton High School in Alaska used Spheros, a programmable ball, to trace the odysseys of characters in *The Adventures of Huckleberry Finn* and study several battles depicted in *Beowulf.* The assignments combined coding skills with deep analysis of the texts and elicited empathy in both classes when students witnessed the characters' trials and tribulations (Schwartz).

The use of robots in education may well be partly student driven, as schools with robust robotics programs tackle mundane problems onsite and solve them. Students at a primary school in South Africa, for example, created a robot to clean Sterkfontein caves that they visited on a field trip. Dismayed by the amount of trash, with some of it in places inaccessible to humans, the students programmed the robot to circumvent sand and water and to remove trash in darker parts of the cave by employing a prong (Evans). When teachers observe students competently and successfully using robots, they may also begin to feel more comfortable sharing their classrooms with them.

As robots begin to invade classrooms throughout our country, school librarians will need to be at the forefront for their adoption and adaptation in not only their libraries but, more importantly, also in classrooms. School districts are notorious for purchasing various technologies and providing limited training to those whom they expect to integrate them into their curricula. School librarians are needed to not only assist with technical problems but also to determine the best practices for assimilating them into a teacher's curriculum.

Applying trend analysis to any proposal for the employment of robots, especially in the instructive assistance area, is essential. Performing background research and subjecting any potential new robotic acquisition to a CIPHER test is also essential. Look for contradictions with a teaching assistant–like robot. Does it assist while simultaneously losing student interest? Where is the inflection point? Is there someone at your school who would be perfect for test piloting a robot, and might their keen reception of it speed up its adoption? Will it violate present practices? At what point might a robot threaten existing teaching methods so that everyone will have to adapt to it? Can a robot be hacked in either good or bad ways? Is it modifiable? Are there robotic functions that a teacher can adjust to the level of a specific class? Could someone change an application of the robot and make improvements on it? Are there aspects of it that invade student privacy? Does a robot possess some extreme quality? Might a student who is withdrawn or suffering from a learning disability interact with a robot more positively than with a conventional teacher?

School district funding is so precarious that schools can no longer afford to invest in technologies that do not fulfill their promises. Lumos Labs, creator of a series of cognitive-based brain games, recently agreed to a $2 million dollar settlement brought by the Federal Trade Commission because it falsely claimed that their games improved student performance (DeSteno).

Critically reading research studies and tech reviews from valid sources is necessary to avoid experiencing the previous example with the acquisition of robots. In 2017, three researchers designed an experiment with the express purpose of demonstrating that robots lack the conversant qualities that mimic true social interaction, especially when nonverbal communication is involved. Their study with four- to seven-year-old children entailed one-half of them hearing a story read by an animated plush creature whose mouth and eyes moved expressively. The other half experienced the same story read by the robot when it was flat—unexpressive and unresponsive to any social cues from the children. To measure the children's understanding and use of new vocabulary words in the story, both groups were asked to retell it immediately and again within a four- to six-week period. As we might expect, the children's learning and engagement were increased in the presence of appropriate social cues. Children who had listened to the expressive robot used more of the new vocabulary words and had the greatest gains in long-term retention of the story. It's also important to note that the expressive robot group did not like the robot more. However, the social cues emitted by the expressive robot made the robot seem more reliable and trustworthy to the children. The moral of this study is to do as much research as possible with new educational technologies and submit them to a CIPHER test before committing taxpayer money for a robot that might not be developed enough to really engage students' attention and consequently positively affect learning (DeSteno).

THE INTERNET OF THINGS (IoT)

If you are wearing a Fitbit band on your wrist; purchased a Mimo monitor that lets you track your baby's breathing, temperature, and sleeping position from your smartphone; or use GlowCaps that send you messages reminding you to take your medication, then you are already experiencing the Internet of Things ("An Internet of Things"). The IoT is simply objects that contain computing power because they have embedded sensors or processors in them that carry information across networks. They are definitely a growth industry, with predictions that there will be 27.1 billion Internet-connected items—three times the human population—by 2021 (Ravipati).

Schools are beginning to realize the benefit of the IoT as they are discovering ways to monitor their energy use by installing lighting that responds to sunlit conditions and turns off when it is evening and the school is closed (Nadel). The IoT provides schools with the ability to issue students smart ID cards. Cincinnati Public Schools, for example, has a partnership with a company that requires students to use their cards when boarding and exiting their school buses. A quick slide into the machine sends a text to a parent that their child has safely boarded the bus, and a swipe upon exiting sends a text that their child has arrived safely at school (Doyne). Students can use a similar type of card to pay for their lunch and obtain snacks from school vending machines. Probably all of us would sign off on these helpful uses of IoT.

The smart card has other functions. In Texas, for example, school budgeting is directly linked to attendance data. Students are counted present in their homerooms each morning. If a student is not present in homeroom but somewhere else in the building, they are not counted as in school. The San Antonio School District invested $261,000 in a smart card ID system, because they hoped to recover a calculated $2 million in lost funding by taking more accurate attendance (Doyne). Both school-based situations and their solutions using IoT are commendable to us. Student safety and funding should be of paramount concern. Yet IoT technologies have the potential to operate as electronic leashes. By issuing smart cards, schools may determine how students traffic their halls, classrooms, lavatories, gyms, and so forth in real time. Attendance, for example, can be taken hourly, and a teacher does not have to take the time from a class to complete it.

A smart ID card can discover with whom students are talking and hanging out. Picture a group of students whose grades are mediocre and whose teacher-reported behaviors suggest total boredom with their courses and school-based extracurricular activities. The software running the program shows that they are regularly congregating in a specific hallway after many of their classes and outside near the auditorium after school. This example of "birds of a feather flock together" may be just the evidence that administrators need for school intervention. Students who are struggling in school and not interested in any outside school-sponsored activities usually fit a profile for dropping out, which would condemn them to a lifetime of high unemployment and a poor standard of living. Imagine being able to perform a targeted intervention where a trusted teacher gains these students' confidence and offers school remedial assistance, counseling, and other support services. All of these uses of IoT would probably meet with our approval.

IoT technologies such as smart card IDs, however, have a potential negative side. Depending upon the level of surveillance that a school wishes to set for the cards, it can potentially constitute an invasion of student privacy that could be taken to extremes. Students, especially teens, reach a natural development stage where they begin separating from their parents and other adult authority figures. They need time to socialize with their peers, form friendships, and just engage in the normal, daily silliness of adolescence. Imagine a second group of teens congregating regularly inside or outside a school to share fast food and soda that an older friend with a car has delivered to them. All of them match the profile for students who are obese. Does the school nurse convene an intervention by calling their parents and lecturing them about the addictive qualities of fast food and its deleterious effects on their health? Many school districts have started down this classic slippery slope without considering more of the up and down sides to the Internet of Things.

SCHOOL LIBRARIES AND THE IoT

The housekeeping part of our jobs will definitely be facilitated with the IoT. Many school librarians are charged with the loan, delivery, maintenance, and storage of multimedia equipment. Sensor beacons are in operation in several academic libraries now that permit linkage between an item and its physical location. In the future, web-connected sensors on each device will be able to indicate when a battery is low and needs replacing or when a device is nearing its targeted lifespan. Having IoT sensors on individual pieces of equipment permits tracking in real time. The IoT in this area should simplify what is usually a more onerous part of our job descriptions (*NMC/CoSN Horizon Report K-12 Edition* 51).

Capturing traffic data in our school libraries from student smart ID cards presents both an opportunity and a temptation. We can determine, for example, how many students visit specific areas or rooms of our libraries and choose to enhance or modify them based on the data. We can collect grade, gender, assignment-related use, and much more based on students with activated smart ID cards visiting our libraries. The data can enable us to broaden our programs and services because we are not even cognizant that we are being insufficiently inclusive. Because big data are going to demand that many of our programs and services be empirically defensible, the data that we could collect may correlate with student achievement on various assessments. Can you picture formulating relational hypotheses demonstrating that students who use the library more frequently tend to have higher GPAs and higher scores on state and national assessments? Will high library circulation data per individual show a correlation with National Merit Scholar commendations, semifinalists, and winners? Years of observing students who are regular users of our libraries has provided us with this evidence, but now we may have an opportunity to objectively measure and evaluate it using an aspect of IoT.

There will be a corresponding dark side to the IoT, even for our libraries. School librarians have always been associated with student privacy issues and consider protecting them one of our core values (Gorman). It will be challenging in the years ahead for us to walk the thin line that the IoT provides in areas of safety, performing time-saving daily tasks such as attendance taking, and equipment management and its potential for helpful intervention.

Where does the IoT become unnecessary surveillance? Smart cards can be activated at different levels to solely track attendance or to monitor student movement anywhere in the school. At what level should smart IDs be set? Where does a school district store all the data it collects, and how long do they archive them? Since schools will need to store these data in the cloud, how will they protect student identities from hacking? If someone obtains a student's ID number, they could easily detect exactly where a student is in a building and plan accordingly.

Remaining current about the potential for the IoT to affect our schools and libraries is vitally important. In 2012, only 3 percent of school districts were employing smart ID cards, but the number can clearly be expected to grow given the understandable exigencies of funding and personal safety (Brown). School librarians will need to attend educational technology meetings and be ready when smart ID cards and other IoT proposals are raised to prompt discussions that include opposing viewpoints, levels of smart card employment, data type collection protocols, data analysis, and storage protection.

M-LEARNING

M-learning or mobile learning (ML) is an understandable outgrowth of Moore's Law, computer transmission speeds, ubiquitous Wi-Fi, and exponential improvements with software (Friedman 71–72). Through the use of smartphones, tablets, and smartwatches, our students can access learning anywhere they have an Internet connection. This easy access is creating unlimited opportunities for school librarians and teachers to provide more meaningful interactions with course content. Teachers in every field can design lessons that leverage ML for data collection, literary analysis, viewing art work, participating in performing arts and sports programs, and lesson review and assessments. In the next few years, ML will dramatically affect student course content and how it is delivered (*NMC Horizon Report 2017 Higher Education* 40).

The use of mobile devices for information searching is continuing to grow, which indicates a readiness on the part of our students to readily adapt to this form of learning. This year, Internet searches using mobile devices and tablets surpassed desktop searching by 55.8 percent, an increase of 4.1 percent over the previous year (Enge). Google's page ranking system is placing mobile search version results ahead of desktop search results, which is going to yield fewer updates for desktop results in comparison to mobile ones (*NMC Horizon Report 2017 Higher Education Edition* 40). More students are also relying upon mobile devices to study, as noted in a recent McGraw-Hill 2016 digital study survey of 2,780 college students. Seventy percent reported that it was important that they study with mobile devices, 81 percent believed them useful for homework, and 79 percent used them to prepare for tests and exams. Seventy-one percent indicated that use of mobile devices increased their engagement with the course content (McGraw-Hill Education 7). For students taking online courses or enrolled in online high schools, ML offers 24/7 access to lectures, assignments, and other course content that allows asynchronous learning opportunities for students engaged in part-time employment or burdened with family responsibilities.

While many of the advancements with ML are occurring at the college level, high schools are also beginning to create ML environments by upgrading their bandwidth and storage requirements and securing their systems from data theft. El Capitan High School in Merced, California, for example, spent $98 million to create an ML environment by providing students with Google Chromebooks plus access to corresponding Google apps, electronic textbooks, and videos. Their librarians are proving essential in assisting teachers with the technological and pedagogical adjustments that are necessary in ML environments (Wong). In 2006–2007, Qualcomm partnered with Onslow County Schools in North Carolina to introduce ML into their mathematics curriculum. Their first step involved installation of fast and reliable Internet and Wi-Fi connections. The second phase distributed smartphones and eventually 1,000 tablets to qualifying students enrolled in math classes ranging from algebra to AP calculus. Math students responded positively, with almost two-thirds of them taking an additional math course after experiencing the ML format. Faculty revamped their content delivery to include the means for online video remediation and use of a digital textbook and social media tools to support peer mentoring (Baker, Dede, and Evans 13).

College ML developments are important to note because secondary school adoptions are usually not far behind. Purdue University, for example, increases the interaction aspect of ML learning with an app called Hotseat. Currently in version 17.0, Hotseat enables students to answer questions in class in real time and anonymously. Professors can poll and quiz students using the app and, more importantly, read the responses to determine which students might benefit from further explanations or examples (Ellison). Using GoPro cameras to produce a food science panoramic-style video is another ML method that gave students at University of Nebraska-Lincoln's College of Education and Human Sciences the chance to experience a VR-like tour of the laboratory. This ML format is an easy and inexpensive one for school librarians to adopt for future new student and faculty library orientations, respectively (Amen).

M-LEARNING AND RESEARCH

On the surface, ML seems a promising development for increasing learning and consequently student achievement. But is it? The research is neither solid nor longitudinal in nature. To our technologically trained minds, ML appears to offer additional student engagement with course material, access to course materials from any location, and a means for teachers to give and receive current and more frequent feedback. Do these obvious ML benefits result in increased student achievement? Fortunately, several studies are indicating that ML is an improved method of content delivery. Professors Elfeky and Masadeh conducted a small study composed of fifty students divided into experimental and control groups. The experimental group received mobile-based access to all course lectures and other relevant materials, while the other group received just face-to-face professor contact. After administering the same achievement tests to both groups, the experimental one scored higher on the achievement tests for learning the material (Elfeky et al.). A second study conducted over a two-year period with anatomy students in conventional versus ML-enabled classes at Middlesex University in the UK revealed that student attendance, achievement, and engagement were higher in classes where the students used iPads to access muscle and skeletal 3D apps and other coursework than in classes that were taught using traditional nonmobile device methods (Wilkinson and Barter 1). While these two studies are not massive, they were designed with scientific rigor and demonstrate that ML may be a promising method for increasing student achievement. What is also important to note with these studies is the ability to replicate them in elementary and secondary school settings. Having access to local results with regard to the implementation of a new pedagogy is probably more relevant to parents and present faculty than citing scores of college-based studies and a few secondary-level ones. The ability to perform A/B testing with parental consent, of course, is in every school district's interest. Results can not only be used for budget requests but also as a means to convince faculty members of the need to retrain for this new method of content delivery.

SCHOOL LIBRARIANS AND M-LEARNING

ML has a set of criteria that are necessary for its success. These conditions are ones where school librarians can make major contributions. The first condition is leadership. While planning, demonstrating, and supporting faculty are understood, school librarians also need to assume a leadership role with new technologies that provide a sense of vision to those who may not be able to see the ability of ML to positively affect student learning. Being able to envision what ML is and present compelling demonstrations, videos, research results, and examples of successful adopters of it will be necessary for its success. Obtaining faculty support will require a school librarian who can inspire by example and include multiple perspectives and approaches to integrating ML into the school's curricula.

Assuming a wide range of professional roles is part of school librarian responsibilities in a time of change, especially when it involves ML (Taylor, Subrmaniam, and Waugh). Too often schools announce new technology-enabled programs with much fanfare but little training or planning on the part of administrators. Faculty, under pressure to show that they are complying with new demands, simply insert one or two irrelevant lessons into their curricula, demonstrate use of it, and afterwards revert to their tried-and-true teaching methods. ML, however, is a potentially transforming technology if proper planning, training, administrative support, and evaluating results are considered.

Planning for ML entails school librarians helping to ensure that their schools have supporting infrastructure relating to sufficient bandwidth and Wi-Fi connections and stable content learning platforms. The 24/7 accessibility of the selected ML platform is paramount. Schools that attempt ML without strong infrastructures provide justifiable excuses for reluctant faculty to resist developing and integrating ML content into their curricula. An ML platform must possess diagnostic and assessment features that give administrators and faculty daily and periodic opportunities to measure and evaluate ML success. Before switching to ML learning, school librarians need to be involved in defining and determining the conditions of what constitutes a successful ML project. Becoming a designer of an A/B type test with a mobile versus conventional class to determine any ML achievement gains should be considered essential to gain future student, faculty, and parent support. The last part of ML planning that school librarians need to become involved in is helping to guarantee that ML success can be leveraged with additional conventionally taught classes throughout the school or district (Baker, Dede, and Evans 12).

School librarians have been creating resource-based instructional units and serving on curriculum committees for years. Knowing that creating an ML curricula that support state and national grade-level learning objectives is something that is intuitive to school librarians. With ML, a balance needs to be struck between static styles of learning (e.g., reading and viewing videos) and mobile forms of learning (e.g., writing, creating, designing, collecting data, and collaborating) (Baker, Dede, and Evans 15). School librarians have been integrating various components of information literacy skills into grade-level units and transitioning to mobile aspects of learning for several years. It will continue to be a smooth process for us. Our faculty, however, will require assistance with evidence-based practices that are starting to emerge with ML. Simply downloading entire videos onto ML platforms or importing thirty-minute videos of lectures are not considered ML best practices. School librarians will need to demonstrate and advise faculty members that not all subject matter loans itself to mobile devices. The two-minute rule, for example, for reinforcing previous content with online polling or three-question quizzes or updating current knowledge is becoming a standard guideline with ML. Devoting no more than five minutes for short interactive game-based learning activities, short videos, or knowledge questions is also considered another ML limit. With evidence-based practices in mind, faculty will begin to develop confidence with integrating ML into their curricula (Chaffe).

Faculty will need assistance in adapting ML techniques to their classes. Devoting one professional development day to it will not imbue teachers with enough confidence and technical skills to thoroughly integrate ML into their curricula. In addition to technical skills, teachers, whose average age is forty, will need to unlearn the "sage on the stage" mentality. The latter set of practices will be challenging to alter for many. Because most school librarians have flexible schedules, we are most suited to providing professional development and technical skill assistance during teacher preparation periods and during pre-/post-school hours. Giving teachers the opportunity to meet with other ML adopters, for example, and co-teach classes with ML-adept school librarians will help provide them with the ongoing support they need to successfully develop improved ML teaching strategies and appropriate ML applications (Baker, Dede, and Evans 20).

ARTIFICIAL INTELLIGENCE

The terms *artificial intelligence* and *machine intelligence* are being bandied about interchangeably. Machine intelligence does not convey the sense of urgency, magic, and wonder that the words artificial intelligence do. When we hear the latter term, we tend to think of conversing with a humanoid robot about the recent book we read or film we watched. When we hear the term machine intelligence and witness Amazon's virtual assistant, Alexa, reading a bedtime story to a child from a smartphone, it comes across as machine-like (Willman). As each term declares itself a subset of the other, it becomes important to distinguish between them, because machine learning is making rapid gains, while artificial intelligence is developing more slowly. As school librarians, we need to monitor both trends, but artificial intelligence may not require our immediate attention in the way that machine learning does, and perhaps its slower development will reduce our anxieties a little as we deal with a host of other technological changes.

Bostrom, in his book, *Superintelligence*, defines artificial intelligence as "machines matching humans in general intelligence" (Bostrom 3–4). In contrast, machine learning is associated with pattern recognition, while artificial intelligence draws deeper, more intuitive, human-like conclusions from those patterns. Up until 2014, the touchstone for artificial intelligence was the Turing Test, which demands that a human being fail to recognize that it is conversing with a computer ("Turing Test"). On June 8, 2014, a computer programmer named Eugene Goostman won the Turing Test challenge by convincing 33 percent of the judges that they were conversing with a thirteen-year-old boy instead of a computer. Although passing the Turing Test is an impressive victory for artificial intelligence, it continues to face numerous impediments. Yet it is making significant strides in overcoming them ("Computer Simulating . . ."). Just like the IoT, it, too, is a growth industry, with predicted earnings from its applications increasing from $8 billion in 2016 to more than $47 billion in 2020 ("Worldwide Cognitive . . ."). It is a technology trend that we definitely need to monitor over the next few years.

One of the major stumbling blocks for artificial intelligence is termed Polanyi's Paradox, named after Michael Polanyi, a Hungarian-British polymath who wrote a book in 1967 titled *The Tacit Dimension*. Its basic perception is that "[w]e know more than we can tell." Installing a light bulb, identifying a hit song based on hearing three notes, and quickly recognizing that someone means us harm and fleeing are actions that we undertake naturally without our brain having to perform a set of explicit tasks (Autor 136). As Polanyi recognized, we do these things tacitly without really being aware of how we accomplish them. The actions that we undertake tacitly require creativity, flexibility, judgment, empathy, and common sense (Autor 136). A medical robot, for example, may be able to discern that a person is bleeding badly and to apply pressure on the wound but not be able to sense that the person's fear of blood is escalating their condition and offer a calming hand or voice. These are the types of the challenges that artificial intelligence is trying to conquer, and is doing so incrementally with the help of machine learning.

THE POWER OF NEURAL NETWORKS

Computer scientists are making great strides in artificial intelligence by developing neural networks rather than hierarchical ones. They facilitate computers in solving problems in a manner similar to the human brain, rather than crunching data in a top-to-bottom formation. Neural-type networks identify patterns of information and delegate various functions to other network parts. They also possess the capacity to improve from errors in various aspects of the network (Craver 1994, 26). Where they are constantly improving is in their extended layering capacity. With one layer, for example, you can discover one pattern within the data. With multiple or convoluted layers of data, the computer can begin to detect patterns that even a human is unable to locate (Lewis-Kraus). Their increased layers provide the means to not only realize improved results but also make them capable of levels of abstraction that can simulate human intelligence. Microsoft, for example, has constructed one with 152 layers (*NMC Horizon Report 2017 Higher Education Edition* 5). Neural networks feed on the intersecting and overlapping continuous improvements that are occurring with the computer chip, big data, algorithms, and the cloud.

One of the most dramatic improvements employing a neural network structure occurred in November 2016 with Google Translate. School librarians first introduced our students to Google Translate in 2006 for quick, sometimes laughable, translations of a French, Spanish, or German word or phrase. Our foreign language teachers pointed out Google Translate's fairly consistent grammatical and translation errors and warned students not to rely upon it for correct interpretation of any foreign language text they were reading. Google Translate previously relied upon a phrase-based machine translation format that broke apart words and phrases and translated them independently of each other. By switching to neural machine translation (NMT), the new Google Translate employs complete sentences as input and translates them as one. Using NMT, which is constructed of a massive database consisting of previously collected foreign words from the old Google Translate and Google Translate Community, a website where users from multiple countries translate sentences from their own language and rate translation by others, the new version of Google Translate begins to comprehend new words and phrases that it is learning over time from all of the additional information it is receiving (Lazzaro). Now when you type in a paragraph from Moliere's play, *Misanthrope*, the translation from French to English is remarkably accurate. It is so improved that it easily passes a type of Turing Test. A French teacher will probably be unable to recognize that it is the work of a machine (Lewis-Kraus 42). With a set of Google's

Pixel Airpods, students can utter the words "help me speak German" and begin speaking and listening using Google Translate (Pierce).

The debut of Google Translate, while having profound educational, social, and cultural implications, is a tremendous advancement for artificial intelligence. Neural networking inches us closer toward replicating human intelligence in an undetectable manner and begins to match the definition of AI. Neural networking is also enabling huge strides in other areas besides translation.

Google, for example, is constantly tweaking its search engines behind the scenes by using improved forms of machine learning/artificial intelligence. Their most significant tweaks concern Google search, the main search engine that our students use and abuse so regularly. For the past five years, Google has increased the semantic qualities of their search engine in an attempt to provide users with more relevant search results. Google Hummingbird and Pigeon are programs that attempt to interpret what a user is actually searching for by the terms they input. Hummingbird delivers results for a posed query even if the exact words were not entered, with the assistance of a massive database of similar terms and synonyms. Google Rank Brain is part of the Hummingbird algorithm and places semantically discovered results at the top of the search results pages. Google's Pigeon and Possum algorithms employ GPS data to furnish improved search results that are dependent upon the searcher's location ("8 Major . . .").

THREE FORMS OF LEARNING

Artificial intelligence is developing in three major areas: supervised learning, unsupervised learning, and reinforcement learning. Supervised learning entails using labeled sets of data as examples for computers to train to understand how to recognize by matching what is desirable versus what is not. An A.I. algorithm can be employed with the data to recognize what is a spam email and what is legitimate email with a supervised learning system. The computer improves its accuracy by learning from the labeled data, with no intervention needed by a programmer or a list of rules. Supervised learning is the type that is presently being used to sort millions of images, detect anomalies in credit card purchases and notify us, and spot malware ("From Not Working to Neural . . ." 4).

Unsupervised learning involves having the computer search for oddities in data, images, text, and so forth that humans do not know exist. This form of A.I. is frequently employed within a network to identify a security breach or by a company to expose new types of fraud. Reinforcement learning is a blend of the two previous forms and entails educating a neural network to communicate with a specific environment and using weighted layers of the neural network to feed back a reward so that it acquires more learning. Teaching a computer to play a game of chess and providing feedback of its winning creates an algorithmic reinforcement for it to improve many times over ("From Not Working to Neural . . ." 4). All three forms of A.I. are being employed in various subject disciplines because computer scientists have discovered that they can be used in combination with one another to obtain accurate results. Google's Smart Reply system, for example, relies upon two neural networks to pose replies to emails ("From Not Working to Neural . . ." 4).

ARTIFICIAL INTELLIGENCE AND EDUCATION

Improvements with A.I. are going to affect education and, eventually, school libraries. Arriving in technological increments, it is already manifesting itself on the educational fringes. Most of us intuitively realize, for example, that students who can afford to pay for PSAT and SAT private tutors can have a significant head start over students who cannot afford them. The tutored students' weakest areas in either English or math are quickly diagnosed by tutors, and work commences to shore up quadratic equations or vocabulary deficits with multiple practice problems and subject-targeted drills. What role can A.I. play in leveling this lopsided field?

Khan Academy has attempted it by forming a partnership with the College Board to help any student improve their PSAT or SAT scores. First, they have the free option to take eight practice tests, which give them excellent, predictive feedback on how they might fare on a real PSAT test. Another link provides them with thousands of practice questions, videos, lessons, and hints. So far none of this requires artificial intelligence—just hard work on the part of students. A.I. kicks in after students take the actual PSAT. Khan Academy uses a form of A.I. that diagnoses students' weaknesses and directs them to lessons that can help fill in the learning gaps ("Khan Academy . . .").

Khan Academy's free A.I.-based assistant is being used by 1.4 million students, and 450,000 of them have linked their College Board scores on the PSAT with Khan Academy to receive targeted assistance on questions they missed (Friedman 228). A.I. assists in two areas with this beneficial event. It immediately relieves students of the necessity for repetitive study in areas where they have already demonstrated subject mastery, and it zones in on students' weak areas, giving them time to devote all of their PSAT study time to improve their performances.

In Mountain View, California, students at the Khan Lab School are experiencing similar A.I. software to take tests and watch instructive online videos from Khan Academy. In this instance, half of the faculty serve as tutors providing academic assistance with various subjects. The other half serve as mentors offering appropriate feedback and encouragement to keep students on task.

In both instances, A.I. is being used to improve learning with its targeted diagnostic features. Some studies, for example, are showing that software that mimics the responsive role of a tutor, rather than producing one question after another, can improve learning. Educational artificial intelligence systems now contain algorithms that adjust their answer rate to about 70 percent of the time, which is the critical success percentage that neither bores nor discourages student interest. A.I. is also improving its diagnostic capabilities based upon the data that students are producing daily in the form of assignments and assessments. Its diagnostic abilities will improve as it becomes acquainted with the students over time ("Machines Learning" 15–16).

ARTIFICIAL INTELLIGENCE AND SCHOOL LIBRARIES

School libraries will benefit from advances in AI in two areas. The first will be with student services. Our OPACs and online databases will improve with access at a deeper level. Students will be able to perform voice-activated, natural language queries, and our resources will be able to supply them with images, text, and data from books, article databases, and media in a form of a micro-federated search process. Our eBooks will produce relevant graphs or images for students to insert and cite for an assignment as easily as they retrieve it. In 2016, at Aberystwyth University, for example, students designed an A.I. catalog that accepts speech-based book requests, locates the hard copy and leads students to the appropriate book shelf (Staufenberg).

A.I. will also make possible research databases similar to Semantic Scholar and Microsoft's Academic. Both new types of search engines permit semantic, full-sentence searching and the retrieval of articles through a ranking of article citations. If students do not enter the relevant keywords, the search engine will be able to infer other relevant synonyms and produce results for them. A.I.-driven OPACs and subscription databases will permit our students to search more naturally without the extent of instruction that is presently required.

The ability of school librarians to develop databases of valid websites for specific assignments that have already filtered out ads and irrelevant commercial sites should also be achievable with A.I. In 1994 National Cathedral School, for example, developed Eagle Eyes, an Internet database of valid websites for various assignments, but it is only searchable by keyword and lacks the ability for Boolean logic applications. With A.I. refinements, a school librarian–generated database similar to Semantic Scholar or Microsoft's Academic could be designed that would bypass the Internet and serve as a platform for other school libraries to input and share their web resources (Craver 2002, 214).

The second area where A.I. will improve school libraries concerns personalized learning opportunities. A.I. is going to furnish school librarians with some useful detours that will enable us to direct our knowledge to yield improved results with academic achievement. We will have the opportunity to transfer our focus to engage our students in deeper forms of learning (Whitehair). Our students will have assigned A.I. tutors that will require information from school assignments and school library research resources to provide them with the extra assistance that they need to help a student in a particular class or with a specific assignment. School librarians will be needed to program A.I. tutoring machines with the applicable information.

Although school librarians provide reading guidance by recommending appropriate interest and grade-level print and nonprint materials to students, we do not have an encyclopedic knowledge of our fiction or nonfiction collections in the way that A.I. will have. We are also quasi-limited by our personal interests, which will not be a problem for A.I. We may read, for example, less in the area of science fiction or fantasy. A.I. will enable us to deliver reading guidance at a deeper, personal level. Because our collections will be searchable at profound levels, we can, for example, recommend additional titles to a student who has devoured just about every dinosaur book or who wants a read-alike after finishing the Harry Potter series.

ARTIFICIAL INTELLIGENCE: PERILS AND PROMISES

While A.I. seems to offer wonderful opportunities for school librarians to dramatically improve our programs and services by individualizing them and deepening access to our resources, it is going to affect society in ways that need to be tackled before major damages occur. Some of the perils of A.I. are already manifesting themselves in ways that school librarians need to address.

On January 13, 2015, 1,000 scientists signed an "open letter" urging the world to study the impact that A.I. was currently having and could have in areas regarding employment, the military, public safety, world economies, and more. The number of scientists who signed the open letter reads like a who's who in the field of A.I. and has already garnered 8,000 additional A.I. scientists' signatures (Russell). Tech titan Elon Musk claims that "with artificial intelligence we are summoning the demon" (McFarland). So what are the issues that we face as a society with this new scientific frontier that we are currently forging? In 2016, the World Forum identified nine ethical questions that we as global citizens need to address concerning the future development of A.I.: (1) What is the potential for unemployment on a vast scale? (2) How will A.I. developments foster inequality? (3) How will human interaction and behavior be affected by A.I.? (4) How can we protect ourselves against A.I. mistakes? (5) What is A.I.'s potential for bias, especially racism? (6) How do we keep A.I. secure against government-sponsored or outside enemies? (7) How do we protect ourselves from the unintended consequences of A.I.? (8) How do we maintain control over A.I. applications and functions? (9) How will we define what is humane treatment of A.I.? As highly trained and certified school librarians, many of us are already witnessing the dark side of A.I. with the types of bot-created information we are encountering on a daily basis and the challenges we confront in determining its validity, reliability, and creditability.

A.I. is making significant advancements with multimedia posing impediments to our abilities as humans to determine the difference between truths and falsehoods. For our students, it is even more difficult because detecting bias in information in all its formats is a skill that does not come easily to them. A recent MIT Media Lab study of twenty-seven children ages three to ten years old arranged for them to play with A.I. devices and toys ranging from Alexa, Google Home, a chatbot named Julie, and Cozmo, a robotic bulldozer. The younger children endowed the A.I. devices with human qualities and asked them personal questions concerning their age and well-being. Nearly 80 percent of them believed that "Alexa would always tell the truth," and many thought they could interact with the devices and teach them something that the children already knew, such as making a paper airplane (Botsman 5). Educating students to think critically is one of the most demanding tasks of our profession, and it will become vitally important in a time of change. School librarians will need to ascertain developmental stages for introducing the idea of information bias and at what grade level students can begin to grasp the subtleties of bias in communication.

In 2017, a French musician appeared in a YouTube video where she is being questioned by an off-screen host about why President Trump told his former press secretary, Sean Spicer, to fabricate the size of his inauguration attendance. In the video, a twenty-ish-looking female musician appears to argue and then states that, "Mr. Spicer gave alternative facts to that." The video was titled "Alternative Face v1.1." In reality, the French musician is seventy-three years old and the voice belongs to Kellyanne Conway, an advisor to President Trump. Mr. Klingemann, the creator of this deceptive desktop-produced YouTube video, used a generative adversarial network (GAN) algorithm that contained old music videos of the musician and a database of short, recorded speech fragments from Ms. Conway that created the pseudo-sentence. This type of GAN uses a neural network to ascertain the data qualities of specific audio sources in question and then reproduces them in any context. If the computer has a database consisting of a sufficient number of words from a person's speeches, then an algorithm can be programmed to have any words that the computer operator wants the attributable person to utter in a completely undetectable manner ("Creation Stories . . .").

For many of us, images and sound are not information formats that we normally apply credibility criteria to, because previously videos and recordings in our collections were from reliable commercial sources. With the presence of YouTube and the availability of A.I., we will be compelled to place all information formats under the microscope for veracity, as A.I. dark hats produce various forms of false information in the form of fake news, rumors, data, and facts.

The cry for metadata is becoming urgent in some quarters. Recordings and videos that contain information showing the where, when, and how they were created are going to be essential for all of us to determine the difference between truth and falsehood, but especially for our students, who inherently place their trust in almost any information source ("Creation Stories . . ." 71).

MIXED REALITIES (AUGMENTED REALITY AND VIRTUAL REALITY)

Augmented and virtual reality are two forms of recent technologies that we are most familiar with and that are starting to arrive in our schools, but there is a new one that is trending right now called mixed reality (MR). Basically, it's virtual reality layered onto the real world, with users wearing sets of semitransparent glasses that permit viewing of their actual environment. MRs are more challenging to develop than immersive virtual reality (VR) that typically provides users with totally artificial images. MRs, however, have much more potential power (Kelly). As school librarians, we need to think like foxes with this new technology and apply trend analysis to determine its possible application to our field. Although many companies are working feverishly to experience a breakthrough with MRs, two major players bear watching. The first is Magic Leap. Based in Florida and extremely secretive about its product, its funders include Google and other notable venture capitalists such as Mark Andreessen, founder of Netscape Navigator. While famous funders do not always predict future success, it's one of the clues that should place Magic Leap and the concept of MRs on school librarians' radar screens. Augmented and virtual realities are already penetrating our schools, but it is MRs that just might leapfrog them, thus making some of the equipment and software that we purchased superfluous overnight. Magic Leap is promising to do away with our desktops by allowing us to conduct our daily lives simply by donning a pair of glasses equipped with a tiny camera at the base of the lens. The camera scans the retina, allowing us to unlock and employ the glasses. The glasses create an MR environment that will be composed of digital avatars of people with whom we will conduct business. Looking at an avatar bank teller's eyes, for example, we will interact with this person even though they are located several states away. Magic Leap means to effortlessly integrate your "family members, plant life, even hobbits into your physical world" (Webb 269). Webb, in her book *The Signals Are Talking,* proposes thinking about it as a super-special form of augmented reality (Webb 270).

Even for technology writers, Magic Leap is challenging to explain. One of the best things to do is watch the YouTube video titled "The Untold Story of Magic Leap, the World's Most Secretive Start-Up" and listen to company president, Romi Abovitz, explain and give us a sneak preview. As we watch the video, school librarians need to engage in active open-mindedness and ask ourselves if Magic Leap is probable, plausible, and possible. Would it pass Google cofounder's toothbrush test? As we explore the developments in AR and VR, can we see the eventual convergence into MR? Is Magic Leap still on the fringe, or is it poised to revolutionize how we instruct our students and interact with them? Right now, it is mentally challenging to picture teleporting a dinosaur into a student's resource-based unit about the Jurassic Age, but with MR, school librarians may be doing it as a matter of course. View the previously mentioned YouTube video and begin asking yourself trend analysis questions, and see if you can envision applications of Magic Leap to school library programs and services.

Dismissing one company's secret project out of hand is easy to do because our minds may not completely grasp MR concepts. Our brains require a prototype, and without one it is easy to classify Magic Leap as an emerging technology. To do so, however, is imprudent. Microsoft has already developed a commercially available form of MR that is being employed in several fields. Using a headset complete with sound, computer processing power, and controls, HoloLens is experimenting with MR to interchange the physical and digital worlds. Users experience immersion while simultaneously being present in their actual surroundings. Doctors, for example, are using HoloLens, because it gives them a form of "x-ray" vision into a patient's body while they perform keyhole surgery. Case Western University medical students are using HoloLens for anatomy classes rather than a cadaver. HoloLens is also being utilized by architects, NASA scientists, automobile manufacturers, and construction workers in a variety of work-related settings (Christian).

It's the field of education, however, where MR is relevant to our profession that really counts, and Microsoft is demonstrating a competitive interest in our profession as well. In 2016, Microsoft partnered with Lifeliqe, a digital education company. In 2017, they began an MR pilot program with Renton Prep Christian School in Washington and Castro Valley Unified College in California to use HoloLens with students to study the circulatory system and electronegativity. The students' reaction to the MR experience was positive, and Microsoft intends to move to a second phase that will measure and evaluate its learning effect soon (Chang).

AUGMENTED AND VIRTUAL REALITIES

For the discussion of AR and VR that follows, it is important to understand current capabilities and applications of AR and VR to our field but also be cognizant of a blending of the forms into MR. If this mix were to occur sooner rather than later, it would affect future equipment acquisitions.

With the exception of nonprototype-stage Magic Leap and the prototype-stage HoloLens, there are two main forms of mixed realities: augmented and virtual. The former provides users with a "live, direct or indirect view of a physical, real-world environment that is modified by computer-generated sensory input such as sound, video, graphics, or GPS data" (Frank, Roehrig, and Pring xiii). Think of it as a close relation to VR with one exception. VR creates a totally artificial world that, while convincingly real, is actually not. Augmented reality relies upon the real world to impose computer-generated information over it. AR is something we regularly experience when we watch a football game on television and see the yardage needed for a first down overlaid on the actual football field. AR usually requires employment of a computer or even a smartphone to experience the visual effects, whereas VR necessitates the use of goggles for the user to experience a three-dimensional world ("Better Than Real" 67).

Although both technologies are beginning to infiltrate education from the entertainment and employment fringes and have promises to enhance learning, it is AR that seems to be gaining market share faster. Digi-Capital, an analyst firm, estimates that out of a predicted $108 billion a year that will be spent on multiple technologies, AR is expected to garner three-quarters of it. The reasons for AR integrating into our lives more readily than VR are several. All of us are more familiar with some of its previous appearances. The game Pokémon Go, for example, used a form of it with the virtual characters imposed over a phone's-eye view of a designated area such as a building or park. Second, most AR does not require the use of spectacles or goggles to experience an enhanced reality, although some computer designers are employing them in factories to provide employees with instructions for assembling parts of a machine and to confirm the proper assembly.

The third reason concerns the type of worlds that we engage in with AR versus VR. The former overlays information on top of a pre-existing image, while VR needs to create computerized worlds from scratch. At present, most users prefer more reality-based worlds than totally artificial ones ("Better Than Real" 67). Both forms of multiple realities are trends that need to be monitored regularly for developments and their applications to education and school libraries, but the one to watch more closely is AR. We also need to be prepared for the differences between the two forms of reality to blur, as headsets can be used for AR and VR and artificial worlds can be created for both. Mixed realities present a number of pedagogical questions. Will students learn more or less with AR and VR programs? To what types of learning are mixed realities suited? Can learning be significantly enhanced by the use of AR and VR? What are the best systems that simulate or permit the visualization of a design, concept, or historic event? Will mixed realities supplant text-dominated learning or augment it?

AUGMENTED REALITY

AR provides us with a responsive level of interactivity that can result in a deeper comprehension of all subject matter. Its immersive qualities introduce an additional layer of understanding as users gain new perspectives from the layers of data that can be imposed on whatever is being viewed (Scholz 149–150). One of the better-known examples, experiencing consistent use in higher education, is TeachLivE. Developed at the University of Central Florida, the AR program is being used at eighty-five campuses across the United States ("TLE TeachLivE"). With this form of AR, pre-service and in-service teachers in STEM-related disciplines are trained to present lessons, manage classes, and experience providing instruction to responsive avatars rather than actual students. The program can be adjusted so that prospective teachers can experience when students are exhibiting typical or atypical behavior, including boredom and class disruption. The mixed reality program is also employed to introduce students with significant disabilities to virtual classrooms equipped with desks, whiteboards, and "other students" (avatars,) so that they can transition more easily to conventional classroom settings ("TLE TeachLivE"). This form of AR furnishes users with the opportunity to practice their pedagogical skills in stress-free environments and does not place real students in human experimental situations that might inhibit their learning progress.

Another use of AR concerns teaching foreign languages. Mentira consists of 70 pages of text, 150 photos, and four short films. It's a game that relies upon AR for an Interactive Storytelling (ARIS) platform. Students play a murder mystery game with directed conversation between players and fictional characters using either an iPod touch or iPhone in Los Griegos, New Mexico, during the Prohibition era. Each conversation is located at a specific site and time within the game's narrative and provides players with the opportunity to converse with the fictional characters to improve their spoken language proficiency. It is a part of the University New Mexico's Spanish 202 course ("Mentira").

A second use of the ARIS platform concerns the Explorez project at the University of Victoria in British Columbia that is designed to provide an immersive contextual learning experience to increase French I students' language proficiencies. Using AR, the campus presents students with a virtual francophone world that requires them to interact with avatars, items, and media to complete various quests, including navigating the university library. Although the study group was not large, the researcher reported that students found the Explorez Project to be meaningful and relevant to improving their French language skills (Perry 2308, 2314).

AR loans itself to history projects by providing students with the opportunity to immerse themselves in the past through the use of primary sources in the form of documents, photos, and data that can be layered on a contemporary location. Dr. Bryan Carter of the University of Arizona designed an AR project as part of his course, "When African Americans Came to Paris." Using an AR program called Daqri, students re-create the jazz scene, cabarets, and artists who frequented Paris when Josephine Baker, Langston Hughes, and other African American expatriates lived there. Over a ten-day Paris visit, students were assigned digital projects that required them to augment an assigned area of the city with various overlays of photos, facts, and art items that illuminated each location's historical importance to the course (Carter 78–79).

The previous examples describe a more traditional form of AR, but it's important to know how much AR is evolving because of advancements with faster and more powerful computer chips, faster processing speeds, neural networks, and machine learning/artificial intelligence. Accelerations in these areas are going to dramatically improve the capabilities of AR and how we and our students interact with it. "Make It Rain: An Augmented Reality Teaching Sandbox" from UCLA is illustrative of the evolution of AR in a short period. Cartography students can sculpt mountains, valleys, rivers, and even volcanoes with their hands and then fill them with water to determine flows and runoffs. Any shape sculpted by the student hands is transmitted to an Xbox Kinect sensor, processed by open-source software, and projected as a color-coded contour map. The video is compelling to watch as the flow of liquids reflects a totally realistic motion. "Make It Rain" is portable and can be delivered to any classroom to enable students to experience their own designs (Snow).

AUGMENTED REALITY AND SCHOOL LIBRARIES

The advent of AR in education will require school librarians to play several roles. The first one is supportive in nature. Since AR is an immersive, context-enhanced environment, we will need to demonstrate how AR can be used to personalize and enrich the learning experience in various classrooms. Pearson Publishing, for example, is teaming up with Layar, an AR company, to introduce interactive contact to their print books via a free, mobile app. Presently it is debuting with a K–5 math text, but its reception with teachers and students will probably result in additional inclusions in other Pearson textbooks. Our role will be to ensure that teachers know how to employ AR-enabled textbooks to their optimum advantage by demonstrating their new features and suggesting AR-enhanced lesson plan ideas (Spina).

Our second role will be as active users of AR in our school libraries. ShelvAR, designed by Miami University in Ohio, is an AR-enhanced form of shelf reading that is 40 percent more accurate and a four times faster method to laboriously reading book shelves. Although it had to cease production because Amazon had a preexisting patent on a similar AR program, Professor Brinkman's YouTube video provides a reality-based glimpse of a future time-saving AR device. As the user scans the shelf with a tablet or mobile device, a mis-shelved book is highlighted with a red "X" on the spine. ShelvAR is also used to generate lists of missing books and reveal shelf areas with either high or low patron activity. Although not currently available to libraries because of Amazon's patent, some AR equivalents can probably be anticipated (Brinkman).

The third role for school librarians with AR will be to acquire, create, and integrate AR elements into our resource-based units and library programs. Software programs remain expensive acquisitions for libraries. Balancing the costs of information in different formats will be a constant concern. What will an AR-based program about U.S. civil rights cost compared to streaming episodes of *Eyes on the Prize* to an American history class? We will have to make acquisition decisions based upon such criteria as access versus ownership and the multidisciplinary aspects of a program and research whether it will enhance learning.

Successful examples of AR-based programs are already appearing in library publications. In 2014, children across the United Kingdom downloaded a Mythical Maze app as part of the Reading Agency's 2014 Summer Reading Challenge. The app employed AR to enable posters and legend cards exhibited around the library to come to life. Mythical AR creatures were hidden around the library, similar to the Pokémon Go characters. When children located a mythical creature, they use the app to unlock mini-games and puzzles. As children read books, they received stickers that unlocked rewards that supplied additional information about the mythical creatures. Needless to say, the Reading Agency reported a record turnout, with 81,908 children joining the library to participate, yielding an attendance increase of 22.7 percent from 2013. The recognition for the Reading Agency was extraordinary since the Mythical Maze app has been downloaded more 10,000 times (Hellyar). This form of AR is adaptable to our school library programs and could easily be replicated to sponsor school vacation–reading programs.

Actively searching for downloadable AR programs and apps at AR-top-ten and best-of-the-year sites will become essential as we determine ways to modify and integrate them in librarian-designed resource units. They will enhance learning and provide our students with more contextual, immersive experiences that hopefully will inspire them to achieve in a time of change (Widder).

VIRTUAL REALITY

Virtual reality is the ultimate artificial format for simulation. By taking three-dimensional images and combining them with special electronic equipment in the form of a visor, helmet, or sensor-fitted glove, our students have the opportunity for educational virtual experiences that will feel incredibly real to them (Hu-Au). While vision and sound are part of this experience, VR developers are already working on haptic technologies that will give users a physical sensation like buzzes and vibrations on their skins as they experience VR programs. In Japan, VR designers have developed a "Synesthesia Suit" that gamers wear to experience tactile-like sensations ("Winner Takes All"). VR can provide teachers and librarians with the technology to design a virtual field trip, to enhance the learning experience, and to possibly develop empathy in their students for others and to provide equity of access for students in rural areas (*NMC/CoSn Horizon Report 2017 K-12 Edition* 47).

So where should we place VR on our library radar screens? With the arrival of Google Cardboards in 1.5 million *The New York Times (NYT)* subscribers' homes in November 2016, the timeline really telescoped for its debut in schools. The Google Cardboard Viewer came with access to a VR program dedicated to showing the plight of 60 million displaced peoples in the world through the eyes of a South Sudanese, Syrian, and Ukrainian child (Hiltner). If you were not an *NYT* subscriber, you could either purchase Google Cardboard Viewer for about $20 or make one from $2 plastic lenses, as Meredith Powers, a YA librarian at Brooklyn Public Library did. Equipped with the viewer and a smartphone, students were able to download other VR-like apps, such as Google Expeditions, to virtually experience the respiratory system; Yellowstone National Park; the Middle Ages; Renaissance buildings in Florence, Italy; or various volcanoes (Marcotte).

For most school districts, Google Cardboard Viewer was their first introduction to VR. In the 2016 market, 100 million VR units were shipped, but 96 percent were Google Cardboard viewers. Two changes on the horizon could influence more widespread adoption of VR in schools. New and affordable cameras equipped with a 360-degree-view option make it easier to take panoramic photos and videos, which can be utilized for VR programs. Second, headsets made by Samsung, Oculus, and HTC are predicted to decline in price with competition from similar headsets from China that are projected to cost $20 or less (Armstrong). Student exposure to Google Cardboard Viewer, educational VR apps, improved cameras, and reduced-cost headsets mean school librarians need to monitor this technology for its latest developments and adaptability to education.

One of the major drawbacks to VR in schools has been the lack of content, but things seem to be improving in this area. Several companies are offering free educational VR programs and even the means for students to create VR content. NASA has produced VR field trips to Mars and the Guggenheim Museum in New York City. YouTube 360 features VR tours of the Hadron Super Collider in Geneva, Switzerland; Jurassic dinosaurs; and one that takes students to the edge of space. The app Timelooper combines AR and VR that allows time travel back to cities such as London, Berlin, and New York to experience iconic events such as the massive London fire of 1666 ("What Is Timelooper?"). Ebeling Elementary School in Macomb Township in Michigan has moved ahead even faster by designing its own VR laboratory. Using a pair of glasses, a stylus, and software called zSpace, students are able to tour the human heart, manipulate organs, determine their function, and place them back into their proper places. Their VR lab also features programs for discovering habitats that support specific animal populations and for experiencing how changing the pH level of a pond can affect the creatures within it (Mathewson).

Nearpod has joined forces with 360Cities to produce VR-based curriculum materials offering VR field trips to national parks, famous landmarks throughout the world, and historic figures with prices ranging from $12 to $20 ("Nearpod"). ThingLink not only offers VR content for elementary schools, with its app that provides VR trips to ecosystems in the French Alps, but also allows students to create VR content with image editing systems, audio annotations, and the ability to combine 360-degree images for immersive VR content (Engestrom). One of the schools to contact as VR moves into curriculum areas is Washington Leadership Academy in Washington, D.C. Winner of the $10 million XQ: The Super School Project Prize, administrators decided to construct a VR chemistry lab instead of a conventional one. Students perform virtual chemical experiments and are able to view chemical molecules at an internal level, something not possible with physical chemicals (Horn).

VIRTUAL REALITY AND RESEARCH

Any school librarian or educator reading the previous section is probably posing some valid questions. Does VR really enhance learning? Can students experiencing VR content actually develop different perspectives and become more empathetic toward others in a specific situation? Can VR be employed to dispel biases and develop an appreciation for our diverse society? Are specific disciplines more suited to VR than others? While there is scant research in the way of formal

A/B testing, some studies are emerging. Foundry 10 conducted a study of 1,351 students across grades 7 to 12 who used VR either as consumers or creators in several schools. Although they only surveyed students and had no control groups, the overall impression of students using VR was positive. The majority of respondents believed that any type of VR that was interactive resulted in a more immersive feeling. VR content that enabled them to experience different places ranked first, and ones that were historic with the element of time travel ranked second (Castaneda, Cechony, and Bautissta 22–23).

A more empirical study was conducted in an astrophysics class in Beijing, China. In this case, students who experienced teaching with VR content scored significantly higher on a test measuring learning, averaging 93 percent versus 73 percent for those experiencing traditional teacher lecturing. The students were tested later for material retention, and VR-delivered content resulted in a 90 percent retention rate versus a 68 percent retention rate for those with traditional teaching. When VR astrophysics students were surveyed about their experience, the majority believed that VR content would also be instructive in physics, biology, and chemistry classes ("A Case Study . . ." 19–20).

The ability of VR to evoke empathy in students is intriguing. Can having students experience VR content that touches their emotions and changes their attitudes be achieved? Some studies conducted at Stanford University's Virtual Human Interaction Lab, for example, are reporting participants assuming avatars of a different race in VR later score lower in racial bias tests, and donning the persona of an elderly avatar seemed to make them more inclined to save for retirement (Berdik).

VIRTUAL REALITY AND SCHOOL LIBRARIES

VR is taking technological steps rather than leaps into our schools, but two companies bear watching for future trends. School librarians will need to be at the forefront of this VR trend by acquiring educational VR content that is not superfluous and counterproductive to learning. Ensuring that students experience VR content that is interactive, creative, and integral to the curriculum will be a goal. The collection standards that we have applied to our print and media acquisitions will need to be redeveloped and applied to VR. Virtual reality has yet to adopt any set of best practices. Questions still remain about which disciplines loan themselves to VR content. At what grade level do students experience difficulty understanding artificial versus real worlds? School librarians will need to research VR's benefits and drawbacks and create evidence-based guidelines for teachers.

Our second VR role will be with employment of this new technology. Modeling how to use it, ironing out tech glitches, and managing an excited class during a VR-based lesson will be our responsibility. Developing resource-based instructional units that seamlessly and appropriately incorporate VR content will be integral to our position as school librarians.

Our third responsibility with VR content will be trying to ensure equity of access. In a virtual world, it is possible for students who live in a rural area to tour the Louvre and get closer to Leonardo's masterpiece, the Mona Lisa, than any conventional visitor. Can they experience the world's largest animal migration from Tanzania to Kenya so profoundly that they will flinch because a lion is roaring right next to them? As they virtually visit Auschwitz, will they be able to empathize with the victims and recognize the need to prevent future genocides? Students can only have these VR experiences when their schools have fast Internet connections, sufficient numbers of headsets or Google Cardboard viewers, and smartphones. School librarians will need to become advocates in schools where many students may not have parity access to the necessary technology that students in affluent schools will have. This is a fast-moving technology that can easily leave many of our students in the digital dust (Snelling).

The last VR content challenge for school librarians is a pedagogical one. Because VR is a visual medium, with an amazing capacity for simulating real worlds, the potential for distortion, increased subjectivity, and emotional manipulation is high. Many VR programs being developed are profit and entertainment motivated and do not have a high degree of government regulation concerning their content. The worlds and games in VR will be incredibly realistic and may have an addictive quality. Are our students going to experience difficulty separating fact from fiction? Will they be able to determine when a VR program contains propaganda and is manipulating their emotions? School librarians will need to teach students media literacy skills so that they can discern when or if VR content is potentially biased.

PRINT OR PIXELS

Readers may well question why a section devoted to the future of a medium whose predicted extinction date keeps getting extended needs any discussion in a technology chapter. But it does. And Marshall McLuhan offers the best reason when he observed that "a new medium is never an addition to an old one, nor does it leave the old one in peace. It ceases to oppress the older media until it finds new shapes and positions for them" (McLuhan and Zingrone 278). For Starbucks addicts, the thought of instant coffee replacing a freshly brewed cup borders on the sacrilegious. Instant coffee did not supplant regular coffee. Passenger trains transport us to work every day, while whizzing past lines of cars snarled in traffic, as their drivers try to distract themselves by listening to the radio. Neither trains nor radios became obsolete. It can be argued that books are a powerful form of technology for "refinement and advancement of thought" with an ancient and adaptable history ("From Papyrus to Pixels" 52). In some ways, print books mirror the technology ideal because they are "portable, hard to break, have high-resolution pages, and a long battery life" ("From Papyrus to Pixels" 51).

The future of print books is also intertwined with an important technology observation by the author of *Megatrends,* John Naisbitt, in 1982. It involves a dynamic balance between high tech versus high touch. Mr. Naisbitt states that "whenever a new technology is introduced into society, there must be a counter balancing human response that is high touch or the technology is rejected" (Naisbitt 39). The high-tech aspects of hospital treatment, for example, when patients are in the final stage of life leads many of us to seek hospice care for our loved ones. As more of us spend our working lives on the screen, new data are suggesting that people are trying to

strike a balance in their lives between high tech and high touch. Yoga is being practiced by 36.7 million people, which is an increase of 16.3 million since 2012. Sixty-
one percent are practicing it to relieve stress, and 37 percent of them are children
under age eighteen ("Highlights from the . . .").

Although it is impossible to mathematically prove the connection between high
tech and high touch, it is an important axiom to monitor with regard to all new
technologies, and especially print books. As ML, bots, diagnostic algorithms, and
A.I.-driven programs affect education, all of us recognize that the library physical
space will need to change to provide additional space for students to collaborate
and use mobile devices. But we need to read, research, and interpret the signals
correctly before we undertake any transition.

In 2010, Cushing Academy in Massachusetts shocked the school library world
by announcing that it was donating 20,000 library books and transforming itself
into a digital center. Their decision was based upon an "explosion of e-Readers and
the rapid acceleration of digital technologies," plus a desire to remain ahead of a
perceived curve in that direction (Houston). Cushing Academy removed their reference desk and stacks and expended tens of thousands of dollars on computer-
friendly carrels and multiple large-format TV screens. Only five years later, as
administrators, teachers, and librarians discovered that many course-required books
were unavailable digitally and that not all students were competent with eReaders,
they began purchasing print books again (Gulon). This flawed decision cost their
school thousands of dollars to reconstitute their collection.

If we were to read the technological tea leaves about Cushing Academy's expensive mistake, where did they fail in their trend analyses? Their first mistake seems
to violate Kahneman's and Tversky's now-famous availability heuristic. Why do
we find it difficult to reason with data? Why do we suffer from tendencies toward
overconfidence in our beliefs (Kahneman 13–14)? Cushing Academy administrators failed to pose critical questions or submit their proposal to discard 20,000 books
to a rigorous set of trend criteria. They needed to raise some of the following questions: When they read about an explosive growth of eReaders, for example, did the
sales represent a new manifestation of sustained change within the school library
world (Webb 182–185)? What age groups seemed to be purchasing eReaders—
teenagers or older adults? Were students visiting the library using eReaders that
they had purchased themselves, or were very few students employing them?

Observing an increase in outside-purchased eReaders by many students may
have indicated a growing trend. Interviewing students who had purchased eReaders on their own would have given school personnel an opportunity to discover what
they liked and disliked about them and possibly revealed that students found them
challenging for immersive types of reading, underlining, and inserting marginalia. Researching whether other independent school libraries had discarded their
book collections and gravitated to eReaders would have been another test of good
trend analysis. Taking representative samples of titles presently in Cushing Academy's library from various subject classifications and ascertaining their availability and cost in eBook form would have been another step. Surveying faculty and
students to see what their support was for eliminating 20,000 books may have
revealed additional questions and concerns that Cushing Academy administrators

had not even considered. Searching through past library resource–based projects may have shown how often faculty change course content, necessitating purchase of materials that are out of print or not in eBook formats for new library-related assignments.

Cushing Academy officials may have also succumbed to belief bias. They were simply unable to recognize the flaws in their reasoning in favor of their own personal beliefs. For example, if eReaders were being purchased by adults rather than teenagers, a significant percentage of secondary-level books were unavailable in electronic format, and no independent school libraries had discarded their book collections for eBooks, would they truly have believed that eBooks were the future of school libraries?

The last trend analysis trap that Cushing Academy administrators encountered was the proverbial "technofix mentality." Faced with a lack of additional library space to accommodate students who needed to collaborate and work on group projects, it is natural in a time technological acceleration to rely upon tech's quick-fix promise as a solution. At the time, Amazon was selling the majority of eBooks for under $10, which was much less than a hard copy or even paperback version of the book. Employing library-trained personnel to maintain a book collection no longer seemed cost-effective, and the cost of creating additional library space was probably prohibitive. Ignoring this dangerous trend analysis trap was the last factor in a serious misreading of the technological tea leaves.

TRACKING THE DATA

With print versus eBooks, school librarians should "never mistake a clear view for a short distance" (Davenport and Kirby 24). Although a change to eBooks may be inevitable, it can still take many years for it to transpire. Predictions of a postliterate society are also premature when we look at the data. In 1960, R. R. Bowker issued 8,100 ISBNs, and by 2013 that number rose to 1.4 million, not counting self-published eBooks that did not contain ISBNs ("From Papyrus to Pixels" 52). The book business remains a highly lucrative one with revenue topping $14.3 billion in 2016 and children's/YA titles accounting for $117.7 million in sales (Price).

In 2016, readers purchased books in a variety of formats, with audiobooks seeing a 25.8 percent increase in revenues compared to eBooks, which saw a 15.6 percent decline. When the children's/YA sectors are examined, the data are even more interesting. Children's/YA sales were up 10.7 percent for hardback, 0.9 percent for paperback, and 7.7 percent for board books. eBooks sales, on the other hand, declined 32.7 percent. Discerning trends from the previous data might lead us to conclude the following: print books continue to be a preference for children and YAs, with eBooks not as much, and books and reading are continuing to play an important role in their lives (Price).

A second part of the eBook equation concerns cost. Most of our students purchase books through Amazon, while the $9.99 price of eBooks was too good to be true. The price easily compensated for the lack of bunny earing and flicking the pages to see how far one had read or needed to go. The tipping point occurred in 2011 when the sales of eBooks actually surpassed print books and then quickly changed (Wood). The sale of eReaders, such as Kindle and Nook, plummeted as readers switched to tablets and smartphones for reading, and the eReader quickly developed a shelf life similar to yogurt (Anderson). So what really happened to eBooks that looked so promising as a solution for our readers and the exponential growth of our print collections? As we visited Amazon regularly to determine if we should purchase a book in various formats for our libraries, we started to see the price of eBooks rise considerably. Although Amazon wanted to price all eBooks at $9.99 and was accepting losses to ensure increased eBook sales, publishers such as Hatchette Book Group, Simon & Schuster, and Harper Collins revolted. The result was an upward increase in prices that was not even subtle. In 2015, eBook prices escalated 30 to 60 percent, and consumers and school librarians began to purchase print books again (Coduti).

KEEP MONITORING THE TRENDS

Watching this Amazon-controlled publishing format war should give us all pause, especially when it comes to eBook collections. A 2015 Follett-conducted eBook usage survey reported that 56 percent of school library collections contained eBooks, which was a decrease of 10 percent since their 2013 survey. Cost continued to be the main factor that was preventing most schools from further eBook acquisitions. The other factor is an interesting and important one. Students still exhibited a clear preference for print books rather than electronic ones. Demand for eBooks was higher in schools that featured one-on-one programs and everyone had a mobile device. Only 17 percent of schools, however, had such programs. Pricing was such a concern to elementary school librarians that they were seeking alternative funding sources so that their print materials budget remained stable ("2015 e-Book Usage . . ." 1–4).

Right now, the area of our collection that is logical to move to an electronic format is reference. Many of our reference questions can be answered by skilled interrogation of valid and reliable Internet sources and subscription online databases. Weeding heavily in this area and contracting with companies like the Gale Virtual Reference Library or ProQuest's Ebook Central for access to electronic reference collections makes sense if it remains affordable. It would also free up space to reconfigure school libraries.

The next area of the collection that is logical for transition is the nonfiction section, especially within specific subject classifications. It will be important, however, as move toward more eBook-based collections that we keep the following caveats in mind. The first concerns high tech versus high touch. Immersive reading that is required for many assignments with nonfiction books loans itself to haptic activities. Flipping back and forth to decide which pages to possibly photocopy and referring quickly to the index at a book's back and reading the cited pages are easily indigenous to print formats. Reading under lamplight instead of on a screen and returning back to a particular passage to grasp its meaning more fully are more easily executed with a print book. Somehow our actually touching the books seems to aid our comprehension of the material (Herman).

The second caveat that was cited in the Follett eBook usage survey is cost. In most cases, school librarians are contracting to purchase access to an eBook collection instead of owning it. When a print book is purchased, it is owned by the library for unlimited use in perpetuity. With an eBook collection, companies charge for the cost of the same book every year, and that price can be expected to increase over time. All of us keep our fingers crossed every year that our subscription databases will not rise and not affect other program and service areas such as author and speaker visits. The same scenario will be experienced with an eBook collection, and we are naive to assume that they will not progress upwards as our database costs have (Herman).

The third caveat applies to subscription licenses and permissions. Permissions and prohibitions concerning eBook use were a major concern of the Follett eBook usage survey participants ("2015 e-Book Usage . . ." 4). eBook use is highly restricted in comparison to print books. Students are limited to printing or downloading a specific number of pages, which is sometimes timed per session. Since most of us are using an access subscription rather than an ownership format, a title can be removed any time by the company. An eBook that has been designated as a course reserve, for example, may no longer be available. eBooks do not circulate via interlibrary loan (ILL), so if your school does have an ILL program with other school districts, it cannot loan the requested material (Herman).

The last caveat is probably the most important. The 2015 Follett-sponsored e-Book Usage survey revealed that students were not as keen about eBooks as school librarians and faculty were. Students are our primary user population and the ones to whom we dedicate almost all of our programs and services. Twenty percent of the school libraries surveyed reported receiving zero eBook requests, which decreased from 23 percent the previous year ("2015 e-Book Usage . . ." 4). It will be vitally important that we survey, observe, and monitor eBook usage with our students before making what is a permanent transition to eBook collections. Our students may be subliminally conveying their preferences for print versus electronic materials without verbally expressing them.

E-READING RESEARCH

Reading is essential to the creation and communication of human knowledge and remains the foundation for the functioning of an advanced society. It is vitally important to learn how a new form of it is affecting our students. E-reading represents a major change in our reading methods. While the benefits of text interactivity; nonlinearity; quick access; and availability of images, audio, and video have enhanced reading, some downsides are present too (Liu 86). Surveys are an important form of data, but reading rigorously conducted research studies is an even more reliable means of discovering trends concerning the impact of digital reading and its influence upon reading in print.

Research over the past fifteen years is starting to reveal a pattern with digital reading that is important to consider when contemplating developing eBook collections. Studies are showing that screen-based reading results in more browsing, keyword spotting, and nonlinear reading, while less time is being spent on in-depth, concentrated reading. Research is also examining the role that touch plays in aiding comprehension and recall of material, which is essential to the accumulation of knowledge. In 2010, a study conducted with fifty Norwegian graduate students divided into two groups showed that the group using Kindles to read a short story by Elizabeth George scored significantly lower in recalling when events occurred in the story and even twice as poorly when asked to place fourteen plot points in a specific order (Heyman). Professors Mangen and Velay conclude that touching the physical pages of a print book may have played a role in helping the control group recall the story's order of events correctly and place them within the correct plot order (Mangen and Velay). Although several contradicting studies found little difference in comprehension and the reading of short articles, they did suggest that paper is better for reading articles that require sustained attention (Liu 89).

The results of this research are also confirmed with several studies involving print versus digital preference. Student preference for digital versus paper reading appears to be contextual in nature. Online reading is their first choice for short documents such as emails, news, and entertainment, but is their second choice for serious immersive reading that entails note-taking, re-reading for understanding, and retention of material. This type of reading is needed when using textbooks, writing research papers, and reading literature as opposed to recreational types of reading (Liu 90). Students are also continuing to prefer print textbooks as opposed to eTextbooks. Studies indicate that they prefer to highlight and write in the margins of a paper text rather than employ any of the similar features offered in many e-Textbooks (Liu 91).

ADMINISTRATIVE AND PARENTAL PRESSURE

Although most administrators and parents are unaware of the extensive research that has already been conducted with digital versus print reading, they are definitely becoming concerned about the amount of time that students are spending online. A Common Sense Media report found that 53 percent of parents have talked to their teenagers about how much time they spend online, and 72 percent of tween parents have done the same ("The Common Sense Census . . ." 15). How much time tweens and teens while away viewing entertainment and using social media, excluding time spent for school and homework, is pretty alarming. According to their report, it's about nine hours for teenagers and six hours for tweens ("The Common Sense Census . . ." 24).

School administrators are also starting to respond to this epidemic of screen addiction. The National Association of Independent Schools, for example, has shown the film, *Screenagers: Growing Up in the Digital Age* to 100 independent schools as a conversation catalyst for students and parents to address the problem ("Schools Tackle Screen Time"). A principal at a Washington, D.C., charter school has promised to pay students $100 each if they can refrain from any form of screen time one day per week during the summer months. She is concerned that her students will not retain what they have learned during the year over the summer months (Matos).

Although many school librarians may be enthusiastic to move toward eBook collections, usually the pressure to do so emanates from administrators and parents. With the growing awareness of the potential educational harm that can befall so many students who overindulge in screen time, administrators and parents may actually become much more disposed toward having students engage more with print materials for part of their instructional experience.

FUTURE OF EBOOKS

As mentioned previously, eBooks offer some advantages that print books will never possess. The ability to embed media provides potential users with a book that actually "teaches, rather than simply informs" and is paced to the user's reading and comprehensive needs ("From Papyrus to Pixels" 56). How-to books, for example, loan themselves to this format, as well as print books that would normally contain two-dimensional diagrams. A Boston-based company has developed an app called Spritz that is designed to send one word at a time to readers at a selected reading speed. The surrounding text is not visible. Developers envision the app helping students with attention deficit disorder and dyslexia improve their reading skills (Tucker).

DIGITAL VERSUS PRINT AND SCHOOL LIBRARIANS

Fortunately, with eBooks and print books, it does not have to be "either/or." School librarians will need to monitor publishing, reading research, and student usage data for both formats diligently to determine the best plan to meet the needs and interests of their students in a time of change. The information that we acquire will need to be privately and publicly disseminated to administrators, faculty, and parents so that they understand what the trade-offs are with eBooks and print books. Observing student behavior with both formats and seeking their opinions about both reading types is paramount since they are our principal responsibility.

Questions

1. Google is presently selling Pixel Buds that utilize a Google Translate app to permit real-time translation between a user wearing the buds and another employing a phone. They are currently selling for $160. What are the upsides and downsides for foreign language instruction in a school and its library?

2. How may the employment of big data assist or hinder the development of the school's and library's programs and services? What are the implications for violating student privacy rights?

3. How may algorithms assist librarians in individualizing instruction within the next five years?

4. What content should be featured on the school library's platform to make it the primary go-to place for all school-related assignments and activities?

5. Describe several realistic scenarios for utilizing an information robot in the library.

6. Provide examples where A.I. will affect supervised, unsupervised, and reinforcement learning in the library.
7. How do you envision the IoT improving library programs and services in the near future?
8. What is the future of print as a medium in the school and its library in the next three to five years?

REFERENCES

"The Algorithm Kingdom." July 15, 2017. *The Economist*. Available at: https://www.economist.com/news/business/21725018-its-deep-pool-data-may-let-it-lead-artificial-intelligence-china-may-match-or-beat-america.

Amen, Alyssa. June 30, 2015. "Engaging Students with Mobile Technology." Available at: https://cehs.unl.edu/cehs/news/engaging-students-mobile-technology.

Anderson, Monica. October 29, 2015. "The Demographics of Device Ownership." Pew Research Center. Available at: http://www.pewinternet.org/2015/10/29/the-demographics-of-device-ownership.

Antolini, Tina. November 9, 2009. "Digital School Library Leaves Book Stacks Behind." National Public Radio. Available at: http://www.npr.org/templates/story/story.php?storyId=120097876.

Armstrong, Paul. April 6, 2017. "Just How Big Is the Virtual Reality Market and Where Is It Going Next?" *Forbes*. Available at: https://www.forbes.com/sites/paularmstrongtech/2017/04/06/just-how-big-is-the-virtual-reality-market-and-where-is-it-going-next/#4c3177194834.

Autor, David. September 2014. "Polanyi's Paradox and the Shape of Employment." National Bureau of Economic Research. NBER Working Paper No. 20485: 1–50. Available at: https://economics.mit.edu/files/9835.

Baker, Angela, Chris Dede, and Julie Evans. June 25, 2015. "The 8 Essentials for Mobile Learning Success." Available at: https://www.qualcomm.com/media/documents/files/the-8-essentials-for-mobile-learning-success-in-education.pdf.

Berdik, Chris. October 10, 2017. "Can Virtual Reality Teach Empathy?" *Slate*. Available at: http://https://hechingerreport.org/can-virtual-reality-teach-empathy/.

Berger, Jonah and Katherine L. Milkman. 2012. "What Makes Online Content Viral?" *Journal of Marketing Research*. 49(2): 1–17.

"Better Than Real." February 4, 2017. *The Economist*. 422(9026): 67–69.

"Big Data—A Visual History." September 26, 2017. Available at: https://www.winshuttle.com/big-data-timeline.

Bostrom, Nick. 2014. *Superintelligence: Paths, Dangers, Strategies*. Oxford, UK: Oxford University Press.

Botsman, Rachel. "Co-Parenting with Alexa." October 8, 2017. *The New York Times*. Available at: https://www.nytimes.com/2017/10/07/opinion/sunday/children-alexa-echo-robots.html.

Brinkman, Bo. October 10, 2017. "Augmented Reality App for Shelf Reading." Available at: https://www.youtube.com/watch?v=NgZVI630SsI.

Brown, Jessica. November 27, 2013. "Cards Let Schools, Parents Keep Eye on Their Students." Available at: https://www.usatoday.com/story/tech/2013/11/27/student-technology-tracking/3757459.

Carr, Nicholas. September 9, 2017. "These Are Not the Robots We Were Promised." *The York Times*. Available at: https://www.nytimes.com/2017/09/09/opinion/sunday/household-robots-alexa-homepod.html?_r=0.

Carter, Bryan. 2016. "Augmenting Reality: Experiencing the Past Through Digital Technologies." In: *Teaching and Learning in Virtual Environments Archives, Museums, and Libraries*, edited by Patricia C. Franks, Lori A. Bell, and Rhonda B. Trueman. Santa Barbara, CA: Libraries Unlimited.

"A Case Study—The Impact of VR on Academic Performance." 2016. Beijing Bluefocus E-Commerce and Beijing iBokan Wisdom Mobile Internet Technology Training Institutions. Available at: https://cdn.uploadvr.com/wp-content/uploads/2016/11/A-Case-Study-The-Impact-of-VR-on-Academic-Performance_20161125.pdf.

Castaneda, Lisa, Anna Cechony, and Arabella Bautissta, 2016–2017. *All-School Aggregated Findings 2016–2017-VR*. Available at: http://foundry10.org/wp-content/uploads/2017/09/All-School-Aggregated-Findings-2016-2017.pdf.

Chaffe, Sophie. March 5, 2016. "Getting Mobile Learning Right: 6 Best Practices. eLearning Industry." Available at: https://elearningindustry.com/getting-mobile-learning-right-6-best-practices.

Chang, Richard. April 7, 2017. "Lifeliqe Piloting Mixed Reality on Microsoft Hololens for Grade 6–12 Classrooms." *The Journal*. Available at: https://thejournal.com/articles/2017/04/07/lifeliqe-piloting-mixed-reality-on-microsoft-hololens-for-grade-6-through-12-classrooms.aspx.

Chatterji, Aaron and Benjamin Jones. September 2012. "Harnessing Technology to Improve K-12 Education. The Hamilton Project." Discussion Paper 2012-05. Available at: http://www.kellogg.northwestern.edu/faculty/jones-ben/htm/thp_chatterjijones_edtech_discpaper.pdf.

Christian, Bonnie. March 3, 2017. "Hololens Trial Gives Doctor's 'X-Ray Vision' to Allow Them to Peer Inside Patients During Surgery." *Wired*. Available at: http://www.wired.co.uk/article/industries-using-microsoft-hololens.

Coduti, Erin. September 8, 2015. "Kindle eBook Prices Have Jumped 30% to 60% in 2015." Available at: https://www.dealnews.com/features/Kindle-eBook-Prices-Have-Jumped-30-to-60-in-2015/1443130.html.

"The Common Sense Census: Media Use by Tweens and Teens." 2015. Available at: https://www.commonsensemedia.org/sites/default/files/uploads/research/census_executivesummary.pdf.

"Computer Simulating 13-Year-Old Boy Becomes First to Pass Turing Test." June 8, 2014. *The Guardian*. Available at: https://www.theguardian.com/technology/2014/jun/08/super-computer-simulates-13-year-old-boy-passes-turing-test.

Craver, Kathleen W. 2002. *Creating Cyber Libraries: An Instructional Guide for School Library Media Specialists*. Greenwood Village, CO: Libraries Unlimited.

Craver, Kathleen W. 2014. *Developing Quantitative Literacy Skills in History and the Social Sciences*. New York: Rowman & Littlefield.

Craver, Kathleen. 1994. *School Library Media Centers in the 21st Century: Changes and Challenges*. Westport, CT: Greenwood Press.

"Creation Stories Fake News: You Ain't Seen Nothing Yet." July 1, 2017. *The Economist*. Available at: https://www.economist.com/news/science-and-technology/21724370-generating-convincing-audio-and-video-fake-events-fake-news-you-aint-seen.

Davenport, Thomas H. and Julia Kirby. 2016. *Only Humans Need Apply: Winners and Losers in the Age of Smart Machines*. New York: Harper.

DeSteno, David, Cynthia Brezeal, and Paul Harris. August 26, 2017. "The Secret to a Good Robot Teacher." *The New York Times*. Available at: https://www.nytimes.com/2017/08/26/opinion/sunday/good-robot-teacher-secrets.html.

Dickson, Ben. June 26, 2017. "How the Cloud Has Changed Education and Training." The Next Web. Available at: https://thenextweb.com/contributors/2017/06/26/cloud-changed-education-training/#.tnw_qvIlBAnX.

"Double, Double, Toil and Trouble." March 12, 2016. *The Economist.* Available at: http://www.economist.com/technology-quarterly/2016-03-12/after-moores-law.

Doyne, Shannon. October 9, 2012. "Should Schools Put Tracking Devices in Students' I.D. Cards." *The New York Times.* Available at: https://mobile.nytimes.com/blogs/learning/2012/10/09/should-schools-put-tracking-devices-in-students-i-d-cards/?referer=.

"8 Major Google Algorithm Updates, Explained." September 19, 2017. Search Engine Land. Available at: http://searchengineland.com/8-major-google-algorithm-updates-explained-282627.

Elfeky, Abdellah Ibrahim Mohammed and Thouqan Saleem Yakoub Masadeh. 2016. "The Effect of Mobile Learning on Students' Achievement and Conversational Skills." *International Journal of Higher Education.* 5(3): 1–31. Available at: https://files.eric.ed.gov/fulltext/EJ1102679.pdf.

Ellison, Jillian. October 8, 2015. "App Makes Being in the 'Hotseat' More Bearable." *The Exponent.* Available at: https://www.purdueexponent.org/features/article_9921c432-223a-508c-b9da-aaf0019fcafa.html.

Enge, Eric. April 5, 2017. "Mobile vs Desktop Usage: Mobile Grows but Desktop Still a Big Player." Available at: https://www.stonetemple.com/mobile-vs-desktop-usage-mobile-grows-but-desktop-still-a-big-player.

Engestrom, Ulla. April 16, 2016. "ThinkLink Launches Virtual Reality Lessons App for Education." Available at: http://blog.thinglink.com/marketing/thinglink-launches-virtual-reality-lessons-app-for-education.

Epstein, Robert and Ronald Robertson. August 18, 2015. "The Search Engine Manipulation Effect (SEME) and Its Possible Impact on the Outcome of Elections." *Proceedings of the National Academy of Sciences of the United States of America.* 112(33): E4152–E4521. Available at: doi:10.1073/pnas.1419828112.

Evans, Jenni. September 8, 2016. "Primary School Kids Invent Cave-Cleaning Robot." Available at: https://www.news24.com/SouthAfrica/News/primary-school-kids-invent-cave-cleaning-robot-20160908.

Frank, Malcolm, Paul Roehrig, and Ben Pring. 2017. *When Machines Do Everything: How to Get Ahead in a World of AI, Algorithms, Bots and Big Data.* New York: Wiley.

Friedman, Thomas. 2017. *Thank You for Being Late: An Optimist's Guide to Thriving in an Age of Accelerations.* New York: Picador.

"From Not Working to Neural Networking Technology." June 25, 2016. *The Economist.* Available at: https://www.economist.com/special-report/2016/06/25/from-not-working-to-neural-networking.

"From Papyrus to Pixels." October 11, 2014. *The Economist.* Available at: http://www.economist.com/news/essays/21623373-which-something-old-and-powerful-encountered-vault.

Gelles, David. August 17, 2014. "In Silicon Valley, Mergers Must Meet the Toothbrush Test." *The New York Times.* Available at: https://dealbook.nytimes.com/2014/08/17/in-silicon-valley-mergers-must-meet-the-toothbrush-test/?_r=0.

Gorman, Michael. 2015. *Our Enduring Values Revisited: Librarianship in an Ever-Changing World.* Chicago: American Library Association.

Gulon, David. May 24, 2017. "What's a Library without Books? Some Bookless Libraries." Available at: http://www.allpurposeguru.com/2017/05/whats-library-without-books.

Hart, Michael. December 2, 2011. "Building a Library in the Clouds." *The Journal.* Available at: https://thejournal.com/articles/2011/12/02/building-a-library-in-the-clouds.aspx.

Heick, Terry. 2015. "30 Trends in Education Technology for the 2015 School Year." Available at: https://www.teachthought.com/the-future-of-learning/30-trends-education-technology-2015.

Hellyar, Diana. April 26, 2016. "On Library Use of New Visualization Technologies MIT Libraries." Available at: http://informatics.mit.edu/blog/guest-post-diana-hellyar -library-use-new-visualization-technologies.

Herman, Peter C. September 30, 2014. "The Hidden Costs of E-book at University Librar- ies." *Times of San Diego.* Available at: https://timesofsandiego.com/opinion/2014 /09/29/hidden-costs-e-books-university-libraries.

Heyman, Stephen. "Reading Literature on Screen: A Price for Convenience." August 13, 2014. *New York Times.* Available at: https://www.nytimes.com/2014/08/14/arts /reading-literature-on-screen-a-price-for-convenience.html.

Hickman, Leo. July 1, 2013. "How Algorithms Rule the World." *The Guardian.* Avail- able at: https://www.theguardian.com/science/2013/jul/01/how-algorithms-rule -world-nsa.

"Highlights from the 2016 Yoga in America Study." January 13, 2016. Available at: https:// www.yogaalliance.org/Learn/About_Yoga/2016_Yoga_in_America_Study /Highlights.

Hiltner, Stephen. November 27, 2016. "Bear Traps and Empathy Engines: Virtual Reality at the *New York Times.*" *The New York Times.* Available at: http://www.nytimes. com/2016/08/24/insider/events/virtual-reality-at-the-new-york-times.html.

"Homework Help." Accessed October 29, 2018. District of Columbia Public Library. Avail- able at: https://www.dclibrary.org/research/homework.

Horne, Michael. September 22, 2016. "Virtual Reality Digs into Brick-And-Mortar Schools." *Forbes.* Available at: https://www.forbes.com/sites/michaelhorn/2016/09 /22/virtual-reality-digs-into-brick-and-mortar-schools/#1e6dc5851707.

Houston, Aaron. February 10, 2010. "Do Schools Need Books." *The New York Times.* Avail- able at: https://roomfordebate.blogs.nytimes.com/2010/02/10/do-school-libraries -need-books.

"How to Devise the Perfect Recommendation Algorithm." February 9, 2017. *The Econ- omist.* Available at: https://www.economist.com/news/special-report/21716464 -recommendations-must-be-neither-too-familiar-nor-too-novel-how-devise -perfect.

"How Voice Technology Is Transforming Computing." January 7, 2017. *The Economist.* Available at: https://www.economist.com/news/leaders/21713836-casting-magic -spell-it-lets-people-control-world-through-words-alone-how-voice.

Hu-Au, Elliot. June 16, 2017. "Virtual Reality and Its Educational Possibilities." Available at: http://virtualrealityforeducation.com/virtual-reality-educational-possibilities.

"Impact of Robots on Productivity, Employment and Jobs." April 2017. International Fed- eration of Robotics. Available at: https://ifr.org/img/office/IFR_The_Impact_of _Robots_on_Employment.pdf.

"Imperial Ambitions." April 9, 2016. *The Economist.* Available at: https://www.economist .com/news/leaders/21696521-mark-zuckerberg-prepares-fight-dominance-next -era-computing-imperial-ambitions.

"An Internet of Things." October 3, 2017. Available at: https://www.postscapes.com/internet -of-things-examples.

Irwin, Neil. October 2, 2014. "Why Ben Bernanke Can't Refinance His Mortgage." *The New York Times.* Available at: https://www.nytimes.com/2014/10/03/upshot/why -ben-bernanke-cant-refinance-his-mortgage.html.

Johnson, Doug A. 2013. *The Indispensable Librarian: Surviving and Thriving in School Libraries in the Information Age.* 2nd ed. Santa Barbara, CA: Linworth.

Kahneman, Daniel. 2013. *Thinking, Fast and Slow.* New York: Farrar, Straus and Giroux.

Kelly, Kevin. May 2016. "The Untold Story of Magic Leap, the World's Most Secretive Start Up." *Wired.* Available at: https://www.wired.com/2016/04/magic-leap-vr.

"Khan Academy Official SAT Practice." October 8, 2017. Available at: https://www
    .khanacademy.org/sat.

La France, Adrienne. January 31, 2017. "The Internet Is Mostly Bots." *The Atlantic*. Avail-
    able at: https://www.theatlantic.com/technology/archive/2017/01/bots-bots-bots
    /515043.

Lazzaro, Sage. March 6, 2017. "Google Is Using Artificial Intelligence to Make a Huge
    Change to Its Translate Tool." *Observer*. Available at: http://observer.com/2017/03/
    google-translate-neural-update.

Lewis-Kraus, Gideon. December 18, 2016. "The Great A.I. Awakening." *New York Times
    Magazine.* Available at: https://www.nytimes.com/2016/12/14/magazine/the-great
    -ai-awakening.html.

Lickteig, Stacy and Jo O'Garro. July 8, 2016. "Data Crunching Proved This School Library
    Program Was Crucial." *School Library Journal*. Available at: http://www.slj
    .com/2016/07/research/data-crunching-proved-this-school-library-program-was
    -crucial/#_.

Liu, Ziming. 2012. "Digital Reading: An Overview." *Chinese Journal of Library and Infor-
    mation Science* (English Edition). 5(1): 85–94. Available at: http://scholarworks.
    sjsu.edu/cgi/viewcontent.cgi?article=1067&context=slis_pub.

"Machines Learning." July 22, 2017. *The Economist*. 424(9050): 15–18.

Mangen, Anne and Jean-Luc Velay. 2010. "Digitizing Literacy: Reflections on the Haptics
    of Writing." In: *Advances in Haptics*, edited by Mehrdad Hosseini Zadeh. Rijeka,
    Croatia: In-Tech, pp. 385–402. Available at: DOI: 10.5772/8710. https://www
    .intechopen.com/books/advances-inhaptics/digitizing-literacy-reflections-on-the
    -haptics-of-writing.

Marcotte, Alison. May 1, 2017. "10 Tech Trends." *American Libraries*. Available at: https://
    americanlibrariesmagazine.org/2017/05/01/top-library-tech-trends.

Marr, Bernard. February 19, 2016. "A Short History of Machine Learning—Everything
    a Manager Should Read." *Forbes*. Available at: https://www.forbes.com/sites
    /bernardmarr/2016/02/19/a-short-history-of-machine-learning-every-manager
    -should-read/#1e90471815e7.

Martin, Jim. September 26, 2017. "What Are Bots?" *TechAdvisor*. Available at: http://www
    .techadvisor.co.uk/feature/software/what-are-bots-3638979.

Mathewson, Tara Garcia. November 4, 2018. "Oh, the Virtual Places Students Can Go."
    The New York Times. Available at: https://www.nytimes.com/2018/10/31/learning
    /bulletin-board.html.

Matos, Alejandra. June 6, 2017. "Can They Unplug? A Principal Will Pay Students to Forgo
    Screen Time This Summer." *The Washington Post*. Available at: https://www
    .washingtonpost.com/local/education/can-they-unplug-a-school-principal-will
    -pay-students-to-forgo-screentime-this-summer/2017/06/09/b22decd.

McAfee, Andrew and Erik Brynjolfsson. 2017. *Machine, Platform, Crowd: Harnessing Our
    Digital Future*. New York: W. W. Norton.

McFarland, Matt. October 24, 2014. "Elon Musk: 'With Artificial Intelligence We Are Sum-
    moning the Demon.'" *The Washington Post*. Available at: https://www.washington
    post.com/news/innovations/wp/2014/10/24/elon-musk-with-artificial-intelligence
    -we-are-summoning-the-demon.

McGrath, Rita Gunther. November 15, 2013. "The Pace of Technology Adoption Is Speed-
    ing Up." *Harvard Business Review*. Available at: https://hbr.org/2013/11/the-pace
    -of-technology-adoption-is-speeding-up.

McGraw-Hill Education. October 2016. *2016 Digital Study Trends Survey*. Available at:
    https://s3.amazonaws.com/ecommerce-prod.mheducation.com/unitas/highered
    /explore/sites/study-trends/2016-digital-trends-survey-results.pdf.

McLuhan, Eric and Frank Zingrone, eds. 1997. *Essential McLuhan.* New York: Routledge.

"Mentira." October 10, 2017. University of New Mexico. Available at: http://www.men tira.org/overview.

Molnar, Michele. September 25, 2017. "EduStar Platform Promises Quick, Randomized Ed-Tech Trials." Available at: https://marketbrief.edweek.org/marketplace-k-12 /early-results-in-from-trials-using-new-ed-tech-evaluation-platform.

Nadel, Brian. February 21, 2017. "School Buildings on Autopilot." Available at: https://www .districtadministration.com/article/school-buildings-autopilot.

Naisbitt, John. 1982. *Megatrends: The New Directions Transforming Our Lives.* New York: Warner Books.

"Nearpod." October 11, 2017. Available at: https://nearpod.com.

"A New Way to Extend Moore's Law." June 8, 2017. *The Economist.* Available at: https:// www.economist.com/news/science-and-technology/21723094-ibm-unveils -transistor-does-not-leak-electrons-new-way-extend-moores.

Nielsen, Jakob. September 12, 2011. "How Long Do Users Stay on Web Pages?" Available at: https://www.nngroup.com/articles/how-long-do-users-stay-on-web-pages.

NMC/CoSN Horizon Report. 2017. K-12 Edition. 2017. Available at: https://www.nmc.org /publication/nmccosn-horizon-report-2017-k-12-edition.

NMC Horizon Report. 2017. Higher Education Edition. 2017. Available at: https://www.nmc .org/publication/nmc-horizon-report-2017-higher-education-edition.

O'Neil, Cathy. 2016. *Weapons of Math Destruction.* New York: Crown.

Palfrey, John. 2015. *BiblioTech: Why Libraries Matter More Than Ever in the Age of Google.* New York: Basic Books.

Perry, Bernadette. February 2015. "Gamifying French Language Learning: A Case Study Examining a Quest-Based, Augmented Reality Mobile Learning Tool." *Procedia— Social and Behavioral Sciences.* 174: 2308–2315. Available at: DOI: 10.1016/j. sbspro.2015.01.82.

Pierce, David. October 4, 2017. "Google Introduces Its Answer to Airpods: Pixel Buds." *Wired.* Available at: https://www.wired.com/story/google-introduces-pixel-buds.

Price, Gary. October 19, 2017. "New Data from AAP Released: Book Publisher Trade Revenues Flat for 2016, Scholarly/Professional Publishing Revenue Down 20.8%." *Library Journal.* Available at: http://www.infodocket.com/2017/06/15/new-data -from-aap-released-book-publisher-trade-revenues-flat-for-2016-scholarlyprofessi onal-publishing-revenues-down-20-8.

Purcell, Kristen, Joanna Brenner, and Lee Rainie. March 9, 2012. *Search Engine Use 2012.* Pew Research Center. Available at: http://www.pewinternet.org/2012/03/09/search -engine-use-2012.

Ravipati, Sri. June 9, 2017. "IoT to Represent More Than Half of Connected Device Landscape by 2021." *The Journal.* Available at: https://www.postscapes.com/internet-of -things-examples.

Reagan, Andrew, Lewis Mitchell, Dilan Kiley, Christopher M. Danforth, and Paul Sheridan Dodds. 2016. "The Emotional Arcs of Stories Are Dominated by Six Basic Shapes." *EPJ Data Science.* 5(1): 1–91.

Russell, Stuart. Accessed October 29, 2018. "An Open Letter: Research Priorities for Robust and Beneficial Artificial Intelligence." Future of Life Institute. Available at: https:// futureoflife.org/ai-open-letter.

Sandoval, Kristopher. September 20, 2016. "What Does the Rise of Bots Mean for APIs?" Nordic APIs. Available at: https://nordicapis.com/what-will-the-rise-of-bots-mean -for-apis.

Scheeren, William O. 2015. *Technology Handbook for School Librarians: Theory and Practice.* Santa Barbara, CA: Libraries Unlimited.

Scholz, Joachim and Andrew N. Smith. March 2016. "Augmented Reality: Designing Immersive Experiences That Maximize Consumer Engagement." *Business Horizons.* 59(2): 149–161. Available at: https://www.researchgate.net/publication /281845545.

"Schools Tackle Screen Time." Winter 2017. *National Association of Independent Schools Magazine.* Available at: https://www.nais.org/magazine/independent-school/winter -2017/schools-tackle-screen-time.

Schwartz, Katrina. July 28, 2016. "How Robots in English Class Can Spark Empathy and Improve Writing." Available at: https://ww2.kqed.org/mindshift/2016/07/28/how -robots-in-english-class-can-spark-empathy-and-improve-writing.

Siegele, Ludwig. 2018. "I Know That Voice." *The Economist—The World in 2018.* Available at: http://www.theworldin.com/article/12760/i-know-voice?fsrc=scn/tw/wi /bl/ed.

Snelling, Jennifer. July 28, 2016. "Virtual Reality in K-12 Education: How Helpful Is It?" *Converge Magazine.* Available at: http://www.centerdigitaled.com/k-12/Virtual- Reality-in-K-12-Education-Is-It-Really-Helpful.html.

Snow, Christelle. July 21, 2015. "Make It Rain: UCLA Unveils Augmented Reality Teaching Sandbox." Available at: http://newsroom.ucla.edu/stories/make-it-rain-ucla -unveils-augmented-reality-teaching-sandbox.

Spina, Carli. 1996–2018. "Keeping Up with . . . Augmented Reality." Association of College & Research Libraries. American Library Association. Available at: http://www .ala.org/acrl/publications/keeping_up_with/ar.

Staufenberg, Jess. February 26, 2016. "Robot Librarian Designed by Aberystwyth University Students." Available at: https://www.timeshighereducation.com/news/robot -librarian-designed-aberystwyth-university-students.

Steiner, Christopher. 2012. *Automate This: How Algorithms Came to Rule Our World.* New York: Penguin.

Stephens-Davidowitz, Seth. 2017. *Everybody Lies: Big Data, New Data, and What the Internet Can Tell Us about Who We Really Are.* New York: Dey Street Books.

Storer, Norman W. January 1967. "The Hard Sciences and the Soft: Some Sociological Observations." *Bulletin of the Medical Library Association.* 55(1): 75–84. Available at: https://www.ncbi.nlm.nih.gov/pmc/articles/PMC198502.

Taylor, Natalie Gree, Mega Subrmaniam, and Amanda Waugh. February 26, 2015. "The School Librarian as Learning Alchemist." *American Libraries.* Available at: https:// americanlibrariesmagazine.org/2015/02/26/the-school-librarian-as-learning -alchemist.

"TLE TeachLivE." October 10, 2017. University of Central Florida. Available at: http:// teachlive.org.

Tucker, Erika. 2014. "How Spritz Technology Flashes Single Words to Double Your Reading Speed." Available at: https://globalnews.ca/news/1174238/how-spritz-technology -flashes-single-words-to-double-your-reading-speed.

"Turing Test." October 4, 2017. Available at: http://whatis.techtarget.com/definition /Turing-Test.

"2015 e-Book Usage in U.S. School (K-12) Libraries. September 2015. Sixth Annual Survey." Follett. Available at: https://s3.amazonaws.com/WebVault/research/School LibraryReport_2015.pdf.

Vogel, Kenneth. August 30, 2017. "Google Critic Ousted from Think Tank by the Tech Giant." *The New York Times.* Available at: https://www.nytimes.com/2017/08/30/us /politics/eric-schmidt-google-new-america.html.

Wagner, Janet. August 3, 2015. "Top 10 Machine Learning APIs: AT&T Speech, IBM Watson, Google Prediction." Available at: https://www.programmableweb.com/news

/top-10-machine-learning-apis-att-speech-ibm-watson-google-prediction/analysis
/2015/08/03.

Webb, Amy. 2016. *The Signals Are Talking: Why Today's Fringe Is Tomorrow's Mainstream*. New York: Public Affairs.

West, Darrell M. September 2012. *Big Data for Education: Data Mining, Data Analytics, and Web Dashboards*. Governance Studies at Brookings. Available at: http://www
.oxydiane.net/IMG/pdf/school_evaluation.pdf.

"What Is Timelooper?" October 11, 2017. Available at: https://www.timelooper.com.

Whitehair, Kristin. February 11, 2016. "Libraries in an Artificially Intelligent World." *Public Libraries*. Available at: http://publiclibrariesonline.org/2016/02/libraries-in-an
-artificially-intelligent-world.

Widder, Brandon. April 19, 2017. "Best Augmented-Reality Apps." Available at: https://
www.digitaltrends.com/mobile/best-augmented-reality-apps.

Wilkinson, Kate and Phil Barter. 2016. "Do Mobile Learning Devices Enhance Learning in Higher Education Anatomy Classrooms?" *Journal of Pedagogic Development*.
6(1): 14–23. Available at: http://eprints.mdx.ac.uk/17589.

Willman, Krzystof. July 5, 2017. "25 Best Amazon Alexa Skills for Kids." Available at:
https://turbofuture.com/consumer-electronics/25-Best-Amazon-Alexa-Skills-for
-Kids.

"Winner Takes All." February 11, 2017. *The Economist*. 422 (9027): 1–6.

Wong, Wylie. January 7, 2014. "How Schools Are Making Mobile Learning Work." *EdTech Focus*. Available at: https://edtechmagazine.com/k12/article/2014/01/how-schools
-are-making-mobile-learning-work.

Wood, Zoe. March 17, 2017. "Paperback Fighter: Sale of Physical Books Now Outperform Digital Sales." *The Guardian*. Available at: https://www.theguardian.com/books
/2017/mar/17/paperback-books-sales-outperform-digital-titles-amazon-ebooks.

"The World's Most Valuable Resource." May 6, 2017. *The Economist*. 423(9039): 7.

"Worldwide Cognitive System and Artificial Intelligence Revenues Forecast to Surge Past
$47 Billion in 2020 According to New IDC Spending Guide." October 26, 2016.
Available at: https://www.idc.com/getdoc.jsp?containerId=prUS41878616.

3

Economic Trends

WHAT'S HAPPENING?

Economics lives up to its sobriquet, "the dismal science," especially for the United States in the twenty-first century. Extreme poverty has been reduced to about 20 percent of the population. Americans work less, commence their working careers later, live longer, and have much more leisure time than our ancestors did in 1820 (Norberg 67). Nonetheless, many of our citizens think that the country is not on a correct economic course and are expressing it in various opinion polls and at the ballot box (Bruni 199). A 2014 economic poll revealed that Americans believed China was the leading economic power. This mistaken belief has been expressed for six consecutive years. A second 2014 economic poll reported that 76 percent of Americans ages eighteen and older no longer believe that their children will fare better economically than they did in the coming years (Bruni 200).

Even though China is not yet the leading economic power, our economic place in the world is no longer unassailable. Between 2000 and 2011, 90 percent of developing countries grew more quickly than the United States by an average of 3 percent per year (Norberg 74). The world is becoming more competitive, and the supremacy and power of the United States are no longer the norms. Our country is undergoing a seismic shift with developments happening in technology affecting almost every aspect of our society. As our economy continues along its path of growth and disruption, our fears regarding debt, income and wages, growing inequality, and lack of funding for education may be well founded (Bruni 198).

The two major forces affecting school libraries are technological and economic. While technologies are not as dependent upon the economy for development and sales, economic forces significantly influence the degree to which school libraries can incorporate such advancements. The economy acts as a catalyst in school libraries by either speeding up adoption and adaption of new technologies or slowing the process down. Because of the size and complexity of the U.S. economy, it is challenging for economists to predict developments regarding future growth, but observing economic trends and taking appropriate action will be paramount for school librarians in the coming years (Kennedy 291).

THE NATIONAL DEBT

By far the dominant variable in the economy is America's debt. It is embedded at every level. In 2018, our national debt skyrocketed to $21.6 trillion. This inconceivable amount that represented about 28 percent of America's gross domestic product (GDP) in 1982 is now up to 105.4 percent of our GDP ("Debt to the Penny . . ."). A critical monetary question arises from these data. When will the federal government owe more than the U.S. economy, or when will financial Armageddon finally occur? Is there a tipping point from which there is no economic return and other countries call in their loans, choose another currency as an international standard, and refuse to lend us additional funds? Based on the current principal that we owe and the interest on the debt, economists predict that the point at which our debt is larger than the entire size of our economy is going to be the year 2032. This date, of course, precludes another war or recession. If either the former or latter event occurs, the date would come even sooner ("The 2017 Long-Term Budget . . ."). It is this breaking point at which the federal government would be unable to pay either the principal or interest on its bonds, creating a financial crisis of catastrophic proportions for programs such as Medicare, Social Security, education, and defense that are dependent upon government financing (Benjamin 2).

The factors that are pushing the U.S. debt to its inexorable financial doomsday are still present and ticking like a clock. The first concerns demographics. The predicted aging of the baby boom generation is starting to take place. In 1960, only 16.6 million Americans were aged sixty-five and over. By 1990, this figure doubled to 31 million. By 2020, the number is predicted to rise to 52 million and then soar to 65.5 million by 2030. Although many aging Americans will not require Social Security and Medicare programs until approximately 2020, the economic impact is already starting to be felt. When Social Security legislation was passed in 1935, the worker-to-retiree ratio was forty-six to one. Currently there are three workers for every retiree, and by 2020, this proportion will have dwindled to two to one (De Rugy). The fiscal crisis generated by the growing debt and aging of America will have serious economic consequences for America's school-aged population.

In 2011, public and private elementary and secondary school enrollment was 55 million. By 2022, this number is expected to grow by 3,300,000 students and fortunately be evenly distributed throughout the United States ("Projections of Education Statistics to 2022"). Simple addition, however, demonstrates that school-aged children will be outnumbered by several million retirees until almost the debt-related projected doomsday date.

As a result, of this major demographic trend, national, state and local governments will be forced to make many draconian decisions in the years ahead. One will be whether to allocate America's stretched-to-the-limit resources to future generations so that they can be economically productive. The other will be whether to divert funds to bolster social and health programs that current generations have already labored to provide. Legislators charged with this unpopular task will also find their decisions challenging to implement. If they decide to place needed monies toward creating educational and employment opportunities, they will encounter

stiff opposition from voting blocs of retirees. Even the best of government intentions may be thwarted at the ballot box. An outbreak of age-based warfare is predicted by many economists, as each generation battles for what it considers its
rightfully earned share of a shrinking economic pie.

The United States has more debt than any other nation, and nineteen foreign
countries hold parts of it. Pardon the pun, but two of them, Russia and China, have
not always had our best "interest" at heart. China, not counting Hong Kong (at
$186.3 billion), holds $1.1 trillion, or 28 percent of our debt, in U.S. treasury bonds.
Russia, which ranks eighteenth as a debt holder, has purchased $74 billion of them
(Moshinsky). Having world-power countries whose governments are often inimi-
cal to ours as stakeholders is worrisome as we approach the year 2032. Most economists believe that China and Russia would not dump their bonds precipitately or
cease purchasing them in the future, because they still represent a sound financial
investment, and international finance imposes a host of intertwined commitments
for all stakeholders. Still we would be somewhat naïve to not consider the economic
leverage that China will have over the country as we approach 2032 and how it
would probably play out with regard to discretionary spending, including funds for
education.

In addition to paying off the principal of the debt, America faces a continual
problem with interest on it. The 2016 interest payment that the government remit-
ted toward the debt totaled $241 billion, or about 1 percent of GDP. It is expected
to rise to 2.7 percent, and the remainder of the budget, which includes defense and
education spending, will decrease from 3.1 percent to 2.6 percent of GDP. As the
debt devours more of the government's budget, economists have sarcastically said
"that in 10 years, the U.S. budget will look like that of a health care company with
a military and a lot of credit card debt" (Benjamin). Nearing the doomsday date,
the nineteen countries holding a percentage of our debt may raise their interest rates
to protect their investments, placing our government in the deleterious position of
slashing even more federally funded programs to meet sovereign investors'
demands. School librarians and educators would experience massive cuts in their
budgets, and every citizen would experience a precipitous drop in their standard
of living (Benjamin).

THE DEFICIT

While the debt is a looming financial abyss, the deficit is here and now. It is simply the annual amount the government spends beyond what is budgeted. It also
indicates a failure on the part of the government to bring in sufficient revenue to
offset spending on various mandated federal government programs and services
such as Medicare and other health programs. The deficit is just as pernicious as
the debt, because it establishes a cycle of cutting other equally important departments' budgets, such as education, just to make payments to congressionally
required ones.

Incomprehensible as it seems in a time of rapid change and global competition in almost every occupational field, education is considered discretionary
spending by the federal government. Funding for this department has dropped to

just 6.4 percent of GDP. In 1993, funding for education equaled 10 percent of GDP. Expenditures by the federal government in 2017 are at 20.7 percent of GDP, but revenues from personal, corporate, and excise taxes are only 17.8 percent of GDP. The projected difference of 2.9 percent in the GDP translates to a $693 billion shortfall. This difference is expected to widen, because the Congressional Budget Office (CBO) projects expenditures to increase to 24.9 percent of GDP in the 2028–2037 period, while tax revenues will increase by less than 1 percentage point to 18.7 percent. Consequently, annual deficits during these decades are expected to average 6.2 percent of GDP ("The 2017 Long-Term Budget Outlook").

SCHOOL LIBRARIES AND DEBT FALLOUT

Deficit spending and increasing national debt are not new to school librarians. These trends have been affecting school library programs for the past four decades. The decline in school library economic fortunes was officially ushered in when President Nixon proposed to reduce spending for libraries to zero. Although a significant amount was restored because of vigorously staged protests, the oil crisis and inflation of the 1970s, coupled with a severe recession, began an erosion of school library collections, programs, and services that has continued through to the present day (Clark 551–567). Dedicated school library legislation has also disappeared as school library funding has been subsumed into large educational acts that have forced us to compete with other eligible departments. The combined results are a slow constriction of library budgets as federal funding diminishes and school libraries are faced with steadily escalating prices for materials. Urban school districts are especially hard-pressed as they grapple with reduced operating hours, staffing, and budget cuts. Less than 40 percent have at least one full-time librarian, and 35 percent report reduced staffing levels over a three-year period. Approximately 50 percent have less than $4,000 allocated for books, while 90 percent work with collections with an average age exceeding five years, and 25 percent have had to reduce their number of subscription databases (Mantel 2).

Although our libraries are primarily funded locally, some of it is derived from grants distributed through the Library and Services and Technology Acts (LSTA). Many school libraries are dependent upon access to subscription databases that are funded by LSTA and continuing education programs for professional development. Threatened cuts to this act would affect school libraries hard since most lack the budget to subscribe to the online databases that states offer gratis through LSTA (Chant). The Every Student Succeeds Act (ESSA) is also in limbo as Congress continues to threaten to overturn various regulations affecting accountability and standards. Still written into the act, however, is a provision that "supporting the instructional services provided by effective school library programs" is part of it (Department of Education 323). Although ESSA does not specifically allot funding to school libraries, Titles I, II, and IV of the act furnish school librarians with the opportunity to apply for them. Funding for using and integrating technology effectively; for improving instruction and student achievement and for professional development, books, and up-to-date materials is available. Even more importantly is a section for funding to revise, update, or develop comprehensive literacy programs ("Opportunities for School Librarians").

While technological trends tend toward acceleration, economic trends present a classic conundrum of danger and opportunity. School libraries are in economic jeopardy because of national trends with the debt and annual deficits. On the other hand, a fighting chance still exists for school librarians to become advocates for the academic needs of their students and, in turn, themselves. Seeking funding at the local, state, and national levels for any type of categorical funding is an essential part of our mission. However, with definite trends involving increased implementation of big data, arguments that employ quantitative data might be more effective as a preemptive measure. At present, school librarians can rely upon the data-based national studies compiled on the American Library Association's (ALA) website for correlational research showing the link between the presence of school librarians and increased student achievement. Collecting and collating usage, circulation, test results, and other data at the local level, however, will also be vitally important for the design of district- or school-based rationales that favor the retention of school libraries.

Public libraries are under the same economic pressure as school libraries and are already devising economic-based arguments for validating their continued existence and budget requests. The Free Public Library of Philadelphia recently showed that the proximity of the city's public libraries added $698 million to home values. Taking the argument further, they demonstrated that homeowners could use this increased home value to borrow for home improvements, financing education, or other expenditures. The additional amount that is produced by living in a home close to a public library produced an extra $18.5 million in property taxes, which was paid annually to the city and its school districts. Several other public libraries in Wisconsin, South Carolina, and Vermont have calculated the return dollar benefits of public libraries for each citizen. Vermont's study reported a benefit of $5.36 per person and South Carolina a $3 dollar return on library investment (Mantel 4). If economic trends continue in a downward direction, these types of evidence-based, economic arguments, along with all the past achievement-based research studies, will need to be employed by school librarians.

STAGNANT INCOMES

Debt is not just a calamitous problem for the federal government. It is also one for the average American. According to Nobel Prize–winning economist Joseph Stiglitz, the U.S. standard of living is maintained by rising personal debt. It is so large that the lower 80 percent of the population is spending about 110 percent of its income (Stiglitz 394). The percentage of Americans living beyond their means is difficult to imagine because money is one of America's taboo topics due to its subtle links to status and class.

Stagnant incomes for American workers are an economic trend that began as early as 1973. While the year should have triggered alarm bells for workers, it didn't because how could they foresee that 1973 would be the peak year for their typical pay? Measured in 2013 dollars, a typical worker engaged in production and non-supervisory work in the private sector earned about $767 per week in 1973. After that peak year, real average wages began a rapid descent that the average worker could not recoup. More than forty years later, a similar worker earns just $644, which represents about a 13 percent decline in wages (Ford 34–35). The share of U.S. economic output that is paid in wages stands at the lowest level since the government started maintaining records in the 1950s (Thompson 5–6).

For almost thirty years after World War II, American workers experienced what economists term the "virtuous circle." As the average hourly pay of the American worker increased, the economy subsequently grew, thus expanding middle-class membership. As the middle class increased in size, so did its purchasing power. The economy grew faster, resulting in new investments and innovations, which further enriched the middle class and completed the circle (Reich 115). The circle, however, is broken, because the hourly pay of American workers no longer rises with their productivity. The United States is still a productive country with gains rising 65 percent since 1979, but workers' median pay has increased by only 8 percent during these years (Reich 123).

Many economists blame stagnant wages on a loss of manufacturing jobs, among other factors. Manufacturing jobs have fallen about 30 percent since 2000, and that percentage has helped to contribute to higher unemployment, which has swelled the working poor to 47 million, or one out of every seven Americans (Thompson 7). By 2013, 25 percent of all U.S. workers had jobs with compensation below the level of full-time, year-round jobs that are necessary to maintain a family of four above the federally defined poverty line. More than 50 percent of the 46 million users of food pantries in 2013 had jobs or were members of working families (Reich 134).

WAGES AND EDUCATION

One of the distinguishing elements of working versus middle class is education. Economists have used a college diploma as a dividing point between these two classes to consistently demonstrate that having a college degree versus a high school diploma will result in increased earnings. Although this finding continues to trend in the same direction, wages are also stagnating for those with a post–high school education. Median earnings for workers with a bachelor's degree equaled $50,000 in 2015 as opposed to $30,500 for high school graduates ("Annual Earnings of Young Adults"). While the difference in earnings between high school and college graduates looks impressive, data show that the median wage for younger college graduates is barely increasing. Between 2000 and 2013, the real average hourly wages of young college graduates declined (Reich 117). In this same span of years, college graduates in the top ninetieth percentile only increased their cumulative income by 4.4 percent (Katel 5). Students with doctorates saw their annual earnings decline from $98,000 in 2000 to about $87,000 in 2016 ("Unemployment Rates . . ."). Entry-level wages of college graduates actually declined 8.1 percent for women graduates and 6.7 percent for men (Reich 210). Adjusted for inflation, hourly average wages for college graduates ages 21 to 24 have barely increased from $18.41 per hour in 2000 to $18.53 per hour in 2016 (Kroeger, Cooke, and Gould 3).

STAGNANT INCOMES AND SCHOOL LIBRARIES

In the latest ten-year survey of school library trends, 96 percent of Americans (224.5 million) reported that "school library programs are an essential part of the education experience because they provide resources to students and teachers" ("The Condition of U.S. Libraries . . ." 4). Ninety-six percent (222 million) also agreed that school libraries are a necessity because they provide children with the "opportunity to read and learn" ("The Condition of U.S. Libraries . . ." 4). It's important to note that this library survey of the American public was taken in 2009, when the United States was still struggling out of the Great Recession and income and wages had been stagnant for quite some time. Despite the fact that most Americans were not experiencing an increase in income, they still believed that school libraries were essential to students' educational future.

These survey results may help furnish us with confidence that school librarians are on the side of the "academic angels" and that our economic-based arguments for continued staffing and support of school libraries need a vocal hearing in our local communities. An interesting study to determine the economic impact that an individual teacher had over a student's lifetime was conducted in 2013. Researchers used school district and tax records of 1 million children and determined that students assigned to a high-value teacher were more likely to attend college and earn high salaries and were less likely to have children in their teenage years. Replacing a teacher whose value-added score was in the bottom 5 percent with even an average teacher was estimated to increase the present value of students' lifetime income by approximately $250,000 per classroom (Chetty, Friedman, and Rockoff). Compiling and calculating similar results for school librarians at the elementary and secondary levels might suggest a similar relationship, and even more so in schools that lack certified librarians or have only part-time ones.

The American Library Association has recently published a handbook titled *The Power of Data* that details not only how to collect useful school library data at the local, state, and national levels but also how to employ it to formulate powerful economic arguments on behalf of our students who desperately need our instructional programs and services. With stagnating incomes and wages throughout the American workforce, parents will be searching for educational resources that are not supplemental to their budgets. Now is the time to demonstrate what school libraries can provide on a 24/7 basis through instruction, borrowing print and non-print materials, access to online databases, and support of school learning standards such as the Common Core.

INEQUALITY

Even the Greeks warned of the dangers of inequality when Aristotle observed that a thriving middle class was an essential requirement for a stable society and Plutarch noted that "an imbalance between rich and poor is the oldest and most fatal ailments in all republics" (Schmidt and McKnight 211, 216). Supreme Court Justice Louis Brandeis also reminded us of it in 1941, stating, "We can have a democracy or we can have great wealth in the hands of a few, but we cannot have both." (Reich 159). Yet in the world of economics, the term equality is not "a morally compelling ideal" (Frankfurt 5). It connotes removing economic gains from citizens who believe that they have rightfully earned them through their own hard work and bestowing them upon those who have not. Frankfurt, author of *On Inequality*, believes that we should not focus on reducing economic inequality, but instead go about making improvements to a society where many have far too little, while others "have the comfort and influence that go with having more than enough" (Frankfurt 5).

In economic terms, the United States is currently a decidedly unequal society. A small percentage of American citizens control an increasing share of the country's wealth. Incomes of this small percentage rival those seen during the age of the "robber barons" during the late 1800s and early 1900s (Schmidt and McKnight 209). Economic data, unfortunately, confirm this tremendous upheaval in Americans' positions on various monetary rungs of the economic ladder. In 1978, a typical household in the wealthiest 0.01 percent had 220 times more wealth than the average household. While this amount seems fairly surprising for a country espousing equal opportunity for all, consider that by the year 2012, those same households at the top of the ladder were 1,120 times richer (Reich 162).

Thomas Piketty, author of *Capitalism in the Twenty-First Century*, reports that the top 1 percent of Americans had doubled their income within thirty years and those in the 0.1 percent quadrupled theirs (Piketty). This means that the upper 1 percent are taking nearly one-quarter of the nation's income every year. In terms of wealth rather than income, the top 1 percent control 40 percent of the wealth. Two countries that share economic inequality with us at this level are Russia and Iran (Stiglitz 88). More than 20 percent of our students live in poverty, and children in Canada, Sweden, France, and Germany have a better chance of exceeding their parents' level of prosperity than our students do (Stiglitz 389). Currently one of every seven Americans is on food stamps (Stiglitz 93).

Enlarging the top percentage just a little reveals a similar shocking pattern of inequality. The wealthiest 10 percent control three-quarters of total family wealth in the United States. From 1989 to 2013, families in the ninetieth percentile watched their wealth increase by 54 percent, whereas those at the fiftieth percentile had only a 4 percent rise. Citizens at the twenty-fifth percentile saw their wealth drop by 6 percent (Sahadi).

Even more revealing are the numbers that relate to generational mobility or death of the American dream. The United States has always been thought of as a land of prosperity and opportunity where children would always do better with regard to income and education than their parents. Data show, however, that the American dream is no longer within reach of most people. Stanford University economists spent months crunching past census data to discover when it started to slip away for so many Americans. It began as early as the 1970s, with the energy crisis, but even then 75 percent of the baby boom generation would make more than their parents. But by the 1980s global competition, the technology revolution, government policies facilitating the accumulation of wealth, a drop in college enrollment, and reduced workforce skills heavily affected America. Children born in 1980 now have only a 50 percent chance of earning as much income as had their parents.

However, when the same economists ran a simulation with the data and removed the post-1970 rise in inequality, 80 percent of children would have outearned their parents rather than the predicted 50 percent (Leonhardt).

One of the contributing factors to our growing inequality is the exorbitant increase in chief executive officer (CEO) earnings. Between 1997 and 2014, executive pay increased by 997 percent. In 2015, the difference between CEO and worker earnings peaked at 644 to 1, when the CEO of McDonald's earned $7.29 million a year and an average McDonald's employee $11,324 a year (Katel 10). When wealth is distributed unevenly, it triggers a reversal of the virtuous circle, with huge consolidations of wealth passing directly to the second generation, resulting in an increase in wealth divisions over time (Stiglitz 209). As this wealth accumulates in the hands of a few, its repercussions throughout American society are pernicious to say the least. The wealthiest 400 Americans have more money than the bottom 50 percent of Americans. The wealthiest 1 percent own 42 percent of the nation's private assets, while the share of wealth maintained by the lower half of households has dropped from 3 percent in 1989 to 1 percent today (Reich 161). The Walton family's Walmart stock, for example, exceeded the wealth of the bottom 40 percent of American families in total. The anticipated transfer shift by wealthy Americans to their heirs within the next fifty years is predicted to equal $36 trillion (Reich 214).

REACTIONS TO INEQUALITY

As statistics, articles, and books are published warning Americans about our growing inequality, questions arise. Why isn't the majority of the public, which constitutes the most unequal part of this dire economic equation, alarmed, if not outraged? When parents comprehend that odds do not favor their children earning more than they do, why do they fail to protest? The answer seems to lie with psychology and not economic data. Psychologists have reported that a person's sense of well-being is linked to their economic position in life (Leonhardt). Psychologists also believe that we all suffer from a phenomenon called the "Lake Wobegon effect," named after Garrison Keillor's invented village "where all the women are strong, all the men are good-looking, and all the children are above average." This effect seems to protect our egos at the expense of objective thinking. A study of hospitalized accident survivors, for example, conducted in 1965 found that all of the patients consistently rated themselves as "better-than-average drivers" even though police records showed that the hospitalized survivors had caused the respective accidents. This type of study has been replicated numerous times and produced similar results. The most surprising one was conducted with college professors who were asked to compare their teaching abilities to those of their colleagues. A whopping 94 percent rated themselves better than average (Payne 16–17).

Despite the fact that we mathematically know that we all cannot possibly be above average with regard to our salaries, intelligence, leadership qualities, SAT scores, etc., we are unable to acknowledge it to ourselves. One particularly startling inequality study researched our ability to deceive ourselves regarding the American dream and its relationship to upward mobility. In a study of 3,000 participants, psychologists asked them to study a five-level income graph and estimate the likelihood that a person born into the lowest quintile would move to any of the other quintiles during their lifetime. Their answers were compared to the correct mobility trends from the Pew Research Center. Respondents in the study overestimated the likelihood of rising from the lowest quintile to one of the top three by nearly 15 percent. In sad reality, only 30 percent of people ever jump three quintiles when they are in the lowest one. Another study found respondents overestimating the number of college students in the bottom economic quintile, who attended college at a rate of five times greater than the actual number (Kraus, Davidai, and Nussbaum). A last study found that the lower placement on the economic ladder resulted in even greater overestimation of one's chances of upward mobility. Ironically, those with the least chances of mobility believed that they had the most opportunity to ascend the ladder (Kraus, Davidai, and Nussbaum).

Fortunately, when Americans are faced with choice regarding inequality, they consistently reveal their dislike of it. After showing more than 5,000 Americans two pie charts with five quintile divisions representing the American and Swedish economies, respectively, 92 percent of them preferred the Swedish one, which does indeed have more equal wealth distribution. Even respondents earning six-figure salaries (89 percent) chose Sweden as frequently as those making less than $50,000 (92 percent). Surprisingly, consensus was also reflected across political parties, with 90 percent of Republicans electing the Swedish pie chart and 94 percent of Democrats doing likewise (Payne 26–27).

INEQUALITY AND OUR STUDENTS

Despite growing data-informed awareness of our increasing inequality, its harmful effects continue to remain below the surface, like an undertow in the ocean. Although we are constantly exposed to economic data about inequality, we continue to employ ego defense mechanisms that enable us to dismiss its reported effects. Perhaps inequality is more relevant when we look at the data concerning our students and how it affects their health, psychological well-being, and educational opportunities.

Because of the disparities in income among Americans, we are rapidly isolating ourselves geographically from one another. The chance that a black child will attend school with white peers is equal to pre-1954 when the Supreme Court issued its landmark decision, *Brown v. Board of Education*, acknowledging that separate schools were essentially unequal (Reich 101). It is becoming more the exception than the rule that the child of a postal worker will attend school with the child of a stockbroker. It wasn't always that way. But within a thirty-year period from 1970 to 2000, families in higher-income brackets began to increasingly live in neighborhoods with other similar families. Low-income families became even more isolated as a result. Since the majority of students attend school near their residences, the gap between high- and low-income children has increased. One study showed that the gap between top and bottom income range jumped 50 percent between 1972 and 2002 (Duncan and Murnane 41). This form of segregation by residence is taking its toll on a growing number of American students, as middle-class parents struggle to provide opportunities for them to prosper in an increasingly unequal country.

The amount of money that a parent can spend on their child is becoming one of the strongest predictors of their cognitive development and a determinant factor with respect to their upward mobility (Putnam 125). Between 1983 and 2007, spending per child by families in the top 10 percent increased by 75 percent in real dollars, compared to a drop of 22 percent in the lowest 10 percent. By 2007, children in the top 10 percent received $6,600 per year in enrichment spending, or nine times the amount (about $750) that a parent of a child in the bottom 10 percent of the economic ladder received (Kornich and Furstenberg 23–25).

As a result of growing geographical segregation between higher- and lower-income classes, two distinct parenting styles are emerging. The first, called "concerted cultivation," entails a variety of investments that a parent intentionally makes to increase a child's educational skills and improve their chances for upward mobility. Enrolling children in preschools that have certified teachers and offer appropriate developmental activities and paying for tutoring if a child requires remedial attention are examples of this type of parenting. "Natural growth" involves less scheduling of activities, more unsupervised play, and reduced attention to school-related work (Lareau 2–3). The former style of parenting demands a considerable investment that affluent parents can afford. Music lessons, trips to museums, summer camp, travel, and even more face time with their children are easily obtained.

A child reared in the natural growth style is at a distinct economic disadvantage because even if their parents desired to engage in a more cultivated growth style of parenting, their placement on the economic ladder makes it completely out of reach. As a result, the class gap between affluent and lower-income parents widens even more (Putnam 124–126). As state and local funding for education declines, schools have had to introduce "pay-to-play" policies for activities such as sports and music, which further widen the divide. More than 50 percent of American high schools have been forced to charge team equipment and participation fees that averaged $300 to $400 dollars per student and affect the participation level between lower- and upper-income students. Lower-income students from those families making less than $60,000 per year participated at the thirtieth percentile, while upper-income families' children participated at the fifty-first percentile ("Pay-to-Play . . ."). If a student in the Poudre School District in Colorado, for example, wishes to participate in the Fossil Ridge High School's competitive marching band, the suggested parent donation is $525. Although both types of activities are considered extracurricular, performing well in either can lead to college scholarships, which lower-income students would definitely benefit from to further their educations (Kyle).

Studies are consistently showing that student learning is affected by the achievement and behavior of their peers. So it actually matters with whom you attend school. Students achieve more when they attend school with other students who are from affluent, educated homes (Logan, Minca, and Adar 287–301). Thirty years ago, the average divergence on SAT type tests between children in the richest 10 percent and bottom 10 percent was about 90 points on an 800-point scale. By 2014, it was 125 points (Reich 140). This span is statistically significant and is a determinant factor in gaining entrance to higher-ranked colleges. Unfortunately, achievement levels and behavior problems tend to be more prevalent among low-income students and when they are the largest demographic in a school, overall achievement declines.

As the middle class continues to compress, more Americans are becoming part of this demographic. In 2015, 120.8 million adults were in middle-income households compared with 121.3 million in lower- and upper-income households combined. The share, however, in the upper tier grew more than the other tiers ("American Middle Class Is Losing Ground"). Once our students fall into this demographic, it becomes more likely that they will suffer from a host of attendant behaviors that will decrease their social mobility and chance for prosperity in the American economy. Studies show that inequality is a strong predictor of an increase in risk-taking behavior, obesity, dropout rates, mental illness, and decreased life expectancy (Payne 48).

WHY IT MATTERS

The economic downsides of inequality should be obvious to all, yet this destructive pattern persists. It is concatenated in its cycle of damage. The share of adults in middle-income households dropped from 61 percent of the population in 1971 to 50 percent in 2015 (Katel 2). As the middle class shrinks, they are unable to spend money, which is what helps drive our economic growth. People with reduced incomes are unable to invest in the future by educating their children or improving their businesses. Our tax base contracts because the middle class is no longer paying the same amount of taxes and the wealthy are not compensating for it with higher taxes. Economic inequality leads to political inequality and eventually to an undemocratic decision-making process (Stiglitz 388). It threatens our most precious resource—our students and future workforce. Their successes and failures will affect our economic and political future in a truly globally connected economy (Schmidt and McKnight 216).

INEQUALITY AND SCHOOL LIBRARIES

Inequality is causing increased polarization in our society, and our schools are starting to reflect an increasing economic homogenization caused by residential segregation. If this economic trend continues, many school libraries will mirror the fortunes or misfortunes of their respective geographic locations. Since school library funding is generated from local taxes, Americans living in more affluent neighborhoods will continue to fund their school libraries at the levels necessary for their children to thrive academically. Even when funds are distributed evenly among upscale and downscale schools within a district, parents' affluence will compensate for shortfalls. "Para-school funding" is the term for parental and community funding. It helps provide the extras such as new books or 3D printers for a school library that only receives its equal share of district funding (Putnam 167). On the Upper West side of Manhattan, for example, parent-teacher associations

(PTAs) raise nearly $1 million to fund extracurricular activities. The parent-funded foundation for public schools in Hillsborough, California, raised $3.45 million that supplemented the school district's budget by 17 percent (Putnam 168). In the years ahead, school librarians will need to take advantage of para-funding to compensate for decreased budgets for library materials. Unfortunately, the amount received will probably be dependent upon the library's geographic location and the socio-economic level of its student body.

Raising awareness of inequality, regardless of the socioeconomic level of school libraries, will be important for the future functioning of American society. One of our core values as school librarians is respecting and promoting diversity. Calling this grave economic problem to the attention of students, regardless of their socio-economic strata, through the use of videos, books, displays, interactive games, and simulations will be vitally important if we are to begin to correct this growing problem of economic injustice. The simulation game *Spent* (playspent.org), for example, asks students to experience the harsh economic choices that someone needs to make living on a low income, and YouTube videos such as "Are the Rich Getting Too Much of the Economic Pie?" visually demonstrate our growing inequality in interesting and understandable ways for teens. The Pew Research Center has designed an income calculator titled "Are You in the Middle Class?" that lets students determine their rung on the economic ladder and compare it to others of similar age, education, race, and ethnicity (Fry and Kochhar). Making our students cognizant of inequality provides school librarians with a golden opportunity to demonstrate why their expertise marshalling resources from a variety of print and nonprint materials is absolutely essential for their educational institutions.

STUDENT HIGHER EDUCATION COSTS AND DEBT

Strolling around a college campus will not enable us to determine if there are fewer students than in past years. Crowds of them still gather at the student union and fill athletic arenas for sporting events. But statistically, there are fewer. Enrollment at college has been in decline since 2011, as our growing inequality continues to wreak havoc with our most precious commodity—our students. College attendance is just over 19 million students from its peak of 20.6 million in 2011 (Korn). Unfortunately, as income levels have stalled, tuition for higher education has skyrocketed.

In America, the best means to obtain an education and the only path for social mobility is to borrow. In 2010, student debt totaled $1 trillion and exceeded credit card debt for the first time (Stiglitz 390–394). By 2016, students owed more than $1.45 trillion in loan debt that is distributed among 44 million borrowers. This exceeds total U.S. credit card debt by $620 billion. Average graduates of the class of 2016 accumulated $37,172 in student loan debt, reflecting an increase of 6 percent over the preceding year ("A Look at the Shocking . . .").

While there are a number of interrelated causes to growing student debt, the main one continues to be tuition increases. In a time of stagnant wages and income growth, it makes for a poisonous economic cocktail. Since the 2007–2008 school year, the average tuition at four-year public universities has risen 28 percent faster than inflation (Douglas-Gabriel). Fees increased even faster than tuition at state schools between the 1999–2000 and 2012–2013 academic years. During that time, inflation-adjusted fees at community colleges rose 104 percent, while tuition moved up 50 percent. At four-year public colleges, fees shot up 95 percent, which made the 66 percent increase in tuition look small by comparison (Douglas-Gabriel).

The hike in student fees coincides with a reduction in state funding for higher education. Beginning in 2004, state support per student plummeted from $9,529 to $6,505, or more than 30 percent when adjusted for inflation. By 2012, tuition exceeded state spending for public colleges. In comparison, during the 1970s, states paid three-quarters of state colleges' bills (Price 2). Although college tuition and fees have declined recently, for a country experiencing increasing inequality, the costs borne by parents and students are formidable. In the 2015–2016 academic year, one year at a four-year public university that includes tuition, fees, and room and board costs an average of $14,120 for a full-time, in-state resident even when grants, scholarships, and tax credits were removed. A year at a private nonprofit college costs even more, totaling $26,400 (Douglas-Gabriel).

As tuition and fees continue to remain out of sight for many students, questions arise about their allocations. What are the monies being spent on? Who is deriving the most benefit from increasing tuition and fees that easily exceed the cost-of-living index? Do the tuition and fee hikes reflect the amount lost from state funding, or is something financially amiss? Are the increases in expenses being spent on faculty?

Unfortunately, stagnant wages are also the norm for full-time faculty members. A long-range outlook from 1971 shows that college teachers' inflation-adjusted salaries have been flat and even declined over the past fourteen years (Price 2). In 2016–2017, the average salary for full professors equaled $102,402. Associate and assistant professors earned on average $79,654 and $69,206, respectively. This average salary, adjusted for inflation, totaled a 0.6 percent increase for a full professor, a 1.2 percent increase for an associate professor, and a 1.5 percent increase for an assistant. Since the cost of living increased at a faster rate in 2016–2017 than it did in 2015–2016, the increase was negligible ("Visualizing Change . . ." 4–5). Often, however, students do not reap the academic benefits from these full-time academicians because the largest percentage of the college workforce consists of part-time faculty. Their salaries, when employed at a single institution, presently average $20,508 per year ("Visualizing Change . . ." 4).

Various economists believe that tuition and fee costs have escalated because of unreasonable expenditures on administrators, athletics, and facilities. Investigative research centers are reporting that the number of administrators doubled at colleges between 1987 and 2012, increasing this budget allocation to 517,636 positions (Price 2). Administrators are also beginning to accrue salaries that mirror those of CEOs at profit-based companies and firms. In 2015, presidents at five public universities earned more than $1 million.

The second reason for increased tuition and fees concerns athletics. Many universities seem to be engaging in an "athletic arms race" that boosts tuition and fee costs considerably. Expenses for a football scholarship player in the National Collegiate Athletic Association's Football Bowl division increased 55 percent from

2005 to 2014. Per-athlete spending on all sports rose 43 percent during this same period, whereas academic spending per full-time student increased only 9 percent ("Athletic & Academic Spending Database . . .").

In addition to an "athletic arms race," many higher education institutions are engaged in costly building projects such as extravagant dormitories, recreation centers, and presidents' homes. Purdue University, for example, constructed a $98 million sports center replete with a climbing wall, vortex pool, and twenty-five-person spa, while Yale and Columbia Universities spent $17 million and $20 million, respectively to upgrade their presidents' houses (Price 7).

It is easy to imagine how many thousands of students would benefit from a redistribution of their tuition and fee dollars, as so many struggle to make payments and incur increasing amounts of debt. The fear of debt is real for millions of students. In 2017, 4.3 million of them (ages 20 to 30 years old) were in default and 1.4 million had loans in the default grace period. Their average student loan payment equaled $351 dollars per month. Those who attended for-profit colleges incurred an average debt of $39,950 per month ("A Look at the Shocking . . .").

SCHOOL LIBRARIES AND THE COST OF HIGHER EDUCATION

If economic trends continue downward regarding stagnant wages and incomes, our library locations will not change the demand for our instruction, programs, and services. The need for our professional reference services can make an economic difference that should be documented. Whether our libraries are situated in affluent or lower-income areas, silently and imperceptibly more Americans will begin a slide down the broken economic ladder. Their children, who are our students, will not arrive in our libraries announcing that they do not have the funds to attend college. This information will remain hidden as long as possible to avoid their peers discovering it. Parents' aspirations for their children, however, will remain the same. The majority of them will want their children to obtain education beyond high school because they still see it as a path to economic security ("Special Report on the Future . . ."). This means that our programs and personalized reference services will become absolutely essential to our students who will need assistance with obtaining scholarships, loans, and grants to help them defray higher education expenses.

Applying our professional searching skills to finding and publicizing the most affordable and reputable colleges and universities will be part of our services. Inserting financial literacy skills into relevant resource-based units will be important so that students become more aware of college debt costs and the long-term implications for their adult lives. A recent global study of financial literacy revealed that Americans had a rate of 57 percent compared to other countries' ranking. Moreover, more than 50 percent of millennials take on student loans without even attempting to calculate the payments ("Should College Students Be . . ."). Finding and demonstrating the financial traps set for them by for-profit colleges will also be critical because student debt at for-profit colleges is even higher ("A Look at the Shocking . . .").

More of our students and their parents are beginning to discern the link between perpetual learning and earning. A recent Pew survey reported that 54 percent of all employed Americans believe that it will be necessary to learn new skills throughout their working lives. For adults under thirty years old, that number rises to 61 percent (Brown). These findings give us the opportunity to stress the need for our students to improve their information literacy skills, and for us to demonstrate their correlation to success in any higher or continuing educational endeavor. Disseminating research studies supporting this connection between proficiency in information-seeking skills and success in performing college-level research assignments will be strategically important for our positions as indispensable to the educational mission of our respective schools.

MONOPOLIES OF THE MIND

Five years ago, science fiction writer Bruce Sterling observed that economists were wasting time discussing the impact of the Internet, iPhones, and the like and should be devoting their research to analyzing how a small coterie of five vertically organized "stacks" were affecting our society (McAfee and Brynjolfsson 295–296). The big five, or "frightful five," as Farhad Manjoo of the *New York Times* dubs them, are Google, Amazon, Facebook, Apple, and Microsoft (Manjoo). These companies have succeeded in harnessing the convergence of technological innovation with reduced cost of technologies, increased network connections, and manufacture of mobile phones at a moment when they perfectly understood the ramifications and could have the edge over all competitors (Manjoo).

Presently, the five companies wield enormous economic, social, and political power, rivaling companies that amassed comparable power and wealth in the Gilded Age (Foer 191). The founders of Amazon, Microsoft, and Facebook are members of an elite club composed of the world's top billionaires (Moskowitz). When looked at monetarily, their dominance is alarming. By 2016, these companies were the "five publicly traded companies with the highest stock market valuations in the world" (McAfee and Brynjolfsson 296). Combined, their collective worth is about $3.5 trillion, which amounts to over 40 percent of the market capital on the NASDAQ stock market (Stewart 56).

Their vast wealth enables them to easily gobble up their competitors, who are smaller and cannot compete with their integrated product lines. Apple's customers, for example, usually purchase numerous peripherals that augment their iPhones because they are designed to work together. When Apple announced their iTunes Store for the purchase of digital music, it cornered a 61 percent share of the downloaded digital music market (Foer 89–90). In 2012, as Instagram grew more popular with young adults and began to compete with Facebook as a primary go-to site, Facebook purchased it for $1 billon. Two years later, it purchased WhatsApp for $22 billion and Oculus Rift for $3 billion ("The New Face of Facebook" 21). Four years later, Microsoft acquired LinkedIn for $26.2 billion. Google bought Motorola Mobility for $12.5 billion just to own the company's trove of tech patents ("Rise of the Superstars" 8). Over the past few years, Google has acquired over two hundred companies (Foer 31). By 2014, Amazon was selling half of all the books published in the United States. Stores such as Borders and thousands of independent bookstores vanished under the onslaught of Amazon's price cuts, stock size, and quick shipping options (Reich 38). In 2017, Amazon purchased Whole Foods for $13.7 billion.

It is sometimes difficult to see the corrosive damage that these five monopolies do to our economy because many of their products appear free or present with reduced costs. Google search and Facebook access, for example, cost nothing. Amazon offers us reduced prices not only on books but also various consumer and grocery items. The big five are so addictively embedded in our lives that we fail to see the "clear and present danger" of their surveillance that occurs with every Google search, photo snapped, or movement from one location to another ("The New Face of Facebook" 23). Facebook owns patents that, when developed, will continuously track our locations, discern our weekly routines and social milieus, and could even predict our amorous intentions based upon clicks to others' pages and profiles (Chinoy). These types of monopolies are more challenging to understand because they are data based, have relatively few employees, and their products are not physically powering our cars or building our factories as monopolies like Standard Oil and Carnegie Steel did during the Gilded Age.

Their dangers, however, are historically similar in nature. They progressively limit our ability to choose by purchasing competing companies. Amazon is the first stop for one-third of all American consumers seeking to acquire anything. Internet clicks to major and reputable news outlets, including network television, are down more than 50 percent, because Google and Facebook are now the first place Americans go to for their news (Reich 38). As these big tech companies amass vast amounts of economic data, they use it to snuff out the competition by purchasing start-up rivals or simply designing competing algorithms that consistently lower prices, denying their competitors market share ("The World's Most Valuable Resource" 7). The big five are accumulating huge profits that enable them to employ large numbers of lobbyists, who in turn obtain the influence of politicians, who do not enforce existing antitrust laws and regulations. As their disproportionate share of the American economy grows, less is returned to American taxpayers who are freely and unknowingly supplying the companies with the product that they need to grow: massive amounts of data about our public and private lives.

For years, Amazon avoided paying taxes in states such as South Carolina and Texas in exchange for constructing distribution centers. Economists at Ohio State University revealed that Amazon's household spending sales dropped 10 percent when individual states began enforcing tax payments on its sales. Years of not paying taxes furnished Amazon with a significant advantage over other online competitors. In 2003, Amazon shifted its assets to Luxembourg, enabling it to save more than $1.5 billion in U.S. taxes. By the close of 2015, Google had followed suit by moving $58.3 billion of its profits to Bermuda and paying no taxes on them. In 2012, Facebook recorded $1.1 billion in profits and paid no state or federal income taxes. Apple and Alphabet, a spin-off of Google, have paid about 16 percent in taxes despite earning huge profits (Foer 197).

The influence that these five tech companies have is hard to document because they do not want the public to know the extent of their economic and political power.

It is, however, considerable. Google spent $17 million on Washington, D.C., lobbyists, and Google representatives visited Capitol Hill on the average of once per week from the beginning of Barack Obama's presidency through October 2016. Their head lobbyist visited the Obama White House 128 times, leading journalists at *The Intercept* to conclude that "Google has achieved a kind of vertical integration with the government" (Dayen).

SCHOOLS AND MONOPOLIES OF THE MIND

As state and local funding for schools becomes imperiled because of our growing national debt, schools will need to contract a devil's bargain with members of the big five in order to provide students with the hardware and software they need to complete school assignments. Many investigative reporters are referring to agreements between Google and school districts as "the Googlification of the classroom" (Singer). In a tech race that used to involve Apple and Microsoft, questions arise about how Google has become dominant. As of 2017, more than half of the country's primary and secondary school students, or more than 30 million, used Google education apps such as Gmail and Docs. Google Chromebooks constitute more than half the mobile devices shipped to schools.

The Chicago Public Schools system has spent $33.5 million on 134,000 Chromebooks. Google's progress toward classroom tech dominance is rather simple. It gains the trust and confidence of technology directors and teachers first, followed by building principals. Bypassing district administrators allows the push for its products to come from below. It encourages teachers who try their apps to post messages in blogs and hosts workshops open to teachers in other school districts to come and experiment with their products. As Google gains market share of the lucrative educational technology market, it creates new apps, such as Google Classroom, that serve as a portal allowing teachers to take attendance, grade papers, assign homework and store all the data in Google Cloud. The savings from using their products can be considerable. Chicago Public Schools, for example, saved $1.6 million just by switching to Google Mail and Docs compared to $2 million for Microsoft's email service, Exchange (Singer).

Google's suite of products are apparently free of technology glitches and integrate so well with each other that they seem the answer to cash-strapped school districts throughout the country. So what is the problem? Critics point to the negative aspects of monopolies and the role that educators are playing in ensuring Google's dominance. First is the idea that tech skills may come before knowledge-based skills, with the underlying concern that students are being trained as skilled tech workers rather than as educated citizens. Second, are schools supplying Google with generations of future customers? High school graduates, for example, are reminded to upload their email accounts and documents to regular Google accounts before they leave the district, thus ensuring that most will stay with Google and its attendant products. Third, Google has been vague about how it is using the data that it collects from student accounts, even after agreeing to comply with the federal Family Educational Rights and Privacy Act (Singer). Naturally questions arise about how student data could be used for the development of new Google products that would further entrench Google's position in the classroom, thus assuring them of complete power in an extremely lucrative market.

SCHOOL LIBRARIES AND MONOPOLIES OF THE MIND

Economic trends involving declining national, state, and local financial support for school libraries may necessitate alliances with tech and publishing companies because the savings can be considerable. In the years to come, school librarians will be wrestling with the problem of "biting the hand that feeds them" as we confront the growing ownership of personal and public information by monopolists of the mind. Siva Vaidhyanathan, in his book *The Googlization of Everything,* bemoans the "increasing privatization of the information ecosystem" (Vaidhyanathan 152). The monopolists of the mind are creating a crisis point where technology is on a crash course with our democracy. In 2012, for example, the Obama campaign employed Google Analytics to assist their election team in discerning the motivation behind increased voter support for candidate Obama, both vocally and monetarily. After President Obama's victory, Google published a paper claiming that it had shaped the information voters received as they searched for answers to questions posed during the debates and that the company was able to deliver answers to those searching directly through various campaign ads (Foer 124).

That same year, a Google engineer with access to Google's street-mapping vehicles reprogrammed Google cars to lock on to Wi-Fi signals emanating from private homes capturing private data and emails. Instead of firing the offending engineer and cooperating with the subsequent investigation, Google thwarted the latter and never fired their Google-based hacker (Lohr and Streitfeld). Similar indifference is exhibited when parents recently discovered that numerous YouTube Kids videos containing disturbing scenes of monsters and other inappropriate content are being viewed by their preschoolers. Many of the videos are animated independently in an attempt to avoid copyright violation detection and are linked to ads that make them profitable to create. Google attributed the influx of unsuitable videos to the huge numbers of uploaded videos and a malfunctioning algorithm. The company did not offer to employ human beings to filter and flag offensive videos in the future (Maheshwari 1, 24).

Given the current monopolists' demonstrated love of excessive profits, it might not take much for them to tip the search engine page rank scales in favor of the more pro-business candidate, or for social media to encourage the proliferation of fake news about a more liberal one. Some investigators of this monopolistic trend believe that our privacy cannot survive the onslaught of technology and that the conditions are prime for the monopolists of the mind to dominate our economy, society, and politics (Foer 230–231).

School librarians have always upheld the values of privacy and diversity in the interest of democracy. Although we may need to cozy up to the monopolists for hardware and software, we can also use their products as a platform to garner economic support for our libraries. The "Saveschoollibrarians.org" is a prime example. Hosted by political action committee EveryLibrary and funded by the publisher Follett, the site requires just one click to initiate assistance for mobilizing parents and other invested groups through Facebook, Twitter, or direct mail to convince school board members and superintendents to revise their budgets to retain librarians in their schools. The site is free, and the campaign can be operative within twenty-four hours. It also features petitions to save libraries in other states and ways to advocate for additional funding (Rogers).

Another platform that is being used successfully is YouTube. The publisher Capstone used it to produce a video titled "School Libraries Matter." Viewed more than 30,000 times, the School Librarians of Rhode Island (SLRL) were inspired by it to raise $8,526 from Kickstarter to fund a video to raise the "profile of their profession" and win support for their ongoing programs and services with critical thinking and science, technology, engineering, and math (STEM) curricula. Capstone reciprocated by agreeing to fund the project (Geddes).

While the trajectory of the big tech companies seems unassailable, it is a propitious time for school librarians to operate in "David versus Goliath" mode. The monopolists of the minds' weaknesses reside in their unwillingness and perhaps inability to curate their content. They are constantly applying a "technofix mentality" to any problem, while all of us can see that the problems with fake news, infiltration of websites by bots, loading of developmentally inappropriate videos, and so forth are proliferating at an alarming rate (Naisbitt 52). As the monopolists continue to combat their problems with algorithms instead of policing their content by employing human beings, our curated collections, services, and programs become more valuable to our school populations. While public librarians make successful connections between the geographic location of their libraries and home values, school librarians should be able to similarly calculate the economic value of our collections of developmentally appropriate, previously reviewed books, non-print materials, and curated assignment-related websites in comparisons to the gazillions of irrelevant sites that our students trawl through on a regular basis.

The next step is to mathematically attribute these collections to our training and skill and articulate cogent human-versus-algorithm arguments. Our excellent collections are possible because we, as professionally trained school librarians, not algorithms, acquired the print materials, websites, subscription databases, and videos after reading numerous reviews, validating websites for creditability, and installing them on a password-protected site. Just as the SLRI is doing, we need to employ the monopolists' own platforms such as Facebook, Google, and Twitter to publicize the economic value of school librarians' curated collections by creating messages, videos, blog posts, and the like. We need to use the same platforms to distribute the research findings concerning the economic value of school libraries to building principals, superintendents, and parents in our communities.

While the economic trends do not auger boom times for school libraries, Google, Facebook, and Twitter executives are beginning to face increasing criticism on Capitol Hill concerning their inability to control the downloading of content to their sites. The most significant example concerned the 2016 election, when thousands of fake Twitter accounts and millions of fictitious Facebook and Google ads were created by foreign governments in a clear attempt to influence the results. As usual, the monopolists made some promises but would not agree to the suggestions of legislators to police their content with additional human labor (Kang, Fandos, and Isaac). So while Goliath remains ascendant, the door may indeed remain ajar for David in the form of school librarians to begin slinging some academic-based content stones.

Questions

1. How should the library position itself in the coming age-based economic conflict regarding the allocation of funds?

2. Devise an economic-based argument employing local library data that will validate the need for funding the library.

3. How do you envision continuing stagnant incomes negatively and positively affecting the library?

4. What is the role of the library in alerting users to the problem of our growing economic inequality?

5. As para-school funding becomes an economic norm, how does the library go about ensuring its continuing share of it?

6. How can the library make a positive economic difference in the lives of its users?

7. What are the economic advantages and disadvantages of contracting with any big five companies for hardware or software in the future?

REFERENCES

"American Middle Class Is Losing Ground." December 9, 2015. Pew Research Center. Available at: http://www.pewsocialtrends.org/2015/12/09/the-american-middle -class-is-losing-ground.

"Annual Earnings of Young Adults." April 2017. National Center for Education Statistics. Available at: https://nces.ed.gov/programs/coe/pdf/Indicator_CBA/coe_cba_2015 _05.pdf.

"Athletic & Academic Spending Database for NCAA Division I. Football Bowl Subdivision. 2013–2017." n.d. Available at: http://spendingdatabase.knightcommission.org/fbs.

Benjamin, Matthew K. September 1, 2017. "National Debt." *CQ Researcher.* 27(30): 1–22.

Brown, Ana. October 6, 2016. "Key Findings about the American Workforce and the Changing Job Market." Pew Research Center. Available at: http://www.pewre search.org/fact-tank/2016/10/06/key-findings-about-the-american-workforce-and -the-changing-job-market.

Bruni, Frank. 2015. *Where You Go Is Not Who You'll Be: An Antidote to the College Admissions Mania.* New York: Grand Central Publishing.

Chant, Ian. March 31, 2017. "What the Trump Budget Means for School Libraries." *School Library Journal.* Available at: http://www.slj.com/2017/03/budgets-funding/what -the-trump-budget-means-for-school-libraries.

Chetty, Raj, John N. Friedman, and Jonah E. Rockoff. September 2013. "Measuring the Impacts of Teachers II: Teacher Value-Added and Student Outcomes in Adulthood." NBER Working Paper No. 1924, National Bureau of Economic Research. Available at: http://www.nber.org/papers/w19424.pdf.

Chinoy, Sahil. June 24, 2018. "Your Life, Patented by Facebook." *The New York Times.* Available at: https://www.nytimes.com/interactive/2018/06/21/opinion/sunday/face book-patents-privacy.html.

Clark, Charles S. June 26, 1992. "Hard Times for Libraries." *CQ Researcher*. 2(24): 553–572. Available at: http://library.cqpress.com.

"The Condition of U.S. Libraries: School Library Trends, 1999–2009." December 2009. Available at: http://www.ala.org/tools/sites/ala.org.tools/files/content/librarystats/librarymediacenter/Condition_of_Libraries_1999.20.pdf.

Dayen, David. April 22, 2016. "The Android Administration." *The Intercept*. Available at: https://theintercept.com/2016/04/22/googles-remarkably-close-relationship-with-the-obama-white-house-in-two-charts.

De Rugy, Veronique. May 22, 2012. "How Many Workers Support One Social Security Retiree?" Mercatus Center. George Mason University. Available at: https://www.mercatus.org/publication/how-many-workers-support-one-social-security-retiree.

"Debt to the Penny and Who Holds It." October 31, 2018. Treasury Direct. Available at: https://treasurydirect.gov/NP/debt/current.

Department of Education. 2015. *Every Student Succeeds Act*. Available at: https://www.ed.gov/essa?src=rn.

Douglas-Gabriel, Danielle. June 22, 2016. "Tuition at Public Colleges Has Soared in the Past Decade, but Student Fees Have Risen Faster." *The Washington Post*. Available at: https://www.washingtonpost.com/news/grade-point/wp/2016/06/22/tuition-at-public-colleges-has-soared-in-the-last-dec (http://tinyurl.com/jxfh2p).

Duncan, Greg J. and Richard J. Murnane. 2014. *Restoring Opportunity: The Crisis of Inequality and the Challenge of American Education*. Boston: Harvard Education Press.

Foer, Franklin. 2017. *World Without Mind: The Existential Threat of Big Tech*. New York: Penguin Press.

Ford, Martin. 2015. *Rise of the Robots: Technology and the Threat of a Jobless Future*. New York: Basic Books.

Frankfurt, Harry G. 2015. *On Inequality*. Princeton, NJ: Princeton University Press.

Fry, Richard and Rakesh Kochhar. March 12, 2016. "Are You in the Middle Class? Find Out with Our Income Calculator." Pew Research Center. Available at: https://www.youtube.com/watch?v=21DrOfLH5WQ.

Geddes, Jennifer Kelly. March 3, 2017. "School Librarians of Rhode Island Raising the Profile of Their Profession." *School Library Journal*. Available at: http://www.slj.com/2017/05/industry-news/school-librarians-of-rhode-island-raising-the-profile-of-their-profession.

Kang, Cecilia, Nicholas Fandos, and Mike Isaac. October 31, 2017. "Tech Executives Are Contrite about Election Meddling, but Make Few Promises on Capitol Hill." *The New York Times*. Available at: https://www.nytimes.com/2017/10/31/us/politics/facebook-twitter-google-hearings-congress.html?_r=0.

Katel, Peter. August 8, 2016. "Future of the Middle Class." *CQ Researcher*. 26(14): 1–24.

Kennedy, Paul M. 1993. *Preparing for the Twenty-First Century*. New York: Random House.

Korn, Melissa. December 19, 2016. "Enrollment at U.S. Colleges Drops by 1.7%." *Wall Street Journal*. Available at: https://www.wsj.com/articles/enrollment-at-u-s-colleges-drops-by-1-7-1450242061.

Kornich, Sabino and Frank Furstenberg. February 2013. "Investing in Children: Changes in Parental Spending on Children, 1972–2007." *Demography*. 50(2): 1–23. Available at: http://paa2011.princeton.edu/papers/110077.

Kraus, Michael W., Shai Davidai, and David Nussbaum. May 3, 2015. "American Dream? Or Mirage?" *New York Times*. Available at: http://www.nytimes.com/2015/05/03/opinion/sunday/american-dream-or-mirage.html?_r=0.

Kroeger, Teresa, Tanyelle Cooke, and Elise Gould. April 21, 2016. "The Class of 2016." Economic Policy Institute. Available at: http://www.epi.org/publication/class-of-2016.

Kyle, Sarah. March 30, 2017. "Pay to Play: Bands March to Different Financial Beats." *Coloradoan*. Available at: http://www.coloradoan.com/story/news/2017/03/31/pay-play-bands-march-different-financial-beats/99478654.

Lareau, Annette. 2011. *Unequal Childhoods: Class, Race and Family Life*. Berkeley: University of California Press.

Leonhardt, David. December 8, 2016. "The American Dream, Quantified at Last." *The New York Times*. Available at: http://www.nytimes.com/2016/12/08/opinion/the-american-dream-quantified-at-last.html.

Logan, John R., Elisabeta Minca, and Sinem Adar. July 2012. "The Geography of Inequality: Why Separate Means Unequal in American Public Schools." *Sociology of Education*. 85(3): 287–301.

Lohr, Steve and David Streitfeld. April 30, 2012. "Data Engineer in Google Case Is Identified." *New York Times*. Available at: http://www.nytimes.com/2012/05/01/technology/engineer-in-googles-street-view-is-identified.html

"A Look at the Shocking Student Loan Debt Statistics for 2017." November 2, 2017. Available at: https://studentloanhero.com/student-loan-debt-statistics.

Maheshwari, Sapna. November 4, 2017. "On YouTube Kids, Startling Videos Slip Past Filters." *New York Times*. Available at: https://www.nytimes.com/2017/11/04/business/media/youtube-kids-paw-patrol.html?_r=0.

Manjoo, Farhad. January 20, 2016. "Tech's 'Frightful 5' Will Dominate Digital Life for the Foreseeable Future." *New York Times*. Available at: https://www.nytimes.com/2016/01/21/technology/techs-frightful-5-will-dominate-digital-life-for-foreseeable-future.html?_r=0.

Mantel, Barbara. July 20, 2011. "Future of Libraries." *CQ Researcher*. 21(27): 1–25.

McAfee, Andrew and Erik Brynjolfsson. 2017. *Machine, Platform, Crowd: Harnessing Our Digital Future*. New York: W. W. Norton.

Moshinsky, Ben. January 12, 2017. "The 19 Countries that Hold the Most US Debt." *Business Insider*. Available at: http://www.businessinsider.com/us-treasury-countries-hold-the-most-us-debt-2017-1/#19-bermuda-659-billion-5479-billion-1.

Moskowitz, Dan. March 6, 2018. "The 5 Richest People in the World." Investopedia. Available at: https://www.investopedia.com/articles/investing/012715/5-richest-people-world.asp.

Naisbitt, John. 1982. *Megatrends: The New Directions Transforming Our Lives*. New York: Warner Books.

"The New Face of Facebook." April 9, 2016. *The Economist*. Available at: https://www.economist.com/news/briefing/21696507-social-network-has-turned-itself-one-worlds-most-influential-technology-giants.

Norberg, Johan. 2016. *Progress: Ten Reasons to Look Forward to the Future*. London: Oneworld.

"Opportunities for School Librarians." 2015. ALA Washington Office. P.L. 114–95. *The Every Student Succeeds Act of 2015*. Available at: http://www.ala.org/aasl/sites/ala.org.aasl/files/content/aaslissues/esea/ALA-ESSA_Library_Opportunities.pdf.

"Pay-to-Play Keeping Kids on the Sidelines." January 20, 2015. Institute for Healthcare Policy & Innovation University of Michigan. Available at: http://ihpi.umich.edu/news/pay-play-keeping-kids-sidelines.

Payne, Keith. 2017. *Broken Ladder: How Inequality Affects the Way We Think, Live, and Die*. New York: Viking.

Piketty, Thomas. October 6, 2014. "What the 1% Don't Want You to Know." Available at: https://www.youtube.com/watch?v=JKsHhXwqDqM.

Price, Tom. November 18, 2016. "Student Debt." *CQ Researcher*. 26(41): 1–24.

"Projections of Education Statistics to 2022." February 2014. National Center for Educational Statistics. U.S. Department of Education. Available at: https://nces.ed.gov/pubs2014/2014051.pdf.

Putnam, Robert D. 2015. *Our Kids: The American Dream in Crisis*. New York: Simon & Schuster.

Reich, Robert B. 2015. *Saving Capitalism for the Many, Not the Few*. New York: Alfred A. Knopf.

"Rise of the Superstars." September 17, 2016. *The Economist*. 420(9007): 3–15.

Rogers, Linda. July 6, 2017. "New Advocacy to Save School Librarians, One Click at a Time." *SLJ Resources*. Available at: http://www.slj.com/2017/07/schools/new-advocacy-to-save-school-libraries-one-click-at-a-time/#.

Sahadi, Jeanne. August 8, 2016. "The Richest 10% Hold 76% of the Wealth." CNN Money. Available at: http://money.cnn.com/2016/08/18/pf/wealth-inequality/index.html.

Schmidt, William H. and Curtis C. McKnight. 2012. *Inequality for All: The Challenge of Unequal Opportunity in American Schools*. New York: Teachers College Press.

"Should College Students Be Required to Take a Course in Personal Finance?" March 19, 2017. *The Wall Street Journal*. Available at: https://www.wsj.com/articles/should-college-students-be-required-to-take-a-course-in-personal-finance-1489975500.

Singer, Natasha. September 2, 2017. "Silicon Valley Courts Brand-Name Teachers, Raising Ethics Issues." *The New York Times*. Available at: https://www.nytimes.com/2017/09/02/technology/silicon-valley-teachers-tech.html.

"Special Report on the Future of Work: Learning and Earning." December 1, 2017. *The Economist*. Available at: http://press.economist.com/stories/10530-special-report-on-the-future-of-work-learning-and-earning.

Stewart, Matthew. June 2018. "The Birth of a New American Aristocracy." *The Atlantic*. 321(5): 48–63.

Stiglitz, Joseph E. 2015. *The Great Divide: Unequal Societies and What We Can Do about Them*. New York: W. W. Norton.

Thompson, Derek. August 19. 2013. "Are the Rich Getting Too Much of the Economic Pie?" Available at: https://www.youtube.com/watch?v=21DrOfLH5WQ.

"The 2017 Long-Term Budget Outlook." March 30, 2017. Available at: https://www.cbo.gov/publication/52480.

"Unemployment Rates and Earnings by Educational Attainment." 2016. Bureau of Labor Statistics. Available at: https://www.bls.gov/emp/ep_chart_001.htm.

Vaidhyanathan, Siva. 2011. *The Googlization of Everything and Why We Should Worry*. Berkeley: University of California Press.

"Visualizing Change: March-April 2017. The Annual Report on the Economic Status of the Profession, 2016–17." *Academe*. Available at: https://www.aaup.org/file/FCS_2016-17_nc.pdf.

"The World's Most Valuable Resource." March 6, 2017. *The Economist*. 423(9039): 7.

4

Employment Trends

On September 19, 1977, Youngstown, Ohio, suffered one of the greatest employment disasters in its thriving manufacturing history called "Black Monday." On that fateful day, Youngstown Sheet and Tube announced the closing of the Campbell Works mill. By 1982, more than 50,000 jobs had disappeared along with $1.3 billion in manufacturing wages. Labor economists label this rare type of employment event a regional depression, but current employment trends reveal that the United States may be about to suffer a similar disaster as technology in the form of robots and other smart machines inserts itself into our workplaces (Thompson 1). Economists have warned us in the past about impending doom when the world transitioned from an agrarian society to a manufacturing-based economy and to a technologically advanced, globally driven system.

Each wave of change has brought significant shifts in the distribution of employment and the nature of work (Perleman 67). In 1920, for example, agriculture employed over a quarter of American workers. By the 1980s, this number had dwindled to 4 percent of U.S. jobs. In the 1990s it represented 2.5 percent of the workforce, and by 2016 equaled 1.5 percent of workers ("Employment by Major Industry"). Manufacturing jobs followed suit, furnishing one of every four American jobs in 1960, then one out of every five in 1980, and finally only 7.8 percent in 2017 (Levinson 1–2).

From 1940 to 1990, service industries' share of total U.S. employment climbed from 45 percent to over 70 percent as millions of displaced workers sought jobs in this sector, which now represents over 80 percent of American jobs ("Employment by Major Industry"). For many years, jobs that involved doing things for other people seemed to be safe from the incursion of automation because they involved personal interaction, which was something that a machine could not successfully do. But automation is encroaching in every economic sector in subtle ways. Unlike the resounding crash that reverberated throughout the Ohio economy when the steel company shuttered its doors, automation is "creeping in silently and unnoticed as if on cats' paws while you marvel at how the modern world grows ever more convenient, customized to you, and efficient" (Kaplan 111). Observers of our technological revolution are concerned about the entire employment picture, not just the plight of the manufacturing and service industries. They believe that we are about to cross into a new frontier where the world of work will be dramatically transformed by smart machines.

A time of change will require that educational institutions charged with the preparation of the next generation for various kinds of work carefully question themselves. What are the general workforce trends? How might advanced technologies affect the nature of work and workers in the next decade? What kinds of jobs might be available in the next ten years? What skills will our students need to perform these jobs? What role can school librarians play to ensure that our students have the opportunity for remunerative jobs in this new world of work?

THE TECHNOLOGICAL LANDSCAPE

The political economist Carlota Perez believes that when the technological landscape of an entire economy is altered or about to be that it responds in a series of phases similar to technological revolutions that it has experienced in the past. Examples would include the technological revolution that America experienced with the invention of the steam engine, electricity, the automobile, and the computer. The first phase titled, *maturity,* involves traditional companies from the previous tech revolution initiating research and development in the new inventions. They use their profits to invest in the new inventions that eventually replace the previous ones. Electric companies, for example, invested in the initial radio and TV companies. Xerox, which manufactured photocopiers, invested in computer user interfaces, and Kodak poured funds into digital camera development. The second phase, termed *irruption,* is the technological quantum leap that occurs when the new invention disrupts the previous technology and the corresponding industries that surround it. The automobile, for example, disrupted the horse business, TV affected radio, the Web unbalanced TV, and so forth. The third phase, called *frenzy,* is where an economy experiences speculative booms, a rise in unemployment, and the beginning of political dissatisfaction. Some tech observers believe that we are currently in the frenzy phase with examples such as the unreasonable valuation of the Tesla car company in comparison to General Motors and Donald Trump, a nonpolitician, being elected president of the United States by a slim majority of disgruntled working-class voters.

In phase three, we experience a *turning point* when the growing inequality between the disenfranchised and the entitled reaches a tipping point and civil unrest ensues, driving the government to enforce existing laws or enact new regulations to curb the disparity in wealth accumulation. Historic examples of the irruption and frenzy phases are illustrated by increased purchases of cars and appliances during the 1920s. This buying spree was followed by the 1929 stock market crash, and the turning point arrived with the enactment of significant social legislation during the New Deal, which curbed much of the financial excesses of the previous era. It also produced the final phase, called *synergy.* This phase is characterized by a more stable, regulated period when more people share in the advantages caused by specific technological innovations (Russell 98–99).

If we are indeed in the frenzy phase of a technological revolution, the road ahead will continue to be rocky, as we continue to navigate the technological landscape without the safety net of reliable employment for many of our citizens. Economists are correct in describing the subtle incursion of robots and smart machines into our workplaces. While it has been a gradual penetration, it still seems to be following a classic pattern concerning the eras of automation. As early as the sixties and seventies, workers in the auto industry welcomed smart machines as they assumed a place on the assembly line installing seats, welding joints, and locking windshields into place (Ford 3). They were industrial robots and represented Era 1 in automation. They relieved us of manually demanding and repetitive, mind-numbing work. Amazon, for example, is currently employing them to pick up large boxes and bring them to employees so that they can stock them.

Era 2 automation was also a welcome relief. Instead of spending hours laboriously typing and, in many cases, manually correcting and retyping misspelled words on a typewriter, the word processor arrived within a personal computer. This gratefully hailed innovation was quickly followed by personal computers and the Internet, giving us the ability to order almost anything our heart desires online, including consumer goods and even humans to perform odd jobs or transport us through companies such as TaskRabbit and Uber. According to Davenport and Kirby in their book, *Only Humans Need Apply,* it is Era 3 that contains "both promise and peril" (Davenport and Kirby 4).

Era 3 is characterized by machines becoming more intelligent and actually making better decisions than we can. Although we are already experiencing Era 3, its impact will be ubiquitously felt within the next decade and possibly more quickly if there is a recession. Although robots appeared in factories during the sixties and seventies, they didn't really begin to replace factory workers until the recessions of 1990, 2001, and 2007 (Thompson 7).

With subsequent layoffs, the recessions provided companies with the opportunity to retool their workplaces with robots instead of human workers (Thompson 7). Automation does not replicate the kaboom effect of the Ohio steel plant closure. It begins with a smart machine mastering one task after another. As with Eras 1 and 2, it is welcomed and not seen as a threat by employees until we begin to realize that it has adroitly assumed a major part of our job description and we are either working beside it or have been replaced by it (Davenport 13–14).

TECHNOLOGY'S PRESENT AND FUTURE INCURSIONS

As workers moved from agrarian to manufacturing to service jobs, many economists observed that in a way they had exchanged their routine jobs on an assembly line in a factory, for example, to flipping hamburgers at a fast food restaurant or scanning barcodes at Walmart. For a long while, there has been an easily mastered congruence between the type of routine work required in a manufacturing economy and in a service-based one. Despite the fact that many of us are employing automated check-outs at grocery stores, most service-related jobs have not been totally breached by automation. Many workers have been able to successfully transition from one to the other because of the low-level skills involved (Ford 252).

The skills needed for jobs in retail sales, food service, and office work, for example, do not require advanced types of reasoning skills or abstract thinking. Smart machines can be easily programmed to successfully complete the routine tasks involved in taking customer orders, locating the requested items, and delivering them to the customers. More importantly, machines can do it day after day with the same quality of service, never call in sick, or disagree with their coworkers or supervisors. These jobs are highly susceptible to automation and employ approximately 15.4 million workers, which is nearly 10 percent of the labor force (Thompson 9). The trade-off for companies may not be parity with smart machines, but actually outperformance as advanced technologies may represent an improvement in service or quality of work in comparison to that of humans. Once smart machines can be shown to outperform human labor at various tasks, the inducement to invest in smart technologies from a personnel management and profit perspective will be difficult to resist.

One of the tried-and-true methods for human labor to prevail over the incursion of smart machines has been our ability to adopt and learn new skills through education (Brynjolfsson and McAfee). In the 1980s a report titled *Workforce 2000* predicted that natural scientists and lawyers would be among the two fastest-growing occupations (Johnson and Packer 98–99). Reich, in his seminal book, *The Work of Nations*, opined that education would need to be centered around a "lifetime of symbolic-analytic work" that encompasses four skills: "abstraction, system thinking, experimentation, and collaboration" (Reich 1991, 227). Both Johnson and Packer and Reich believed that advanced education would ensure employment that was secure and remunerative in a perpetual, competitive economy.

If there is one employment-related trend to remember with Era 3 technology, it is that "if work can be codified, it can be automated" (Davenport and Kirby 14). Unfortunately, this axiom is now holding true even for those working in cognitive domains. It will be increasingly more difficult for Americans in all walks of life to work in jobs that are immune to automation (Brynjolfsson and McAfee). Automation is no longer just consuming low-level and routinized jobs. The increasing employment of smart machines, bots, algorithms, and artificial intelligence demonstrates that new advanced technologies can equal or surpass the abilities of people who are currently "dermatologists, insurance claims adjusters, lawyers, seismic testers in oil fields, sports journalists, financial reporters, crew members on guided-missile destroyers, psychologists, retail salespeople and border patrol agents" (Rainie and Anderson 2). In addition, advancements with A.I. and the like are threatening to render millions of workers redundant "who drive trucks and cars, analyze medical tests and data, perform middle management chores, dispense medicine, trade stocks and evaluate markets, fight on battlefields, perform government functions, and even software programmers" (Rainie and Anderson 2).

To alert governments about the gravity of this problem, labor economists have been trying to quantify and rate the susceptibility of various occupations to automation within the next decade. The largest study, published in 2013, assigned automation risk factors to 702 detailed occupations, including librarians, kindergarten teachers, airline pilots, and nuclear engineers. Their analysis estimates that by 2023, 47 percent of total U.S. employment is at risk for automation

(Frey and Osborne 1). Even a profession such as psychologist that requires a high degree of empathy, compassion, and personal care is vulnerable to automation. Studies reveal that patients are more forthcoming in therapy sessions when inter-acting with a computer, because they believe that the computer is not judging them (Thompson 8).

A second study by the McKinsey Global Institute estimates that "knowledge work automation tools and systems" could complete tasks that would be the equiv-alent to the labor of 110 million to 140 million full-time workers (Manyika et al. 3). Jobs in knowledge work fields encompass 25 to 50 percent of all workers in developed economies, including all the professions already mentioned, are vulner-able to automation (Davenport and Kirby 4–5). As computers are able to read words and comprehend images, perform manual labor, and analyze data, we are fast approaching what computer scientists term the convergence point where machines become self-aware and able to make their own decisions. The implica-tions for employment in the twenty-first century are profound, especially for edu-cators who are charged with preparing students for the future. Fortunately, however, all of the studies are predictive in nature, and their extended timelines give K–12 schools time to prepare and plan.

GENERAL WORKFORCE TRENDS

The impact of technology in the employment sector has been subtle in its incur-sion into various occupations and professions. Even though America's unemploy-ment rate remains low, economists crunching the data tell a different story about how we are remaining productive. In 1998, workers in the U.S. business sector totaled 194 billion hours of labor. Fifteen years later, the value of goods and ser-vices produced by American businesses increased by about $3.5 trillion after adjust-ing for inflation, which represented a 42 percent increase in output. The total amount of human labor that was required to achieve this productive output was 194 billion hours, even though the U.S. population had increased by more than 40 million people and created thousands of new businesses between 1998 and 2013 (Ford 281). If labor cannot account for this enormous profit, what does? The answer is automation of the workplace.

While we were experiencing a Great Recession, work environments that in the past contained human beings were being replaced by advanced technologies. Even when the U.S. economy is officially no longer in recession, economists see auton-omous cars, drones, and digital assistants rather than humans on the labor horizon (Thompson 2). It is hard to envision a profession like law that requires three years beyond college and significant reasoning ability being vulnerable to algorithms and machine learning. Since 2012, however, applications to law schools have dropped nearly 30 percent and salaries are down almost 17 percent. Even more importantly, employment of attorneys is down, with more than 35 percent of new graduates fail-ing to gain employment in the legal field. Although some of the data reflect our economic downturn, several automated programs have rendered many lawyerly tasks superfluous. Sifting through thousands of documents; drafting commercial agreements, licenses, and loans; and even identifying relevant case law can now be performed by legal software such as eDiscovery, FairDocument, and Judicata (Kaplan 145–146).

The ancient practice of medicine is also not immune to technology's advances. As medicine is becoming more data driven and specialized, the amount of published research about a disease such as cancer can easily overwhelm a doctor charged with a patient's care. IBM and Wellpoint, one of the biggest healthcare providers, have entered into a partnership to employ *Jeopardy!*'s winning smart machine Watson to sift through thousands of articles, research trials, and the like to identify the most efficacious treatment options (Kaplan 150–151).

Lest we dismiss doctors' and lawyers' professions as synthetic intelligence aberrations, we must consider our own profession: education. Providing instruction online or offline is also susceptible to automation. Many of the tasks that teachers perform, such as taking attendance, grading, and delivering subject matter, are already being automated as noted in previous chapters. The flipped classroom, however, as educationally enhancing as it sounds, places teachers in the same quandary as the legal and medical professions. Videotaping lectures so that students can learn and even review subject matter at home and then complete homework at school makes excellent sense. Once the lectures are digitized, however, they can be mass-produced and utilized in a multitude of classrooms. Consequently, school districts can employ fewer teachers or teaching assistants instead as "learning coaches" to monitor students' academic progress (Kaplan 151).

INTEGRATION OF THE WORLD'S ECONOMY

One of the most important forces affecting America's workforce is the integration of the world's economy. Fostered by gradual improvements in transportation and telecommunications, the economy of the United States is now inextricably intertwined with those of Japan, China, Germany, Great Britain, France, and other developed countries. World markets, not nations, decide the prices not only for commodities such as fuel but also for manufactured products.

Within the past decades, capital and labor markets have also become globally integrated. Multinational corporations borrow and invest in foreign markets. Individual Americans regularly purchase stocks in the Japanese stock market, and the Japanese in turn invest in American companies and real estate.

Labor, once thought stationary, has become a fluid global commodity with heads of corporations constantly seeking the cheapest source of it to produce their goods (Johnson and Packer 1–2). Workers in Mexico, for example, at maquiladora factories assemble Japanese car parts into finished automobiles, which are shipped back to the United States (Reich 1991, 210–211). A similar labor trail can be traced for products such as Apple's iPhone, which is manufactured in countries with lower labor costs, including Mongolia, Taiwan, South Korea, and China. When wages for specific jobs and services are cheaper in other countries, the loss of jobs and wages for American workers can be considerable. In 2011, for example, Apple sold 70 million iPhones requiring the skills of 63,000 American laborers working either in the United States or abroad versus 7,000,000 foreign workers (Kabin).

As the world economy becomes further connected, the United States' economic destiny is tied to that of other nations. Our monetary markets, corporations, and banks are so intertwined with those of other countries that America's economic pulse can only be evaluated in the context of the world's economy. The fortunes of multinational companies and individual nations, unemployment patterns, and shifts in other countries' production must be planned for and monitored globally. Policies can no longer be arrived at unilaterally but must be negotiated with other countries.

Despite the formulation of international trade and monetary policies designed to equalize economic opportunity for all countries, the United States is going to experience increasing competition not only from smart machines and their increasing incursion into the workplace but also competition from other countries that are able to produce better products at lower prices. Companies are forever being driven by the bottom line and will continue to seek out the least expensive way to produce their product and sell it at a competitive cost. Their loyalty is to their stockholders, not their country where their products are manufactured or where they are sold.

OFF-SHORING VERSUS RE-SHORING

With no allegiance to a nation, companies can be characterized as geocentric. Their sole goal is to sell their products globally at the most competitive prices. To do so requires constant evaluation of advanced technologies and balancing their automation installment and maintenance costs versus remaining with human labor. At present, there are ongoing off-shoring and re-shoring trends in flux within the American labor market. Unfortunately, neither labor shift pattern is cause for celebration because of the impact of advanced technologies.

With advanced technologies, it is now feasible to ship jobs that were previously performed by highly educated and skilled American workers, such as radiologists, lawyers, computer programmers, and tax preparers, to countries with similarly high-skilled workers who can accomplish the same tasks at much reduced costs. India, for example, has scores of tax preparers who are completely current on U.S. tax code regulations and attorneys trained in U.S. law who can do legal research much more cheaply than can American workers.

In the past, shipping costs may have proved an obstacle to off-shoring arrangements, but electronic forms of off-shoring have no shipping costs. Some writers see electronic off-shoring as virtual immigration and more pernicious to the U.S. employment picture than the type of off-shoring that necessitates transportation of products back to the United States. At least the traditional form of off-shoring employs drivers and other tangentially related occupations to gain some small share of the off-shoring process. Electronic off-shoring, on the other hand, provides jobs for millions of workers who do not live in or pay taxes in the United States. While we as consumers are benefiting from the product's low cost, the estimate of off-shoring is projected at 30 to 40 million lost jobs. This electronic form of off-shoring would make one-quarter of the U.S. workforce vulnerable to job loss (Blinder).

Off-shoring's opposite is re-shoring, or companies returning to the United States to manufacture their products. While it sounds like a reversion to normal, it is not.

Re-shoring represents only a partial improvement of the overall employment picture because of the impact of advanced technologies. The opening of the Parkdale Mills textile plant in Gaffney, South Carolina, in 2013 was indeed the impetus for celebratory articles in various newspapers, but the resulting employment numbers did not amount to many workers. The plant only employs 140 workers to achieve the same level of production that it did with 2,000 textile workers in 1980. While the textile industry was decimated between 1990 and 2012 from off-shoring to China, India, and Mexico, its economic rebound has not seen huge employment gains. U.S. economists, however, welcome re-shoring because at least it creates additional peripheral jobs for drivers and other smaller suppliers of parts and the like. The move back to the United States was purely an economic decision on the part of the textile company. China's manufacturing companies raised workers' pay by 20 percent, thus making re-shoring more profitable for Parkdale.

As an employment trend, re-shoring could be one of the bright spots in an otherwise dismal employment picture. A 2013 survey of American manufacturing executives with profits exceeding $10 billion indicated that they were either deciding on or researching re-shoring back to the United States (Ford 9). In 2016, there were indications of a slight turnaround when textile plants opened in Georgia but with a more reduced workforce. Now managers oversee smart machines that are doing the "spinning, scouring, and weaving of the cotton" and are doing the work of thousands of former employees. As for Thomaston, Georgia, one-half of the residents are living below the poverty line compared to 23 percent in 1999, and their average income has dropped 20 percent (Bhattari).

Unfortunately, re-shoring is only a miniscule positive blip on the employment screen. Waiting in the wings are an increasing number of robots that will become even more dexterous and intelligent—meaning that the American workers in the manufacturing sector can easily be replaced. While companies will probably remain in the United States to be closer to suppliers and reduce shipping costs, former workers will probably be looking in the factory windows and remembering times past.

ARE AMERICANS REALLY WORKING?

Despite the unemployment rate hovering at less than 4 percent and dropping precipitously from 10.6 percent in the 2009 recession, Bureau of Labor Statistics data may be masking employment trends that we need to study ("Databases, Tables . . ."). For example, counting Americans who have given up searching for work and those working part-time would raise the rate considerably higher (Sorrentino 3–4). Currently the country has 6 million open jobs but more than 8 million people out of work. Even though these figures are a definite improvement since the Great Recession, they muddy the bright employment picture that a low unemployment rate indicates. Just looking at "the percentage of people participating in the labor force" compared to other years should give us pause. Labor force participation stood at 62.7 percent in September 2018, which is the lowest level in four decades ("Databases, Tables . . ."). In April 2000, the labor force participation rate stood at 67.3 percent (Meyer 20). During this time, we have been experiencing a technology boom with the tech big five continuing to acquire new companies with alacrity.

Common sense would dictate that there should be more jobs with a new emerging industry. Data, however, show the opposite, with only 0.05 percent of American workers employed in industries that have appeared since 2000. The reason is that technology is actually creating fewer jobs because its business is really automating them ("Return of the Machinery Question . . ." 10). More than two-thirds of job losses are currently directly attributable to having one's function taken over by a machine (Rushkoff 49). Most workers, when faced with layoffs, lack the education and qualifications to move up the employment ladder to temporary places of employment safety. They cannot reach rungs that are secure from the constant claws of big data and analytics that will determine their corporate worth almost to the minute. Instead they join the millions of Americans who will become part of an on-demand workforce or the entrepreneurial gig workforce.

THE CONTINGENT LABOR FORCE

One of the employment trends that big data, algorithms, and smart machines enable is the ability to design an online, demand-based labor system where companies can hire and release workers based on their specific job needs. Workers can be hired for a year, month, labor unit, or several hours or even minutes. Labor economists call it a contingent workforce or gig economy (Rainie and Anderson 19). Although the data are limited concerning the size and scope of it, the federal government estimates that 7.9 percent of workers in 2010, or 12.2 million, participated on a contingent labor force basis ("Contingent Work Force . . ."). The number continues to grow appreciably. In 2013, contingent workers represented 3.4 million people, about 2.3 percent of the national total employment. From 2008 to 2012, contingent jobs increased by 41 percent (Lifsher). Since the recession, contingent labor has surpassed overall employment growth rates, increasing from a weekly average of 2.2 million jobs in 2009 to 3.2 million in 2014 (Poole and Berchem).

Some labor experts, however, believe that these figures are misleading because they do not account for all the freelancers, part-timers, moonlighters, self-employed, perma-temps, and independent contractors who may drive for Uber, walk dogs, tutor, provide day care, and cater from their homes but do constitute a contingent workforce.

In April 2015, the U.S. Government Accountability Office stated that the "size of the contingent workforce can range from less than 5 percent to more than a third of the total employed labor force" (Meyer 25). The fast-growing Freelancers Union states that full-time employees who perform some types of part-time work should be also considered members of the contingent workforce. When they are counted, according to their 2017 Freelancers Union survey, 57.2 million people, or one-third of the work force, would fall into the contingent worker category ("Freelancing in America 2017").

Even when the number disparity of Americans in the contingent labor force is disputed, increasing numbers are working part-time as cited by the federal government. It is a clear indication of an employment trend that has moved away from access to permanent jobs that offer vacation time, sick pay, retirement plans, health insurance and job security.

Many economists believe that a contingent labor force is the wave of the future. Companies that used to bear the risks and costs associated with developing and selling a product are now going to reduce their employee expenses by no longer hiring them on a permanent basis (Meyer 5). Relying on big data that can analyze customer impact almost to the hour, companies are also utilizing it to schedule workers for short-term peak times when, for example, a supermarket is especially busy or to handle increased shopping on the day after Thanksgiving (O'Neil 124–125).

In some cases, companies in the newspaper, drug, and public relations businesses are releasing their workforces and hiring them back en masse as freelancers or independent contractors to avoid paying benefits (Gordon). Some experts view a contingent type of workforce as a return to the nineteenth-century piecework system where workers completed parts of products for companies using their own sewing machines and were paid by the number they completed. They see the contingent economy as spelling doom for workers by isolating them, reducing wages, and creating tedious tasks (Meyer 5). Other experts see a possible migration towards a "gray economy" where members of the contingent workforce barter skills for work they need performed or complete tasks where they are remunerated in cash and do not pay taxes (Meyer 25).

Critics of this viewpoint see the contingent workforce model as saving the U.S. economy in a time of increasing automation and global competition. If U.S. companies are to remain flexible in times of rapid change, they need to unburden themselves of employees for whom they need to pay benefits so that their labor costs are reduced and profits remain high for demanding stockholders. Statistics show that a company's labor cost can go down by as much as 30 percent by eliminating benefits to its employees (Meyer 25). Some experts, however, see this model of a contingent work force spreading to all types of work as companies using big data and algorithms to determine almost to the dollar employees' value on the corporation's ladder (Rainie and Anderson 19). In 2016, even the Obama administration conceded that "major macroeconomic trends of the past two generations— particularly loss of benefits that once went with formal employment relationships— are largely irreversible" (Scheiber).

Despite the security that comes with full-time jobs replete with retirement, healthcare, and other benefits, many members of the contingent workforce like this new arrangement for its flexibility to pursue leisure activities, to further their educations, to care for loved ones, to pursue an avocation that they are passionate about such as acting or music, and to break bonds with the corporations that have betrayed them (Thompson 19). Even though stagnant wages, reduced standard of living, and job insecurity are omnipresent, a 2015 survey taken by the Freelancers Union shows how a contingent working model favors many Americans. Seventy-five percent of freelancers are motivated to choose contingent work because of the flexible schedule it presents, and the same percentage like being their own boss.

In a labor market where many workers are on an electronic leash in the form of 24/7 work-related email and summons to work on-call, the ability to manage one's own worktime and be in charge of one's work product can be welcome amenities. Seventy-three percent expressed satisfaction with being able to choose their work location. Much of gig economy work is electronic in nature and can be completed anywhere around the globe. Being able to live in a warm climate during the winter months while working, for example, is an understandable attraction for contingent workers. Pursuing professional (70 percent) and personal (69 percent) passions were also motivations for contingent workers. So many first-choice careers for workers in the performing arts, for example, have been typically marginal for steady employment and remuneration, so part-time work has always been characteristic of these professions. Sixty-seven percent are motivated to freelance because they can spend more time with friends and manage their own financial futures, while 64 percent do it for the extra pay. The latter three categories, while separate from each other, are all commonsense motivations for working part-time (Meyer 6).

TWO SIDES OF THE GIG ECONOMY

Although there are two sides to the contingent workforce model, most economists detect an exploitive side to it. Its sustainability and lack of security for many workers are alarming. With many types of contingent work, one is truly at the mercy of a corporation to employ workers with absolutely no guarantee how long they will be employed, any mutual discussion of their pay, and absolutely no benefits' safety net. Amazon Mechanical Turk, for example, pays people to labor at tiny repetitive tasks that computers cannot yet complete. Aspiring workers log into a platform from anywhere they choose and select from a series of tasks. For every photo subject they identify or sentence they transcribe from a video lecture, they are paid approximately three cents. These temporary Amazon employees are called click workers and number in the millions. Working for Amazon Mechanical Turk might satisfy some of the positive aspects of freelancing in that one can be flexible about the schedule and do it from anyplace in the world but without even a minimum wage law in force. Nearly 18 percent of laborers in Amazon Mechanical Turk are full-time workers, and Amazon pays them less than $2.00 per hour (Rushkoff 50).

Not knowing how long your current job may last and when it ends or how soon you will be able to obtain another one induces an aspect of insecurity with workers that may not be sustainable over a lifetime of work. In the assertion of the need for corporate growth, profit, and a competitive posture globally, there is little concern for the security of workers who may no longer be able to afford to buy the products that they have helped produce (Pfeffer).

There are some positive sides to a contingent labor force. It provides some workers with the opportunity for entrepreneurship who may never have had the opportunity and gives them a chance to prosper. Toiling away as a contingent labor force member provides a flexible work schedule that can allow time for starting a business that will take time to develop into a commercially successful entity. Employees in the computer science field, for example, may be constricted by noncompetitive clauses that stifle workers' creativity and entrepreneurial drive. Working part-time allows this type of worker to perhaps flourish as they establish a new business or create a new product.

Being your own boss has many positive aspects, as workplace environments are increasingly monitored, bureaucratized, and regimented. An online interview with

601 Uber drivers in twenty regions reported that more than three-quarters of them were satisfied with their jobs, and 61 percent felt that they were "more financially secure than before." Although their average pay was $10 per hour, 75 percent believed that Uber gave them an opportunity to earn more income to support themselves and their families and needed a flexible schedule to balance work and family (Meyer 8).

IMPACT OF ADVANCED TECHNOLOGIES ON EMPLOYMENT

The role technology has played in shaping America's economy has always been dramatic, beginning with inventions such as the telephone, automobile, airplane, and computers. All of these inventions brought significant changes in employment patterns, but in a rather slow, manageable fashion. The impact of Moore's Law, big data, increased computer storage, and processing speeds, coupled with powerful algorithms, is accelerating technological change, making it difficult for workers to cope with the present, let alone the future. Advances are occurring so rapidly with smart machines that change is affecting almost every field of endeavor. Economists seem torn as to whether humans will work alongside machines or whether they will eventually consume all of our jobs by engineering the labor out of them (Rush-koff 49).

THE DARK SIDE OF EMPLOYMENT TRENDS

Are the times so different that advanced technologies are going to create a jobless future? Will we be traveling in autonomous cars with no employment destination? Is there something different from this technological revolution that should make us fearful of our future employment? Some labor experts think that the impact of advanced technologies is more pervasive than it has ever been in previous industrial revolutions. Norbert Weiner, an early expert on information technology, believed that the computer was more uniquely positioned than any technological predecessor to possibly wreak havoc on society (Ford 33). During other times of technological disruption, workers moved from routine jobs on the farm to the factory and to routinized jobs in the service economy. But this time it may be different, because the type of work that a computer is exactly matched for is routine. Computers thrive on routine and do it 24/7 with few errors and no need for time off.

A second factor that makes this revolution different for employment is the speed at which software is becoming a game changer. An application that tracks your fitness levels can be manufactured and used by millions within months. The last factor concerns labor density. Unlike previous revolutions that required vast numbers of people to manufacture products, this one is much less labor intensive ("Return of the Machinery Question . . ." 10).

Amazon is an example of a company birthed with every advanced technology and is the world's largest online retailer. In 2017, for every dollar Americans spent shopping online, Amazon garnered 53 cents of it (Kim). Their average earnings per employee over the past five years equals $85,500. Walmart is a conventional store and also has one of the highest profits of any retailer. Its earnings per employee are $213,000. Translated into per worker-revenue speak, it means that for each $1 million in sales that Walmart generates, it does so by employing about five people. On the other hand, Amazon only employs slightly more than one person. So "for every $1 million in sales that shift from Walmart to Amazon, four jobs are potentially lost" (Kaplan 139).

Data reinforce this employment trend. There are ten times fewer employees per dollar earned than with conventional companies (Rushkoff 51). What's more is the troubling growth in online retail sales, which has been increasing at about 15 percent yearly for the past four years. If this trend continues, e-tail will be hiring more people to work, but not nearly as many workers as conventional retailers have in the past (Kaplan 140).

The three pessimistic factors in employment trends are unfortunately present with an occupation that employs more than 8.7 million Americans—truck driving. One out of every fifteen U.S. workers drives a truck, and according to the more pessimistic economists, their jobs are in jeopardy ("Truck Drivers in the USA"). The Australian company Rio Tinto is already operating 150 trucks remotely from Perth, 932 miles away from the Pilbara region, to move tons of iron ore. The autonomous trucks run 24/7 and have traveled more than 280,000 miles. Adhering to a predefined GPS course, the trucks move autonomously between loading and dump sites (Kaplan 142).

Truck driving as an occupation possesses the three vulnerabilities to advanced technologies. For commercially licensed drivers, it is especially routinized work. They supervise the loading of the truck, drive onto an interstate freeway, put the pedal to the metal, and deliver the goods to the destination. Yearly, however, drivers of large trucks are involved in as many as 273,000 accidents, which cost 3,800 lives and cost more than $4.4 billion (Kaplan 142). The savings in lives and property damage will make this occupation more than cost-efficient to automate before it will be to mass-produce autonomous cars. Trucks can be equipped with 360-degree vision instead of a driver looking primarily straight ahead, drive in blackout conditions, and continuously share data about highway surroundings. More importantly, they can be "platooned"—driving with only inches of space between them—thus helping to reduce traffic congestion and economizing on fuel (Abt). They can also travel 24/7 and deliver goods faster because, unlike human drivers, they will require neither rest nor food. The accident and property damage rates should also plummet with autonomous trucks (Kaplan 141).

This example of an almost completely routine job being automated, possibly within the next five years, poses questions about where these workers will find work. Economists on the pessimistic side predict an enormous growth in service jobs as workers searching for employment migrate to occupations that seem less prone to automation (Rainie and Anderson 15). In 2011, for example, McDonald's announced the hiring of 50,000 new workers in a single day, and more than 1 million people applied (Ford 13). Years ago, these jobs would have been taken by entry-level workers in their teens working perhaps during summer vacation or after school. Now, nearly 90 percent of fast food workers are twenty years or older, and the median age is thirty-five. Many rely upon a job at McDonald's to support themselves and their families at a median wage of $8.69 per hour (Ford 14).

By 2013, the Bureau of Labor Statistics (BLS) projected that the category "food preparation and serving workers" would be a top employment area in the number of job openings up through 2022. Predictions ranged from half a million new jobs opening and 1 million jobs available to replace those leaving the industry. In 2017, however, McDonald's joined Wendy's and Panera in adding touchscreen ordering systems at their restaurants. In San Francisco, a robotic barista was serving freshly brewed coffee. The fast food industry, which was heralded by the BLS as a growing source for new jobs, is already installing software that will make millions of those jobs redundant way before the projected growth date of 2022. Some economists predict that robotic food production and touchscreen ordering may reduce the fast food workforce by 50 percent or more (Ford 15).

Most of us do not think of writing as a routine occupation. We think of it almost as an art that requires creativity, originality, and strong organizational and grammar skills. Traditionally, it is an occupation that is revered by librarians for the author's ability to conjure imaginative worlds and plausible characters. Much of writing, however, is scientific and journalistic and loans itself to automation. Companies such as StatsMonkey and Quill are poised to make serious inroads into a formerly knowledge-based occupation with automation. The former company, which was created by Northwestern students and researchers, employs sports data from memorable events of a game, notes the key players involved, and weaves together readable text that appears written by a human sports writer. The company merged into a new one in 2010 called Narrative Science and designed a powerful algorithmic-based A.I. machine that is now writing articles about sports, business, and politics. Quill can produce a news story every thirty seconds and is "employed" by many websites that wish to remain anonymous. Termed robo-journalism by critics, its owners think that more than 90 percent of articles will be written by Quill-like software within the next fifteen years (Ford 84–85).

Education is not going to remain immune to advanced technologies' encroachment and subsequent threat to future employment. One of the most routine tasks that teachers perform is grading assessments. For most faculty, it is a form of sheer, but essential, drudgery if we are going to be able to measure and evaluate our students' academic progress. Essays take the most time to grade because of their supposedly subjective natures and resulting feedback comments that are usually required for future academic growth. Without a doubt it is a teacher's task that is frequently an impetus for procrastination.

In 2012 against the protests of nearly 4,000 professors, the University of Akron's College of Education analyzed 16,000 pregraded essays from six different public U.S. schools and pitted them against nine companies' machine-graded software. The automated essay-grading software resulted in "virtually identical levels of accuracy with the software in some cases proving to be more reliable" ("Man and Machine . . ."). The previous paragraph stimulates us to pose all kinds of questions, including whether students will write to please the algorithm and will teachers in the future be able to return written assignments more quickly with more detailed comments? The incursion of A.I.-generated software into education has important employment implications. Teaching assistant jobs in K–12 schools and higher education could become redundant and the profession of teaching devalued as advanced technologies continue to apply a downward pressure on numerous occupations, regardless of their educational requirements (Thompson 5).

THE OPTIMISTIC SIDE OF EMPLOYMENT TRENDS

Some economists believe that we should be more optimistic about automation because of its beneficial counterbalancing effects. In the past, automation created more jobs than they eliminated because of a technology balancing effect. As a task was automated so that it could be performed faster or more inexpensively, the damaging effect was counteracted by increasing the demand for laborers to complete other tasks surrounding it that had not been automated. A nineteenth-century example of this technology counterbalancing effect concerns the swift increase of weavers during the Industrial Revolution creating an economic virtuous circle. When the automated looms arrived, the amount of coarse cloth that a weaver could create multiplied by a factor of 50 and the amount of work needed per year of cloth dropped by 98 percent. This scenario would seem to render almost all weavers in the factories redundant, but it did not because it made cloth less expensive and consequently created more demand for it. In turn, demand was created for additional weavers whose numbers between 1830 and 1900 increased fourfold. In this case, technology altered the type of job the weavers did and changed the tasks but did not totally replace the occupation ("Return of the Machinery Question . . ." 9).

A twentieth-century example exists with bank tellers. We would have expected that the arrival of ATMs would have made bank tellers as extinct as dinosaurs, and their average number did actually fall from twenty per branch in 1988 to thirteen in 2004. But most of us have witnessed a mini-boom in bank branches opening throughout the country. Again, automation reduced various banking costs, permitting banks to open more branches in response to consumer demand. The number of urban bank branches increased by more than 43 percent during this period and so did the total number of bank tellers. Their work tasks moved from simply cashing customers' checks to sales and marketing other bank products that automation is still unable to accomplish ("Return of the Machinery Question . . ." 9).

In 1992, a similar job transformation occurred with cable TV technicians. Previously their tasks consisted of simply hooking up a coaxial cable to a nearby telephone pole and bringing the cable into a home. Since then, their tasks have increased to include Internet installation, troubleshooting wireless routers for the Internet, working with Voice over IP (VoIP) telephony, and remotely solving cable connection problems on home personal computers. With each additional task, the job was transformed by advanced technologies but not eliminated by them (Frank, Roehrig, and Pring 39).

A similar technology counterbalance occurred in school libraries when catalogs became automated and the boring rituals of typing, sorting, and filing printed catalog cards entered the dustbin of history. Neither we nor our staff disappeared from schools, even though maintaining a card catalog had previously consumed a significant portion of our time. Instead, online catalogs allowed us to direct our work to increasing the amount of instruction, consulting with faculty, reading to classes, and providing other personalized library services.

Economists claim that the technology counterbalancing effect is observed in countless industries where computers have arrived. Instead of eliminating work, automation redefines it in ways that reduces costs for some aspects of the job but also boosts demand for other areas of it. Between 1982 and 2012 employment prospects for occupations entailing enhanced use of computers, like graphic designers, grew as opportunities and demand for their skills increased ("Return of the Machinery Question . . ." 9). According to some economists, even the legal and health fields, which are currently undergoing a major incursion from algorithms and robots, are experiencing the technology counterbalancing effect.

One would expect that smart machines capable of reading and analyzing huge numbers of legal documents would make legal clerks redundant. Automation, however, has lessened the cost of discovery and consequently increased demand for it. Judges are open to discovery because it's less expensive and easier. Between 2000 and 2013, the number of legal clerks has increased by 1.1 percent per year. The use of Enlitic, for example, to read x-rays increases the expertise of an average radiologist, providing a higher standard of care in rural hospitals ("Return of the Machinery Question . . ." 9).

In the future, teachers will be able to use machine-graded software on students' daily journals or short written assignments and have additional time to make incisive comments about the organizational structure and logic needed to improve student writing skills. Again, educators will not be replaced, but can move to helping students with the professional expertise that reflects their concomitant training and high intelligence.

Economists in the optimistic employment camp ask us not to fall into what is called the "lump of labor" trough. The idea that there is only a fixed amount of work to do and if it becomes automated we can say good-bye to an entire occupation is fallacious. They believe that advanced technologies will not generate mass unemployment, but the jobs that can be performed by human beings rather machines will have increased value ("Return of the Machinery Question . . ." 10).

COUNTERINTUITIVE EMPLOYMENT TRENDS

One of the most disturbing employment trends concerns a term called deskilling and its counterintuitive opposite—hiring overqualified workers. The former term has been used by labor experts for years to describe the effect that automating a task has upon an industry or discipline. Revisiting the weavers' jobs in the nineteenth-century textile industry provides an apt example. Prior to automating their looms, weavers were considered artisans, because their weaving could not be learned overnight and required hours of practice and even apprenticeship to master the techniques. With automation, while they did not lose their jobs, their weaving skills were no longer needed. Their new position necessitated maintaining the automated looms, and their jobs consequently were deskilled. Workers without any weaving experience could assume them with little instruction or training (Frey and Osborne 8).

Deskilling has always been part of labor history, but workers have successfully remained employed by moving from manufacturing industries to service industries and perhaps taking on additional part-time jobs to compensate for the wage difference. But the threat of deskilling is raising more of an alarm now with the advent of artificial intelligence, robots, neural networks, and algorithms (Davenport and Kirby 15–16). The role of "physician advisor," for example, calls for higher-order thinking skills and diplomacy, as the position needs to review physicians' treatment plans involving tests and hospital stays to keep with recommended guidelines set by insurance companies and the federal government. IBM's Watson, however, is assuming the cognitive skills of this position by providing doctors with a knowledge base far vaster than any single physician advisor could possibly retain in memory. While Watson has not been able to deskill the physician advisor yet, it is well underway because it has already assumed the knowledge-based tasks and the recommendations of the essential job description, and the remaining part of the position could easily be assumed by a nurse or perhaps a nurse practitioner (Davenport and Kirby 14–15).

WorkFusion, designed in the MIT Computer Science and Artificial Intelligence Lab, is a machine-learning-driven project management system. It assigns human tasks, such as writing a report involving data, and then evaluates the worthiness of the research and writing. If the finished product is not acceptable, the program assigns another human to it. While this does not sound like a form of deskilling, it is because the software algorithms are learning constantly how to further automate the process. Even as the writers compose their projects, the software is searching for ways to replace skilled writers with smart writing machines (Marshall).

As smart machines assume more knowledge-based tasks, they will affect the field of education and school librarianship. While computers will not be able to deskill a teacher who is expert in motivating students and maintaining an atmosphere conducive to learning, these positions have the potential to become deskilled through A.I. diagnostic software that will personalize educational content and be able to discern mastery of it. The role of teachers and school librarians could be assumed by mentors and teaching coaches rather than credentialed instructors and school librarians with subject expertise (Davenport and Kirby 16).

OVERQUALIFIED WORKERS

One would think that deskilling would result in more employees with lower skills being able to assume the jobs of workers who are more educated and qualified for those positions. But the opposite seems to be occurring. Research is revealing that almost 50 percent of college graduates find jobs that really require college degrees, even though such degrees are a stated qualification on the job description. Almost 20 percent of U.S. college graduates are deemed overeducated for their present occupations. Lest we think that this problem is indigenous to our country, it reflects a global phenomenon as citizens on three continents grapple with the challenge of locating meaningful, remunerative work in a period of accelerating change. Estimates in Europe approximate 30 percent of college graduates are overqualified for their positions (Buckley). Canada is experiencing a similar pattern, reporting

40 percent of their college graduates are overqualified for their current jobs (Blatchford), while China with its booming population reports 43 percent of its workforce is overeducated for current occupations (Zhu).

Looking for causation is natural so that we can understand and perhaps redirect our future workforce toward jobs that truly match their qualifications. But ferreting out the possible causes of this growing employment trend is challenging. Some experts fault students' major choices, believing that their failure to opt for a career in the physical sciences, especially engineering and computer science, dooms them to working in jobs where they are overcredentialed. Data, however, belie this criticism, finding that about one-third of U.S. students who dutifully obtain degrees in these disciplines fail to locate a position that employs their qualifying degrees. In the fields of computer science, information science, engineering, and other technical fields, U.S. colleges are graduating 50 percent more students than are hired in these disciplines each year. "For every two students that colleges graduate with STEM degrees, only one is hired into a STEM job" (Salzman, Kuehn, and Lowell).

As the world wrestles with more people entering the workforce at the same time that more machines devise ways to remove them from the workforce, employment trends toward overcredentialing. Credential inflation ensues where jobs that once required a high school diploma can only be obtained by those with a four-year college degree. Occupations that used to demand a bachelor's degree can advertise for a master's degree and weed out applicants whose degrees were obtained from for-profit colleges or online universities. Ford, in his outstanding book, *The Rise of the Robots*, envisions the employment schemata as a pyramid rather than a ladder, with only so much room for those at the top tier working in jobs that require creative, innovative work. The larger base of the pyramid is characterized by work that still is routinized in many aspects and thus highly susceptible to machine learning (Ford 252).

THE EDUCATION/INCOME CONNECTION

As the employment trends of deskilling and overeducated workers occur simultaneously, it is also important to keep our focus on the present employment picture for students with and without education beyond high school. The level of education workers attain is still strongly related to their income level. Even in a time of change, this correlation between increased education and income is direct. Labor experts report that each additional year of education translates into an 8 to 13 percent increase in hourly earnings ("Learning and Earning" 4). Those with college educations, even if they are in positions for which they are overqualified, will manage better than those lacking education beyond high school. In 2013, for example, U.S. workers with four-year college degrees fared far better, earning 98 percent more per hour on average than workers without college degrees (Reich 2015, 209). The college advantage has increased over the years, showing that there is a distinct edge for college graduates, whose earnings were 89 percent more than nongraduates in 2008, and only had a 64 percent advantage over nongraduates in the early 1980s (Reich 2015, 209). Over a lifetime, the average earnings of U.S. college graduates are $2.3 million, while the average high school graduate earns approximately $1.3 million (Kaplan 113).

While the employment picture is not exactly rosy for college graduates, it is positively grim for those high school graduates and high school dropouts. Dropping out of high school or not obtaining education/training beyond it is associated with a host of economic, social, and physical ills. In a time of change, it is a noxious cocktail for a lifetime of woe. Unfortunately, data from the U.S. Department of Education confirm this prediction. In 2012 the median income of persons ages 18 through 67 who dropped out of high school was about $25,000 compared to $46,000 for those with at least a high school education, including a General Educational Development (GED) certificate.

Throughout a person's lifetime, this lack of education converts to a loss of $670,000 in income for a student who graduated from high school compared to one who dropped out. Finding gainful employment is also a continual problem for high school dropouts, and a much lower percentage of them are unemployed compared to those who earned high school certification. The toll that marginal employment and unemployment take on high school dropouts is considerable. The average dropout suffers from worse health, constitutes a high percentage of the prison population, and actually costs the economy about $250,000 over their lifetimes because they pay lower taxes, require public assistance, and need to rely upon Medicaid and Medicare more often than do high school graduates (Stark, Noel, and McFarland 1).

SKILL REQUIREMENTS IN A TIME OF CHANGE

In the face of counterintuitive employment trends surrounding deskilling and overqualification of workers, there lurks the omnipresent word—unemployment. According to Kaplan, author of *Humans Need Not Apply*, we will not suffer from a lack of jobs, but instead be engaged in a race against developing human skills to match the rate of automation skills (Kaplan 13). Will machine learning outdistance the rate at which we can train our workforce to adapt to a new work environment replete with nano-speed algorithms and other forms of machine learning? What skills will be needed to secure and then hold jobs that in the future may be accessible to anyone with equal skills anywhere in the world (Friedman 205)?

In general, employment is rising in occupations that require education, job training, and experience beyond high school. In 2015, about 83 million Americans worked in occupations that required an average or above-average level of preparation. This tier of additional education represented a 68 percent increase since 1980. On the other hand, there was only a 31 percent increase in employment in positions needing a below-average level of job preparation. Low-level jobs in this category rose from 50 million to 65 million from 1980 to 2015. Occupations that favor higher social and analytical skills showed an overall increase of 50 percent over ones that did not from 1980 to 2015. Jobs that called for average or above-average social skills, such as interpersonal, management, and communications skills, increased by 83 percent, whereas those requiring analytical skills, including critical thinking and computer skills, increased by 77 percent. Occupations needing manual labor and physical skills only increased by 18 percent (Brown 1–2).

Although the increased skill requirements were somewhat stagnant from 1990 to 2015, there were wage increases in occupations requiring higher social or analytical skills. The average hourly wage for social skill occupations rose from $22 to $26 per hour, and for analytical skills they increased from $23 to $27 per hour. For jobs only requiring manual skills, however, the average hourly wage only increased from $16 to $18 (Brown 1–2).

The big question concerning these employment trends is will Americans recognize the need for lifelong learning in a time of change? Evidence garnered from Pew Research Center concerning the changing job market is finally beginning to indicate that a shift is occurring in the mind-set that American workers hold concerning their employment. They are starting to realize that retraining and upgrading their skills will require a lifetime commitment (Brown 1). Approximately 54 percent of adults in the workforce expressed the opinion that it will be necessary for them to obtain additional training and develop new skills throughout their workspans in order to remain competitive in the workplace. An additional one-third consider it important but not imperative. Those workers with the highest level of education deem it essential (Brown 2). Thirty-five percent of American workers report that they lack the education and training they need to compete in the workplace. Many of them, 45 percent, are presently pursuing extra training to either maintain or improve their current job skills (Brown 2).

Disappointingly, and perhaps because of the growing trend of obtaining work in jobs for which they are overqualified and their assumption of college debt, American workers are ambivalent concerning the value of a college degree in the job market. Sixteen percent of all Americans believe that a bachelor's degree prepares one for a remunerative job in the current workplace. Fifty-one percent think that a college degree prepares students "somewhat well" (Brown 2).

Colleges and K–12 schools do not have to hypothesize about the skill requirements for employment in a time of change because numerous surveys have been conducted that provide us with a blueprint for ensuring that our graduates can succeed in an increasingly automated work environment. Given the first imperative of hiring the most educationally qualified workers that they can, what other more delineated skills do employers seek to remain competitive? In a survey of 302 employers, whose organizations numbered at least twenty-five employees, employers are searching for a combination of liberal and applied learning. They desire subject expertise in students' majors and the ability to apply this knowledge in a work environment. They are looking for students to have the ability to perform research and use evidence-based analysis. Because so many companies have a global reach or are in a potentially globally competitive situation, they need employees to comprehend the global context of various projects and directives. Future employees will need to be aware of the role the United States plays in the world and understand the diversity in American society and the extent of it in other countries ("Raising the Bar . . ." 1).

The intellectual and practical skills that employers need are similar to ones that K–12 schools are either teaching or inculcating in various curricula subjects.

Companies want students with good communication skills both orally and in writing. They need them to be able to think critically and to apply analytical reasoning skills to a project and to solve complex problems. Collaboration is a key job requirement, encompassing the ability to get along with coworkers and work on a team to complete projects and solve problems. Employees of the future will need to be comfortable with innovation and finding creative solutions for an employer. In an age of information overload, employers want them to be able to locate, organize, and evaluate information from multiple sources. They also need them to be able to work with numbers and understand statistics ("Raising the Bar . . ." 2).

A significant number of surveyed employers expressed a need for employees with a well-developed sense of personal and social awareness. Students will be expected to make the connections between their own personal work decisions and a company's ethical code or practices. Future employees who get involved in their communities by participating in various civic events were considered an asset ("Raising the Bar . . ." 2).

WHAT ARE THE JOBS OF THE FUTURE?

For the first time, labor experts seem to be ducking the prediction of future jobs. In the past, they prophesized an increase in the number of lawyers, computer scientists, and healthcare professionals. But something is different this time. Thomas Friedman, in his book, *Thank You for Being Late*, believes that securing and holding jobs in a time of change will necessitate workers living by means of "dynamic stability" and that they will need to be extremely self-motivated (Friedman 205). A Pew Research Center Report about the future of jobs and job training cites the ability to adapt and continuously learn and that people who can do it best and most quickly will be the winners (Rainie and Anderson 15–16). Both viewpoints imply a form of social Darwinism that will be challenging for many Americans who do not discern the need for additional preparation in the form of education or training beyond high school.

Despite the fact that the demand for data analysts has grown by 372 percent over the past five years and that the demand for workers with data visualization skills has risen 2,574 percent, some labor analysts are suggesting that future jobs may also reside with the development of skills that machine intelligence cannot replicate ("Learning and Earning" 4). What are the skills that define us as human beings? How are we able to sense and reflect the feelings and thoughts of other people? What makes us able to work cooperatively in groups and solve problems together? How are we able to express ourselves emotionally in the way that a robot cannot that enables us to persuade others to successfully accomplish a task or project (Colvin 4)? These are skills that future jobs may entail even as our students work side by side with algorithmically driven machines. Think of them as "STEMpathy jobs" where humans will work in concert with machines because their intelligence about the subject will be greater than ours, but we will be essential to communicating their output to others through the use of our superior intellectual and personal skills (Friedman 239).

Machine intelligence is already more accurate at diagnosing certain forms of cancer than a specialist is, but a patient needs to learn of such a life-threatening diagnosis from a physician who exudes empathy and concern and can explain possible treatment options (Frank, Roehrig, and Pring 3). Reliance on a machine to objectively render a cancer verdict will cross technology's high-tech versus high-touch barrier, and there will be a predictable opposite reaction to it despite the machine's improved accuracy. High-touch occupations in the future may become more viable as humans learn to leverage advanced technologies to work in concert with them (Rushkoff 66–67).

The Bureau of Labor Statistics foresees that healthcare professionals will be in high demand by 2022. The country is slated to need 527,000 registered nurses, 424,000 home health aides, and 312,000 nursing aides within the next decade, and all of these positions will require highly developed personal skills that include empathy and sound judgement and an ability to work with advanced medical technologies to maintain patient health (*Occupational Outlook Handbook*).

EMPLOYMENT TRENDS AND SCHOOL LIBRARIANS

The trends in employment have political, technological, and pedagogical implications for school librarians. For years most of us have passively shared the economic fate of our schools. If budgets were reduced, we quietly bore our share of the cut in the interests of the whole school. If greater reductions were necessary, many of us closed our doors and departed, leaving future generations bereft of the most essential resource in a time of change—information and knowledge. Now the employment evidence suggests that the availability of technologically advanced school libraries is probably the best resource that schools can have in their battle to improve the quality and quantity of jobs for their students. Convincing fiscally strapped school boards and state legislatures, however, will be a problem.

GOVERNMENT AND SCHOOL LIBRARIES

As the U.S. economy becomes more integrated with the world economy and jobs become increasingly mobile, it will be difficult to protect American workers against competition from workers in other countries willing to perform the same job tasks for less money. Machine learning is already making inroads into jobs requiring high cognitive skills and education beyond high school. Simultaneously, the jobs that remain will require additional preparation but will not necessarily pay better. Some workers will experience the deskilling of previously well-paying positions, while others will be cut out of the job market because employers can obtain more educated workers.

Students, parents, and administrators will be puzzled at first by these trends and then, as they become permanent, will probably react negatively. A recent Pew Research Center survey bears this discontent out. Although 72 percent of U.S. adults believe that workers should take responsibility for ensuring that they have the right skills and education in today's work environment, 60 percent think that public K–12 schools should have a lot of responsibility for ensuring that they do. Forty percent of them fault their state government, and only 35 percent think that the federal government should bear responsibility (Brown 1–2). These figures indicate that the failure of state and local governments to help prepare workers for future employment shock will not be the only source of dissatisfaction. Instead, parents will probably vent their frustration on their local schools. Teachers and administrators will be accused of not doing their jobs, especially in districts with significant numbers of dropouts and low standardized test scores. School librarians in these schools will be challenged to justify expenditures for print and nonprint materials when so many of their students desperately need to improve their reading and comprehension abilities.

Increasingly the employment picture for students capable of only routine-production services work will be grimmer, as more jobs are assumed by robots and machines equipped with advanced technologies. Many of these students can be expected to flock to service jobs that require interpersonal skills as a last resort. For those lacking these essential skills, future employment may cease to exist. These individuals will continue to swell the rolls of those already on some form of public assistance. The creeping effect of social Darwinism will not be lost on the vast numbers of deserving children who are doomed to chronic unemployment because of inadequate school libraries. Their discontent with the status quo may well be manifested in increased crime and other forms of social unrest.

On the other hand, students, parents, and administrators in affluent schools will be prepared for the changing employment trends. They will continually voice their concerns over the educational and subsequent employment future of their children. In the meantime, they will try desperately to ensure that their children have stimulating teachers who structure learning situations to increase higher-order thinking skills. They will continue to fund school library budgets, even if this entails raising outside monies, sponsoring book fairs, or vigorously protesting any reductions to their local school boards funding. This one-fifth of the population will labor incessantly to guarantee that their children get the 20 percent of American jobs that require critical thinking skills and college education and that might remain immune to future automation.

School librarians, regardless of the economic status of their respective districts, will be challenged to respond to this situation. There will be demands for materials that improve literacy and/or raise standardized test and SAT scores. Career materials will be needed and, as a matter of course, will change frequently because the employment picture will be so fluid. Information that monitors the employment situation in local areas, as well as globally, will be requested as schools try to halt a steady decline in employment opportunities for four-fifths of the population. School librarians will be involved in helping to raise the aspiration levels of many students through the use of their library collections, speakers, and career programs. They will probably be requested to disseminate comparative data concerning the relationship between earnings and education to parents, teachers, and administrators.

TECHNOLOGY AND SCHOOL LIBRARIES

As jobs are either complemented or subsumed by machine learning, schools will need to invest in diverse information technologies to assist future generations to obtain employment. A dichotomy will probably emerge as schools in the top twentieth percentile try to secure their students' gainful employment by providing instruction that employs higher-order thinking skills with advanced technologies rather than basic, rote coding skills that may become obsolete with new iterations or A.I. While computer parity exists between affluent and less affluent school districts, the discriminating factor will be how they will be utilized to foster learning rather than for memorization or routine-like work (Bulman and Fairlie 6).

School librarians in either type of school library will be charged with creating high-tech environments that provide the types of learning experiences that employers will require of their employees. Access to school-based and remote online networks and interactive media will be prevalent in both types of schools. The critical operating variable will be how advanced technologies are used. In schools without dedicated faculty and Common Core Standards curricula, school librarians may observe much of the material being used as entertainment or plug-in drugs until the period ends. In progressive school districts, school librarians will need to design course-related units that require the use of critical thinking skills to retrieve, organize, interpret, and evaluate the information that students access.

INSTRUCTION AND SCHOOL LIBRARIES

Much of the employment trend information indicates that teaching higher-order thinking skills to students is an absolute necessity if the United States is to have a highly productive and remunerative economy. Evidence of off-shoring further suggests that employers are demanding skill sets that completely match the information-seeking skills taught across the K–12 curriculum by school librarians. In a time of rapid change, they are an absolute necessity. Our students will need to be able to discern patterns and meanings in information so that it can be equated, formulated, analyzed, or categorized. This form of abstract reasoning will need to be coupled with a form of system thinking so that students are able to see how patterns of information relate to a complete process or cycle. They are going to need to develop skills about how to identify cause and effect and especially with big data how they differ from correlation. Skills that compete with machine learning will entail solving problems that are complex, require the input of several workers, do not have a formulaic means of arriving at the solution, and may have more than one answer.

Since many of the resource-based units we design are group oriented, students will need numerous opportunities to work in teams and to collaborate with one another to develop the reasoning and interpersonal skills that make their human qualities essential to any organization that employs them.

Most importantly, school librarians will be called upon to consistently stress one of our core values—the need for lifelong learning. Previously cited surveys show that Americans are finally agreeing with the labor experts, economists, and educators who have warned of the danger of obtaining an education, a job, and then performing it in a similar manner for the duration that an employee is in the workforce. By 2020, it is predicted that 65 percent of all U.S. jobs will necessitate some postsecondary education and training (Carnevale et al. 7). In the future, few workers will hold jobs that will not require acquiring new skills to augment their abilities and deepen their expertise by taking courses or additional training.

REFERENCES

Abt, Neil. September 13, 2017. "Senate Told of Safety, Efficiency Benefits of Autonomous Trucks." Available at: http://www.fleetowner.com/autonomous-vehicles/coverage-senate-hearing-go-here.

Bhattari, Abha. March 16, 2016. "Factory Jobs Trickle Back to the U.S. Giving Hope to a Once-Booming Mill Town." *The Washington Post.* Available at: https://www.washingtonpost.com/business/capitalbusiness/factory-jobs-trickle-back-to-the-us-giving-hope-to-a-once-bo.

Blatchford, Andy. March 25, 2017. "Growing Proportion of University Grads Overqualified for Their Jobs: Study." *The Globe and Mail.* Available at: https://www.theglobeandmail.com/news/national/growing-proportion-of-recent-university-grads-overqualified-for-their-jobs-study/article.

Blinder, Alan S. May 6, 2007. "Free Trade's Great, but Offshoring Rattles Me." *The Washington Post.* Available at: http://www.washingtonpost.com/wp-dyn/content/article/2007/05/04/AR2007050402555.html.

Brown, Ana. October 6, 2016. "Key Findings about the American Workforce and the Changing Job Market." Pew Research Center. Available at: http://www.pewresearch.org/fact-tank/2016/10/06/key-findings-about-the-american-workforce-and-the-changing-job-market.

Brynjolfsson, Erik and Andrew McAfee. 2011. *Race Against the Machine: How the Digital Revolution Is Accelerating Innovation, Driving Productivity, and Irreversibly Transforming Employment and the Economy.* Lexington, MA: Digital Frontier Press.

Buckley, Stephanie Gruner. October 5, 2012. "30% of European Workers Are Overeducated for Their Jobs." Quartz. Available at: https://qz.com/12551/30-of-european-workers-are-overeducated-for-their-jobs.

Bulman, George and Robert W. Fairlie. October 2015. *Technology and Education: Computers, Software and the Internet.* Bonn, Germany. IZA Research Network. Available at: http://ftp.iza.org/dp9432.pdf.

Carnevale, Anthony P. et al. 2015. *Iowa: Education and Workforce Trends through 2025.* Georgetown University Center on Education and the Workforce. Available at: https://cew.georgetown.edu/wp-content/uploads/Iowa_Wrkfrce2025.pdf.

Colvin, Geoff. 2015. *Humans Are Underrated.* New York: Penguin.

"Contingent Work Force: Size, Characteristics, Earnings, and Benefits." April 20, 2015. U.S. Government Accountability Office. Available at: https://www.gao.gov/products /GAO-15-168R.

"Databases, Tables & Calculators by Subject." November 15, 2017. Bureau of Labor Statistics. Available at: https://data.bls.gov/timeseries/LNS11300000.

Davenport, Thomas H. and Julia Kirby. 2016. *Only Humans Need Apply: Winners and Losers in the Age of Smart Machines.* New York: Harper.

"Employment by Major Industry." November 13, 2017. Bureau of Labor Statistics. Available at: https://www.bls.gov/emp/ep_table_201.htm.

Ford, Martin. 2015. *Rise of the Robots: Technology and the Threat of a Jobless Future.* New York: Basic Books.

Frank, Malcolm, Paul Roehrig, and Ben Pring. 2017. *When Machines Do Everything: How to Get Ahead in a World of AI, Algorithms, Bots and Big Data.* New York: Wiley.

"Freelancing in America 2017." September 2017. Upwork and Freelancers Union. Available at: https://www.slideshare.net/upwork/freelancing-in-america-2017/1.

Frey, Carl Benedikt and Michael A. Osborne. September 17, 2013. "The Future of Employment: How Susceptible Are Jobs to Computerisation?" Available at: http://www .oxfordmartin.ox.ac.uk/downloads/academic/The_Future_of_Employment.pdf.

Friedman, Thomas L. 2016. *Thank You for Being Late: An Optimist's Guide to Thriving in the Age of Accelerations.* New York: Farrar, Straus & Giroux.

Gordon, Claire. April 27, 2012. "How Employers Can Legally Strip Your Job of Benefits." Available at: https://www.aol.com/2012/04/27/how-employers-can-legally-strip -your-job-of-benefits.

Johnson, William B. and Arnold E. Packer. 1987. *Workforce 2000.* Indianapolis, IN: Hudson Institute.

Kabin, Benjamin. September 11, 2013. "Apple's iPhone Designed in California but Manufactured Fast All Around the World." *Entrepreneur.* Available at: https://www .entrepreneur.com/article/228315.

Kaplan, Jerry. 2015. *Humans Need Not Apply.* New Haven, CT: Yale University Press.

Kim, Eugene. February 2, 2017. "More Than Half of Online Sales Growth in the US Came from Amazon Last Year." *Business Insider.* Available at: http://www.businessinsider .com/amazon-drives-more-than-half-us-ecommerce-growth-2016-2017-2.

"Learning and Earning." January 14, 2017. *The Economist.* 422(9023): 3–6.

Levinson, Marc. May 5, 2017. "Job Creation in the Manufacturing Revival." Congressional Research Service. Available at: https://fas.org/sgp/crs/misc/R41898.pdf.

Lifsher, Marc. May 7, 2014. "Rising Use of 'Perma-Temp' Workers Is Stirring Up a Legislative Fight." *Los Angeles Times.* Available at: http://www.latimes.com/business/la -fi-permatemp-worker-bill-20140507-story.html.

"Man and Machine: Better Writers, Better Grades." April 12, 2012. University of Akron. Available at: http://www.uakron.edu/im/online-newsroom/news_details.dot?news Id=40920394-9e62-415d-b038-15fe2e72a677.

Manyika, James et al. May 2013. *Disruptive Technologies: Advances That Will Transform Life, Business and the Global Economy.* McKinsey Global Institute. Available at: https://www.mckinsey.com/business-functions/digital-mckinsey/our-insights /disruptive-technologies.

Marshall, Patrick. September 25, 2015. "Robotics and the Economy." *CQ Researcher.* 25(34): 793–816. Available at: http://library.cqpress.com.proxygw.wrlc.org/cqre searcher/document.php?id=cqresrre2015092500&type=hitlist&num=0.

Meyer, Eugene L. March 18, 2016. "The Gig Economy." *CQ Researcher.* 26(12):1–44.

Occupational Outlook Handbook. October 24, 2017. Bureau of Labor Statistics. Available at: https://www.bls.gov/ooh.

O'Neil, Cathy. 2016. *Weapons of Math Destruction.* New York: Crown.

Perleman, Lewis J. 1992. *School's Out: Hyperlearning, the New Technology and the End of Education.* New York: William Morrow.

Pfeffer, Jeffrey. July 30, 2015. "The Case Against the Gig Economy." *Fortune.* Available at: http://fortune.com/2015/07/30/freelance-vs-full-time-employees.

Poole, Cynthia and Steven P. Berchem. 2014. "The Climb Continues: Staffing and Recruiting Industry Growth Outpaces Economic Growth and Labor Market Improvements." American Staffing Association. Available at: http://altstaffing.org/wp-content/uploads/2015/06/American-Staffing-2014_The-Climb-Continues.pdf.

Rainie, Lee and Janna Anderson. May 3, 2017. "The Future of Jobs and Job Training." Pew Research Center. Available at: http://www.pewinternet.org/2017/05/03/the-future-of-jobs-and-jobs-training.

"Raising the Bar: Employers' Views on College Learning in the Wake of the Economic Downturn." January 20, 2010. Hart Research Associates. Available at: https://www.aacu.org/sites/default/files/files/LEAP/2009_EmployerSurvey.pdf.

Reich, Robert B. 2015. *Saving Capitalism for the Many, Not the Few.* New York: Alfred A. Knopf.

Reich, Robert B. 1991. *The Work of Nations.* New York: Alfred A. Knopf.

"Return of the Machinery Question: Artificial Intelligence Special Report." June 25, 2016. *The Economist.* 419(8995): 1–4.

Rushkoff, Douglas. 2016. *Throwing Rocks at the Google Bus: How Growth Became the Enemy of Prosperity.* New York: Penguin.

Russell, Stuart. Winter 2015. "An Open Letter: Research Priorities for Robust and Beneficial Artificial Intelligence." Future of Life Institute. Available at: https://futureoflife.org/ai-open-letter.

Salzman, Hal, Daniel Kuehn, and Lindsay B. Lowell. April 24, 2013. "Guestworkers in the High-Skill U.S. Labor Market." Economic Policy Institute. Available at: http://www.epi.org/publication/bp359-guestworkers-high-skill-labor-market-analysis.

Scheiber, Noam. February 9, 2016. "Obama's Budget Seeks to Ease Economic Fears." *The New York Times.* Available at: https://www.nytimes.com/2016/02/10/us/politics/obamas-budget-seeks-to-ease-economic-fears-for-us-workers.html?_r=0.

Sorrentino, Constance. June 2000. "International Employment Rates: How Comparable Are They?" *Monthly Labor Review.* Available at: https://stats.bls.gov/opub/mlr/2000/06/art1full.pdf.

Stark, Patrick, Amber M. Noel, and Joel McFarland. June 2015. *Trends in High School Dropout and Completion Rates in the United States: 1972–2012.* U.S. Department of Education. Available at: https://nces.ed.gov/pubs2015/2015015.pdf.

Thompson, Derek. July/August 2015. "A World Without Work." *The Atlantic.* Available at: http://www.theatlantic.com/magazine/archive/2015/07/world-without-work/395294

Zhu, Jin. "More Workers Say They Are Over-Educated." February 8, 2013. *China Daily.* Available at: http://europe.chinadaily.com.cn/china/2013-02/08/content_16213715.htm.

5

Educational Trends

By 2023 approximately 7,750,000 children will be in America's schools. Public schools alone are projected to spend $699 billion to educate these children—27 percent more than they did in 2008–2009. Per pupil these expenditures are also expected to increase 18 percent, to $13,200, from 2009 to 2023 ("Projections of Education Statistics to 2022" 16–17). As the problems of illiteracy and declining tests scores continue, educators, parents, and school administrators hear the drumbeats clamoring for reform and listen to the demands for academic accountability. Everyone who pays taxes, has school-aged children, or has been educated in an American school will have an opinion on this multibillion-dollar investment. More of them can be expected not only to voice their opinions but also to exercise them locally and nationally at the ballot box.

Years ago, education came to be viewed as a means to citizenship and a universal privilege. This philosophy of education, with its corresponding need to tax people to provide for all children, gradually replaced private schools and academies with public schools (McGill 6–11). As America industrialized and waves of immigrants swept ashore, public schools reflected the factory assembly-line style of production. The curricula were tidily divided into subjects, taught in a preset period of time, categorized by grade level, and measured by standardized tests designed to identify students who were suitable for routine production work or higher education (Reich 1991, 226).

This system served America well when companies such as GM, Westinghouse, and U.S. Steel employed millions of workers to perform monotonous assembly line–style tasks. For more than two centuries, America's public education system was the envy of the world. The result was an impressive increase in the percentage of our students who graduated from high school. To enable them to acquire even more advanced skills, America established thousands of affordable state colleges, universities, and community colleges (Duncan and Murnane 143). But by the 1980s, many employers no longer needed as many routine production type workers, and the educational system had failed to produce potential employees with corresponding higher skills. Unfortunately, as the demands for a more literate and skilled workforce increased, educational systems seemed to deteriorate, creating a crisis that presently threatens the social, economic, and personal well-being of all Americans.

The severity of the problems afflicting American schools, from the poorest to the most affluent, centers around literacy and academic achievement. Educators and school librarians will continue to be heavily involved in the process of improving literacy and halting the decline in academic achievement for years to come.

LITERACY

A country's literacy rate can affect not only its citizens' employment prospects but also decrease their lifespans. Illiteracy threatens democracies when its citizens lack the ability to comprehend fact from fiction because they cannot understand context or make inferences from their reading. It has the gravest educational, economic, and civil consequences for a nation and places it at extreme risk. In a society as wealthy as the United States, the word *illiteracy* evokes feelings of defenselessness and anger. Witnessing adults placing Xs on the backs of their checks and implicitly entrusting bank tellers to correctly credit their accounts has a deep emotional impact. Worse still are the numbers of workers who must fearfully conceal their illiteracy from their employers, children, and peers (Breivik 1–7).

Economically literacy is thought of as a "classical relational good" (Norberg 132). The more people who can read and write, the more everyone stands to reap the rewards (Norberg 132). In a society where the majority of citizens can read and write, those who cannot or who do so at a minimal level are condemned to suffer economic, social, cultural, and civil consequences. More than 700,000 students drop out of U.S. high schools each year with low literacy skills ("Adolescent Literacy" 1). The literacy problem is baffling many because in 1980 the census reported a literacy rate of almost 100 percent. Since then, studies have discerned that between 17 and 21 million American adults cannot read at all or can only read at the level of a nine-year-old (Kennedy 306). Among the 155 United Nations member countries, America reports an 86 percent literacy rate, with countries such as Cuba, Russia, Latvia, Tajikistan, and Barbados having literacy rates ten or more points higher ("25 Countries . . .").

Literacy used to be defined as the ability to sound out words from print and did not measure whether an individual could comprehend their meaning or context. But the shift in jobs requiring enhanced literacy has led the United States to develop a three-scale literacy test devised by the National Assessment of Educational Progress (NAEP). The survey measures (1) prose literacy, the ability to understand narrative texts; (2) document literacy, the ability to locate information in charts, tables, and graphs; and (3) quantitative literacy, the ability to use basic mathematics to solve everyday problems involved in making a bank deposit, dining in a restaurant, or reading and interpreting an advertisement. Administered to young adults (twenty-one to twenty-five years old) in 1985, the test yielded results further reinforcing bad news by finding that 80 percent of America's young adults could not interpret a newspaper story, 63 percent could not follow written map directions, and 5 percent lacked the language and literacy skills of nine-year-olds (Breivik 2).

More literacy-related tests added to this educational misery index, reporting that many students could not identify the president of the United States or correctly state the location of New York City. Nearly one-third of American seventeen-year-olds did not know the author of the Emancipation Proclamation, and nearly one-half could not tell who Josef Stalin was (Sowell 3). With these findings, it became apparent that literacy involved more than being able to spell, define words, and pronounce them correctly. Literacy took on the connotation of specific background knowledge about particular subjects. Words and concepts could not be learned in isolation but required an understanding of their cultural context as well.

The increasing qualifications for employment, coupled with competition from countries filled with workers who can accurately complete our tax returns, read our x-rays, and perform legal work, should have triggered an avalanche of local, national, and federal government literacy programs similar to the science and math ones generated when the Russians launched Sputnik in 1957, but regrettably it did not. The literacy needle remains stuck in the same position that it was in 1971 (Clemmitt 2008, 10). From 1973 to 2015, the share of positions in the U.S. economy that required education beyond high school rose from 28 percent to 61 percent ("Adolescent Literacy"). Yet seventeen-year-olds' average reading scores have dropped to 1971 levels. From 1992 to 2005, the percentage of twelfth graders at or above a proficient level dropped from 40 percent to 35 percent. With the exception of those students in the ninetieth percentile, scores for all students dropped (Clemmitt 2008, 4). For minority students, the literacy profile is even worse. NAEP reading assessment reveals that only 27 percent of American Indian and Alaska native students, 24 percent of Latino students, and 16 percent of African American students scored at or above the proficient level compared to 44 percent of white students and 48 percent of Asian students ("Adolescent Literacy").

One of the major causes for America's literacy needle not budging is the lack of pleasure reading by students. The research continually shows a positive correlation between reading for pleasure and reading achievement. Just the simple act of reading a book brings a cavalcade of positive benefits, from increased vocabulary and comprehension to higher achievement on standardized tests. The possession of a large number of books at home even correlates with high academic achievement, regardless of a family's income status. Children of families with graduate school education who possess few books perform less well academically than do children in poorer, less well-educated families with many books (Clemmitt 2008, 10).

Twenty years have passed, however, and pleasure reading by teenagers has dropped significantly. From 1984 to 2004 reading for pleasure has declined steadily, with only 30 percent of thirteen-year-olds stating that they read for pleasure. The percentage of thirteen-year-olds reporting that they hardly ever read for fun rose from 8 percent to 13 percent (Clemmitt 2008, 10).

LITERACY GAP MIRRORS THE INEQUALITY GAP

Educators indicate that we are experiencing a literacy crisis and that it is worsening with students in the upper grades. More than 60 percent of eighth graders and 60 percent of twelfth graders scored below the proficiency level on the NAEP in reading achievement ("Adolescent Literacy"). Most alarming about the twelfth-grade decline in reading achievement is that it appears in the lower 75 percent of students, which signals a growing literacy gap similar to the one occurring with economic inequality. Scores continue to hold steady for those in the ninetieth percentile, but all the others are beginning to sag or have already dropped (Clemmitt 2008, 10). Just as the economic gap between rich and poor is widening, so it is with literacy. The offline reading achievement score gap between 1976 and 2001 increased by nearly 40 percent for students raised in families at the tenth income percentile compared with those in the ninetieth percentile. This gap translates roughly to three to six years of schooling in the middle and high school years (Leu et al. 4). Literacy experts are projecting that as income inequality increases, the reading achievement gap will expand over time (Leu et al. 4).

It is important to note that some educators think our literacy problem is not a crisis and simply reflects how technology is shaping our reading, because current literacy assessments do not measure online reading. Even though book and periodical reading has declined precipitously, these educators hold that Americans are reading similar amounts and simply doing it online. The same educational skeptics purport that Americans have replaced reading with watching YouTube videos, playing electronic games, and trawling the Internet. Since most of our occupations involve work on computer screens that take up a great deal of "mental energy," they believe that our literacy skills have been redeployed into our daily work. After a day of work, the mind requires a different form of stimulation other than traditional reading (Clemmitt 2008, 6). Some questions naturally arise from these differing viewpoints. Will additional harm be done to our literacy skills if the use of various technologies muscles in on reading for pleasure? Will future generations not develop essential skills that are engendered by reading and acquiring subject knowledge (Clemmitt 2008, 6)? Is online reading that different from offline reading in terms of its skill and factual knowledge base?

Researchers concur that online reading is different from offline reading. It is actually a more focused type of reading where the online reader is intent on solving an information problem. While this information inquiry can easily take place offline, online readers are confronted with a different set of tools (Leu et al. 3). When reading online occurs, the reader has to (1) develop a specific information question, (2) find relevant online information, (3) critically evaluate the worthiness of the information, (4) read to synthesize the information, and (5) read and write to communicate online information (Leu et al. 3).

Online reading studies are showing that online research and comprehension skills are similar to offline research and comprehension skills in many aspects, but online research and comprehension require additional skills. A study conducted with 336 seventh graders in two economically different middle schools found a significant gap in online research and comprehension scores when controlled for pretest differences in offline reading, offline writing, and prior knowledge scores. Students in the lower income school, with prior gaps in their offline research and comprehension skills, maintained those gaps when asked to locate, evaluate, synthesize, and communicate information from their online research. There was no improvement in their ability to successfully complete online research versus offline research. Researchers concluded that estimates that define the offline reading gap based upon income may be even higher when similar comparisons are conducted for online research. Sadly, researchers may be grossly underestimating the real problem of the reading achievement gap in an age of advanced technologies (Leu et al. 1–8).

CAN EDUCATORS AND SCHOOL LIBRARIANS REVERSE THE DECLINE?

Outstanding valid and reliable reading research that has been successfully replicated numerous times has been conducted for decades and presents us with an almost foolproof formula for how to raise our literacy rate. One of the primary goals is to enlist the support of parents, since by the time a child reaches school age lasting damage has been done if they have not been academically prepared to start school. The benchmark three-year Kansas study showed that by the time children entered kindergarten, children in professional families had heard more than 19 million more words than the children of working-class families, and 32 million more words than children in families receiving welfare. A related study found that 72 percent of students in middle-class homes knew the alphabet before starting school compared to only 10 percent of poor children (Putnam 116).

Recent studies indicate that parents at the lower income levels are beginning to realize how important the first years of life are for literacy growth and may be trying to narrow the gap for their children. Studies are showing that children entering kindergarten today are more equally prepared than they were in the 1990s and that the school readiness gap narrowed by 16 percent in reading between low- and high-income children. Researchers attribute the narrowing to access to better preschool programs and the fact that poor children have more books, read more with their parents, visit libraries more often, and do more activities with their parents than they did in the 1990s (Reardon).

When a child enters kindergarten, the definition of literacy begins to change because it involves much more than increasing vocabulary, sounding out words, and making the connections between the words and sounds. Literacy at the level necessary for a country to remain globally competitive, socially equal, and politically aware involves accumulating factual knowledge about subjects so that their context can be comprehended. Once context is understood, the mind can more easily ascertain inferences in the text and begin the process of reasoning abstractly, if necessary, to gain the truth or additional knowledge about the subject. Willingham, author of *The Reading Mind*, provides a relevant example of why we need to read constantly to close factual gaps. He rightly asserts that knowledge of a subject furnishes the reader with context and provides the fake-news headline, "Pope Francis Shocks the World, Endorses Donald Trump for President" as an illustration. Anyone reading the headline possessed of background knowledge about the Pope would automatically know that no Pope has ever endorsed a presidential candidate.

Reading studies bear out the need for factual knowledge in order to score well on reading tests. Even poor readers in a study conducted of third-graders who knew a lot about soccer were able to score better on a soccer reading passage than good readers with little knowledge of the game. Poor readers were three times as likely to make correct inferences about the reading passage compared to good readers who lacked soccer factual knowledge. A second experiment posed questions of eleventh graders about their general knowledge of science, history, geography, civics, athletics, and literature. High scores on the general knowledge test correlated directly with higher reading scores (Willingham).

Since comprehension is directly related to an accumulation of factual knowledge, Willingham proposes a restructuring of literacy instruction to make it more factually based. Right now, third graders devote 56 percent of the time to literacy activities and only 6 percent each on science and social studies. Devoting more time to acquiring factual subject knowledge by reading books would improve students' comprehension and in turn boost their reading achievement. Willingham also recommends using "high information texts" in place of current textbooks (Willingham).

The language in American textbooks was perilously simplified after both world wars. For example, textbooks published for grades four through eight have had the average sentence length dropped from twenty words to just fourteen, which has the effect of making the sentences much less complex. Over the years, the vocabulary has also become simplified. English texts used in high school are below the level of books read by seventh graders in the 1940s (Stier 63). The third change that would improve literacy is to imbue every aspect of the curriculum with subject knowledge. While the Common Core Standards specify that students be able to reason abstractly and think critically, they do not refer to precise content through which this type of reading and necessary comprehension will occur (Willingham).

SCHOOL LIBRARIANS AND LITERACY

The role that school librarians can play in remediating our literacy crisis is highly significant at every grade level. We are in the perfect position within schools to positively affect change regarding reading, because we represent the academic heartbeat of our schools with print and nonprint collections of fiction and nonfiction materials that are age appropriate, relevant to the curricula, and stimulating and entertaining for our student populations. Research has validated that we are an essential link in helping children and young adults improve not only their reading and comprehension with print materials but also their skills with locating, evaluating, synthesizing, and communicating online research.

All of our libraries are equipped with collections of books and nonprint materials that support resource-based instructional units but also contain or have access to computers that allow us to teach online information-seeking skills to our students from elementary through high school. Of all the departments within schools, we have the ability to see the big picture regarding a child's online and offline reading progress, because we have them as students as they move from one grade to the next. In the coming years, it will become exceedingly important to assume the role of literacy expert within our schools by informing administrators and faculty about the deleterious effects that poor reading skills can have on students medically, economically, socially, and civilly.

Students who leave our schools with poor reading skills are at risk medically. Many medical directives assume a patient's ability to read and understand sometimes complex prescriptions. Studies of older Americans, for example, report that

Americans with poor reading skills had higher death rates. Their poor reading skills corresponded with weak understanding of instructions concerning hypertension, diabetes mellitus, asthma, and heart failure medications. Lack of comprehension of the importance of vaccinations and cancer screenings was another factor attributed to a low rate of literacy (Clemmitt 2008, 5).

Encouraging students to read fiction and nonfiction for pleasure, and pointing out the reasons why, is something that most of us have practiced for years, but the need is now more urgent for economic and employment reasons. We have a duty to warn our students of the economic and employment situations they face when their reading and comprehension skills do not register proficient on standardized tests and to initiate a personalized program to remedy that lack.

The connection between literacy and democracy could never be more paramount after witnessing the intrusive role that the Russians played in the 2016 presidential election. Studies reveal that only 21 percent of college-age Americans read a daily newspaper, which represents a downward trend from the 46 percent that read newspapers in 1972. Only 20 percent of teens and young adults say they read some news daily on the Internet. Thirty-two percent of teens and 46 percent of young adults actively sought Internet news, whereas the remaining 54 percent just came across it by accident (Clemmitt 2008, 5). This news does not augur well for democracy, which demands constant, active interest and full participation at the ballot box. School librarians are going to be playing one of their most important roles by teaching students how to detect bias in information. Technology advancements have ushered in the ability for anyone, anywhere to publish rumors, lies, gossip, and fake visuals and recordings without sophisticated technical editing skills. We will need to be on the front line in equipping our students with the offline and online skills to successfully navigate through a maze of information that may be either fact or fiction.

ACHIEVEMENT: PERFORMANCE AND DECEPTION

Although tests should not constitute the be-all and end-all for measuring and evaluating our students' academic progress, they remain one of the most objective criteria that local, national, and federal governments can employ to determine improvement or slippage and make subsequent course corrections. Years ago, one of the standard assessments for evaluating our students' achievement by the close of their high school careers was to analyze the results from the SAT test administered by the College Board. While it remains a standard form of assessment, a second test, titled Programme for International Students Assessment (PISA), was devised in 2000 that compares our students' achievements to their peers from seventy-two countries or regions ("What the World Can Learn . . ."). Both tests are useful for determining American educational trends because the SAT provides useful, national data and PISA furnishes information about how our educational system is faring on a global level.

The SAT is characterized by questions that are sometimes subtle in nature, and they compel students to apply logic and contextual suggestions to derive the correct answer (Stier 144). Scores range from 200 to 800 points. Like income and wages, America's SAT scores have been stagnant for a long time. In 1986–1987, for example, the mean score for critical reading was 507, and in 2015–2016, it was 494. The same year, mathematics was 501 and then 508 in 2015–2016. SAT writing assessment was initiated in 2005–2006, and the average mean score was 497. In 2015–2016, it dropped to 482 points ("NCES National Center . . .").

A question naturally occurs. When did the decline start, and how did Americans react to it? SAT scores began to slip as early as 1963 when verbal scores fell from 475 to 425. Average mathematics scores declined 30 points from 500 to 470 points. As scores decreased, parents and school officials did not respond with a hue and cry for more rigorous curricula or increased homework. But the College Board did react to it. Their solution was to "re-center" the score. Other euphemisms for this action in twenty-first-century educationese include curving or massaging the score. So students who took the SAT in 1982 and received a 500 on the verbal (presently called reading section) now had a score of 580. Mathematics scores were also bumped up, but not as much as the reading section. Someone who received a 500 on the mathematics section in 1982 moved up to a 520 score.

As massaged SAT scores continued to stagnate, academics proffered a host of rationales, including that the test had become more difficult and that more students were taking it who were not qualified. Both arguments were found to be fallacious. A Harvard reading specialist analyzed SAT reading passages and declared that they were actually harder between 1947 and 1975 (Stier 61–62). The second rationale was punctured when researchers showed that the largest increase of students taking the SAT occurred during the 1950s and not the 1960s. Average scores did not change at all during this time and only began their sad descent after the huge influx of 1950s test-takers. Some "Cassandra academics" like Thomas Sowell emerged in the 1980s to sound the alarm with books including *Inside Education* and *The Vision of the Self-Anointed: Self Congratulation as a Basis for Social Policy* and Alan Bloom with *The Closing of the American Mind*, but America continued along its path of educational complacency.

During this period, it is important to note that the decline in reading skills really struck those at the top. Only the most qualified students who were taking the SAT were being affected. In other words, those who were college-bound students taking the courses required by higher education for entry were experiencing a decline in scores. A twenty-year PSAT study employed a "representative sample to estimate what the average score of *all* high school seniors would have been if they had taken the test" revealed that the scores of "average" students had not declined during those years (Stier 64).

The drop in test scores was, and continues to be, experienced by higher education instructors and employers. In 2015 only 46 percent of high school graduates who took the ACT (or SAT equivalent exam) reached the reading readiness standard, which is the level required to successfully complete first-year college courses ("Adolescent Literacy"). Only 28 percent reached or exceeded the same standards for reading, mathematics, and science ("Adolescent Literacy").

As students continue to be educationally unprepared for higher education or training beyond high school, they pay a price, and so do their employers. Many have to take remedial courses at an estimated cost of $3.6 billion annually.

Employers spend about $3.1 billion to improve literacy levels for their employees. Students do not receive college credits for remedial courses, yet they not only have to pay for them, but the extra time taking the courses extends the years that they spend in higher education with its exorbitant tuition and fees ("Adolescent Literacy").

The "re-centering" of America's SAT scores conjures up Kahneman's and Tversky's "availability heuristic" or bias belief that was referred to in Chapter 1. The bumping up of the scores, with the exception of several "Cassandra academics" who tried to warn us, tricked our collective brains into thinking that perhaps all of us had actually performed better on our SAT scores, especially when the data came out in our favor. It helped enable teachers, parents, and administrators to ignore the real educational data concerning America's educational performance and deceive ourselves for many years.

THE NEW SAT TEST

In 2015 the College Board debuted a new SAT test based on Common Core standards, which stress evidence-based reading and research. The test favors students who are habitual readers and who are accustomed to doing immersive reading. The prose passages need to be read carefully, and test-takers need to be able to infer the meaning of words from the text. The test no longer requests students to complete sentences or recall the definitions of vocabulary words. Instead, students will need to comprehend the meaning of the words within the passage that they are assigned. The most fundamental change is that there are "many, many more words," which is going to demand an even higher level of reading and thinking on the part of high school students (Hoover 8).

GLOBAL EDUCATION COMPETITION

In 2000 the Organisation for Economic Co-operation and Development (OECD) designed a test for selected groups of fifteen-year-olds that measures mastery of specific skills in science, mathematics, and reading ("Programme for International Student Assessment"). It is administered every three years to approximately 540,000 students in seventy-two countries or regions. The average result in each subject area is about 490 points. If a student scores 30 points above the average score, it is considered the equivalent of completing an extra year of education ("What the World Can Learn . . ."). In 2016 Singapore topped the world in all three areas with an average pupil's math score of 564 compared to an American student's score of 470. In years ahead, these scores imply that Singaporean adolescents are about three years ahead of American teens in mathematics.

The United States scored 496 in science and 497 in reading, which placed it behind almost two dozen countries and rendered us below average in mathematics and average in science and reading among developed countries (Ripley 1). America's reading score of 497 also reflects a computer-based reading section that PISA incorporated into the test. It measures students' proficiency in "evaluating information from several sources, assessing the credibility and utility of what they read using criteria that they have generated themselves" and requires them "to locate information related to an unfamiliar context" (Song). Comparisons among sections of the test showed that students with strong reading skills performed well on both the paper-and-pencil sections and computer-based sections (Song).

The PISA test results are revealing to the United States in economic, social, and educational terms. PISA math scores, for example, are considered a reliable predictor of children's future earnings. Spending money on education, however, is not a predictor of high PISA scores, since none of the world's biggest education spenders, including the United States, Luxembourg, and Norway, excelled on the PISA exams. Socially, immigration does not account for our average results, because Canada has more immigrant students than does America and Canada scored better on the PISA test than we did. Educationally, America did improve by passing the No Child Left Behind Act, which introduced some national accountability and government support for lower-income students. The 2015 PISA result showed that one of every three of our disadvantaged students improved in science by scoring in the top quarter of disadvantaged students globally (Ripley 4–5). The bad educational news is that "nearly one-third of America's fifteen year-olds are not functioning at a basic level of ability—the lowest level that the OECD concludes that children must reach in order to thrive as adults in the modern world" (Ripley 4).

HOW DO THE TOP COUNTRIES SUCCEED?

What are the educational achievement best practices of countries who top the PISA charts? Can the United States emulate them in our educational institutions? Duncan and Murnane, in their book, *Restoring Opportunity*, believe that the adoption of the Common Core Standards by forty-two states and the District of Columbia represents a definite form of progress (Duncan and Murnane 134). They believe that having school choice, accountability for results, and social intermediary and organizational support, plus evidence-based, best education practices are positive ingredients for future academic success.

Ripley, author of *The Smartest Kids in the World and How They Got That Way*, reinforces Duncan and Murnane more specifically with an educational prescription that includes making teaching a high-status profession, directing funds towards lower-income children, providing access to quality preschool education, building a mind-set of constant improvement, and instituting a uniform set of demanding standards that are applied equally to all subject areas (Ripley 3).

The author of *Cleverlands* is also worth consulting for her keen observations of five of the top PISA-performing countries in 2012—Finland, Canada, Shanghai, Singapore, and Japan. Crehan visited them, spending four weeks in each country observing, assisting, and posing questions to educators about their countries' teaching practices, philosophy of education, and more. She, too, concluded that the profession of teaching needs to be elevated and that teachers and students seem to thrive in an environment of constant improvement. Working hard and being persistent in the face of obstacles was a common denominator of Asian countries when compared to Western ones. The teachers in Asian countries believe that every child has equal potential, and those countries do not use IQ tests to predetermine intelligence or class placement.

Memorization, which is antithetical to Western educational concepts, is also an important component of their educational systems, because it builds a knowledge base for future reference and advancing to the next subject level. Teaching skills such as critical thinking and problem-solving through specific subjects rather than in isolation was another characteristic that all the top performing countries shared. Lastly, there is less breadth to the top performing countries' curricula than there is depth. Students acquire mastery of the subject matter, rather than experience a survey-like course that American schools offer (Crehan 91, 242–243).

SCHOOL LIBRARIANS AND ACHIEVEMENT

The dawning realization that a substantial portion of American children will not enjoy the standard of living that their parents now experience may fuel the fires for educational reform. The adoption of a set of common educational standards by forty-two states and the District of Columbia is the first step in a direction that may improve scores. Although President Trump has called for a repeal of the Common Core, it may be difficult for him and his Secretary of Education Betsy DeVos to repeal them. They were not created by the federal government and are technically outside their jurisdiction. National education standards are the foundation for every high-performing PISA country that currently ranks above us on the score rankings (Ripley 4). School librarians reading these trends can easily envision a role for themselves at every educational level. Supporting Common Core standards with print and nonprint sources, as well as designing Common Core–based resource units, should be a priority in the years to come.

An analysis of American student performance on literacy, SAT, and PISA tests is a siren call for emphasizing all types of reading, but especially immersive reading. No place in the school is better situated to provide our students with a wealth of fiction and nonfiction material that is designed to increase subject knowledge, vocabulary, and comprehension than a school library's collection. As school librarians we are only limited by our imaginations as to how we expose students to this treasure trove of reading. Booktalking, reading aloud to them, creating book trailers, sponsoring book fairs, holding reading contests, hosting authors, and celebrating readers are just some of the activities that can help tip the scales in favor of greater literacy and stronger achievement.

Disseminating data about literacy and achievement scores will also become essential if our schools are not to lapse into our former pseudo-complacency. Parents, teachers, and administrators have to realize what's on the line, especially with growing competition for jobs from countries where English is the first language and their PISA scores are higher than ours.

In the future, school librarians may have access to diagnostic data that will help them target students who need remedial reading assistance before they fall far behind their peers and suffer a fatal loss of confidence and interest in their education. New and improved software programs should be available that monitor student reading progress more quickly and easily, thus enabling remedial interventions. Our online catalogs should also be more sophisticated in producing read-alike recommendations that will enhance our ability for reading guidance activities and other reading-related programs and services.

To achieve all of these goals will require school librarians who are tenacious in their belief that reading—especially the immersive type—must be the hallmark of entire school curricula. It cannot be the province of the English and school library departments, but must be integrated into all subject areas if America is going to provide all of its children with equal educational opportunity.

DIGITAL EDUCATION

Digital education is learning that is facilitated by technologies that provide students with the opportunity for individualized instruction that may be at their own pace and time of their choosing ("What Is Digital Learning?"). The transformative shift toward digital education is being driven by technological, economic, and employment forces. It is an educational movement that is important to apply trend analysis to by submitting any potential acquisitions to the CIPHER (contradictions, inflections, practices, hacks, extremes, and rarities) and F.U.T.U.R.E. (foundation, unique, track, urgency, recalibrate extensible) tests (Webb 152–153, 239).

As America faces an educational reckoning, it will also be tempting for educators to fall back on the "technofix mentality," rationalizing that new bots, apps, and A.I.-powered software programs will magically imbue our students with enhanced literacy skills without them needing to spend time reading and accumulating knowledge (Naisbitt 52). While there have been significant improvements in digital education with computers that can comprehend speech, correct pronunciation, and monitor and evaluate progress, it is also time for caution because of the costs involved and the lack of evidence-based research results (Clemmitt 2011,1). Technology will be presented to us as a quick solution that we all crave to make our educational system the envy of the world again.

Across the country, school administrators are grappling with how public funds should be spent on educating children for a digital world. Common sense tells us that student educational experiences should be infused with state-of-the-art technologies so that they are prepared to cope with the latest software version, know how to search for relevant information online, and communicate information to others using a variety of online-based formats such as videos, podcasts, slide presentations, and the like. A search of school storage closets, however, tells a sad tale of expensive, fast-occurring obsolescence. Laptops that need replacing every three years, cables that no longer comply with the latest equipment purchase, and monitors that cannot support high memory programs are just some of the obsolete computer items that are piled up in school EdTech graveyards (Trip and Richtel).

Economic forces will also be pushing us in a similar direction, as throughout America school budgets are tight. In impoverished states, such as Ohio and Michigan, legislators are contemplating having a teacher–student ratio of 1 to 50, because of blended learning and other types of online learning that feature use of advanced technologies (Clemmitt 2011, 1). As early as 2011, Idaho had the honor of being the first state mandating that students complete two or more courses online to meet their graduation requirement (Bonner). Within a year, online courses skyrocketed, with one in ten students taking courses solely online (Hicks).

Cash-strapped school districts are not the only factor in this troubling economic equation. The industry is also gearing up to cash in on a potentially huge EdTech market. Market analysts project the combined value of North American and European EdTech markets, including postsecondary and higher education fields, to rise from $75 billion in 2014 to $120 billion in 2019 ("Machines Learning" 15). Pressure will be on school districts to purchase the latest programs that promise to improve test scores and boost achievement.

Schools have always faced a philosophical dilemma when educating students. Should we prepare them for postsecondary education and training by instructing them in the physical sciences and humanities, thus ensuring that they do not require remedial work to enter a first-step job or first year of college? Instead, should we offer opportunities to elect classes such as computer science and computer coding that might improve students' immediate chances in the local job market? Is it our responsibility to train future programmers and coders for an increasingly digital workforce? What are the trade-offs? With the predicted growth and expansion of digital learning, we are already encountering the education/employment role that the big five (Amazon, Microsoft, Google, Apple, and Facebook) are going to play in this evolving educational picture.

WHERE'S THE RESEARCH?

Companies such as the big five argue that access to the latest technologies enhances learning and is necessary to ready students for an increasingly digital work environment. Proponents of this view believe that computers also offer multiple tracks to academic success. Students, for example, may have more options about how to visually present data or deliver assignment results with technology than with traditional communication forms. Critics, however, argue that schools would increase achievement if they focused their funds and attention on hiring outstanding teachers who are trained in their subject areas and methods of delivering instruction that results in learning (Clemmitt 2011, 13). Opponents of game-based learning cite how students engage in "repeated blind-based guessing" to avoid learning the material, thus defeating the entire learning objective (Clemmitt 2011, 3).

As the digital argument rages on, costing schools millions of dollars in obsolete hardware and software, EdTech companies are poised to offer still more seductive software as the pressure mounts from parents and state legislators to halt America's educational decline. The most devastating report that measured the impact of technologies on educational outcomes is interesting to contemplate. Published in 2015 by the Institute for the Study of Labor (IZA), it spanned thirty-two countries, including the United States. Their findings revealed a statistically insignificant correlation between academic achievement and the availability of school computers. The study focused on classroom use of computers in schools and home use by students. Shockingly, the research suggests that there may be even a negative effect on most test scores and that computer instruction may be less effective than traditional instruction.

Even with governments, such as the U.S. government, increasing the spending cap up to $3.9 billion per year for discounted e-rate programs that include funds for schools to purchase equipment and Internet access at reduced costs, there was no increase in academic test scores or other academic outcomes (Bulman and Fairlie 15–17). Only the state of Maine showed some improvement. After providing every Maine public school seventh- and eighth-grade student and teacher with a laptop, Maine's writing scores for this demographic improved by approximately only one-third of a standard deviation (Bulman and Fairlie 17).

Writers of this important global research study also focused on six reading and four math software products for students ranging in grade K–12. Nine of the ten products revealed no statistically significant improvement, while the tenth had a positive outcome with fourth graders. The same study also looked at how usage and effects changed over a two-year period, hypothesizing that additional teachers' experience might produce a positive outcome. Surprisingly they found that usage of the programs decreased in the second year and there were no positive effects on learning (Bulman and Fairlie 20).

Lamentably, this detailed global study showing no relationship between the use of technology and increased learning will not stop companies from shopping their wares equipped with new bells and whistles that promise increases in learning and achievement to school districts that are mandated to increase student achievement. Demanding longitudinal, randomized trials and pilot studies for EdTech products, however, may arm school administrators and teachers as they face the fast tech-talkers who present programs at education conventions, visit school districts, and offer other incentives to purchase the latest product that digital education has to offer.

Using the site What Works Clearinghouse is another possible source for discovering if an educational computer-based program, product, practice, or policy has research behind it to back up its claims. Run by the Institute of Education Sciences (IES) and the National Center for Education Evaluation and Regional Assistance (NCEE), users simply click on categories including math, science, English learners, Pre-K, K–12, and Literacy to locate the latest research and evidence about the effectiveness of various EdTech developments ("What Works Clearinghouse").

MEASURING LEARNING WITH DIGITAL EDUCATION

As digital education continues to make inroads into K–12 classrooms, its new development, termed telemetric education, offers a tantalizing ability to electronically measure, track, and evaluate learning. The lure of this latest tech enhancement is going to be irresistible, because it promises to quickly diagnose learning problems that students face in the classroom faster than a teacher can detect them. We all have encountered students in our classes who seem to be daydreaming or not paying attention to the instruction. Sometimes it is just the temporary distraction of warm spring air wafting into the classroom after a long winter that's the cause. But what if software equipped with motion sensors, video cameras, and other tracking devices reveal that this is a more frequent occurrence and that it necessitates an intervention on the part of the teachers or school learning specialists?

Welcome to the new world of learner multimodal analytics, or LMS. This type of learner analytics centers on the "biological and mental processes of learning in real world environments" (*NMC Horizon Report 2017 Higher Education Edition* 14).

Software combined with hardware will give educators the ability to track and capture voice and tonal inflections that could be used in teaching foreign languages, facial gestures that would indicate attention or distraction during a lecture, and timely analysis that monitors student grasp of a lesson. Lest we think that this is a technological pie-in-the-sky trend, LMS is already emerging with digital tools such as Edpuzzle for a flipped math class at the Bullis School outside of Washington, D.C. Students complete their homework via Edpuzzle's video platform. Before the class enters the next day, the teacher can determine from the learner analytics how many had trouble with specific problems and adjust their lessons accordingly (Madda). An LMS program called Student Dashboard is being used at Nottingham Trent University in the UK to initiate interventions by tutors and other college personnel to ensure college engagement. The software collects data from student visits to the library and all learning assignments and provides them with benchmarks that track their academic progress compared to their classmates, alerting tutors who can provide immediate assistance (Madda).

The future of LMS programs will involve data analytics programs that enable teachers to manage their classroom environments physically and mentally. They will be able to monitor social interactions, identify where students need to work more cooperatively, and who is not interacting in the class at all. LMS will be used to track personal data with sensors that monitor posture, attention, rest, and stress and discover ways to increase personal learning. LMS will abet autonomous learning because students will receive almost instant feedback and will be able to adjust their learning approaches in quicker and more responsive manners. The last part is going to hit the high-tech versus high-touch nerve because LMSs will make teachers dependent upon the computer for almost every aspect of their teaching—from managing the class to conducting class discussions and measuring and evaluating student progress.

It will be the last trend where developments will be interesting (Ferguson et al. 1–5). An outstanding teacher, for example, already possesses many of the qualities that a computer is going to coldly embody. An excellent instructor is characterized as having strong subject expertise with the ability to correctly choose the best pedagogical tools to deliver content and diagnostic capabilities to identify common student mistakes. Their unique ability to inspire and motivate students will be the final hurdle for a computer to match (Crehan 233).

SCHOOL LIBRARIANS AND DIGITAL LEARNING

Despite the studies that continue to be issued showing no positive relationship between academic achievement and the availability of school computers, school librarians will need to have a choice seat at the EdTech table to educate and alert faculty and administrators of the perils and promises of digital education. Digital education is a growing trend in K–16 education, and its negative and positive aspects will need to be researched and addressed.

Three charter schools in Arizona report that the Galileo learner analytics system helps them "focus on the whole child" (*NMC Horizon Report 2017 K-12 Edition* 17). On the other hand, nine schools in New York City show that becoming "data-driven" by recording every answer, giving children rankings where they stand compared to others, and having them endlessly complete one worksheet after another with little instruction for the purpose of collecting more data seems to be continuing America on the path to educational stagnation (Neuman 24–29). Both articles, while informative, can be classified in the "glad tidings versus bad tidings" category. Although they do serve as contact points for further investigation, they do not provide the evidence-based research that is so essential to a school before it invests in a sophisticated learner analytic data system.

School administrators need to start posing educational outcome questions about learner analytics and thoroughly investigate whether they have any positive impact on student achievement. To do this, they need to rely upon the research skills of fully certified school librarians. We are the ones with access to education research databases and have unparalleled searching skills to query them on behalf of faculty and administrators. Arming all the decision makers with research data will provide them with the basis for informed decisions, rather than the temporary hypes about products that they encounter while attending conferences, conventions, and workshops.

LMSs that enable us to measure learning should be welcomed into our schools when they are directly linked to improving student achievement. In the future, they probably will be, and it will then be incumbent upon school librarians to train teachers in best practices. Countless studies show that computers are not appropriately employed in K–12 schools because teachers are inadequately trained and lack technical support when software or equipment falters. School librarians will need to remain at the forefront of these new data-driven systems by training teachers, troubleshooting problems, and exploring the best aspects of them.

We will also need to assiduously apply trend analysis techniques to any digital education proposals to identify ones that are trendy from those that represent valid and reliable programs that will be fully supported technically and educationally in the future. Recall that a trend usually follows an S-curve. It appears on the fringes and slowly becomes mainstream. Use CIPHER to try and discern the contradictions in measuring learning. As schools invest heavily in recording every student assignment, assessment, and class participation contribution, is *contradiction* present? Educators hypothesize that we should witness increased achievement because we can intervene, diagnose, measure, and evaluate instruction in real time. Is that occurring, or is the evidence contradictory?

Watch for *inflection* with digital education. Is something occurring that may act as a catalyst with digital education? Would the passage or defeat of a local bond issue, for example, either speed up the adoption of an LMS program or slow it down? Pose a *hacking* question: Are there aspects of digital education that can be employed to supplement other programs and services? Would a swipe card program that tracks student movement throughout the school provide your library with data to discern if high-achieving students use the library more often than less achieving students? Search for *extremes* with digital education: Is there something unexpected that you might achieve with a form of digital education? If your district established a virtual school, would it enable you to establish a required student-interactive information literacy program?

The last step is to watch for *rarities.* Is there something such as a new educational practice or policy that either addresses a basic human need or changes some aspect of society that digital education could affect? How might students over time react to being monitored physically and academically almost 24/7? What library programs and services might need to be designed for them to escape the educational electronic leash that may tighten around them?

PRIVATIZING EDUCATION THROUGH CHOICE

The demand for better-educated students has created a reciprocal demand for better schools. A 2017 EdNext poll found that almost half of all respondents supported vouchers and tax-credit scholarships, whereas almost forty percent liked the idea of education savings accounts (School Choice FAQs . . ."). Through the years, the education establishment has been attempting to respond by providing a smorgasbord plan of schools and programs to satisfy disillusioned parents, ranging from magnet, performing arts, alternative, and virtual to charter schools (Perleman 193). Proponents of choice plans argue that affluent families have a variety of schools to select from, either by paying increased school taxes in academically oriented communities or by sending their children to private institutions. In turn, why shouldn't less affluent parents be given a choice within their communities? A corresponding benefit would be overall improvement in quality of education because students and parents would choose only effective schools. Therefore, to maintain their student populations, all schools, regardless of their location, economic status, or reputation, would be forced to improve schooling (Murnane and Levy 10).

Some education experts believe that something deeper than solving dilemmas concerning education inequality is occurring. There seems to be a movement toward the privatization of education that may threaten the foundation of public education that has been one of America's building blocks since the 1850s (Clemmitt 2011, 13). After many years of hammering out Common Core Standards that are acceptable to the majority of states and which educators believe is a first step toward improving our declining test scores and achievement levels, there is a drive by President Trump's administration to repeal the Common Core Standards, remove the watchdog role of the federal government in overseeing funding expenditures for educational programs, decentralize educational development by empowering it at the local level, and encouraging the development of all types of schools other than the traditional ones. The implications for traditional public schools—and subsequently school librarians—bear our closest attention (Clemmitt 2011, 13).

CHARTER SCHOOLS

Of all the types of schools cited earlier, it is charter schools that are growing the fastest. Currently there are about 6,800 charter schools functioning in forty-three states educating 5 percent of America's public school population (Clemmitt 2011, 1). Critics on one side of the debate argue that few raise student achievement scores, while their counterparts cite for-profit BASIS and KIPP charter school chains that are running successfully in several states and possess evidence of achievement based on test scores and college acceptance rates, especially with low-income, inner-city children. Most charter schools, however, are tragically flawed by their lack of libraries and certified school librarians. During the 2011–2012 school year, 49 percent of charter schools reported having school libraries compared to 93 percent of conventional schools. Only one-third of charter schools had full-time, paid, state-certified school librarians compared to two-thirds of public schools (Chandler).

Charter schools' structures reflect the privatization of the education movement. While they are required to have appointed boards in many states, they lack the accountability and transparency that are present within locally elected boards of education that regularly expose accounts of fraud, administrative incompetence, or corruption at public hearings. One liberal watchdog group estimates that charter schools have squandered at least $216 million in the former activities since 1994 (Northern). The profit motive also seems forever lurking within the charter school trend. More than 900 charter schools are managed by for-profit companies, and charter schools are enticing investment by hedge fund managers and real estate companies, who can receive tax credits for establishing charter schools in disadvantaged areas (Baker and Miron). The Walton and Gates Foundations, respectively, also support charter schools ("Billionaires Are Boosting . . ."). The current secretary of education, Betsy DeVos, a strong proponent of charter schools, has a family investment in K12, Inc., that has been accused of questionable practices in several states, with students logging in for only minutes per day in order to receive public school funding (Clemmitt 2011, 16).

VIRTUAL CHARTER SCHOOLS

As education budgets continue to be squeezed at the local, state, and federal levels, virtual charter schools are another growing option within the privatization panoply of K–12 education. They sound like the culmination of a technophile's dream. There is no need for physical buildings, and all students need in the way of supplies are a computer and Internet connection. Students can communicate with their teachers by email, telephone, web, or video conference (Gill et al. xi). According to a 2015 online charter schools report, about 200,000 students are enrolled in approximately 200 virtual charter schools (VCS). Most of the VCS population is distributed fairly evenly in three states: Ohio, Pennsylvania, and California. While the majority of the schools instruct high school students, significant numbers also serve elementary and middle school students. Whereas some VCSs are small, 79 percent of them have enrollment of 1,000 plus students (Gill xi).

Students attending VCSs select them for a number of reasons that range from those who are being homeschooled to students with special needs ranging from disabilities, transience, geographic isolation, and aversion to conventional schooling. Seventy-one percent of the VCS students are white, with 14 percent black students and 12 percent Hispanic. Most students attend a VCS for only two years

(Gill et al. xii). Their class size averages twenty-five per full-time teacher in elementary school to thirty at the secondary level. Larger virtual charter high schools average fifty or more students per class (Gill et al. xv).

Most of the instruction is self-paced, with independent study being the main method for knowledge acquisition. The most frequently employed instructional delivery method is teacher–student discussions, and collaboration is rarely used. The lecture method, so common to conventional schooling, is employed only in about one-fourth of virtual charter schools (Gill et al. xiii). Synchronous instruction, which is another common feature of conventional schools, is much reduced in virtual charter schools. Students experience less synchronous instructional time in one week than do conventional school students in one day.

Virtual charter schools offer little individualized instruction that is constantly seen in conventional schools. Students are expected to engage independently with the material, and parents are expected to help. Since there is no way to monitor student attention during the instructional period, teachers give assessments much more frequently. Three-quarters of VCSs purchase their curricula through a school management company. Fifty-seven percent of VCSs are associated with school management companies such as K12, Inc., and Connections, the present dominant ones in this potentially growing educational market.

Again, the salient question for this tech-utopian form of school is student achievement. How do America's virtual charter school students fare when compared to their counterparts in traditional schools? A New York University study found that VCS students across all grades and subjects performed worse on standard tests and that high school students were less likely to pass the Ohio state graduation test ("Students in Ohio's Online . . ."). New York University's findings were confirmed even more starkly with a study by Stanford University's CREDO that analyzed six years of assessment VCS data. Their summation revealed that students going to a VCS dropped behind "their peers by 72 days' worth of learning in reading and 180 days in math in a single 180-day school year." According to the CREDO's study director, VCS math scores were equivalent to not attending school for the entire year (Karaim 23). One of the study's directors at New York University concluded that VCSs in their present state are not sound pedagogical delivery platforms for K–12 students. She stated that "learners still need the presence of teachers, mentors, or peers to help them through the learning process" ("Students in Ohio's Online . . .").

Although the study's results should probably be cause for the closure or suspension of any new VCSs, too many privately owned and managed ones exist for that to happen. Instead, the companies who manage VCSs will continue to try and tweak their models, promising unsuspecting parents and their children that they are going to receive a comparable education to that of traditional schools.

EARLY COLLEGE AND DUAL ENROLLMENT PROGRAMS

Many colleges and universities face a perfect economic storm as enrollments drop and tuition and fees become intolerable burdens to prospective students. Searching for students from within local high schools who can even partially defray their costs will probably become more prevalent. It is a mixed blessing, for it removes students who are usually strong academic role models from the public school demographic. On the other hand, it affords high school students the opportunity to take more challenging courses, and sometimes low-income and first-generation students the means to receive two years of college credit tuition-free, plus get a head start on obtaining higher education. Two types of programs have current working models, but more can be expected to establish themselves in the coming decade.

The first, titled early college, has support from the Bill & Melinda Gates Foundation Early College High School Initiative (ECHSI) and other charitable organizations. Early college allows high school students to take college classes either at a local community college or college while still in high school and receive two years of college credit. It has an outstanding track record with low-income and first-generation students. Started in 2002 by ECHSI, it targets students who might not have dreamed of attending college, let alone graduating from one because of their present economic situations.

There are approximately 240 early college programs operating throughout the country showing a growth rate of 20 percent over a fifteen-year period. The ECHSI's achievement record is remarkable ("Six Years and Counting . . ."). More than 92 percent of early college students graduate from high school, and 86 percent enroll in college the following semester. Seventy percent of them are students of color, and 59 percent are eligible for free lunch programs, which is a student category indicating low income ("Report Confirms Early College High School . . .").

Middle College High School at LaGuardia Community College in New York City and Bard High School Early College at Simon's Rock, New York, are examples of successful early college programs. Their campuses reflect a working collaboration with their respective high schools and colleges, while offering students ages thirteen to eighteen the opportunity to take college courses tuition-free. In Burhana's book, *Informed Transitions,* librarians describe their experiences working with high school students who have never faced the array of print and electronic databases that college-level institutions provide. As a result, Bard College requires that students take a series of information literacy seminars that entail writing assignments and integrated practice sessions. Librarians also offered individualized assignment-related assistance and a place that was almost a home away from home for students as they successfully navigated not only a college campus but also a path through more challenging courses and a social milieu (Walk et al. 133–136).

The establishment of an actual place for high school students to find academic research assistance, friends to socialize with, and a place to study seemed to be the hallmarks of how to successfully transition from secondary school to the college level. Even though students could have completed all their work by using the electronic resources of the library, the conventional library seemed to play a significant stabilizing role in their academic lives (Walk et al. 139).

The second type is known as dual enrollment, dual credit, concurrent enrollment, or the postsecondary option. In this type of program, students in grades nine through twelve can simultaneously earn both high school and college credit. Dual enrollment has existed since the 1970s, and by 2003 48 percent of degree-granting institutions that were eligible for Title IV federal funds offered dual enrollment programs. Funding for dual enrollment programs, however, is becoming problematic because tuition is usually paid for by states, federally funded colleges, and local school districts. Several U.S. senators have proposed legislation to fund dual enrollment, but none of it has made it into law. With these funding sources under potential cutbacks, students and their parents can be expected to bear more of the financial burden (Reinsfelder and Thompson 183–185). Local community colleges are the main place for students to participate in dual enrollment, with 98 percent reporting that high school students were taking college credit courses compared to 77 percent at four-year public colleges and universities. Only 40 percent of secondary-level students took courses at four-year private institutions.

Overall studies indicate that dual enrollment students are more likely to attend college and complete a degree than non–dual enrollment students, but their success rate is not as high compared to that of early college students. Still, the college completion rate for dual enrollment students was 66 percent versus 54 percent for non–dual enrollment students ("Research on Dual and Concurrent . . ."). Other researchers found that student performance increased effectively for dual enrollment students even though some professors indicated that dual enrollment students were not prepared as adequately as non–dual enrollment students (Reinsfelder and Thompson 184–185).

The lack of library instruction stands out as a major stumbling block to dual enrollment students successfully completing various research assignments. An example of a local high school librarians and Penn State (Monto Alto campus) librarians collaborative allowed for only one day for students to become acquainted with the college's print, electronic resources, and other services that the library had to offer. Teaching college-level information-seeking skills in one session and in isolation rather than integrating them into a required research assignment cannot furnish students with the structured and individualized support that is noted earlier in the model early college programs (Reinsfelder and Thompson 186–187). It is evident that there needs to be closer partnerships with local high school and college librarians in institutions where dual enrollment is occurring.

SCHOOL LIBRARIANS AND EDUCATIONAL CHOICE

School librarians can expect the desire for choice in education to be a trend during the next decade. Although some states, such as Massachusetts, have voted for an annual cap on charter schools based on a funding formula and enrollment levels, the Trump administration is strongly promoting the idea of school choice with promised vouchers directed at low-income students (Karaim 10–11). The desire for increased school choice and charter schools also features a demographic variable. Data show that the younger generation favors charter schools and choice more than older generations, with millennials expressing opinions that they should choose the school that their child attends (Karaim 13). This desire for more choice, rather than less, will probably manifest itself in battles for funding as charter schools attempt to obtain a larger share of public funds for their programs.

Although we will not be able to support students enrolled in independent charter schools with our programs and services, we can increase our information literacy instruction for students who attend state-run, dual enrollment, and early college programs. These students are even more in need than our traditional school populations for information literacy skills, because they cannot easily stroll into our conventional libraries for spur-of-the moment or after-school help that so many school librarians provide to students during term paper time or exam periods. School librarians are going to need to be assertive in attempting to identify this somewhat invisible but increasing population quotient and coordinate their efforts to teach them information literacy skills in concert with the librarians on the college campuses where they are attending classes. Furnishing them with access to and promoting the resources on the school library's website and ensuring that they have our contact information may help extend our resources and librarian hands to a demographic in equal or even greater need of our assistance.

TRENDING PEDAGOGIES

America has practiced many different pedagogies with the promise that they will boost test scores and halt declining achievement with our children and future workforce participants. They are too numerous to mention and touch upon a profound irony. Beginning in the 1980s, research companies and universities throughout the United States instituted strict rules and regimens for human experimentation in any form, including even surveying students on campuses. While the rules were necessary to prevent some well-publicized cases of abuse from recurring, they did not apply to our children. Generations of them have been offered up to the pedagogical altar of multiple intelligences, discovery-based learning, schemas, scaffolding, schools without walls, or differentiated instruction without ever requiring that any new education proposal be tested on a large scale with control and test groups and then piloted. The sole reasons for enacting any changes should be because they would unequivocally increase student achievement. Sadly, no legal impediments will probably be put in place to stop this form of unhealthy experimentation with a resource that is more precious than oil or gold: our children.

With America floundering to solve its education problems, new pedagogies are being proposed. Of the myriad of new teaching methods being put forth, three might bear some promise for the future. They are deep learning, blended learning, and collaboration. All three are cited as current or pending trends in the various editions of NMC's *Horizon Reports* and may help improve achievement outcomes with digital education, which is not going to stay its technological hand despite proven failings.

DEEP LEARNING

The William and Flora Hewlett Foundation is associated with the term deep learning. In 2010 they established grants for educational institutions willing to implement pedagogies that foster proficiencies in learning challenging subject matter, developing critical thinking skills, solving problems creatively, collaborating to achieve shared academic goals, communicating content cogently, learning independently, and building a disposition favorable to lifelong learning. Although all of the skills seem like a tall order for helping to get America's educational system back on the right track, the foundation promulgated this new pedagogy because it is practiced by countries such as Canada and Japan that consistently surpass America on the PISA tests. The foundation was also responding to the incessant testing born of the No Child Left Behind Act that required rote memorization and a teach-to-the test mentality on the part of faculties ("Deep Learning").

Before distributing $100 million in deep learning grant monies, the William and Flora Hewlett Foundation established a goal of having 15 percent of America's students assessed for the six proficiencies by 2017. With great effort and collaborative work with other foundations, nongovernmental organizations (NGOs), and deep learning education advocates, the foundation lobbied various state legislatures to incorporate the six competencies into states' yearly assessments and also tied them to the Common Core Standards. A recent evaluation of the Deeper Learning Grant program shows that at the beginning of the 2015–2016 academic year, over 43 percent of students were in a state using a high-quality deep learning assessment. While the new tests do not measure all six competencies, significant inroads are occurring that indicate progress.

In 2016 a national sample of U.S. teachers revealed that considerable and increasing activity is happening with instituting deep learning pedagogies into classrooms. Between 52 percent and 79 percent of teachers surveyed reported that deep learning competencies are being emphasized during professional development times. Between 41 percent and 52 percent of teachers reported that they themselves are emphasizing more deep learning competencies in their curricula than they did during the previous year (Warkentien et al. 3–5).

The Stanford Center for Opportunity Policy in Education has developed one of the best websites for locating high-quality deep learning assessment tools, curriculum units, rubrics, deep learning tasks, and a progression of deep learning frameworks. More importantly, it contains a section devoted to research, with statistical evidence showing the efficacy of introducing pedagogies that foster the development of deep learning competencies ("Performance Assessment Resource Bank . . .").

BLENDED LEARNING

One after another, studies are beginning to appear that reveal the educational pitfalls of online education with regard to achievement. Although all of us have experienced the benefits of advanced technologies in our classrooms and libraries, discovering that the majority of Ohio's high school students who enrolled in their state's virtual charter schools are approximately a year behind in math and reading than their peers in traditional schools should give us pause.

According to a 2013 study, only 5 percent of students taking one of seventeen Coursera classes offered by the University of Pennsylvania actually finished their classes. Other completion rates for online classes come in at below 13 percent. Completion rates are one important aspect of taking online courses, but passing them is what really counts. Regrettably, studies are showing that passing online courses is even more of a challenge for online students. When Udacity partnered with San Jose State University in California, the overall passage rate across three courses in a sample amounted to 33 percent. Only 25 percent of San Jose State students passed the online remedial algebra course. Overall, the achievement rate also indicates a more dismal online portrait. A Columbia University economist crunched data obtained from more than 40,000 students in thirty-four colleges within Washington State. She found that online students received lower grades and were less persistent than students taking conventional courses (Konnikova).

Blended learning is being offered as a possible solution to the low completion and achievement levels that are frequently being reported with online learning that takes place solely within a digital environment. Just like its title, it attempts to combine the employment of advanced technologies for delivering content combined with face-to-face learning. With the exception of the flipped curriculum, blended learning has been the province of higher education, but the technologies that it employs are becoming more affordable and easier to use, so its eventual arrival in K–12 classrooms is imminent.

Law students at Wake Forest University take a blended learning course in "Professional Responsibility" by watching videos, listening to podcasts, and responding to multiple-choice questions remotely. In class, they sometimes work on problems in groups, participate in course-related discussions, and react to various hypotheticals posed by the professor. For a law school class, the blended learning pedagogy offers professors an opportunity to delve deeper into course material and explore issues that are more challenging to understand (Friedman). The University of Central Florida offers an online Blended Learning Toolkit that features guidelines for developing model blended learning courses, best practices, evaluation resources, and journals featuring the latest blended learning research ("Blended Learning Toolkit"). For K–12 schools desiring to implement blended learning courses, it provides an excellent starting point.

Before embarking on developing blended learning courses at the K–12 level, it's important to apply trend analysis to this fairly new pedagogy. A 2010 meta-analysis of various online learning studies conducted by the Department of Education found that "instruction combining online and face-to-face elements had a larger advantage relative to purely face-to-face instruction than did purely online instruction" (Means et al. xv). Researchers also believed that the data analytics provided by the online part of the course gave instructors the opportunity to target students experiencing difficulties for early intervention and that the face-to-face part of the course enabled more engaging class discussions (Means et al. xv). Please note, however, that these studies have been conducted at the higher education level. As of 2014 a literature review conducted by the Michael & Susan Dell Foundation located only five studies where the blended learning model was employed to teach courses at the K–12 level.

In their 2011–2012 school year blended learning evaluation conducted with thirteen lower-income charter schools, blended learning courses using online instructional programs such as Dreambox and Istation encountered reports from teachers of technical and student attention problems ("Blended Learning Report" 10–15). Because of the technical difficulties experienced with Internet connections and the like, the foundation's researchers were unable to conclude whether students in the control groups versus the blended learning groups experienced higher achievement because of the blended learning pedagogy ("Blended Learning Report" 10–15).

Students enrolled in blended learning classes at the higher education level have two advantages that students lack at the K–12 level. The first benefit concerns the sometimes complex mechanics of providing consistent support for reliable Internet connections and other computer fixes essential to supporting curricula that are engaged with project-based learning, the flipped classroom, student-response systems, and remote Internet access on a daily basis. All of us have experienced the "terror by technology effect" when technology systems are a "go" during the first two class periods and dead in the water for the last two. Always having a Plan B and having to constantly implement it to further daily instruction can be time consuming and discouraging no matter how pedagogically relevant blended learning sounds.

Timely technical support is more readily available for instructors at the higher education level. In most colleges, instructors can request that their classes be taped from a central location and placed on the school's portal. Higher education possesses readily available state-of-the-art facilities replete with taping studios that are equipped with more than one camera and permit student interaction from remote locations. If technical difficulties arise, glitches can be repaired by trained technicians whose sole responsibility is technical support for class taping and does not include responding to multiple technical problems throughout the entire school.

The second advantage is subtler and is the reason for applying trend analysis before investing in funds for equipment and teacher training to initiate blended learning. It pertains to student dispositions. Higher education students are a self-selected response group for blended learning. Unlike students at the K–12 levels who are legally required to attend school, higher education students are enrolled in courses by their own volition. They have also chosen a field of study that already interests them, whereas our student demographic is under the tutelage of a mandatory curriculum with little room for electives until almost the last year of high school. K–12 students are also younger, and their level of concentration, motivation, and eventual understanding that learning is a vital undertaking to their economic survival takes years to develop. Consequently, blended learning may not offer K–12 students the amount of face-to-face time that many students require to remain motivated and concentrated on courses.

COLLABORATIVE LEARNING

Collaborative learning also goes under the name cooperative learning. Most of us can adequately define it without the use of a dictionary by apprehending each word in the term and correctly intuiting that it means students working together in small interactive groups to accomplish various assigned or learning activities in an interdependent fashion ("Cooperative Learning"). Unspoken is a secondary purpose that intends to expose students to different viewpoints and peers with whom they may not have previously interacted. This form of learning has been in existence for a long time, but technology has greatly enhanced its potential effectiveness.

With the availability of wikis, Google Docs, social media, and messaging apps, teachers have the opportunity to structure group projects that no longer require students meeting during free periods or after school to complete assignments. It is a pedagogy that is also related to deep learning activities and can be initiated throughout grade levels and subjects (*NMC Horizon Report 2017 Higher Education Edition* 20).

Research at Cornell's Center for Teaching Innovation confirms that collaborative learning fosters higher-order thinking skills, boosts self-esteem, and improves student leadership skills ("Collaborative Learning Group Work"). More than eighty studies conducted at the University of Minnesota College of Education and Development also concluded that collaboration increases student learning, but it requires correct implementation and attention to the following caveats: (1) assignments must be structured so that students are not only accountable for their own work product but also to other group members for learning; (2) every individual within the group must learn the material; (3) group members must assist one another in learning the material and sharing knowledge; (4) leadership and constant communication need to occur within the group; and (5) the teacher and the group need to assess how well they are collaborating with one another. The instructor is the key to making collaboration work properly and needs to teach collaboration techniques in addition to the class subject matter (Reed 1–6).

A positive example of implementing the five criteria for successful collaborative learning is exemplified at the College Preparatory School (College Prep) in Oakland, California. According to a 2010 *Forbes Magazine* article, College Prep ranks among the twenty best prep schools in the United States, with a 100 percent graduation rate and acceptance to college. Average student SAT scores are in the top tenth percentile in math, critical reading, and writing. More than one-third of their students are enrolled in advanced placement classes, with 95 percent scoring a three or higher each year. Collaborative learning techniques are employed in English and math classes almost throughout the entire class on a daily basis. College Prep follows the five collaborative criteria that research shows are critical to successful implementation (Vega and Youki).

Arranged in groups of four, College Prep math students solve problems involving the same mathematical concepts with worksheets where each student has a different set of numbers to prevent copying. When stumped for solutions, the students have been taught to collaborate to explain and understand the material. More than 1,200 collaborative research studies confirm that this type of cooperative learning increases student retention of the material compared to traditional lecture and diagram methods where students are more passive course material consumers (Vega and Youki). A large meta-analysis performed with K–16 students involved in collaborative learning concluded that groups of three or four worked best and achieved more than students who worked individually (Vega and Youki). Over forty studies conducted with K–12 English students revealed that discussion-based cooperative learning increased comprehension of the text and critical thinking skills, regardless of students' ethnic backgrounds or income levels.

The rigorous research studies conducted about this form of learning and the increases in achievement are so significant that it would seem a pedagogy worthy of adoption and implementation by K–12 schools throughout the country. Higher education institutions are recognizing an increased need for collaboration not only to increase achievement levels while students are taking college classes but also to better prepare them for work environments that are already employing collaborative learning techniques to innovate and maintain their productivity (*NMC Horizon Report 2017 Higher Education Edition* 21). Collaboration is a significant part of an employee's job. It's what businesses do with each other as well as governments. A leading investment bank, for example, requires that a candidate interview with sixty executives before being hired. The company is not looking at test scores or even college transcripts. The reason for multiple interviews is to determine if the interviewee possesses the ability to successfully collaborate with others (Summers 2).

SCHOOL LIBRARIANS AND TRENDING PEDAGOGIES

Although many new pedagogies are being discussed in educational literature, deep learning, blended learning, and collaborative learning seem to have the most potential to improve achievement and increase learning. School librarians can play a critical role with each pedagogy. Deep learning requires immersive reading of factual and fictional material at every grade level. Our print and electronic collections of materials will be essential for students and teachers who will need additional reading material beyond the text to support higher-order thinking skills. Deep learning is also reflected in the Common Core Standards, which school librarians have wholeheartedly adopted and are helping to implement. Assisting teachers with developing new lesson plans that do not require rote memorization but instead employ evidence-based analysis of material will be essential in the coming years.

Blended learning seems to be emerging as an antidote to total online education. However, school librarians will need to urge caution and further research in this area is needed to confirm that blended learning increases student achievement to a greater degree than does face-to-face time. Urging faculty members and administrators to experiment with it over a period of years, with sections of classes rather than an entire grade, will be necessary if we are to avoid falling for another educational -ism that does not improve learning.

When teachers decide to employ blended learning in their classes, our role should be totally supportive. Most of our schools lack the consistent technical support that will be necessary for teachers initiating student-response systems or videotaping their classes. As school librarians, we have been trained in how to employ the latest blended learning technologies. Our teachers should be able to rely upon us for assistance with their appropriate use in their classrooms.

School librarians and teachers have been collaborating for years to teach reading and information literacy skills together. We have designed units that called for group work and over the years have incorporated technologies that have facilitated students to continue to work together after the classes have ended. In the future, some advanced technologies will permit collaboration on school levels so that school librarians may become involved in intervention-like roles where we supply students with supplemental reading materials when they have been identified as needing remedial help or increased academic challenges. Assessment scores used to be the sole domain of teachers, but technology will allow a much more administrative, cooperative approach to each student's education. In the near future, school librarians will probably find themselves attending meetings where teachers, reading specialists, counselors, and administrators collaborate to design improved, more personalized learning experiences for their students.

Questions

1. What instructional programs do librarians need to initiate to improve U.S. literacy scores?
2. What do you think are the implications of increasing income inequality for reading achievement and future employment of students?
3. Is the United States entering a postliterate age that will not require immersive reading skills or deep factual subject knowledge to perform most job-related tasks?
4. Should literacy instruction be more factually based? If so, what is the role of the librarian in implementing more factual-based reading?
5. How can a low literacy rate threaten a nation's democratic institutions?
6. What role can librarians play to boost academic achievement as measured by various standardized assessments?
7. How can librarians assist students taking online courses or enrolled in virtual schools with course-related research and information-seeking skills?
8. What instructional role do you see librarians having with future trending pedagogies, including deep learning, blended learning, and collaborative learning?

REFERENCES

"Adolescent Literacy." May 2016. Alliance of Excellence in Education. Available at: https://all4ed.org/wp-content/uploads/2016/01/FINAL-UPDATED-AEE_AdolescentLiteracy_FactSheet_May-2016.pdf.

Baker, Bruce and Gary Miron. December 2015. "The Business of Charter Schooling: Understanding the Policies That Charter Operators Use for Financial Benefit." National Education Policy Center. Colorado University. Available at: http://nepc.colorado.edu/publication/charter-revenue.

"Billionaires Are Boosting Charter Schools Across America." July 16, 2018. CBS News. Available at: https://www.cbsnews.com/news/billionaires-are-boosting-charter-schools-across-america.

"Blended Learning Report." May 2014. Michael & Susan Dell Foundation. Available at: https://www.edweek.org/media/msdf-blended-learning-report-may-2014.pdf.

"Blended Learning Toolkit." n.d. University of Central Florida. Available at: https://blended.online.ucf.edu.

Bonner, Jessie L. November 3, 2011. "Board Approves Idaho Online Class Requirement." *Boston News*. Available at: http://archive.boston.com/news/nation/articles/2011/11/03/idaho_online_class_requirement_up_for_final_ok.

Breivik, Patricia Senn. May 1991. "A Signal for the Need to Restructure the Learning Process." *NASSP Bulletin*. 75(5): 1–7.

Bulman, George and Robert W. Fairlie. October 2015. *Technology and Education: Computers, Software and the Internet*. Bonn, Germany. IZA Research Network. Available at: http://ftp.iza.org/dp9432.pdf.

Chandler, Michael Alison. March 10, 2015. "Charter Schools Less Likely to Have Libraries." *The Washington Post*. Available at: https://www.washingtonpost.com/local/edu cation/charter-schools-less-likely-to-have-libraries/2015/03/10/5e5e723a-c739.

Clemmitt, Marcia. December 2, 2011. "Digital Education: Can Technology Replace Class-room Teachers?" *CQ Researcher*. 21(42): 1–22.

Clemmitt, Marcia. February 22, 2008. "Reading Crisis?" *CQ Researcher*. 18(8): 1–22.

"Collaborative Learning Group Work." October 18, 2008. Cornell University Center for Teaching Innovation. Available at: https://teaching.cornell.edu/teaching-resources /engaging-students/collaborative-learning.

"Cooperative Learning." 2012–2018. University of Tennessee Chattanooga. Walker Cen-ter for Teaching and Learning. Available at: https://www.utc.edu/walker-center -teaching-learning/teaching-resources/cooperative-learning.php.

Crehan, Lucy. 2017. *Cleverlands: The Secrets Behind the Success of the World's Educa-tion Superpowers*. London, UK: Random House.

"Deep Learning." 2018. William & Flora Hewlett Foundation. Available at: https://www .hewlett.org/strategy/deeper-learning.

Duncan, Greg J. and Richard J. Murnane. 2014. *Restoring Opportunity: The Crisis of Inequality and the Challenge of American Education*. Boston: Harvard Education Press.

Ferguson, Rebecca et al. April 25–29 2016. "6th International Learning and Analytics and Knowledge Conference." Available at: http://oro.open.ac.uk/45312/1/LAK16%20 LACE%20panel%20final.pdf.

Friedman, Jordan. November 7, 2016. "Law Schools Experiment with Partially Online Learning." *U.S. News & World Report*. Available at: https://www.usnews.com /education/best-graduate-schools/top-law-schools/articles/2016-11-07/law-schools -experiment-with-partially-online-learning.

Gill, Bill et al. October 2015. *Inside Online Charter Schools*. Mathematica Policy Research. Available at: https://eric.ed.gov/?id=ED560967.

Hicks, Kristen. May 15, 2015. "2015's Top Education Technology Trends." Available at: http://www.edudemic.com/education-trends-keep-tech-front-center.

Hoover, Eric. October 28, 2015. "Everything You Need to Know about the New SAT." *The New York Times*. Available at: https://www.nytimes.com/2015/11/01/education /edlife/everything-you-need-to-know-about-the-new-sat.html.

Karaim, Reed. March 10, 2017. "Charter Schools." *CQ Researcher*. 27(10): 217–240.

Kennedy, Paul M. 1993. *Preparing for the Twenty-First Century*. New York: Random House.

Konnikova, Maria. November 7, 2014. "Will MOOCs Be Flukes?" *The New Yorker*. Available at: https://www.newyorker.com/science/maria-konnikova/moocs-failure -solutions.

Leu, Donald J. et al. January/February/March 2015. "The New Literacies of Online Research and Comprehension: Rethinking the Reading Achievement Gap." *Reading Research Quarterly*. 50(1): 37–59. Available at: DOI:10.1002/rrq.85.

"Machines Learning." July 22, 2017. *The Economist*. 424(9050): 15–18.

Madda, Mary Jo. October 25, 2016. "Not Just Numbers: How Educators Are Using Data in the Classroom." Available at: https://www.edsurge.com/news/2016-10-25-not-just -numbers-how-educators-are-using-data-in-the-classroom.

McGill, Michael V. Fall 1991. "Humanity and Technology in the School of the Future." *The Bookmark*. 50(3):6–11.

Means, Barbara et al. September 2010. *Evaluation of Evidence-Based Practices in Online Learning: A Meta-Analysis and Review of Online Learning Studies*. U.S. Depart-ment of Education Office of Planning, Evaluation, and Policy Development Policy and Program Studies Service. Available at: https://www2.ed.gov/rschstat/eval/tech /evidence-based-practices/finalreport.pdf.

Murnane, Richard J. and Frank Levy. Spring 1993. "Why Today's High School–Educated Males Earn Less Than Their Fathers Did: The Problem and an Assessment of Responses." *Harvard Educational Review.* 63(1): 1–20.

Naisbitt, John. 1982. *Megatrends: The New Directions Transforming Our Lives.* New York: Warner Books.

"NCES National Center for Education Statistics Fast Facts SAT Scores 1986–2016." 2018. Available at: https://nces.ed.gov/fastfacts/display.asp?id=171.

Neuman, Susan B. November 2016. "Code Red: The Danger of Data-Driven Instruction." *Educational Leadership.* 74(3): 24–29. Available at: http://www.ascd.org/publica tions/educational_leadership/nov16/vol74/num03/Code_Red@_The_Danger_of _Data-Driven_Instruction.aspx.

NMC Horizon Report 2017 Higher Education Edition. 2017. Available at: https://www.nmc .org/publication/nmc-horizon-report-2017-higher-education-edition.

NMC Horizon Report 2017 K-12 Edition. 2017. Available at: https://www.nmc.org /publication/nmccosn-horizon-report-2017-k-12-edition.

Norberg, Johan. 2016. *Progress: Ten Reasons to Look Forward to the Future.* London: Oneworld.

Northern, Amber M. July 1, 2015. "Buckets of Water into the Ocean's Non-Public Reve- nue in Public Charter and Traditional Public Schools." Thomas B. Fordham Insti- tute. Available at: https://edexcellence.net/articles/buckets-of-water-into-the-ocean -non-public-revenue-in-public-charter-and-traditional-public.

"Performance Assessment Resource Bank: Resources for Deeper Learning." 2014. Stan- ford Center for Opportunity Policy in Education. Available at: https://www.perfor manceassessmentresourcebank.org.

Perleman, Lewis J. 1992. *School's Out: Hyperlearning, the New Technology and the End of Education.* New York: William Morrow.

"Programme for International Student Assessment (PISA)." 2000. U.S. Department of Edu- cation National Center for Education Statistics. Available at: https://nces.ed.gov /surveys/pisa/faq.asp.

"Projections of Education Statistics to 2022." February 2014. U.S. Department of Educa- tion National Center for Education Statistics. Available at: https://nces.ed.gov /pubs2014/2014051.pdf.

Putnam, Robert D. 2015. *Our Kids: The American Dream in Crisis.* New York: Simon & Schuster.

Reardon, Sean F. August 28, 2016. "The Good News about Educational Inequality." *The New York Times.* Available at: http://www.nytimes.com/2016/08/28/opinion/sunday /the-good-news-about-educational-inequality.html.

Reed, Zachary A. 2014. "Collaborative Learning in the Classroom." Available at: https:// www.usma.edu/cfe/Literature/Reed_14.pdf.

Reich, Robert B. 1991. *The Work of Nations.* New York: Alfred A. Knopf.

Reinsfelder, Thomas L. and Jill E. Thompson. 2013. "Dual Enrollment Students: Starting the Library Connection." In: *Informed Transitions*, edited by Kenneth J. Burhanna. Santa Barbara, CA: Libraries Unlimited, pp. 183–190.

"Report Confirms Early College High School Students Much More Likely to Earn a College Degree." January 15, 2014. AIR (American Institutes for Research). Available at: http://www.air.org/news/press-release/report-confirms-early-college-high-school -students-much-more-likely-earn-college.

"Research on Dual and Concurrent Enrollment Student Outcomes." n.d. National Alli- ance of Concurrent Enrollment Partnerships. Available at: http://www.nacep.org /research-policy/research-studies.

Ripley, Amanda. December 6, 2016. "What America Can Learn about Smart Schools in Other Countries." *The New York Times.* Available at: http://www.nytimes .com/2016/12/06/upshot/what-america-can-learn-about-smart-schools-in-other -countries.html?_r=0.

"School Choice FAQs What Does the Public Think about School Choice?" 2019. Available at: https://www.edchoice.org/school_choice_faqs/what-does-the-public-think -about-school-choice/.

"Six Years and Counting: The ECHSI Matures." August 2009. Available at: http://www .air.org/sites/default/files/downloads/report/ECHSI_Synthesis_Report_Summary -_Final_0.pdf.

Song, Ji Soo. November 28, 2016. "PISA and Digital Literacy." Alliance for Excellent Education. Available at: https://all4ed.org/pisa-and-digital-literacy.

Sowell, Thomas. 1993. *Inside American Education.* New York: Free Press.

Stier, Debbie. 2014. *The Perfect Score Project: One Mother's Journey to Uncover the Secrets of the SAT.* New York: Harmony.

"Students in Ohio's Online Charter Schools Perform Worse Than Peers in Traditional Schools." February 16, 2017. New York University. Available at: https://www.nyu .edu/about/news-publications/news/2017/february/students-in-ohios-online -charter-schools-perform-worse-than-peer.html.

Summers, Lawrence H. January 20, 2012. "What You (Really) Need to Know." *The New York Times.* Available at: http://www.nytimes.com/2012/01/22/education/edlife/the -21st-century-education.html.

Trip, Gabriel and Matt Richtel. October 8, 2011. "Inflating the Software Report Card." *The New York Times.* Available at: http://www.nytimes.com/2011/10/09/technology/a -classroom-software-boom-but-mixed-results-despite-the-hype.html.

"25 Countries with the Highest Literacy Rates." December 4, 2017. Available at: http:// www.worldatlas.com/articles/the-highest-literacy-rates-in-the-world.html.

Vega, Vanessa and Terada Youki. December 5, 2012. "Research Supports Collaborative Learning." *Edutopia.* Available at: https://www.edutopia.org/stw-collaborative -learning-research.

Walk, Meghan Suzanne et al. 2013. "Libraries and Early College: Notes from the Field." In: *Informed Transitions: Libraries Supporting the High School to College Transition*, edited by Kenneth J. Burhanna. Santa Barbara, CA: Libraries Unlimited, pp. 133–140.

Warkentien, Siri et al. February 2017. "Charting the Progress of Hewlett Foundation's Deeper Learning Strategy 2010–2015." RTI International. Available at: https://www .hewlett.org/wp-content/uploads/2017/04/Deeper-Learning_2017_RTI-.pdf.

Webb, Amy. 2016. *The Signals Are Talking: Why Today's Fringe Is Tomorrow's Mainstream.* New York: Public Affairs.

"What Is Digital Learning?" n.d. Governor's Office of Student Achievement. Available at: https://gosa.georgia.gov/what-digital-learning.

"What the World Can Learn from the Latest PISA Test Results." December 10, 2016. *The Economist.* Available at: https://www.economist.com/news/international/21711247 -reforming-education-slow-and-hard-eminently.

"What Works Clearinghouse." n.d. Available at: https://ies.ed.gov/ncee/wwc.

Willingham, Daniel. November 25, 2017. "How to Get Your Mind to Read." *The New York Times.* Available at: https://www.nytimes.com/2017/11/25/opinion/sunday/how-to -get-your-mind-to-read.html?_r=0.

6

Social and Behavioral Trends

WHAT DO WE CALL THIS GENERATION?

What term do we apply to a generation of students who believe that the Internet has been here forever? When asked for a synonym for the word tablet, they answer iPad rather than pill. If handed a map to drive a sibling to a birthday party, they request only an address because their GPS-enabled device does the navigating for them and they have no need for a map (Seemiller and Corey). The present generation that we are engaging with and serving as librarians doesn't care for labels. They like to think of themselves as individuals with all the uniqueness that the word bestows. There are, however, events, inventions, fads, music, and the like that are indigenous to their generation and that already trigger mutual shared memories and reactions.

For the purpose of studying future social and behavioral trends and their influence on students born between 1995 and the present, social psychologists refer them as Generation Z, Post-Millennials, the Homeland Generation, or iGeneration. The latter term is most appropriate for librarians because it encapsulates all the technological applications that we observe our students using and perhaps abusing on a regular basis (Bromwich). Many of our students will not necessarily mirror the current research studies reporting the iGeneration's lack of confidence, need for political independence, positive relationships with parents, and decreasing use of alcohol. However, survey data involving millions of them provide us with sufficiently large numbers of respondents to support many social and behavioral conclusions about them. Although labeling can infer stereotyping, it is essential to study a generation's behavioral and social characteristics so that we can adapt, strengthen, and change our library programs and services to meet their changing needs.

WHAT DOES THE "I" STAND FOR?

Jean Twenge, in her excellent book *iGen*, employs the letter "i" to represent ten characteristics that help define the current generation with whom we are currently and will be working. The first, "*in no hurry*," reflects the prolonging of childhood, while the word "*Internet*" expresses the inordinate amount of time they spend on the Web. "*In person no more*" acknowledges the lack of face-to-face time spent with peers, and "*Insecure*" notes the increasing rates of mental health issues that members of the iGeneration are exhibiting. "*Irreligious*" observes their declining spirituality and interest in organized religions, whereas, "*Insulated but not intrinsic*" stands for their worries about physical and emotional safety and lack of community involvement. "*Income insecurity*" reports their changing views toward employment, and "*Indefinite*" indicates a growing acceptance of differences regarding gender identities and sexual orientation. Finally, "*Inclusive*" shows the iGeneration's awareness of the need for inclusivity and equality concerning various constitutional amendment issues (Twenge 2017, 3).

Many of these characteristics are ones that we are currently observing or will react to with our future students as they make their way through the American school system. iGeneration students, unlike previous generations, do not seem in a rush to grow up and are content to have a parent drive and accompany them to a mall or the movies (Twenge 2017, 73–74). Nickelodeon's survey of 900 children ages eight to fourteen revealed that 85 percent of them agreed with the statement "I like my age" (Alpert). The Internet is consuming more of their time, and smartphone use has completely saturated their lives. Ninety-five percent of teens report that they either own a smartphone or have access to one, and 45 percent state that they use them on a "near-constant" basis (Anderson and Jiang 2).

As Sherry Turkle, in her ground-breaking book *Alone Together*, notes, children and teens are increasingly isolated from one another in a conventional sense and are spending their time communicating solely through social media (Turkle xi–xvi). As more of their time is devoted to this pastime, the iGeneration is also exhibiting a significant uptick in issues involving their mental health. The number of children ages five to seventeen visiting children's hospitals for suicidal thoughts or attempts was twice as high in 2015 than in 2008. Half of the visits occurred among fifteen- to seventeen-year olds, 37 percent with twelve- to fourteen-year olds, and 13 percent with five- to eleven-year-olds (Haelle). Unfortunately, this development has coincided with the introduction and increasing use of smartphones by children within these age ranges.

Social psychologists are also noticing a concern with physical and emotional safety among members of the iGeneration. They seem afraid of engaging in the risky type of behavior such as driving and drinking that previous generations ritualistically did in the previous century. The accident and ticket issuance rates for teens are down dramatically, with only 20 percent getting into a car driven by someone who was drinking as compared to 40 percent in 1991. They are also more peaceable and avoid physical fights with one another more. In 1991 50 percent of ninth graders had physically fought with a peer, but by 2015, only 25 percent had gotten into a fight. Emotional risks are also being avoided. Students of this generation don't like disagreements and are wary of vigorous debates concerning issues where they may be on the opposing side (Twenge 2017, 147–154).

Despite schools requiring a specified number of hours of in-school and after-school community service, the iGeneration seems disinterested in the plight of others. They tend to take a more standoffish approach to caring about others by agreeing with survey statements such as "It's not really my problem if others are in trouble and need help." Their measure of willingness to contribute or make actual donations to charities plummeted to the lowest level in 2015 (Twenge 2017, 173–174). Perhaps their lack of empathy and charity toward others is influenced by their income insecurity. The present iGeneration seems aware of future employment trends and the insecurity that it may bring to their future prospects. They feel the pressure to obtain a college degree and that it is linked to maintaining a standard of living that they are accustomed to. Their income insecurity seems to arise from the bind of paying for higher education at a time when the tuition and fees have soared, forcing them to assume significant debt. Possibly, as a result, more of them are searching for occupations and jobs that offer stable and remunerative work with an opportunity of paying off their loans rather than something that they feel passionate about doing (Twenge 2017, 186–187).

What has changed for the better seems to be the iGeneration's attitudes toward sex and relationships. This area is somewhat intertwined with the iGeneration's concern with physical and emotional safety and their reduced face-to-face time with each other. For years, school officials were concerned with adolescent pregnancy and its severe educational and economic consequences for all involved, but their fears may be alleviated in the future. While members of the iGeneration express more tolerance for their peers having sex outside of marriage, regardless of race and ethnicity, they are actually engaging in less of it. Data from the 2015 Youth Risk Behavior Surveillance survey reported that 59 percent of all ninth to twelfth graders had not yet had sex. From 1991 to 2015, the percentage of students who had engaged in sexual intercourse decreased from 54 percent to 41 percent ("Statistics: Sexual Activity").

Relationships with the iGeneration are more fraught, perhaps because they suffer from income insecurity and a greater need for emotional and physical safety compared to members of previous generations. While the boomer generation ranked "having a good marriage and family life" higher than any other life goal, iGeneration high school seniors in 2015 ranked it fourth, indicating that finding stable work, becoming successful at it, and "giving my children better opportunities than I had" were more important goals (Twenge 2017, 219).

THE INCLUSIVITY CONUNDRUM

Inclusivity is a wonderful word, and in some ways members of the iGeneration embrace it, but in other ways they are ambivalent about it. Members of the LGBT community still suffer a disproportionate share of violence in the form of physical assaults and cyber and school-grounds bullying than do straight students. Evidence shows, however, that their acceptance by their iGeneration peers improves with the existence of a supportive school community, including the presence of LGBT support groups such as gay–straight alliances and affinity groups ("Lesbian, Gay, Bisexual, and Transgender Health").

In another area of inclusivity, race, the findings are also problematic. In 1966 *Newsweek* dedicated an entire issue to survey results from 775 male and female teenagers ages thirteen to seventeen years old living across the United States concerning their opinions about race. In 1966 44 percent of them predicted that racial discrimination would be a generational concern. When *Newsweek* writers posed the identical question in 2015 to 2,057 adolescents, a whopping 91 percent of them predicted a similar problem (Jones). While a Pew Research Center poll reported that 60 percent of white respondents ages eighteen to thirty supported the Black Lives Matter movement, a survey reported in Monitoring the Future, 1976–2015 reveals that only 25 percent of surveyed twelfth graders believe that diverse environments "in which some people are of another race—are desirable" (Twenge 2017, 244).

Because the iGeneration seems especially tuned to emotional and physical safety issues, their understanding and interpretation of free speech as defined by the First Amendment is undergoing a generational change. In pursuit of a sincere goal of eliminating offensive language from public discourse, members of the iGeneration are more likely to support free speech restrictions than do previous generations (Twenge 2017, 250). A supporting Pew Research Center poll reported that 40 percent of millennial and iGeneration participants ages eighteen to thirty-four were in favor of preventing people "from making offensive statements about minority groups" compared to 12 percent of the Silent generation, 24 percent of the boomers, and 27 percent of GenX'ers (Poushter). iGeneration students seem to be struggling between preventing the proliferation of offensive language directed at any group and the deleterious effects of censorship and its harmful effects to a democratic society (Gillman and Cherminsky).

IGENERATION DEMOGRAPHICS

We are either presently or going to be teaching 74 million iGeneration students. That number represents about 24 percent of the entire population and is equal to about 25 percent of all Americans (Twenge 2017, 10). Approximately 50 million students are presently enrolled in K–12 public schools, and the majority, for the first time in American history, are children of color (Friedman 448). Twenty-five percent are Hispanic and 5 percent are termed multiethnic. Fifty-three percent are non-Hispanic whites (Twenge 2017, 11–12). While no group is currently dominant, demographers predict a change. Census data from 2010 indicate that students of mixed race increased by 46 percent, which was faster than any other group within the past decade. Hispanic children increased by 39 percent and Asian and Pacific Islanders by 31 percent. Washington, D.C., and ten other states have school populations where non-Hispanic white children are less than 50 percent. Almost 75 percent of the student population of America's one hundred largest cities are composed of nonwhite children (Flowers 6).

Members of the iGeneration are not living in conditions of parity. As growing economic inequality slowly reduces parents' ability to provide for their children's basic needs, including food and housing, students of this generation relied on free and reduced lunch programs in record numbers in 2016 (Friedman 448). Many of them, especially children of color, are living in neighborhoods of concentrated poverty. These are areas where more than 40 percent of Americans subsist on an income below the federal government poverty level, which totals $25,100 for a family of four. Almost 14 million of our citizens, including children, live in these areas compared to 7 million in 2000 ("Coming Apart"). Race and ethnicity are decisive elements of this demographic portrait. Twenty-five percent of poor blacks, 17 percent of poor Hispanics, and 8 percent of poor whites reside in neighborhoods of concentrated poverty. iGeneration students living in these areas must cope with a myriad of life-threatening problems, including higher crime rates, and schools that do not foster learning or a sense of hope ("Coming Apart").

Segregation by residence is one of the largest impediments to poorer members of the iGeneration. Americans are continuing to group together by income and education, with the wealthiest top 10 percent living in affluent areas where the schools are better. Their ability to afford housing in these areas is afforded them by income. In 2016 the Pew Research Center reported that the net worth of black households, characterized by someone with at least a bachelor's degree, totaled $26,300 in 2013. White households of the same definition showed a net worth of $301,300, which was eleven times greater than black households ("Demographic Trends and Economic Well-Being"). The numbers speak to the opportunity to live in safer areas where schools have better-performing students and there is an emphasis on achievement rather than simply survival.

SCHOOL LIBRARIANS AND OUR ROLE WITH THE IGENERATION

Our school libraries' geographic locations will somewhat determine our role with members of the iGeneration. Although they will all share some generational characteristics, many will have needs and interests that are based on their positions on the economic, racial, and ethnic ladders of society. Their increased desire and angst for emotional and physical safety can be addressed in any school library by making sure that we continue to provide a welcoming, comfortable, and safe environment for them to study and learn. The Internet will be a challenge for them as they are truly living in an age of distraction. School librarians are especially suited for assisting them with time management and organizational problems that are the natural results of time ill spent on the Web. Providing online quizzes about how they are spending their time can be revealing and helpful for them. Introducing planners to help them keep track of assignment deadlines and other activities is an essential role that we can play.

Even though the presence of the Internet characterizes their generation, it does not have to dominate. Fortunately, students and parents are developing a growing awareness of its positive and negative aspects. Disseminating the differences in gender, race, and ethnic use of the Internet to administrators and faculty is our responsibility. Approximately 5 percent of children ages five to twenty have a learning disability. Our user group for disseminating digital media study results should be wider in the future to include parents, many of whom have been ignorant, slow, or reluctant to monitor screen time with their children. Elementary school librarians especially need to make parents aware of the dangers of too much screen time and their link to attention and learning deficits.

We also have to be alert to growing income insecurity among our students even if we are employed in an area where salary and employment levels are high. Twenty-two percent of our children live in families with incomes below the poverty level. The number of unemployed young adults ages sixteen to twenty-four is at a record high of 22.7 percent. Even with these dismal data, approximately 3 million teens drop out of school each year. Although it may be temporary, more than 1.3 million children and adolescents are homeless each year (Flowers 7). Chances are that some members of this demographic will be attending our schools and require assistance from social services and other supportive agencies. Our role in helping to identify them and put them in touch with assistance is crucial.

Members of the iGeneration tend to insulate themselves not only from each other, but by default, the world. What better place to open their minds and hearts to new friends and places than through our carefully curated collections of online and print materials? We need to devise innovative ways to engage them with reading and learning, including creating book trailers, giving book talks, reading aloud to them, telling stories, presenting puppet shows, and initiating captivating reading contests.

Encouraging inclusivity in the purest sense of the term is a necessity if we are to continue to reap the benefits of a democratic society. While sensitivity regarding offensive language should be uppermost, the rights that are bestowed on all Americans pertaining to free speech cannot be restricted because students do not agree with the content, message, or viewpoint. School librarians at all levels are perfectly situated to lead the charge in this area. Consider teaming up with American government teachers to host debates in the library about pro and con issues. Sponsor the debate team and help them research different sides of an argument. Show films and videos that feature First Amendment issues followed by discussions. Broaden students' concept of inclusivity by planning exhibits and book displays showing that the United States was not and still is not inclusive for all Americans.

Our library communities are unique, and not every student will present with some or all of the characteristics of the iGeneration. The majority of them, however, will conform to some of the qualities attributed to them by various surveys, and this information will be invaluable in formulating new programs and services for them.

IGENERATION AND THE WEB

In the book *The Attention Merchants,* by Tim Wu, he observes that "[t]echnology does not follow culture so much as culture follows technology" (Wu 303). This statement seems especially true for members of the iGeneration, for it is their cultural and behavioral relationship with the Internet that distinguishes them from previous generations. Members of this generation know it as a true constant in their lives. It is less a tool in their lives than "a way of life of thinking, appearing and preferring" (Fairfield 105). The Internet is not only defining their generation, it is influencing it in ways that we as educators and librarians have not even fathomed.

The iGeneration's access to the Internet is almost ubiquitous. Some 95 percent of adolescents report either having a smartphone or having access to one, and

88 percent of them have access to a laptop/desktop computer at home. Again, the classic divisions caused by inequality start to emerge when it comes to multiple device ownership. Ninety-six percent of teens with household incomes of $75,000 or more per year report having access to home computers, whereas only 75 percent from households making less than $30,000 per year do. Access also varies by education levels, with 94 percent of teens with a parent with an undergraduate degree or more reporting home computer access versus 78 percent for teens whose parents have graduated high school (Anderson and Jiang 8).

HOW MUCH TIME ARE THEY SPENDING ON IT?

As most of us know from observing student behavior with smartphones and computers, it is their usage of these devices that intrigues and concerns us. Questions naturally arise about how much time they are spending on screen activities and what effect it will have on their ability to learn now and in the future. Starting with the youngest members of this generation, preschoolers spend more than four hours per day watching a screen. The average age onset of habitual screen viewing has declined since 1970 from four years to four months old (Christakis 12). By grade eight, students are devoting 1.5 hours to texting, 1.5 hours to gaming, and approximately 30 minutes to video chatting. In their senior year, screen time increases to 2.25 hours of texting, 1.5 hours of gaming, and 1.5 hours of video chatting. These hours are for new media and do not count an additional 2 hours per day for TV viewing. If 17 hours per day are allotted for time spent in school, sleeping, doing homework, and extracurricular activities, any cogent reader would discern a total of over 24 hours. What is not factored into the total, however, is the amount of multitasking occurring with students sending texts while watching TV, trawling the Web while posting to Snapchat, and talking on the phone while completing homework. What is most alarming about this sum, however, is that when 17 hours spent in school are removed from the total, the remainder of iGeneration's leisure time is devoted totally to screen activities (Twenge 2017, 51). About one-third of a student's life is spent sleeping, another third at school, and a third captivated by new media (Alter 237).

ARE THERE DIFFERENCES IN USAGE AMONG STUDENTS?

Screen activities are entrancing girls more than boys. Fifty percent of teenage girls report "near-constant online use" in comparison to 39 percent of boys. Usage rates are different for minority children as well. They watch 50 percent more television than white children and are on computers 1.5 hours longer per day than their white peers. White children devote more than 8 hours to screen activities per day, and black and Hispanic children spend 13 hours (Riley). Unfortunately, researchers already know that there is an educational price to pay for excessive screen viewing. Research studies as early as 2004 report a link between TV viewing and attentional problems, finding that one standard deviation in the hours watching TV at age one was related to a 28 percent increase in the chance of having attentional problems by the age of seven. Each additional hour upped a child's chances for attention problems by 10 percent. By 2010 doctors were confirming the findings, noting that exposure to TV and video games was related to increased attention problems in students. A study conducted at Penn State and University of California, respectively, confirmed that black children are more likely to exhibit symptoms of attention deficit disorder than their white counterparts (Riley).

Even when students use the Internet for similar amounts of time, there are class/income differences. Students from upper-class backgrounds are more likely to employ the Internet for jobs, education-related activities, health, and news items and less for entertainment and recreation. Putnam, in his excellent book, *Our Kids,* reports that upper-class students are utilizing the Internet in "mobility-enhancing" ways, whereas poorer, less educated students are not using it in ways that will further their educations (Putnam 212). When upper-class students search for assignment-related information, they also are either taught or develop stronger digital literacy skills that include the ability to efficiently locate relevant information and evaluate sources for creditability (Putnam 212).

WHAT ARE THEY ON ALL THE TIME?

Platform preference is evolving for the types of new media that students prefer to communicate with, and differences exist among genders, income, races, and ethnicities. Students ages thirteen to seventeen report preferring YouTube, Instagram, and Snapchat to Facebook. Only 51 percent of them report using Facebook now. Seventy percent of teens residing in families earning less than $30,000 per year still prefer Facebook compared to 36 percent of teens whose families earn $75,000 or more. Forty-two percent of girls prefer Snapchat to 29 percent of boys. Boys are more likely to use YouTube as their preferred platform, 39 percent versus 25 percent. Forty-one percent of white teens compared to 29 percent of Hispanic teens and 23 percent of black teens elect Snapchat as their preferred online platform (Anderson and Jiang 4).

WHAT'S THE ALLURE OF NEW MEDIA, AND SHOULD WE BE CONCERNED?

What do our students see in the new media? Why do they seem so captivated by it that many take their smartphones to bed with them just in case someone sends them a text or a picture? Hanson, in her book, *The Social Media Revolution,* sees social media as a means to "friend others, follow others, text others, and connect to others" (Hanson 320). When this can be accomplished at lightning speed from anywhere and at any time, it can have an almost hypnotic effect on teenagers who are in the classic developmental stage of wanting to belong to a group, form friendships, and separate from authority figures including parents and teachers. Hanson believes that social networks are in their adolescence just as so many of our students are and will need to mature (Hanson 328).

In the meantime, our students remain in the throes of it at the expense of so many other choices where they could devote their precious time. Are they and their parents becoming aware of the siren call of social media and its threat to their attention spans and the need to study, learn, and achieve? An epiphany appears to be slowly occurring between parents and students about the dangers of social media. According to the latest Pew Research survey taken of 743 students, ages thirteen to seventeen, more than half of them are concerned that they are spending too much time on their smartphones. Seventy-two percent of them report checking for messages as soon as they awake, while 40 percent report feeling anxious without access to their cell phones. Fifty-six percent of them experience anxiety, loneliness, and upset without the presence of their phones. More than 90 percent view excessive screen time as a problem facing their generation, and 60 percent see it as a major problem. Eight percent of them report losing focus in school because of their cell phones.

Fortunately, their parents share their concerns. More than 66 percent of parents believe that their children are spending too much time on their cell phone, but only one-third worry a great deal about it. Fifty-seven percent are setting some type of screen restrictions regarding when and for how long their children can go online or use a cell phone. What is welcoming about this response is that it crosses income levels and demographics regarding gender, race, and ethnicity (Jiang).

SCHOOL LIBRARIANS AND SCREEN TIME

As school librarians we face one of the most significant challenges to instruct the generation who we are entrusted to educate concerning the positive and negative aspects of new media. Social networks possess capital, and many benefits accrue to them. They help us learn from each other and are essential for civic and political involvement. Their ability to enable us to feel connected to others is also a vital facet. Our students can experience a sense of community within them when they may be feeling isolated because of gender, sexual orientation, disabilities, or other issues. They can establish the means to participate in a cause greater than ourselves, such as raising awareness of gun violence in schools or victims of a natural disaster. Most importantly, they may offer students a broader sense of identity, aiding students in moving from their individualism to a "we mentality" (Hanson 325).

On the other hand, Nicholas Carr, author of *The Glass Cage,* believes that Google, Facebook, and creators of new media "are demeaning and diminishing qualities of character that in least in the past, have been seen as essential to a full and vigorous life: ingenuity, curiosity, independence, perseverance, and daring" (Carr 182). School librarians will need to bridge the pros and cons of social media, especially since it seems in the process of maturing. Sounding the alarm about its potential for misuse is our responsibility, particularly in neighborhoods where parents may be unaware of the link between screen time and attention disorders. Distributing sustainable media use guidelines to the entire school population, including parents, will be necessary.

Encourage students who may be unwittingly wedded to Facebook to consider other platforms like Snapchat and Instagram. Social media platforms that feature short and individual posts rather than group messaging protect users from spending time curating their images, running the risk of viral dissemination and worrying about the number of "likes." Snapchat and Instagram are also semi-permanent types of social media and lessen the chances of students' media missteps following them forever in cyberspace (Twenge 2017, 295).

Jana Partners is a shareholder in Apple. In January 2018 they sent a letter to the company warning that its products "may be having unintentional consequences (Herman). The companies that have manufactured social media apps are slowly becoming aware of their addictive qualities. Some have designed apps and options on their devices that cede parental control when selected. School librarians need to provide information to all concerned about apps such as Freedom, In Moment, Space, App Detox, Off the Grid, and Antisocial as possible solutions to restricting students' screen time ("Limit Your Screen Time . . .").

DISTRACTION AND MULTITASKING WITH THE IGENERATION

Distraction and multitasking are inextricably linked. The screen devices that students are constantly attuned to seem to be shrinking their attention spans. Listening to music, drinking coffee, texting a friend, and finishing homework almost simultaneously are as natural to them as breathing. But it seems to be resulting in a subsequent inability for students to focus on one particular assignment or project and immerse themselves in it. Their devices constantly distract them and encourage multitasking. Prado, in his book, *Social Media and Your Brain*, believes that our students are experiencing an "akratic attention" problem. Their devices have become so addictive that they lack the self-control to cease multitasking (Bermudez 66).

Distraction research is confirming our observations of this new behavioral trend. One study conducted with mothers of two-year-olds instructed them to teach their children two new words and then deliberately interrupted them with a phone call. The interruption alone was sufficient to prevent the children from learning the new words, while those in the control group succeeded in learning their new words (Christakis 13). Researchers studying college students multitasking activities used screen capture software that let them discern what application or task students were paying attention to every five seconds. The median length of remaining on one screen was only nineteen seconds (Yeykelis, Cummings, and Reeves 167–180). A related study of office workers found that the average office email goes unread for only ten seconds. Seventy percent of emails are read within six seconds. While this response speed sounds gratifyingly responsive to a potential client, it results in a twenty-five-minute recovery time for the responder to become re-immersed in their interrupted activity ("Paying No Mind").

This constant attention to our screen devices appears to be having an effect on our students' attention spans and self-control. In 2000 Microsoft Canada announced that the average human attention span was twelve seconds. In 2013 the number had dropped to eight seconds (Alter 28). Multitasking is also affecting the ability of our students to learn and retain information. One study used a simulated classroom to study the effects of laptop use in the classroom. All the students who multitasked during the lecture scored significantly lower than the control group did on the subsequent test. Unfortunately, even those who were seated near a multitasker suffered from lower test scores compared to those who were seated without a view of them (Sana 24).

The question that arises from these studies concerns our students' capacities for self-control and what screen activities seem to be doing to erode it. Studies with children show that self-control and the ability to delay gratification offer long-term educational and economic rewards. The famous marshmallow delayed gratification experiment that placed children in a room with no distractions for fifteen minutes and told them to resist consuming them showed that the self-control that some of the children exhibited correlated with their ability to focus their attention elsewhere. Those who did not partake of the marshmallows were found to possess "higher academic scores, more stable emotional lives, richer relationships, and lower Body Mass Indexes" (Bermudez 58).

SCHOOL LIBRARIANS AND DISTRACTION AND MULTITASKING BEHAVIORAL TRENDS

All school librarians probably correctly identify distraction and multitasking among our students as a trend rather than a fad and must rightly be concerned for students' future success in higher education and occupations requiring their consistent attention. Questions naturally arise about how the increased use of digital media will affect the use of legacy media, which consists of print books, magazines, newspapers, TV, and movies. Twenge and her fellow researchers conducted a rigorous trend analysis study of 1,021,029 U.S. eighth, tenth, and twelfth graders' media use from 1976 to 2016. Lamentably, their results indicate that students substantially prefer digital media to legacy media. Sixty percent of twelfth graders reported reading a book in the late seventies versus 16 percent by 2016. The number of seniors who reported not reading any books for pleasure decreased to one out of three by 2016. Declines for tenth graders are similarly disappointing. In the early 1990s 33 percent of tenth graders said they read newspapers every day. By 2016 only 2 percent did. Eighth graders' data are only reported for TV viewing, revealing that they are watching one hour less of television than they did in the early 1990s (Twenge 2018, 1–24).

For the past few years there have been two schools of thought regarding legacy media. The first group of researchers, from the complementary one, hypothesized that the same amount or more of legacy media would be consumed as digital media use increased. The second version, termed displacement, hypothesized that preference for digital media would increase over time, thus eclipsing use of legacy media altogether (Twenge 2018, 3). When the Pew Research Center surveyed students of similar ages in 2014, the results were surprisingly more promising because books assigned for school projects were counted in the survey and it looked as if students were actually reading less than in previous years but not drastically. In Twenge's study, the survey did not count school-assigned reading, and the results revealed a serious displacement pattern for legacy media of all types (Twenge 2018, 14).

The most alarming aspect of this significant trend study is that use of digital media is increasing even at the expense of homework. Eighth graders are spending two weeks less on homework per week than they did in the early 1990s (Twenge 2017, 61). Time is a finite commodity in a competitive information economy, and with every daily given set of hours, choices need to be made regarding their expenditure. This study indicates that for many students, digital media, with all of its addictive qualities, is well on its way toward displacing legacy media.

Given the huge inroads that digital media have made in our students' lives and the shortening of their attention spans with accompanying multitasking, what should we expect our roles to be in assisting them in an increasingly competitive society? Trends show that remunerative employment for the poorly educated will be hard to come by, and many will also be working in positions where they are even educationally overqualified. It goes without saying that all types of reading will be required in many occupations and professions even in the near future. We are going to have to educate our students to become smarter digital media users. Agosto consulted with ninety-eight active digital media–friendly high school students who suggested a set of guidelines to assist them in becoming smarter users.

Some of the recommendations where librarians can play a role include developing strong adult–teen relationships where students are open to learning about the latest research concerning multitasking or distraction, and inviting students to live demonstrations that incorporate information about sustainable use of digital media such as at "lunch 'n learn" events (Agosto and Abbas 46–47). In a 2015 survey of 2,600 tweens and teens conducted by Common Sense Consensus Media, only 3 percent of them indicate that they spend time on content creation. As librarians, educators, and physicians begin to develop sustainable technology use guidelines, inculcating using digital media to create with our students should be considered. Rechanneling students' constant viewing of digital media by teaching them how to become creators of their own videos, images, and artwork provides an opportunity to employ digital media to communicate with classmates over assignments, collaborate online to complete assigned group projects, and connect them to others who may be espousing worthy causes and concerns. It may help them re-evaluate how they can use various forms of social media such as Twitter, Snapchat, and Facebook for more educational purposes (Dodds 13–16).

HOW ARE OUR STUDENTS FARING EMOTIONALLY AND PSYCHOLOGICALLY?

Causation is a term that can only be used when researchers find evidence that a change in something is the direct result of a second event or occurrence. A house that is blown off its foundations by a confirmed tornado is an example of causation. The relationship between the destroyed house and the tornado is causal. On the other hand, correlation is a statistical measure that provides a description of the size and direction between two or more occurrences or events. It indicates but does not prove, for example, that there may be a direct relationship between voluntary reading and higher scores on reading achievement tests ("Correlation and Causation").

Social psychologists who study the emotional and psychological well-being of our students are starting to report strong correlations between the iGeneration's use of the Web and increased reports of loneliness, an inability to be empathetic toward others, feeling depressed, and attempting to take or taking their own lives. While no causation has been established by their studies, their research results definitely bear reading and monitoring for future social and behavioral trends.

EMPATHY SEEMS TO BE ON THE DECLINE

Empathy is having the psychological ability to place oneself in another's shoes and imagine and try to understand what they are experiencing ("All about Empathy"). It is linked to employment in occupations and professions that may in the future not be affected by technology as much and will require the ability to persuade, motivate, inform, and inspire other human beings (Colvin 140). A meta-analysis of seventy-two studies concerning empathy finds that it has declined significantly among college students from 1979 to 2009. Researchers reported that students exhibited less ability to assume the perspective of the other person and demonstrated less concern for other people (Konrath, O'Brien, and Hsing 180). Twenge, in her correlational research work, is reporting similar findings that indicate continuing declining empathy among members of the iGeneration. More of them agree or on the fence with statements such as "It's not really my problem if others are in trouble and need help" and "Maybe some minority groups do get unfair treatment, but that's no business of mine" (Twenge 2017, 174).

What seems to be the connection between the decline of empathy among our population demographic? Is the decline of empathy related to increased digital media use among our students? Social psychologists are hypothesizing that the more time our students devote to digital media activities, the less likely that they are to apprise community involvement. Students termed heavy users of social media are 45 percent more likely to value material possessions such as new cars and second homes and are 14 percent less likely to ponder national and international issues (Twenge 2017, 176). Other researchers have published studies that found that distance and even proximity affect communication. Communication between two people seems to decline in proportion to the physical distance between them. Human beings require a physical closeness to one another to communicate optimally. It is this type of closer communication that researchers believe is also associated with the ability to build empathy (Colvin 174–175).

Our students' increasing predilection for communicating via digital media rather than in person precludes all the messages that are perceived through verbal and nonverbal expression, including tone of voice, facial expressions, and other body language (Prado 106). Reading each other's nonverbal expressions helps develop empathy skills. In 2012 fifty-one children attending a summer camp, with no access to any form of electronic communication, took pre- and post- nonverbal reading tests. At the close of the camp, their error rate on the nonverbal reading test declined by 33 percent (Alter 238–239).

Empathy is going to become a highly valued skill in a time of change because our students are going to be trying to obtain remunerative employment in a world where they will be competing against robots who will be able to execute many of their basic job functions. In the future, schools may be teaching empathy as an essential employment-related skill. One successful program titled, *Roots of*

Empathy, for kindergartners through eighth graders introduces a local infant into the classroom periodically. The lessons are designed to see if students can determine what the baby is feeling, what it needs, and how it is changing throughout the year. Research results with the program find that it builds empathy, decreases aggression, and increases socialization that includes sharing and helping others. The benefits seem to be lasting for years (Colvin 83–84).

LONELINESS AND UNHAPPINESS ARE INCREASING

It's hard to fathom our students feeling lonely and being unhappy when they are supposed to be having the time of their lives. The overwhelming majority do not suffer from health problems at their age and can look forward statistically to long lifespans. They are physically together with hundreds of their peers who share many of their interests and have the electronic means to communicate with them in a nanosecond. Yet studies are painting a different portrait of them. More of them are reporting being lonely and feeling left out, socially isolated, and unhappy.

In yearly surveys conducted by Monitoring the Future with 1.1 million eighth, tenth, and twelfth graders from 1991 to 2106 concerning their psychological well-being, the results are dramatic in their findings. Students were asked to rate their feelings regarding self-esteem, life satisfaction, and happiness. They were also queried about the amount of time they spent emailing, instant messaging, gaming, shopping, searching, downloading music, and other web activities. The last set of questions concerned the time that they devoted to in-person activities, including personal social interaction, attending parties, hanging out with friends, shopping, and dating. Within the span of survey years, 2012 is pivotal. It is the year when psychological well-being declined significantly for all three grades. The year corresponds to an increase in the amount of time students reported spending online versus a decrease in time spent in personal interaction activities as previously described (Twenge 2018, 765–780). It is also the beginning of the period in 2015 when teens' access to smartphones surged from 37 percent to 73 percent (Lenhart).

One of the most important findings to emerge is that students who devoted more time to offline activities that involved not only face-to-face interaction but also reading, doing homework, and playing sports reported higher psychological well-being. With the eighth and tenth graders, every single offline activity correlated with greater happiness and every onscreen activity with less happiness (Twenge 2017, 72).

As psychologists try to puzzle out some of the possible causes behind our students' declining sense of psychological well-being, one possible cause is being reported more frequently than others. Documented by Sherry Turkle in her excellent book, *Alone Together*, its text-speak letters are FOMO, which translates as Fear of Missing Out (Turkle 255–256). In previous decades it was referred to as "Keeping Up with the Jones." Basically, it's a new term for *electronically* keeping up with the Jones. For students within our instructional demographic, FOMO is taking on some critical dimensions. The term incorporates some of the seven deadly sins in many of our students' psyches, and the result appears to be increased loneliness and decreased feeling of happiness in them. A Facebook study conducted in 2014 with 736 college students was one of the first to show how the ability to remain in constant touch with one another by posting status updates, links, photos, responding to news and images with likes, and so forth represents an omnipresent form of peer surveillance. It seemed to engender in many of the participants feelings of envy and jealousy. Researchers concluded that for heavy users, viewing others' social information created competitive feelings because of the comparisons they made with their own social lives (Tandoc, Ferruci, and Duffy 139–146).

ARE MORE OF OUR STUDENTS SUFFERING FROM DEPRESSION?

The envy that heavy Facebook users in the study experienced was also linked to a more serious mental health condition, that of depression. More than one study has linked social media use to depression, and unfortunately it is not just among college students. Of all the age groups using digital media, children and adolescents may be the most vulnerable to its siren call because they are experiencing more physical, psychological, and social changes than other age groups. During the tween and teen years students begin to value their peer group, and its opinions of their status are life-affirming. They connect their physical appearance to their self-worth and are extremely vulnerable to criticism. Filled with self-doubt about how they look and feel, many are compelled to present themselves in the best possible light on social media sites at the expense of their psychological well-being and mental health (Salomon and Brown).

A 2018 study of 142 seventh graders, controlled for diversity, examined how the frequency of overall social media use was related to posting selfies and also placing some students at risk for body shaming and increased body surveillance. Again, students who reported using social media four or more hours per week posted more selfies, requested more peer ratings of them, and had higher levels of body surveillance than did the group that spent less time. Body surveillance presaged body shaming, and the high social media use group reported feeling worse about their appearance. High social media use girls were seen to be more susceptible to social pressure and vulnerable to its effects than were high social media use boys (Salomon and Brown).

As students exchange the hours that they used to spend playing with toys and others for uploading pictures of themselves, counting their likes on Facebook, and posting videos, psychologists are reporting much higher incidences of depression among them. Family income, race, and ethnicity are no barriers to this alarming trend. Yearly the National Survey on Drug Use and Health (NSDUH) employs a representatively diverse sample and trained interviewers to query more than 17,000 students, ages twelve to seventeen, for major depressive symptoms. Utilizing the *Diagnostic and Statistical Manual* (DSM) of the American Psychiatric Association, students are asked if they have experienced "depressed mood, insomnia, fatigue, or markedly diminished pleasure in life for at least two weeks (Twenge 2017, 108). The results were nothing short of astonishing. In 2015 56 percent more teens experienced a major depressive episode compared to teens in 2010. Sixty percent more of them suffered from severe impairment. More students are not just exhibiting symptoms of depression and anxiety, they are being medically diagnosed with major depression. More than one in nine teens are experiencing major depression. Clinically diagnosed depression is gender-balanced. The increase is higher in girls, which fits with their overuse of social media, when compared to boys. In 2015 one in five adolescent girls suffered a major depressive episode (Twenge 2017, 108).

A diagnosis of depression by a psychologist or psychiatrist is cause for serious concern not only for students' parents but also for all the school personnel who are charged with their care, especially during school hours. Depression, while not causative of suicide, is considered a primary risk factor. Recent data bear witness to this direct correlation. In 2015 46 percent more teenagers ages fifteen to nineteen committed suicide than they did in 2007. During that same time span, two and a half more twelve- to fourteen-year-olds did likewise (Twenge 2017, 110). The most recent statistics from 2016 continue to show suicide as the second leading cause of death for people ages ten to thirty-four ("Suicide").

One of the reasons posited for this shocking rise in tween and teen depression and suicide rates concerns academic pressure. Dwyer, in an article about academic anxiety, cites the burdens of a more rigorous curriculum, including taking Advanced Placement courses and the increasing challenge for admission into competitive colleges (Dwyer). Twenge, however, cites two countervailing statistics that lead us to suspect the increased use of digital media by students ages ten to eighteen may be the culprit rather than increased academic pressure. First, the amount of homework that students reported doing between the critical depression/suicide periods should have increased because of additional academic pressure, and it did not. Actually, students have been doing less homework or similar amounts during this period. Second, in the yearly surveys of 1.1 million students, those who spent more time on homework and reading reported feeling less depressed (Twenge 2017, 111).

A third possible cause concerns sleep deprivation. Historically, tweens and teens have been notoriously negligent about getting sufficient sleep. Some see it as badge of honor to state how late they stayed up burning the midnight oil before an exam or finishing off a term paper. But there are three important social and behavioral trend questions concerning their lack of it. Is sleep deprivation among adolescents increasing? Is there a link between sleep deprivation and abuse of digital media? Finally, is there a direct correlation between lack of sleep and the risk of depression and even suicide?

Another robust study conducted by Twenge and other researchers examined 2015 survey data from 360,000 eighth, tenth, and twelfth graders and found that about 40 percent of them reported sleeping less than seven hours per night, which was 58 percent more students than in 1991 and 17 percent more than in 2009. Twenge makes the point that the key year for smartphone use adoption by this age cohort was 2009. Her results showed that the more time students spend online, the less sleep adolescents receive ("More Teens Than Ever . . ."). The relationship between sleep deprivation and increased susceptibility for depression and suicide is also direct. A Columbia University Medical Center study of 15,000 U.S. adolescents found that not sleeping a sufficient number of hours made them 42 percent more likely to suffer from depression, and 30 percent were more likely to have had suicidal thoughts in the past year (McBride).

CYBER BULLYING

Data are showing that cyber bullying is also putting many of our students at risk for depression and increases their suicide risk. Social media provides our students with a 24/7 opportunity to relentlessly torment each other with derogatory pictures, messages, false rumors, nasty videos, and threats. The medium creates a distance that for children and adolescents in various developmental stages seems to envelop them with an imaginary cloak of invisibility. Perhaps since they never personally witness their cyber victims' initial reactions to their abhorrent behavior, they have difficulty empathizing with them (Bowler, Knobel, and Mattern 1275). Unfortunately, the data show that cyber bullying continues to be prevalent among our students, with 20 percent of 4,441 students in a recent survey between the ages of ten and eighteen years old reporting an incidence of it during their school careers. Sadly, a similar percentage admitted to being perpetrators by sending hurtful comments and spreading rumors.

While girls are more often on the receiving line (25.1 percent versus 16.6 percent) than boys are, girls tend to report it more often (21.3 percent versus 17.5 percent). Boys tend to keep it to themselves. If one were to hypothesize percentages for students who are nonheterosexual, our fears would be confirmed for their psychological well-being. More than 17 percent of nonheterosexual participants in the study reported being cyber bullied in the previous thirty days when compared to less than 7 percent of heterosexual students ("Cyberbullying Research Center"). Although social psychologists are collecting data, reporting on incidences, and making recommendations for reducing cyber bullying, school librarians can probably expect to be play an important role in helping to reduce incidences of it in the years to come.

SCHOOL LIBRARIANS AND THE IGENERATION'S PSYCHOLOGICAL WELL-BEING

School librarians are the proverbial canaries in the coal mine. We are the frontline educated witnesses to major social and behavioral trends that research demonstrates are threatening not only the psychological well-being of our students but is also placing them at risk educationally because of their misplaced attention. While the direct cause-and-effect link between use of digital media and decreased psychological well-being cannot be proved yet, there is sufficient correlational smoke in our schools to begin sounding the alarm. As the studies continue to reveal the decline in our students' desire to emphasize with others, we have the means at our electronic and nonelectronic fingertips to counteract it. We have known for years that fiction educates the heart. More than ever before, we need to read and provide quality fiction to our students that reveals characters' feelings and thoughts and helps our students vicariously understand and experience others' point of view and perspective. We have to pose questions about stories and other fictional readings that cause students to understand how a character might feel in a specific situation. Selecting books for discussion and reading aloud evoke emotional responses in our students and are ways to develop empathy. Encouraging parents to read aloud to children and pose questions to them about each characters' feelings are empathy-building activities that fit easily into our fundamental job description.

Unsupervised play and time for silent sustained reading (SSR) are in short supply in schools given the pressure for our students to excel on various state-mandated tests. Think of these activities as essential empathy building blocks that may help ensure that our students are not replaced by robots in the future. The former activity gives children the opportunity to assume pretend roles where they describe to each other why a character would feel a certain way because of the situation that their imaginations have placed them in (Colvin 84). SSR provides librarians with the opportunity to recommend fiction books that tap students' abilities to identify and empathize with a character's plight to a degree not possible with any multimedia.

In our future economy, work that our students will perform with other human beings will be highly valued. Our students' ability to inform, persuade, motivate, and influence others is related to their capacity to empathize with them. It is an essential attribute that will need to be encouraged and nurtured with members of the iGeneration (Colvin 140). Some of the most interesting results of the behavioral studies cited earlier concern the positive relationship between reading books and magazines and sleep deprivation. Teens who use legacy media, including TV viewing, right before bed are less likely to suffer from sleeplessness (Twenge 2017, 115). This also means that they are less likely to suffer from depression and are at reduced risk for suicide.

Publicizing research that shows students who used social media less and who read and did homework more frequently are less lonely and unhappy is imperative for us now. It is time to reverse some of the social and behavioral trends that social psychologists are showing are having such a negative effect on many of our students' psychological well-being and mental health. Our administrators, faculty, and parents are already showing signs acknowledging the problem and beginning to urge digital media use restrictions. It is our responsibility to provide them with the research that supports their observations regarding technology's negative effects and helps reinforce restriction decisions that will probably meet with some resistance on the part of our students. Wieseltier, a book reviewer for *The New York Times*, holds that "every technology is used before it is completely understood" (Wieseltier). In the case of digital media, no statement could be truer. We need to use legacy and digital media to reduce incidences of cyber bullying not only because it is pernicious to our student population but also because of its more serious effects concerning depression and possible suicide.

Several possible solutions worth exploring include the FearNot! Project that employs interactive storytelling involving an on-screen avatar that connects with students eight to twelve years old through virtual storytelling dramas to self-empower them. Librarians without access to this software could also easily replicate the format by selecting an appropriate story that features bullying and posing self-empowerment questions and role-playing situations for students. MIT's Media Lab's Time Out Project and the BullyBlocker project at Arizona State University are examining the use of word analysis software to detect hurtful language and then send a warning message to parents that their child may be being bullied. MTV's

The Thin Line and It Gets Better projects can help us identify and define inappropriate online behavior and provide psychological support for those suffering from it. Yale Center's Center for Emotional Intelligence has worked with Facebook to develop a Bullying Prevention Hub that assists students and parents with privacy and security settings and includes tools for reporting, unfriending, and blocking links when cyber bullying occurs (Bowler, Knobel, and Mattern 1277).

As librarians on the front lines with technology and legacy media, we can and will need to play a significant role in locating legacy and digital resources that can help address and possibly alleviate some of the social and behavioral trends that are affecting our students regarding loneliness, unhappiness, depression, suicide prevention, and cyber bullying. As technology continues to produce more digital media applications that may have dark sides, we will also need to help develop sustainable digital use policies for our schools that may help improve our students' psychological well-being and make them feel emotionally supported during a time in their lives when they have everything to look forward to.

CALL ME IRRESISTIBLE

In 2010 Apple founder Steve Jobs told *The New York Times* reporter, Nick Bilton, that his children never used the iPad and that he and his wife had restrictions on how much technology they allowed their children to use at home. Curious if similar limitations are imposed by other techies, Bilton learned that Chris Anderson, the former editor of *Wired*, also had placed time restrictions on his five children regarding all electronic devices (Alter 2–3). The chief technology officer of eBay and employees of Google, Apple, and Hewlett-Packard send their children to the Waldorf School of the Peninsula where computers are banned and home use of them is strongly discouraged (Richtel). In Silicon Valley, parents employed in the tech industry are requiring that their children's nannies sign no-technology contracts that totally ban any screen time, including TV (Bowles). What did these titans and workers in this social- and behavioral-transforming industry know so early in the game that educators, psychologists, and non–technology-employed parents didn't?

Scientists are showing us that digital media has an impact on the brain that is almost irresistible to our students. Alter, in his excellent book, *Irresistible,* holds that many forms of digital media contain addictive elements that make it an almost mesmerizing experience when using them. As we learned from various digital media use surveys, the majority of them report almost constant use of them. Are the majority of our students addicted? If so, what does it bode for the future with regard to their attention spans, ability to learn and retain information, maintain will power and self-control, and delay gratification in the interest of future educational and economic rewards?

Addiction is an alarming word that conjures victims nodding off or slumped over in some kind of substance-induced stupor. We associate the word addiction correctly with harmful effects. Alter characterizes something as addictive when "the rewards it brings now are eventually outweighed by damaging circumstances" (Alter 20). It can also be thought of as a learning disorder where an individual develops learned patterns of behavior that instead of helping them engage in useful activities encourages just the opposite. It involves the substitution of pleasant activities for a purpose such as procrastinating doing homework or completing an assignment (Szalavitz). The most vulnerable period for behavioral addiction is during adolescence when students are more independent and searching for ways to entertain themselves, discover their identity, try to belong and fit in, and seek approval from their peer group (Alter 74).

Would Ivan Pavlov, the Russian physiologist famous for his conditioning and reinforcement experiments with dogs, felt at home in today's Silicon Valley? Many neuroscientists believe that he would be experiencing a techno-nirvana. Although a new subfield has been created called *captology* (an acronym for "computers as persuasive technology"), its principles involving stimulus, response, and reward are based on Pavlov's discoveries concerning behavior modification (Weisberg). Employees of this field learn how to capture our students' attention and make it more challenging for them to escape.

Their steps are classic behavior modification techniques accompanied by trigger colors, fonts, catchy music, videos, and images. Their first step is to establish an ingrained habit so that the activity can be performed with almost no conscious thought. Tech companies study how frequently a user is on their site and try to determine how useful and rewarding performing the activity is compared to other pastimes. Compare the time-saving rewards gained from shopping at Amazon as opposed to getting in a car, driving to a store, and standing in line. The second step is to create a *habit zone* so that using the site becomes the default behavior. A company's site needs to fulfill sufficient pleasure needs so that it creates some pain when the user is not on it.

The next stage involves employing a series of external and internal triggers. The first one is to change users' behavior with some sort of call to action. Where Pavlov used a bell to summon his dogs, captologists use the ring of a phone or the lighting up of a brightly colored icon. They make the desired action explicitly understandable and almost instinctive. To limit the spreading of fake news to members' friends groups, Facebook is making it less explicitly clear by adding a second button. Their assumption is that many of their users will not bother to take the time to press a second one to disseminate the news to additional parties, thus reducing its spread. After a while individuals are conditioned to checking their devices without need of a stimulus because many will feel anxious when too much time has elapsed without engaging with it—hence the introduction of the pain factor (Eyal and Hoover).

Tech companies also introduce internal triggers, which are more insidious because they are subliminal in nature. They try and design their products to intersect with a thought, emotion, or pre-existing routine. For example, students may habitually check their email while eating their breakfasts. When tech companies can connect an internal trigger with use of their product, they consider it scoring a perfect ten. Of the three internal triggers, emotions are probably the most addictive to our students. When students are feeling bored, lonely, frustrated, confused, or indecisive. the feeling stimulates a slight pain or irritation along with the need to suppress the sensation. Boredom can be relieved by texting a friend, posting an image, or scrolling through a newsfeed. If students discern that the product eases that slight pain or irritation, they will usually form an attachment to the product over time. Once the attachment becomes fixed, the product's stimuli in the form of colorful icons, buttons, or emojis are no longer essential for its continued use. The tech company can safely rely upon students' automatic responses. Using the product has become a habit, and habits, as we all know, are challenging to break and may become addictive (Eyal and Hoover).

IRRESISTIBLE FUTURE TECHNOLOGIES

As we observe how irresistible smartphones and other tech devices are to our students, what may the future hold for these emerging technologies that have been explored in Chapter 1? One type of irresistible product may be mixed realities that incorporate the augmented and virtual. They are immersive and interactive and can introduce worlds that are so realistic, mysterious, beautiful, frightening, informative, and entertaining that our students may prefer them to the humdrum world of learning, lessons, and assessments. VR games have the potential to become totally immersive, containing features with perfectly realistic graphics that may offer fantasy worlds far preferable to the real one. Readers of this chapter may wish to either read the book or view the film *Ready Player One*. Set in the 2040s, it depicts people spending all of their waking hours within a virtual reality game (Hendricks).

Online games already have a built-in formula for success that includes immersion, a sense of achievement, and the ability to communicate with other players synchronously (Alter 230). The latest Pew Research Center report found that 84 percent of teens ages thirteen to seventeen years old have game consoles at home, and 90 percent of them indicate that they play video games on either consoles, computers, or smartphones. Game console ownership is especially high among lower-income families (less than $30,000 a year), with 85 percent of survey participants reporting access to a game console in 2018 compared to 67 percent in 2015 (Anderson and Jiang 9). This income segment usually lives in communities characterized by high degrees of poverty, crime, and schools that are not preparing them for the future as much as higher-income communities are doing. Mixed realities games will present a temptation that may be difficult for many of our students to resist because they represent a delicious, shielded form of escapism from neighborhoods that are not safe to play in or hang out with friends. Students who are experiencing learning, family, or school relationship problems may also be especially vulnerable to the addictive qualities of mixed realities.

SCHOOL LIBRARIANS AND IRRESISTIBLE TECHNOLOGIES

In future years, school librarians are going to be facing commercial adversaries that are causing our students to undergo significant social and behavioral changes. They will affect their learning and ability to succeed in school. While technology has brought convenience, speed, and innovation, the social costs have been high.

We will be pitting ourselves against captologists who are highly competent. As discussed in Chapter 2, they can run thousands of A/B tests to determine what background colors, fonts, and audio tones to employ with an application to maximize engagement and reduce frustration. As our students engage with these apps, they can become irresistible to most of them (Alter 5).

We will need to develop strategies that can educate our students to think of digital media in ways that they are unaware of at present. One strategy that can be employed is teaching students that tech companies are using an intermittent variable format that is similar to how a slot machine operates. They are designed to cause FOMO, increase our students' craving for social approbation, reinforce their compulsion to respond to others' communications, and alert them of any notifications (Harris). Introduce students to the Time Well Spent site and encourage them to do the following: (1) Turn off all banners, badges, and notifications except where real people require their attention. (2) Set their smartphone to grayscale to remove reinforcements that are activated by color. (3) Dedicate their home screens solely to tools such as maps, calendar, and notes to lessen the temptation to click game-playing and other time-wasting applications. (4) Encourage students to log on to irresistible apps by typing. The extra time may make it too troublesome for them to waste their time. (5) Have them charge electronic devices outside their bedrooms. They will avoid experiencing the need to immediately check them before getting out of bed. (6) Persuade them to delete all social media from their cell phones and use only a computer for access, if at all. (7) Send audio messages instead of texting because the tone of voice will convey additional information and make their messages less likely to be misinterpreted. (8) Employ a texting shortcut using iOS by pressing and holding on a text message and choosing one of the assent/dissent graphics to indicate their responses. (9) Finally launch apps and extensions that are designed to reduce distraction such as Flux, uBlock Origin, Thrive, Inbox When Ready, Freedom and others ("Center for Humane Technology").

Recommendation #6, deleting all social media apps from one's phone, will be a shocking one for most students who truly believe that they cannot live without social media. Inform them of the 2015 Facebook Denmark study conducted with 1,095 participants. It is one of three studies to attempt to establish cause and effect with Facebook and decreased psychological well-being. After taking tests that measured happiness and general life satisfaction, one half of the respondents agreed to continue to use Facebook in their usual manner. The other pretested group deleted Facebook and discontinued using it. Both heavy and passive users of Facebook in the treatment group experienced a positive effect in general happiness and life satisfaction compared to those who remained on Facebook. Gains were greatest for heaviest users of Facebook and for those who expressed envious tendencies on it (Tromholt 661–665).

CAPTURE THEIR ATTENTION

A second strategy that might assist students in the throes of irresistible technologies now and in the future might be to ask them to think of their attention as a commodity. It is a product that they personally own and is a limited asset. Ask them to contemplate its worth. How much of it are they willing to sell, and to whom are they willing to sell it (Wu 335–336)? Our attention is a reservoir similar to mental capacity or mental capital. Although our students are furnished with it at a constant rate, they are the ones deciding every day how to apportion it.

Thorngate, in an excellent article about the economy of attention, formulated four axioms about it. The first is that we need to pay attention to be informed. But as the quantity of available information has exploded, our attention did not do so at the same rate. Our students, unlike previous generations, are facing torrents of information at their fingertips. It would be challenging for them to state that they had ever mastered even the smallest discipline because of the constant creation of new information and knowledge that is daily being published in print and digital media. This explosion of information is new and transformative and should make us more compassionate when we observe their information-seeking skills.

Axiom two is that our attention is a fixed asset. Paying attention requires the expenditure of time, which is limited by our human need to sleep, eat, attend school, and learn. Only a few activities such as walking and listening to music can be multitasked. Ones requiring careful and measured thought cannot. Even when our students think that they are multitasking, they are simply diverting their reservoir of attention solely to one activity and then quickly switching to the other (Thorngate 263). One study found that performing tasks while taking phone calls and responding to emails lowered the participants' IQs by about 10 points compared to those who labored in uninterrupted quiet ("Paying No Mind").

Axiom three is that our attention is shared among others as well as across time. There is a social aspect to our attention reservoir. As members of society, some of our students' attention will be devoted to exchanging information about what they are doing because they thrive on the attention from others. They need teachers, librarians, parents, and peers to listen, to read what they have written, and to comment on what they have designed and produced. The attention they receive is rewarding to them. What they need to realize, however, is that even the act of choosing with whom, where, and when to share requires an additional attentional investment (Thorngate 263). Raising their level of consciousness about the economy of attention so that they become more cognizant of how they are choosing to expend it may help them learn to husband their time resources more than the majority of them are doing at present.

Axiom four states that attention is invested in anticipation of emotional returns. Psychologists report that there is a strong connection between attention and emotion. It is natural for our students to invest their attention in activities that arouse, excite, and interest them. With the constant allure of the Internet, it is extremely challenging for librarians and educators to compete against the wealth of entertainment furnished to students through the Web (Thorngate 264). Our role will be to show students that every day their choices about where to direct the finite reservoir of their attention can result in unfavorable or favorable results concerning their academic success and future in a time of significant social and behavioral changes.

Questions

1. Why does understanding the social and behavioral trends of the iGeneration help comprehend the future?
2. How might the social and behavioral characteristics of the iGeneration directly affect the library's programs and services?
3. What strategies, approaches, or changes do you intend to pursue to better engage iGeneration students?
4. What may be lost or gained when social technologies cease being tools and change our students' ways of communicating, thinking, and learning?
5. What role do you see librarians playing in encouraging students to read, write grammatically correct sentences, listen to diverse points of view, lengthen their attention spans, and think critically?
6. If you were asked to write a sustainable technology use policy for your school, what components would it include?
7. If the displacement of legacy media takes place completely, what will be lost? How crucial will it be?

REFERENCES

Agosto, Denise and June Abbas. March/April 2016. "Simple Tips for Helping Students Become Safer, Smarter Social Media Users." *Knowledge Quest*. 44(4): 42–47.

"All about Empathy." 2018. Available at: https://www.psychologytoday.com/us/basics/empathy.

Alpert, Emily. July 21, 2013. "Kids Like Being Kids, Study Finds, Perhaps Thanks to Parenting." *Los Angeles Times*. Available at: http://articles.latimes.com/2013/jul/21/local/la-me-growing-up-20130722.

Alter, Adam. 2017. *Irresistible: The Rise of Addictive Technology and the Business of Keeping Us Hooked*. New York: Penguin.

Anderson, Monica and Jingjing Jiang. May 31, 2018. *Teens, Social Media & Technology Report*. Pew Research Center. Available at: http://www.pewinternet.org/2018/05/31/teens-social-media-technology-2018.

Bermudez, Juan Pablo. 2017. "Social Media and Self-Control: The Vices and Virtues of Attention." In: *Social Media and Your Brain*, edited by C. G. Prado. Santa Barbara, CA: Praeger, pp. 57–74.

Bowler, Leanne, Cory Knobel, and Eleanor Mattern. 2015. "From Cyberbullying to Well-Being: A Narrative-Based Participating Approach to Values-Oriented Design for Social Media." *Science and Technology*. 66(6): 1274–1293.

Bowles, Nellie. October 28, 2018. "Silicon Valley Nannies Are Phone Police for Kids." *The New York Times*. Available at: https://www.nytimes.com/2018/10/26/style/silicon-valley-nannies.html.

Bromwich, Jonah Engle. June 31, 2018. "We Asked Generation Z to Pick a Name. It Wasn't Generation Z." *The New York Times*. Available at: https://www.nytimes.com/2018/01/31/style/generation-z-name.html.

Carr, Nicholas. 2014. *The Glass Cage: Automation and Us*. New York: W. W. Norton.

"Center for Humane Technology." 2013. Available at: http://humanetech.com.

Christakis, Erika. July/August 2018. "The Dangers of Distracted Parenting." *The Atlantic*. 322(1): 11–16.

Colvin, Geoff. 2015. *Humans Are Underrated: What High Achievers Know That Brilliant Machines Never Will.* New York: Portfolio.

"Coming Apart." April 17, 2018. *The Economist.* Available at: https://www.economist.com /united-states/2018/04/04/fifty-years-after-martin-luther-kings-death-a-divided -america.

"Correlation and Causation." July 3, 2013. Australian Bureau of Statistics. Available at: http://www.abs.gov.au/websitedbs/a3121120.nsf/home/statistical+language+-+correla tion+and+causation.

"Cyberbullying Research Center." 2016. Available at: https://cyberbullying.org.

"Demographic Trends and Economic Well-Being." June 27, 2016. Pew Research Center. Available at: http://www.pewsocialtrends.org/2016/06/27/1-demographic-trends -and-economic-well-being.

Dodds, Liz. January 1, 2017. "Students as Social Media Content Creators." *CSLA Journal.* 40 (2):13–16. Available at:http://csla.net/wp-content/uploads/2012/09/CSLA_Journal _40-2_Winter2017_V3.pdf.

Dwyer, Lucy. October 3, 2014. "When Anxiety Hits at School." *The Atlantic.* Available at: https://www.theatlantic.com/health/archive/2014/10/when-anxiety-hits-at-school /380622.

Eyal, Nir and Ryan Hoover. July 31, 2017. "Hooked: How to Build Habit-Forming Prod- ucts." *Book Notes.* Available at: https://medium.com/@skueong/hooked-how-to -build-habit-forming-products-book-notes-a59d30fc4f9b.

Fairfield, Paul. 2017. "Social Media and Communicative Unlearning: Learning to Forget in Communicating." In: *Social Media and Your Brain*, edited by C. G. Prado. Santa Barbara, CA: Praeger, pp. 105–118.

Flowers, Sarah. 2017. *Crash Course in Young Adult Services.* Santa Barbara, CA: Librar- ies Unlimited.

Friedman, Thomas L. 2016. *Thank You for Being Late: An Optimist's Guide to Thriving in the Age of Accelerations.* New York: Farrar, Straus & Giroux.

Gillman, Howard and Erwin Cherminsky. March 31, 2016. "Don't Mock or Ignore Stu- dents' Lack of Support for Free Speech. Teach Them." *Los Angeles Times.* Avail- able at: http://www.latimes.com/opinion/op-ed/la-oe-chemerinsky-gillman-free -speech-on-campus-20160331-story.html#.

Haelle, Tara. May 16, 2018. "Hospitals See Growing Numbers of Kids and Teens at Risk For Suicide." NPR. Available at: https://www.npr.org/sections/health-shots/2018/05/16 /611407972/hospitals-see-growing-numbers-of-kids-and-teens-at-risk-for-suicide.

Hanson, Jarice. 2016. *The Social Media Revolution: An Economic Encyclopedia of Friend- ship, Following, Texting, and Connecting.* Santa Barbara, CA: Greenwood.

Harris, Tristan. December 6, 2017. "How Technology Hijacks People's Minds." *Huffing- ton Post.* Available at: https://www.huffingtonpost.com/tristan-harris/how-tech nology-hijacks-peoples-minds_b_10155754.html.

Hendricks, Scotty. May 8, 2018. "If the Future Is Full of VR Addicts, Should We Bring Them Back to Reality?" BigThink.com. Available at: https://bigthink.com/scotty -hendricks/how-will-we-treat-vr-addiction.

Herman, John. February 27, 2018. "How Tiny Red Dots Took Over Your Life." *The York Times.* Available at: https://www.nytimes.com/2018/02/27/magazine/red-dots-badge -phones-notification.html.

Jiang, Jingjing. August 22, 2018. "How Teens and Parents Navigate Screen Time and Device Distractions." Pew Research Center. Available at: http://www.pewinternet.org /2018/08/22/how-teens-and-parents-navigate-screen-time-and-device-distractions.

Jones, Abigail. May 12, 2016. "What Do American Teens Want? Less Racism." *News- week.* Available at: https://www.newsweek.com/2016/05/27/american-teenagers-race -458942.html.

Konrath, Sara H., Edward H. O'Brien, and Courtney Hsing. February 2011. "Changes in Dispositional Empathy in American College Students Over Time: A Meta-Analysis." *Personality and Social Psychology Review.* 15(2): 180–198.

Lenhart, Amanda. August 9, 2015. "Teens, Social Media & Technology Overview 2015." Pew Research Center. Available at: http://www.pewinternet.org/2015/04/09/teens-social-media-technology-2015.

"Lesbian Gay, Bisexual, and Transgender Health." June 21, 2017. CDC. Available at: https://www.cdc.gov/lgbthealth/youth.htm.

"Limit Your Screen Time with These Six Apps for iPhone and Android." January 6, 2018. Available at: https://www.digitaltrends.com/mobile/apps-to-reduce-screen-time-iphone-android.

McBride, Hugh C. September 12, 2018. "Is Sleep Deprivation Putting Your Teen at Risk for Depression and Thoughts of Suicide?" CRC Health. Available at: https://www.crchealth.com/troubled-teenagers/sleep-deprivation-putting-your-teen-at-risk-for-depression-or-suicide.

"More Teens Than Ever Aren't Getting Enough Sleep." October 19, 2017. *Science News.* Available at: https://www.sciencedaily.com/releases/2017/10/171019100416.htm.

"Paying No Mind." December 7, 2017. *The Economist.* Available at: https://www.economist.com/finance-and-economics/2017/12/07/are-digital-distractions-harming-labour-productivity.

Poushter, Jacob. November 11, 2015. "40% of Millennials OK with Limiting Speech Offensive to Minorities." Pew Research Center. Available at: http://www.pewresearch.org/fact-tank/2015/11/20/40-of-millennials-ok-with-limiting-speech-offensive-to-minorities.

Prado, C. G. 2016. *Social Media and Your Brain: Web-Based Communication Is Changing How We Think and Express Ourselves.* Santa Barbara, CA: Praeger.

Putnam, Robert D. 2015. *Our Kids: The American Dream in Crisis.* New York: Simon & Schuster.

ReCAPP. 2015. "Statistics: Sexual Activity." Available at: http://recapp.etr.org/recapp/index.cfm?fuseaction=pages.StatisticsDetail&PageID=555.

Richtel, Matt. October 22, 2011. "A Silicon Valley School That Doesn't Compute." *The New York Times.* Available at: https://www.nytimes.com/2011/10/23/technology/at-waldorf-school-in-silicon-valley-technology-can-wait.html.

Riley, Naomi Schaefer. February 11, 2018. "America's Real Digital Divide." *The New York Times.* Available at: https://www.nytimes.com/2018/02/11/opinion/america-digital-divide.html.

Salomon, Ilyssa and Christia Spears Brown. April 21, 2018. "The Selfie Generation: Examining the Relationship Between Social Media Use and Early Adolescent Body Image." *The Journal of Early Adolescence.* Available at: https://doi.org/10.1177/0272431618770809.

Sana, Faria, Tina Weston, and Nicholas J. Cepeda. September 2012. "Laptop Multitasking Hinders Classroom Learning for Both Users and Nearby Peers." *Computers & Education.* Available at: http://dx.doi.org/10.1016/j.compedu.2012.10.003.

Seemiller, Grace and Meghan Corey. October 31, 2013. "Move Over Millennials, Generation Z Is Here." Available at: http://www.satest.arizona.edu/symposium/files/2013/MoveOverMillennialsGenerationZisHere.pdf.

"Suicide." September 11, 2018. National Institute of Health. Available at: http://www.nimh.nih.gov/health/statistics/suicide.shtml.

Szalavitz, Maia. August 4, 2014. "Most of Us Still Don't Get It: Addiction Is a Learning Disorder." *Pacific Standard.* Available at: https://psmag.com/social-justice/us-still-dont-get-addiction-learning-disorder-87431.

Tandoc, Edson, Jr., Patrick Ferruci, and Margaret Duffy. 2015. "Facebook Use, Envy, and Depression among College Students: Is Facebook Depressing?" *Computers in Human Behavior.* 43:139–146.

Thorngate, Warren. 1990. "The Economy of Attention and the Development of Psychology." *Canadian Psychology.* 31(3): 262–271.

Tromholt, Morten. 2016. "The Facebook Experiment: Quitting Facebook Leads to Higher Levels of Well-Being." *Cyberpsychology, Behavior, and Social Networking.* 19(11): 661–666.

Turkle, Sherry. 2016. *Alone Together: Why We Expect More from Technology and Less From Each Other.* New York: Basic Books.

Twenge, Jean M. 2017. *iGen: Why Today's Super-Connected Kids Are Growing Up Less Rebellious, More Tolerant, Less Happy—and Completely Unprepared for Adulthood.* New York: Atria Books.

Twenge, Jean M. August 20, 2018. "Trends in U.S. Adolescents' Media Use, 1976–2016: The Rise of Digital Media, the Decline of TV, and the (Near) Demise of Print." *Psychology of Popular Media Culture.* Available at: http://dx.doi.org/10.1037/ppm0000203.

Twenge, Jean M., Gabrielle N. Martin, and W. Keith Campbell. 2018. "Decreases in Psychological Well-Being Among Adolescents After 2012 and Links to Screen Time During the Rise of Smartphone Technology." *Emotion* 18(6): 765–780.

Weisberg, Jacob. February 25, 2016. "We Are Hopelessly Hooked." *The New York Review of Books.* Available at: https://www.nybooks.com/articles/2016/02/25/we-are-hopelessly-hooked.

Wieseltier, Leon. January 7, 2015. "Among the Disrupted." *The New York Times.* Available at: https://www.nytimes.com/2015/01/18/books/review/among-the-disrupted.html.

Wu, Tim. 2016. *The Attention Merchants: The Epic Scramble to Get Inside Our Heads.* New York: Vintage.

Yeykelis, Leo, James J. Cummings, and Byron Reeves. February 2014. "Multitasking on a Single Device: Arousal and the Frequency, Anticipation, and Prediction of Switching Between Media Content on a Computer." *Journal of Communication.* 64(1): 167–192.

7

Instructional Trends

IS THE WRITING ON THE SCREEN?

Looking at job loss data for full-time equivalent (FTE) school librarians over the past several years is alarming. Using trend analysis, there is no indication that it is an educational blip or hiccup. Since 2,000 more than 10,000 of us have lost our jobs. The crisis in school funding does not account for the losses, because during the same period the number of teachers has remained stable but the number of instructional coordinators has greatly increased. From 2005 to 2015, "for every FTE school librarian lost on average, slightly more than three instructional coordinator positions were added" (Kachel and Lance 15). Many of us who peruse the American Library Association's (ALA) job descriptions are also observing openings for positions titled "digital learning specialist, reading interventionist, innovation specialist, or instructional technology teacher" along with school librarian (Kachel and Lance 15).

In interviews conducted with sixteen school library leaders, school librarian job losses were largely attributed to principals feeling increasing pressure to find competent educators who could provide faculty with hands-on technical support for new programs involving reading, the Common Core, blended learning, and the flipped curriculum. For school librarians on a fixed schedule, these mandates made them ineligible because they were bound to a daily schedule of classes. In districts where there were strong advocates for teacher librarians in the form of school library coordinators/supervisors, the trend has been allayed, and in several, such as Oakland, California; Portland, Oregon; Tacoma, Washington; and Westborough, Massachusetts, the trend has actually been reversed (Kachel and Lance 16).

Reading recent job descriptions posted by the ALA and school districts serve as a blazing trail marker to lead us toward revamping our instructional role toward our students, faculty, administrators, and parents. To survive extinction as a profession, we must master and instruct our user populations with the latest educational technologies. In a time of rapid change, our instructional role will be somewhat schizophrenic. On the one hand, we will need to be at the forefront of the latest technologies—separating fad from trend—and teaching and guiding users to help them become information literate. On the other hand, we are also charged with developing strong reading programs and services that require us to instruct our students in more subtle ways. The question is "where shall the twain meet?" In a time of rapid change, school librarians who ignore, slight, or deny their instructional role with technology do so at their own peril (Palfrey 165).

The Colorado Department of Education Highly Effective School Library Program report states that planning for the future is a crucial role for a teacher librarian. An exemplary one needs to be able to work with administrators to develop a curriculum that is aligned with the school's goals for growth and change. The state envisions a teacher/librarian's instructional role in equal terms with any collaborating teacher. They are tasked with integrating digital information skills into their teaching, being actively involved in the educational process, and assisting with the development of assessments for measuring the effectiveness of their resource-based units. In addition, they need to encourage reading by employing a variety of digital and legacy media to motivate students and faculty to become perpetual learners (Colorado Department of Education).

The state of Colorado is not alone in recognizing that the instructional role of the teacher librarian is evolving. In the years to come, we will be meeting our users' needs in physical and virtual spaces. Working with classroom robots and virtual worlds will eventually become part of our job descriptions (Hill 225–227). Doug Johnson, in his excellent book, *The Indispensable Librarian*, believes that we must do the following if we wish to survive as a profession: (1) develop an integrated "information/technology" course of study with measurable, grade-level bench marks; (2) design instructional units that provide students with the opportunity to acquire those competencies within various disciplines; (3) consult with teachers to create assessment rubrics that measure a unit's effectiveness; and (4) be responsible for reporting assessment results through grade reports and the like (Johnson 5).

GETTING A SEAT AT THE TABLE

School librarians are already in the catbird's seat when it comes to providing the lead instructional role with technology and reading. We are doubly qualified. While our instructional technology counterparts have elected a course of study in the operation and integration of hardware and software into a school's curriculum, we have not only taken similar courses but also have years of research demonstrating how our presence and development of a strong legacy and digital media collection results in increased student achievement. More than sixty studies link the presence of our libraries and services with increased student academic success ("School Library Impact Studies . . .").

Administrators deciding between hiring an instructional coordinator and a school librarian are placing their schools in academic jeopardy. A meta-analysis of numerous reading studies measuring the positive role that school librarians play in improving student reading is unassailable (Krashen 58). The classes that we provide for students to listen to stories, partake in book discussions, engage in voluntary reading activities, obtain reading guidance, and choose material from our attractive displays result in improved reading achievement. The ability for a child to read at or above grade level is the strongest link to their present and future academic and employment success. The training, background knowledge, and skills required for this essential curriculum role cannot be replicated by an instructional coordinator.

Studies show that administrators seem to be understanding the changing instructional role to be played by school librarians, which may help us obtain our rightful membership on technology, curriculum, and strategic planning committee meetings. A principal's perception survey of school librarians acknowledged that they valued school librarians' skill and proficiency with "technology integration" or technology infusion. More elementary school principals than secondary ones emphasized school librarians' implementing reading incentive programs as important hiring criteria. Overall, more than 82 percent were satisfied or very satisfied with their current school librarian (Shannon 1, 6). The job loss data, however, seem to indicate that it may not be happening with sufficient speed and that our invaluable roles with information literacy and reading need to be more widely disseminated.

To survive in a time of accelerating change requires changing teachers' perceptions of our role also. Kansas introduced a state certification requirement that school librarians at elementary and secondary levels have two years classroom teaching experience. One of the courses required of elementary education majors entailed collaborating with a school librarian to develop lessons for literature-based instruction. By the end of the course, elementary education majors' perceptions of school librarians as partners in teaching showed that they strongly agreed with the collaborative role school librarians should have with their own classes (Dow, Davis, and Vietti-Okane 41–49). Introducing courses involving coteaching with K–6 elementary education majors showed promise for changing the understanding that elementary school teachers hold toward the instructional role of school librarians.

Our role as instructors is going to be vital to our continued existence. A study conducted with 800 elementary schools in Ontario, Canada, reported exemplary school libraries were characterized by three elements: (1) the presence of teacher librarians who are focused on instructing students, (2) the active role that teacher librarians played in finding continuing opportunities for teaching students, and (3) how teacher librarians worked to change the perception of their teaching role within the context of the school (Lee and Klinger 81–85).

While our instructional role in improving reading achievement is supported by many research studies, our essential role with teaching information-seeking and critical thinking skills lacks a similar research-based foundation. A 2014 EBSCO-sponsored study showed that when teachers and school librarians teamed up to teach grade nine students database research skills, it resulted in a higher confidence level in research-seeking skills that even transferred to college. Sending students to the school library to seek research assistance from a librarian did not improve their confidence levels. The study showed that when the teacher and school librarian collaborated to instruct students in information-seeking skills and repeated the instruction by providing opportunities to practice the skills, the results were even more effective (Barack 14).

Our administrators, teachers, and school board members need to become aware of our unique dual qualifications. Working with teachers to design resource- and project-based units, instructing students in the use of legacy and digital media, and preparing lessons that teach critical thinking skills must be articulated for every grade level and be operative within every discipline. Our role in measuring and evaluating the effectiveness of our instruction is also critical to our continued survival as a profession. Playing an equal role in assessing student learning enables us to begin building the research foundation that supports the need for our continued presence within our schools (Levitov 2012, 13–18).

DO MEMBERS OF THE IGENERATION LEARN DIFFERENTLY?

Assuming that we are members of the technology, new course development, curriculum, and strategic planning committees, what information can we provide them about instructional trends looming on the horizon regarding the iGeneration? How will our instructional methods and curriculum need to change to meet their needs and interests? What pedagogies and instructional techniques will we need to rethink, especially when we integrate more technology into our teaching units? Articles about the learning characteristics of the iGeneration indicate that they prefer obtaining information rapidly from a variety of multimedia sources, while their teachers evince a desire for slowly introducing information, usually from a textbook or a reduced number of sources. Our students' attention can be diverted easily from one task to another, thereby increasing their chances of missing important information or concepts. They are accustomed to reading visual images and less likely to want to learn from texts. iGeneration students process digital media in the form of videos, podcasts, images, and pictures before text, whereas educators usually start instruction with text. Many of them are adept at playing video games that meld the physical and virtual worlds. Adjusting to mixed realities (augmented and virtual) in the future will be less of a challenge for them. Members of the iGeneration like accessing information randomly through hyperlinks and multimedia sites. Teachers, however, tend to furnish information in a linear and sequential fashion. iGen'ers favor discovery over lecture. This learning style loans itself to project- and resource-based learning. Fast is their normal speed because they are used to operating their smartphones and other devices so rapidly. It tends to make them more impatient with learning that requires extended explanations. Our students enjoy working with others synchronously through wikis and Google-like apps, while teachers prefer they work independently prior to consulting or networking with their peers. An iGen'er does not fret over learning just for the moment, whereas teachers want them to learn something because they might need it for an assessment or for their knowledge base. Students in a time of rapid change have trouble delaying gratification concerning learning. They want to be rewarded for it right away. Teachers, on the other hand, see learning as a process with gratification occurring over a longer period. Instructional trends show that this generation likes to learn when they discern that it is relevant, presently useful, and fun. Teachers, however, realize that some aspects of learning must involve memorization, which is anathema to iGen'ers (Jukes, McCain, and Crockett 37; Scheeren 219).

From the learning differences and approaches described earlier, how are teachers and school librarians going to support the iGeneration with instructional programs and services that enable them to experience academic success? How can we change our instruction to meet their needs for increased information literacy and critical thinking? The first step is to remain the go-to person for information and all research-based assignments. We will need to provide personalized service to help students find relevant, accurate information. Acknowledging that they have many search choices, including their favorites, Google and Wikipedia, we need to teach them how to use all of their bells and whistles. Teaching Google tips such as advanced search, highlighting key words in text, and accessing primary sources through Wikipedia's bibliographies are just a few good search techniques. The Web has also helped create a generation of consumers who turn to Yelp and other evaluative sites before they purchase even a bagel or latte. Employing that similar consumer mentality to teach them about the different qualities of information they can access via Google versus online subscription databases will be important to them. Providing them with information about organization tools like Evernote, Google Keep, and Microsoft One Note to help them organize the multitude of sites, notes, images, and videos that they collect during an information search will be invaluable.

Supporting this new active means of learning loans itself to instructional design involving project-based assignments that can increase students' data, visual, textual, and aural literacies. Demonstrating how to incorporate creditable survey data, interviews, videos, primary sources, experiments, and scholarly documents into assignments will not only appeal to their learning characteristics but also furnish faculty and librarians with the opportunity to teach evaluative and critical thinking skills with forms of literacy that are quickly gaining market share with the iGeneration.

Text can no longer be the end-all, be-all of information types. Information in the form of picture books and graphic novels is an effective form of communicating information, entertainment, and background knowledge and stimulating the imagination. This generation likes to present projects and research in visual, aural, and data formats so we, in turn, need to teach them how to take the best photographs, create relevant digital movies, incorporate appropriate images and pictures, and prepare interesting podcasts. The Web has created an environment where our daily information needs can be met more easily and learning can be personalized. Students can satisfy their curiosity about almost any subject with one click. We will need to tap into those personal interests to help design project-related research that can be tailored to a student's interest in whales for a science assignment or fashion for researching clothing worn during the Middle Ages (Johnson 9).

Instruction in the future will no longer take place in a conventional library but is going to occur asynchronously. While our digital libraries are stocked with access to online databases, the online public access catalog (OPAC), sample assignments, and reading recommendations, responding to students' emails and texts with recommendations for sources and assistance for research assignments is also going to be a growing instructional trend. An enduring characteristic of every generation that we instruct is their predilection for procrastination and need for immediate assistance to meet a deadline. Making ourselves available to them online up until a certain time after school hours is going to become part of our new instructional role (Johnson 9).

WHAT IS THE STATE OF THEIR INFORMATION LITERACY SKILLS?

This generation of students is confronting a deluge of information that previous generations with limited access to legacy media never experienced. Information can assume the form of fake news, machine-generated tweets, and robotically produced opinions (Wu 346). To decipher fact from fiction will require consummate information literacy skills on the part of our students as software programs enable voice and visuals to blend so seamlessly that it will be a challenge to correctly detect their falsity. Are our students up to this challenge with their information literacy (IL) skills?

In 2006 the Education Testing Service piloted a core and advanced levels iSkills assessment that involved 1,016 high school students, 753 community college students, and 4,585 college and university students. Most of the students performed poorly on both level tests, obtaining about 50 percent of the possible points on them. Only 44 percent correctly selected a statement that encapsulated the assignment request, only 35 percent correctly identified a more narrowly revised assignment statement, and only 40 percent employed multiple search terms to narrow their search results. With regard to website evaluation, the results were just as ominous. Only 52 percent correctly judged the site's objectivity, 65 percent selected the authority correctly, and only 49 percent of the respondents were able to correctly identity the one site that satisfied all the evaluative criteria (Katz 10).

In 2009 LaTrobe University Library in Melbourne, Australia, also tried to assess the state of incoming students' IL skills. Among the surprises they encountered when examining 1,000 responses were students' seemingly complete confidence in their ability to successfully locate information. Their perceptions of their skills were inflated, and when they met with a searching obstacle, their confidence in using the library quickly eroded (Salisbury and Karasmanis 46). The questionnaire evaluated their skills concerning (1) identification, (2) search strategy, (3) document types, (4) search tools, and (5) understanding of scholarly information. When asked to prioritize their search tools for finding information on a topic, their first, second, and third preferences were Google, a friend, and a book. When asked to indicate which search tool they would employ to locate scholarly articles, only 14 percent selected a database, 35 percent chose Google, 21 percent chose the OPAC, and 15 percent chose journals within the library. While 77.3 percent understood the relationship between keyword choice and search results, only one-third were able to isolate the key concepts in an information query. In evaluating the quality of an Internet site, 27 percent counted the accessibility of a site as being an indication of quality, and only 23.8 percent cited date, author, and responsibility of the site as criteria. Even fewer students, 23 percent, were able to correctly identify a journal article citation within a bibliography (Salisbury and Karasmanis 49).

These results were echoed seven years later in a similar study conducted with Illinois University libraries at 700 data collection points. Again, the librarians noted that while students were quick to learn the technology of the databases, they exhibited significant gaps in their understanding of basic concepts of academic research. They lacked the ability to correctly read and understand citations, comprehend the OPAC, formulate a cohesive search strategy, and correctly evaluate sources in different formats. The saddest aspect of the study concerned their failure to consult a librarian (Asher, Duke, and Green 8–9).

Additional studies also confirm these findings regarding students' inability to define the information problem, identify keywords in a research question, formulate a search strategy, expand or narrow the results accordingly, and synthesize and evaluate the information (Head). All of these IL skills can be remedied with appropriate course-integrated instruction in the future, with the exception of one—the ability to judge the credibility of an online source. A recent study shows librarians what changes are needed. In 2015 Stanford University began assessing middle school, high school, and college/university students' ability to correctly evaluate the credibility of sites that inundate their social media accounts, Google searches, and other online sources of information. The test designers collected 7,804 student responses. The highlights are extremely worrisome for librarians at every academic level. "More than 80 percent of middle school students surveyed believed a native ad, identified with the words 'sponsored content' was a real news story." ("Evaluating Information" 10). Only 9 percent of AP history students were able to correctly discern that the MinimumWage.com site was a front group for a Washington, D.C., lobbyist ("Evaluating Information" 5). When shown a photo titled "Fukushima Nuclear Flowers," nearly 40 percent of 454 high school students indicated that the picture provided strong evidence because it presented pictorial evidence about conditions near the power plant ("Evaluating Information" 17). University students failed to note that a tweet sent out by the National Rifle Association (NRA) was actually based on a poll conducted by a professional polling firm, thus rendering the information more credible ("Evaluating Information" 23).

The state of our students' information literacy skills is disturbing and dangerous. It indicates that school librarians need to make teaching information skills a top priority. First, because we are charged with preparing them for an age where they will be competing against robots, artificial intelligence, and machine learning in addition to their peers for remunerative employment. All of the jobs available to them now and in the future are going to require various forms of continuing education and will assume high degrees of information literacy. We have more than a mandate to prepare them for this coming age—we have an imperative to do so.

Second, the results of failing to instruct our students to evaluate the credibility of legacy and digital media materials can endanger their participation in a democracy. Seventy-five percent of young adults obtain their news online. Their vulnerability to influence by those who seek to change their minds by altering the facts or presenting partisan viewpoints is clearly evident in the latest studies

(Breakstone et al.). Our mission as school librarians now and in the future will be to teach information literacy skills and ensure that evaluating the credibility of online sources is integrated into every school discipline, including mathematics.

WHAT DO WE NEED TO TEACH THEM IN A TIME OF CHANGE?

We need to ask ourselves what information literacy skills are essential not only for entry into higher education but also for continued achievement and success in any work environment. Numerous studies are showing that the Internet is changing the way our population demographic reads and processes information. Because students are incorporating images, graphics, pictures, videos, sound, and text into assignments, our information literacy instruction needs to evolve to include different types of literacies. Researchers are using the term "transliteracy" to refer to a different information-seeking behavior that we are observing in our school libraries. It means the ability to "read, write, and interact across a range of platforms, tools, and media" (Flowers 23). It encompasses multiple literacies, including (1) textual, (2) visual, (3) data, (4) aural, and (5) ethical. These skills are not meant to be taught in isolation but integrated into various project-based units that align with various standards such as the Common Core and Association of College and Research Libraries (ACRL) standards for information literacy (Ipri).

TEXTUAL LITERACY

For years, our students read to gain information and knowledge in a linear pattern, but that is no longer the case when they read online. Access to almost all information is now online. Less than 0.1 percent of current information is on paper, whereas 99.9 percent of information is only digitally available ("Kids and Teens Online"). When our students read online, they engage in scanning. And as a study conducted at University College of London found with youngsters between twelve and eighteen years old, they are six times faster than we are at it. Their eyes follow an "F-shaped pattern," reading the first two lines of text, then scrolling to the left side, and then focusing on the center. Reading in this manner results in their absorbing only about 20 percent of the content on a page, with about 69 percent of their attention devoted to the left side of the screen and about 30 percent to the right side ("Kids and Teens Online"). For teaching purposes, this type of reading has positive and negative aspects. Fortunately, when our students are scanning they are actually hunting for keywords. This is one of the tenets of IL skills—identifying keywords and then formulating a search strategy with them. We can also use this natural scanning technique to recommend that they think of keywords before they initiate their searches and employ the highlighting function to make their scanning more efficient and possibly rewarding.

The negative aspect, however, is that scanning constantly seems to deplete the brain's capacity for deeper processing, which allows "conscious acquisition of knowledge, inductive analysis, critical thought, imagination and reflection

(Greenfield 71). Immersive reading is needed to counterbalance the effects of constant scanning. As students engage more in the former textual reading, our instruction for immersive reading will need to emphasize patience, reflection, linear eye movement throughout the text, printing the online source when appropriate, and using marginalia.

VISUAL LITERACY

Colors, icons, photos, videos, animations, symbols, and emojis dominate the online world of our students. Advertisers, employing the brightest developmental and behavioral psychologists, already know what colors, fonts, type size, and graphics cause them to gaze, purchase, download, or recommend their products. Information for time-saving and persuasive purposes has gone visual. Diagrams, schematics for assembling electronic devices, and instructions for use contain pictures and, in many cases, helpful videos rather than text. Our students, however, are unaware of their power to influence them (Jukes, McCain, and Crockett 119). Visual literacy can be defined as "the ability to comprehend, analyze, evaluate, create and communicate with images (Cordell 1). It's an aspect of information literacy that embraces every aspect of the curriculum from historical maps, astronomical charts, and mathematical diagrams to primary sources in the form of pictures, ancient coins, and cartoons. As school librarians, we have naturally been preoccupied with teaching text-based IL skills, but with the learning characteristics of the iGeneration, we must address visual literacy skills and integrate relevant lessons about visual information's purpose, market effect, intended audience, and how the images are used to evoke emotions and convey a perspective to us (Cordell 65). Visit *The New York Times* site What's Going on in This Picture? and The Literacy Shed for ideas about how to introduce visual literacy elements into project-based assignments.

DATA LITERACY

There's a deluge of data behind the algorithms that are making decisions about our preferences for adventure movies, chick flicks, and Italian comedies. And we and our students are the ones supplying social media and big search companies with it. What we click on and even hover over is being diligently recorded and used for modifying our behavior (O'Neil 9–10). Never before in our history do our students need to be taught the elements of data literacy. Students need to understand how search engines and social media sites are constructed to produce filter bubbles that push specific newsfeeds and political viewpoints at us, thus making it more difficult to obtain contrasting opinions. As librarians, we do not have to be mathematically inclined to explain how Google designs its relevancy rankings and the implications of the pros and cons.

Data literacy can be made cool for a variety of collaboratively designed project assignments at any grade level. Many of our students' classes are requiring inclusion of infographics in the form of surveys, bar graphs, and pie charts. The class assignments provide the opportunity to introduce a variety of learning strategies that instruct students about data visualization, appropriate usage, and privacy concerns with big tech companies. For IL teaching ideas and inspiration, download two free books titled, *Data Literacy in the Real World: Case Studies and Conversation* and *Creating Data Literate Students*, from the latter-named site.

AURAL LITERACY

One of the reasons that we may have trouble commanding students' attention is because they are 24/7 wired into listening devices. As we watch them stroll down a sidewalk, they are constantly listening to music, news delivered orally, or phone messages. Aural literacy is not just about sound and its effects on our emotions and moods, it's about deciphering the tone with which words are spoken and interpreting whether they are unimportant or important. Sound is an essential component for deciding whether to believe someone or trust them. Learning how to interpret sound with videos, speeches, music, and messages is essential for deigning if its purpose is to educate, inform, entertain, inspire, motivate, or persuade us. As school librarians, we usually confine storytelling and reading-aloud activities to the elementary level, but as more of our students devote time to wired listening, perhaps we should experiment with hiring a professional storyteller or reading a passage from a new book, essay, or op-ed piece to them. Hosting a student-sponsored poetry slam, exposing them to oral histories in primary sources, and onsite political debate are all ways to stimulate this literacy form.

The second aspect of aural literacy concerns sound production. As more teachers become accepting of different media formats, they are permitting presentations that involve sound in the form of podcasts, documentary films, and short vides embedded into students' reports. These types of assignments provide us with the perfect teaching vehicle to introduce aural literacy concepts and give our students opportunities to critically analyze the impact and influence that this sense has on their learning ("Aural Literacy"). Visit the Aural Literacy website for examples of sound and its effects with aural examples from nature, speech, film, commercials, and, of course, music.

ETHICAL LITERACY

Issues of right and wrong are more evident to students in the physical world than they are online. The possible consequences for stealing, bullying, or being malicious toward others are more obvious in the physical world. The online world provides students with pseudo-cloaks of invisibility and impunity from recrimination or discipline. The temptation to insert a photo, image, video, sound effect, or text without attributing its source is just a click away. The ability to alter the facts, neglect to acknowledge contradictory research findings, or cite dubious sources is ever present for them (Johnson 149).

Ethical literacy is the final product of textual, visual, data, and aural literacies. It can also be considered a form of higher-order thinking involving the ability to think critically about the use and misuse of information in any material format. Once students have learned how to examine text, visual images, numbers, and sound with a critical eye, they can begin to understand the moral obligation to (1) acknowledge the intellectual ideas and property of others, (2) report all the facts when researching an issue, (3) use visual and aural media appropriately, (4) respect the rights of others to hold opposite opinions, and (5) respect the rights of others to privacy.

School librarians can provide students with the opportunity to analyze media content and discuss the ethical implications of rhetorical strategies at course-related sites. How do the site authors/sponsors use language, images, color, sound, or videos to persuade and influence users? Researching the veracity of online scientific claims and discussing the deleterious effects that false health information could have on noncritical readers can be part of a science class. Ask students what the ethical considerations are for engaging in public discourse through social media. How can students become involved online in a political, health, or environmental cause and maintain their ethical standards when participating in online discussions, sharing, or posting (Krutka and Carpenter 54–55)? This form of literacy should not be taught separately, because it can be easily integrated into exiting resource-based units. Weaving in questions and short exercises that reinforce ethical literacy into existing assignments ensures its relevancy. Members of this generation, as we know, value education that is applicable to their daily lives. Visit the Center for Journalism Ethics site for resources and a detailed discussion of the meaning of ethical literacy and its boundaries and Newseumed.org for classroom activities that help students explore the ethical literacy implications with various media scenarios.

IN GOOGLE THEY TRUST?

Google is used for 90 percent of all searches and is the first stop for our students when initiating any information search (Epstein). Surveys are also revealing that it is completely trusted by children and teens. A United Kingdom survey reported that one in five children ages twelve to fifteen "believed information returned by a Google search must be true" (Temperton). Google and Facebook are also the main places where our students are retrieving their news, and we are now learning that news and information from these sources is skewed in favor of their personal views. A 2016 study that researched 376 million Facebook users' interactions with over 900 news outlets confirmed that people tend to seek information that accords with their opinions and perspectives (Anderson and Raine). Receiving information that only aligns with students' viewpoints renders them extremely vulnerable to accepting, sharing, and distributing false information. Teaching them how to think critically about the accuracy, reliability, and creditability of the information they retrieve is essential not only to their success in higher education endeavors but also as citizens of a functioning democracy. The social and learning characteristics of members of the iGeneration make them especially vulnerable to misinformation because they prefer to collaborate and share information quickly among their peers (Anderson and Raine).

CAN TEACHING CRITICAL THINKING SKILLS SOLVE THE PROBLEM?

Critical thinking skills can be defined as "the intellectual disciplined process of actively and skillfully applying, analyzing, synthesizing and/or evaluating information gathered from, or generated by observation, experience, reflection, reasoning or communication as a belief or action" (Balto). Researchers contend that learning to think critically can be taught and integrated into any discipline. It is an essential element that permeates instruction in every grade level of the Common Core Standards ("Common Core Standards Initiative"). Reasoning critically about any idea or subject will need to become both a skill and a habit for our students in future years. They will need to become information skeptics (Farkas).

As school librarians and educators, we are up against a formidable opponent when teaching critical thinking skills in a time of change. Without realizing it, our students are providing computer coders and programmers with huge amounts of data in the form of likes and other responses to information that they are using to subliminally influence them in directions that they think they want to go. Computer code in the form of bots has responsibilities in this win/lose information-seeking contest. Beneficial ones trawl the Internet and retrieve content that is used for relevancy rankings, measuring market share of a product, and disseminating information. Bad bots are employed to send spam, mine users' data, and manipulate public opinion by artificially boosting the popularity of a site or pushing specific content more frequently. Bad bots can appear as if they come from a friend, a political candidate, or a family member (Burkhardt 16–17).

Studies have reported that humans make poor lie detectors. In a meta-analysis of 206 lie detection experiments with documents, humans detected lies in text only 54 percent of the time (Bond and De Paulo 214). When news or other forms of information seems to come from a peer, it can be unbelievably difficult to mentally challenge the accuracy, reliability, and creditability of that information. Although content analysis software is being developed to counteract bad bots, they presently account for 30 percent of all web traffic, thus making it imperative that we teach critically thinking skills throughout the curriculum, beginning at the lowest grade levels (Burkhardt 15).

HOW SHOULD WE TEACH CRITICAL THINKING SKILLS?

For our students, even at the secondary level, Google is a magical search engine. With its semantic and predictive searching functions, it requires little intellectual work on their parts and almost instantaneously rewards them with what they think are valid results. Since Google is their main starting source for information queries, we need to begin to remove the magic curtain and show n' tell how Google operates. Explaining how search engines rank sites and keep track of the sites they have searched so that they push others within their filter bubble are beginning steps for introducing skepticism about their search results. Go further and teach them all of Google's bells and whistles. If our students are choosing it as their first search site, at least they can become critical users of it. Invite them to a lunchtime or after-school Google Fest and challenge them to find information using the advanced search option and other Google applications.

TEACH THEM TO SEARCH LATERALLY

One of the unlikely discoveries in the Stanford History Education Group study was that students were reading vertically through websites when trying to evaluate them. Some were applying site evaluation guidelines concerning the author, date, and publisher of the website just as they had been previously taught by school librarians. Unfortunately, it led most of them astray with the study's questions because most of them never investigated the source or possible bias of the website's publisher/author ("Evaluating Information") Recent observations of journalists and fact-checkers showed that they do not read down the site searching for a checklist of identifiable, but not necessarily verifiable, markers. Instead they initiate multiple lateral searches until they locate the true source of the page and confirm whether it is a biased or neutral site and can be relied upon for accurate information ("Evaluating Information"). Becoming a critical and skeptical thinker when evaluating information does not happen overnight, and our students do not bring a subject expert's oeuvre to the library. They will need assistance from their teachers and us to change their thinking process from the default belief mode to one of initial doubt when tackling assignments.

Showing students how to use verification sites and educational strategies to determine trustworthiness of sites is vitally important. Visit The Trust Project at Santa Clara University in California, where articles are flagged showing that verification has already taken place. For validating news stories, have them look at the National Institute for Computer-Assisted Reporting, Investigative Reporters and Editors Association, and Document Cloud. Public Data Lab features A Field Guide to Fake News, which outlines methods for lateral searching to detect the source of fake news (Burkhardt 27).

There are also a number of curricula that, while designed primarily for the detection of fake news, do provide a mind-set for inculcating skepticism and critical thinking skills for middle and high school students. The Stanford History Education Group has produced an online Checkology that helps students develop their own news stories that are fair and unbiased. They also have lessons for "reading like a historian" and other civic reasoning activities, all of which are designed to teach critical thinking skills and are aligned with the Common Core Standards (Stanford History Education Group). Their curriculum has been adopted by several large school districts and downloaded more than a million times. Their study cited in an earlier section served as the impetus for California and several other states to pass new media literacy laws that will require schools to teach critical thinking skills when evaluating all types of media (Graber). The News Literacy Project also features tools and strategies for students to become more adept at critical thinking with regard to finding and citing online sources (Burkhardt 27). Finally, plan to check out *The New York Times*' site Evaluating Sources in a

"Post-Truth" World: Ideas for Teaching and Learning about Fake News for additional curriculum ideas and lessons.

READING TO ACQUIRE KNOWLEDGE

As our students continue to prefer scanning to immersive reading, will their ability to remember facts and store knowledge be diminished? If they read less deeply, will they still be able to think critically and discern the difference between propaganda and the factual transmission of information (Hedges 45)? As Google "Suggest" supplies key search terms and corrects their spelling, will their database queries become more perspicacious or lazier? Already, educators are writing articles that indicate they are witnessing an epistemological shift in how students are learning (Doyle). Are we moving, as the late writer Philip Roth predicted, to a postliterate age (McGrath)? With programs such as PBS's The Great American Read that garnered over 2 million votes, generated thousands of local and nationally staged book club groups, and author appearances for 100 best-loved titles, perhaps the prophecy is premature. Deep reading seems to be fulfilling a need for a cultural and intellectual life for many citizens in a time of accelerating change (Roberts).

School librarians observe the need for immersive reading on a daily basis. Our students need to acquire facts and knowledge to take assessments that enable them to advance their education and gain entrance into colleges and universities. To think critically, they need to build up the store of background knowledge that is available to them, not at the click of a mouse, but even more quickly, from their memories. Nicholas Carr, author of *The Glass Cage*, reported on several experiments published in the peer-reviewed journal *Science* that found that "the ready availability of information online weakens our memory for facts" (Carr 79). One of the experiments requested participants to read and then type several dozen factual statements into a computer. Half of them were told that the computer would save what they typed, and the other half were told that the statements would be erased. Those who were told that they could rely on the computer remembered significantly fewer facts than those who knew that the computer would not save their work. For the experimental group, simply knowing that the information would be available to the participants seemed to reduce the likelihood that their brains made the effort to retain the information (Carr 79).

The instructional challenge for school librarians in the coming years will be how to balance the two forms of reading. Scanning is a required form of reading for the computer, but immersive reading is essential for constructing knowledge about various subjects. We will need to introduce evidence in the form of research and confirmation from national and state standards that immersive reading is critical to our students' academic success. The new American Association of School Librarians standards affirm that reading is "the core of personal and academic competency" and urge us to promote motivational reading initiatives to ensure that our students become perpetual learners (American Association of School Librarians). Cite statements from your own state standards or the Six Shifts adapted from

Engage NY. They are recommending (1) a 50 percent balance of fiction and non-fiction texts, (2) constructing knowledge by analyzing the texts and building arguments from them and providing students with the opportunity to construct their own, (3) increasing the complexity of texts and scaffolding learning activities to increase comprehension, (4) creating evidence-based questions around text that increase students' comprehension of the work, (5) that students cite evidence from texts as their sources when engaged in writing assignments, and (6) building their vocabularies by reading increasingly complex texts and using similar vocabulary when referring to the texts (Harada and Coatney 32).

Refer to the "School Library Impact Studies" that show the more students visit the library, the better their test scores and that access to books instills lifelong reading habits that will enable them to succeed in all future academic endeavors ("School Library Impact Studies . . ." 3).

Start practicing researcher Krashen's, Lee's and Lao's winning, research-based reading combination. In elementary school begin with read-alouds because they expose children to stories and build language proficiency and make written text more comprehensible, including vocabulary, grammar, and how knowledge is constructed. Move on to free, self-chosen voluntary reading, which bridges the division between conversational language and academic language. Graduate them to specialized reading that is self-selected and compelling as their reading interests naturally change and progress. Krashen, Lee and Lao claim that all the by-products of reading will fall into place, including increased vocabulary, the ability to read and comprehend more complex texts, and students' eventual evolution into life-long readers with all the academic and career benefits that accrue from this achievement (Krashen, Lee, and Lao 13–15).

CAN WE FIND THE HOME-RUN BOOKS?

One of Krashen's more startling research findings is that one positive book, which he titles a "home-run" book, can create a reader (Krashen 8). It seems almost implausible that a single book can hook a child just the way the addictive call of an application on their iPhones can, but it does. Our role in the future will be to initiate programs and services that motivate and hook children on immersive reading. David Sax, in an op-ed piece for *The New York Times*, penned an eloquent ode to the power of analog books. He believes that it engages nearly all of our senses from the brightly colored cover design, to the smell of paper and glue, to the sound of the pages being turned. More importantly, it places the reader in a walled garden far away from the technological world with its insistent need to respond. It serves as an avenue to creativity and imagination, just the ingredients for success in our schools (Sax).

Our instructional role with reading demands that we build library collections containing home-run books and to know those collections so intimately that we can guide our students to them. In Europe, for example, there is a growing movement among bibliophiles to prescribe books for clients with personal problems and to treat them with personalized recommendations that sound very akin to home-run books. At the 2016 Frankfurt Book Fair, a bibliotherapist even dressed as a doctor, complete with white coat and stethoscope, and provided a line of "patients" with personalized book recommendations who were suffering with everything from relationship problems to feeling overwhelmed by technology (Sloat).

We will need to achieve a personalized level of reading guidance in this time of change to compete with various captivating technologies. Unfortunately, there is something sinisterly appealing about observing our students sitting at computers compared to seeing them curled up with a book in their favorite library lounge chair. Observing students in the act of voluntary reading does not register favorably with many administrators, teachers, and sometimes even parents because they cannot physically witness the chemical release of oxytocin from the pituitary gland that occurs when a student is reading a "good story" and the emotional and learning effects that reading for pleasure are having on them (Colvin 153). While administrators, teachers, and parents are beginning to awaken to the abuse of screen time, they will need to be educated about the amazing effects that free, voluntary reading has on our students' test scores and emotional and psychological well-being during a time of accelerating change.

HOW DO WE MOTIVATE OUR STUDENTS TO READ?

School librarians will need to don two instructional hats in a time of change. One will entail working with technology, and the other will be to create a literacy-centered school. In a period of technological acceleration, it is going to take a community, not just a school, to raise a reader. Making books available in classrooms in addition to the school library encourages voluntary reading. It broadens the library's reach and places reading uppermost on the educational radar screen. It is especially helpful to faculty members as they move to differentiated instruction, which future technological trends predict will be possible (Pitcher and Mackey 62–63).

Involve parents at all grade levels. Our focus needs to be not only on parents of preschool and elementary-aged students but also on engaging parents of adolescents. Communicate and involve parents with a monthly newsletter that informs them of new acquisitions, invite them to join a parent/child book club, start a classics book club that culminates in viewing the film, and design and offer craft activities centered around the reading of a story or book. At parent/student gatherings model discussion questions that derive deeper meaning from the selection. Parents can observe and learn how to pose active and reflective questions that help advance students to the next reading level (Pitcher and Mackey 81–87).

Make the need for voluntary free reading a shared goal of your faculty. Once they see the research-based need for it, they should become your strongest advocates. Begin a faculty book club. Create posters of teachers holding their favorite book and display them throughout the school. Ask faculty and administrators to create "celebrity booktalks" and post them as podcasts on the school library's website. Encourage them to speak about what they are reading in front of their students and to always model the behavior during a sustained silent reading period.

Provide reading guidance with books that might enhance their teaching units for students who are interested in a topic beyond the textbook (Pitcher and Mackey 127–137).

While there is not a great deal of research concerning whether motivational reading contests improve reading achievement, they do assist by making the school library a happening place and promote the idea of a literacy-centered school. As school librarians, we should not be averse to implementing any ideas, no matter how outlandish, if it results in reinforcing reading for learning and enjoyment. A middle school librarian in Larchmont, New York, using Google Data Studio, created a digital dashboard to encourage her students to log their reading choices. Students can see what books are trending, share their reading choices with each other, and observe the number of books being read from week to week. It also succeeded in widening the circle of interested teachers. The data were employed to recommend other types of reading to students, give reluctant readers first choice of classroom library returns, and provided the librarian with ideas for future acquisitions (Cohen 28–29).

Despite analyzing the employment trends for the next five years, it is still challenging to predict what new businesses will be created and what ones will become obsolete. What will become invaluable will be the ability of our students to adapt to rapid change and become perpetual learners (Krashen, Lee, and Lao 85) Our instructional role is twofold. First, we must provide them with the skills to define an information problem, design a search strategy that will allow them to locate appropriate sources, evaluate the credibility of the sources, synthesize what they have learned, and present it in a variety of media formats. This type of instruction is direct and involves our collaboration with teachers and their presence in classrooms in every subject area. Our second and equally important role entails creating programs, displays, clubs, contests, and activities that encourage them to become lifelong readers. The latter entails a more indirect form of instruction but is absolutely essential to our schools. These two roles cannot be duplicated by instructional coordinators or digital librarians who lack the coursework and training for producing readers and inquiring minds. School librarians, however, fulfill the position perfectly.

Questions

1. Our students are operating in transliterate mode when seeking information. How should our instruction change to meet their instructional needs?
2. Will the information-seeking practices of students outpace the digital shift that our school libraries need to make?
3. What role should librarians play in balancing the scales regarding scanning and immersive types of reading?
4. How may future technologies help us in providing our students with personalized reading choices?

REFERENCES

American Association of School Librarians. 2018. "National School Library Standards. Common Beliefs." Available at: https://standards.aasl.org/beliefs.

Anderson, Janna and Lee Raine. October 19, 2017. "The Future of Truth and Misinformation Online." Pew Research Center. Available at: http://www.pewinternet.org /2017/10/19/the-future-of-truth-and-misinformation-online.

Asher, Andrew, Lynda Duke, and David Green. May 17, 2010. "The ERIAL Project: Ethnographic Research in Illinois Academic Libraries." Academic Commons. Available at: http://www.academiccommons.org/commons/essay/erial-project.

Aural Literacy. September 2015. Available at: http://www.21stcenturyschools.com/aural -literacy.html.

Balto, Mark. January 3, 2018. "Fostering Critical Thinking and Information Literacy Skills: An Inquiry into What Librarians Could Do to Support Students." Library Blog for the Touro College Community. Available at: https://tclibraryblog.wordpress.com /2018/01/03/criticalthinking.

Barack, Lauren. September 2014. "Good Research Habits Pay Off." *School Library Journal*. 60(9): 14.

Bond, Charles F., Jr. and Bella M. De Paulo. March 2006. "Accuracy of Deception Judgments." *Personality and Social Psychology Review*. 10(3): 214–234.

Breakstone, Joel et al. March 8, 2018. "Why We Need a New Approach to Teaching Digital Literacy." *Phi Delta Kappan*. Available at: http://www.kappanonline.org /breakstone-need-new-approach-teaching-digital-literacy.

Burkhardt, Joanna M. 2017. "Combating Fake News in the Digital Age." *Library Technology Reports*. 53(8): 1–33.

Carr, Nicholas. 2014. *The Glass Cage: Where Automation Is Taking Us*. New York: W. W. Norton.

Cohen, Kelsey. June 2018. "Supporting Middle School Reading." *American Libraries*. Available at: https://americanlibrariesmagazine.org/2018/06/01/supporting-middle -school-reading.

Colorado Department of Education. 2016. "Highly Effective School Library Programs." Available at: https://www.cde.state.co.us/cdelib/2016heslprogram.

Colvin, Geoff. 2015. *Humans Are Underrated*. New York: Penguin.

"Common Core State Standards Initiatives." 2018. Available at: http://www.corestandards.org.

Cordell, Diane M. 2015. *Using Images to Teach Critical Thinking Skills: Visual Literacy and Digital Photography*. Santa Barbara, CA: Libraries Unlimited.

Dow, Mirah J., Tonya Davis, and Angela Vietti-Okane. 2013. "Influencing Instructional Partnerships in Preservice Elementary Education Teachers." In: *School Libraries Matter: Views from the Research*, edited by Mirah J. Dow. Santa Barbara, CA: Libraries Unlimited, pp. 39–49.

Doyle, Christopher L. March 31, 2014. "K-12 Education in a Post-Literate Age." *Education Week*. Available at: https://www.edweek.org/ew/articles/2014/04/02/27doyle_ep .h33.html.

Epstein, Mark. December 18, 2017. "The Google-Facebook Duopoly Threatens Diversity of Thought." *The Wall Street Journal*. Available at: https://www.wsj.com/articles /the-google-facebook-duopoly-threatens-diversity-of-thought-1513642519.

"Evaluating Information." November 22, 2016. The Cornerstone of Civic Online Reasoning. Executive Summary. Stanford History Education Group. Available at: https:// stacks.stanford.edu/file/druid:fv751yt5934/SHEG%20Evaluating%20Information %20Online.pdf.

Farkas, Meredith. June 2018. "Beyond Fake News." *American Libraries*. Available at: https://americanlibrariesmagazine.org/2018/06/01/beyond-fake-news.

Flowers, Sarah. 2017. *Crash Course in Young Adult Services.* Santa Barbara, CA: Libraries Unlimited.

Greenfield, Patricia M. January 2009. "Technology and Informal Education: What Is Taught, What Is Learned." *Science.* 323(2): 69–71.

Harada, Violet H. and Sharon Coatney. 2013. *Inquiry and the Common Core: Librarians and Teachers Designing Teaching for Learning.* Santa Barbara, CA: Libraries Unlimited.

Head, Alison J. *Learning the Ropes: How Freshmen Conduct Research Once They Enter College.* December 4, 2013. Project Information Literacy Research Report. Available at: http://www.projectinfolit.org/uploads/2/7/5/4/27541717/pil_2013_freshmen study_fullreportv2.pdf.

Hedges, Chris. 2010. *Empire of Illusion: The End of Literacy and the Triumph of Spectacle.* New York: Nation Books.

Hill, Valerie. 2016. "The Future of Libraries in the Digital Age." In: *Teaching and Learning in Virtual Environments: Archives, Museums, and Libraries,* edited by Patricia C. Franks and Lori A. Bell. Santa Barbara, CA: Libraries Unlimited, pp. 225–236.

Ipri, Tom. 2010. "Introducing Transliteracy: What Does It Mean to Academic Libraries." *College & Research Libraries.* 71(10): 532–567. Available at: https://crln.acrl.org /index.php/crlnews/article/view/8455/8698.

Johnson, Doug A. 2013. *The Indispensable Librarian: Surviving and Thriving in School Libraries in the Information Age.* 2nd ed. Santa Barbara, CA: Linworth.

Jukes, Ian, Ted McCain, and Lee Crockett. 2010. *Understanding the Digital Generation: Teaching and Learning in the New Digital Landscape.* Kelowna, BC. 21st Century Fluency Project.

Kachel, Debra E. and Keith Curry Lance. April 2018. "Changing Times: School Library Staffing Status." *Teacher Librarian.* Available at: http://teacherlibrarian.com/2018 /04/11/changing-times-school-librarian-staffing-status.

Katz, Irwin R. September 2007. "Testing Information Literacy in Digital Environments." *Information Technology and Libraries.* 26(3): 3–12. Available at: https://ejournals .bc.edu/ojs/index.php/ital/article/view/3271.

"Kids and Teens Online." October 29, 2013. Available at: https://kidsandteens online .com.

Krashen, Stephen. 2004. *The Power of Reading: Insights from the Research.* 2nd ed. Santa Barbara, CA: Libraries Unlimited.

Krashen, Stephen D., Sy-Ying Lee, and Christy Lao. 2017. *Comprehensive and Compelling: The Causes and Effects of Free Voluntary Reading.* Santa Barbara, CA: Libraries Unlimited.

Krutka, Daniel G. and Jeffrey P. Carpenter. November 2017. "Digital Citizenship in the Curriculum: Educators Can Support Strong Visions of Citizenship by Teaching with and about Social Media." *Educational Leadership.* 75(3): 50–55.

Lee, Elizabeth A. and Don A. Klinger. 2013. "The Role of the School Library: Building Collaborations to Support School Improvement." In: *School Libraries Matter: Views from the Research,* edited by Mirah J. Dow. Santa Barbara, CA: Libraries Unlimited, pp. 79–88.

Levitov, Deborah D. 2014. "School Librarians and the CCSS: Knowing, Claiming, and Acting on Their Expertise." In: *Inquiry and the Common Core,* edited by Violet H. Harada and Sharon Coatney. Santa Barbara, CA: Libraries Unlimited, pp. 31–48.

Levitov, Deborah D. 2012. "Teaching and Learning: The Heart of Advocacy." In: *Activism and the School Librarian: Tools for Advocacy and Survival,* edited by Deborah D. Levitov. Santa Barbara, CA: Libraries Unlimited, pp. 13–26.

McGrath, Charles. November 17, 2012. "Goodbye, Frustration, Pen Put Aside, Roth Talks." *The New York Times.* Available at: https://cn.nytimes.com/culture/20121126/c26roth/en-us.

O'Neil, Cathy. 2016. *Weapons of Math Destruction.* New York: Crown.

Palfrey, John. 2015. *BiblioTech: Why Libraries Matter More Than Ever in the Age of Google.* New York: Basic Books.

Pitcher, Sharon M. and Bonnie Mackey. 2013. *Collaborating for Real Literacy: Librarian, Teacher, Literacy Coach, and Principal.* 2nd ed. Santa Barbara, CA: Linworth.

Roberts, M. B. August 9, 2018. "Two Million Votes—and Counting—as PBS' Great American Read Continues the Tally for America's Best Loved Novel." Available at: https://parade.com/692090/m-b-roberts/two-million-votes-and-counting-as-pbs-great-american-read-continues-the-tally-for-americas-best-loved-no.

Salisbury, Fiona and Sharon Karasmanis. 2011. "Are They Ready? Exploring Student Information Literacy Skills in the Transition from Secondary to Tertiary Education." *Australian Academic & Research Libraries.* 42(1): 43–58.

Sax, David. November 20, 2017. "Our Love Affair with Digital Is Over." *The New York Times.* Available at: https://www.nytimes.com/2017/11/18/opinion/sunday/internet-digital-technology-return-to-analog.html.

Scheeren, William O. 2015. *Technology Handbook for School Librarians.* Santa Barbara, CA: Libraries Unlimited.

"School Library Impact Studies: A Review of Findings and Guide to Sources." August 2013. Available at: https://www.baltimorelibraryproject.org/wp-content/uploads/downloads/2013/09/Library-Impact-Studies.pdf.

Shannon, Donna M. "Principals' Perceptions of School Librarians." 2009. *School Libraries Worldwide.* 15(2): 1–22.

Sloat, Sarah. December 18, 2016. "Book Doctors' Say What's Good for You." *The Wall Street Journal.* Available at: https://www.wsj.com/articles/book-doctors-say-what-you-need-is-a-good-read-1482091512.

Stanford History Education Group. Accessed October 2018. Available at: https://sheg.stanford.edu.

Temperton, James. November 20, 2015. "One in Five Kids Believe Everything Google Tells Them." *Wired.* Available at: https://www.wired.co.uk/article/digital-natives-children-trust-online-ofcom.

Wu, Tim. 2016. *The Attention Merchants: The Epic Scramble to Get Inside Our Heads.* New York: Vintage.

8

Organization and Management Trends

INSURGENTS WITHIN BUREAUCRACIES

The goal of every school librarian should be to organize and manage a school library so that it is the proverbial "academic heartbeat of the school." To do so in a time of rapid change requires us to become insurgents in our bureaucracies. Insurgent behavior does not mean operating in a void. It does, however, mean organizing and managing the school library so that it is the most powerful and influential department within the institution. Power can be thought of as possessing influence and social control. It means having sufficient esteem within an organization to successfully promote one's goals. This power is not characterized by autocratic behavior but is meant to provide us with control over our achievements at work and our professional self-concept (Grimes 724–728). To position a school library to be the most powerful department within the school demands that we develop formidable organization and managerial skills. Fortunately, the training we receive in organizing information and providing access to it for all of our users readies us for this challenge.

By design, schools fit the definition of a bureaucracy. They are characterized by varying degrees of personal freedom (Waters and Waters 76–79). While school librarians do not possess total freedom within our institutions, any of us experiencing a flexible schedule has the liberty to contact faculty members during their preparation periods or at a time in between their classes. This personal freedom places us in a unique position to expand our access and to provide numerous programs and services ranging from classroom instruction to individualized assistance or instruction integrating a new technology.

Bureaucracies are constructed around an interwoven concept of dependency. School librarians are dependent upon several hierarchies of authorities for our funding, allotted space, and staffing. Within the hierarchy, each person is granted jurisdiction over a specific area and is responsible to others for exercising power within a given sphere. In looking at a flow chart of the school's power structure, a person's title and job description demonstrate their position and ranking within the bureaucratic structure. These interlocking hierarchies ensure that we must work with everyone in the school to gain power and influence. As librarians, we are not given carte blanche within our schools to command faculty to collaborate with us or supervise our sustained silent reading programs. Even though we are placed in a work environment that provides us with a semblance of autonomy, it may isolate us from other parts of the organization that we need to connect to and with whom our destiny is bound. Developing power and influence within this bureaucracy is a means for fostering independence and gaining control over our professional lives (Hartzell 3).

Gary Hartzell, in his outstanding book, *Building Influence for the School Librarian*, believes that it is essential that we understand how bureaucratic dependencies work so that we can become successful insurgents in them. He recommends identifying the people/positions that are most important to the success of school library programs and services and determining how dependent school librarians are upon them. If their support is essential to our success, rank them high. If their support is critical to achieving school library goals, give them a medium priority, and assign a low ranking if their support is important to the quality of the library's programs and services (Hartzell 4).

Without consulting any research studies, most of us would prioritize people in the following positions as having significant influence with the school's library: principal, assistant principal, department chairs, prominent faculty, parents, students, staff members, curriculum coordinator, technology specialists, superintendent, board of education, and the state and federal governments (Hartzell 4). Coincidentally, we would also identify the bureaucratic titles that a study of exemplary school libraries conducted with Ontario, Canada, schools noted. They cited board-level policies, administrative support, principal knowledge, and community and parent involvement, among other factors, as essential to establishing an outstanding school library program (Klinger et al. 18). School board–level policies and support, funding, and staffing models for a school library are all derived from decisions by school board members that are, in turn, guided by a school superintendent. Building-level administrative support is determined by a principal and assistant principal who gain knowledge from teachers, students, demonstrated librarian skills, and parent involvement (Oberg 13).

After creating a bureaucratic dependency map, school librarians need to consider each title's physical proximity to the school library and assess the strength of the relationship. If the school library is physically proximate to various bureaucratic titles that we rank essential and critical to the school library's programs and services, our interactions with people in these positions will probably be more frequent. Librarians need to ensure that our interactions are positive, mutually supportive, and able to fulfill "each other's needs and goals" (Hartzell 6). School librarians risk isolation in our positions, and we are currently in a time of significant technological, economic, and employment-related change. We need others to pay positive attention to our programs and services. Without that attention, our ability to gain power, funding, and influence will depreciate just like a new car or video game.

Pretend that you are playing a word-association game with your teachers, administrators, students, and parents. Ask them to say the first word that occurs to them when they hear the words book, school, and technology. School librarians need to make a prime organizational goal that the word *library* is the first word associated with book, online resources, technology, and, of course, school (Hartzell 81).

ORGANIZING TO THRIVE

Even though school librarian job losses have slowed, they have been continuing in a downward trend ever since the economic recovery began. While 2014–2015 data showed a little upward bump, the decrease recommenced in 2016–2017 with a 2.8 percent decline in school librarian positions. Since 1999 19 percent of school librarians have lost their jobs (Lance). The ability to access information at any hour or location has changed how students use our physical space. When college students receive a research assignment, an EBSCO survey revealed that 68 percent of them initiate their research by consulting Google and Wikipedia first ("Why Are Digital Research Skills . . ."). Now with access to a wealth of online databases, our students can successfully complete a research assignment, especially if it requires scientific or current information sources, using their personal computer while sipping coffee in a local café or sitting on their beds.

Collins, in *How the Mighty Fall*, isolated several factors that organizations experience before they bow to the inevitable. All of the elements can be characterized as ignoring the signals of change. First is a "hubris" that gives librarians a sense of entitlement to the present state of our libraries. Our hundred-plus-years' existence in schools makes it easy to think that school librarians will always be needed to organize and manage libraries. A second stage concerns "denial of risk and peril." School librarians in this stage engage in magical thinking and ignore declining circulation data, lower library attendance, and fewer collaborative activities because we may attribute the changes to a passing fad that our students are having with social media. The penultimate stage involves administrators looking for some sort of salvation in the form of instructional coordinators who can bring about the technological and collaborative changes that they are seeking to raise student achievement. Collins believes that the bright side of this staged decline is that it is usually self-inflicted and can be arrested. The path to a secure and trusted position within our schools is within our organizational and managerial hands (Collins 27).

IMPACT OF CHANGE AND BECOMING ITS AGENT

School librarians are already aware that our physical libraries are evolving and will continue to do so in the future. Technology will move us to modify our learning environment and propose alternative means of delivering information. We will need to make organizational changes in our conventional libraries to support the educational standards of our schools. (Sullivan 1). Change hastens three effects. The first consequence is that it accelerates loss. Faculty miss doing something in a certain way. They wish that they could rely upon former methods of teaching as a guarantee for student achievement. Principals are less confident of the role that librarians need to play within their schools, and parents are perplexed about the time and devotion students give to their smart devices instead of engaging in face-to-face conversation. Change also threatens competence. Faculty members were formerly masters and mistresses of their classrooms, standing at the front lecturing and passing out assignments afterwards. Now they need to learn to be "guides on the side," proficient in the use of Google Suite apps, student-response systems, and interactive whiteboards. Administrators are challenged to manage their schools with all these new technologies, make wise budgetary decisions with staffing, and ensure that their student achievement levels improve under the onslaught of state-mandated reforms. Parents are unsure of the role they need to play in regulating the amount of screen time with their children. What are the trade-offs when children are content to remain in their rooms texting one another as opposed to engaging in personal interaction? What can parents do to help when their child is being cyber bullied?

Change also causes conflict. Every technological advancement is presented as an improvement for all, but that is seldom the case. Members of a department may rise or fall as a result of a school instituting a new grading, accounting, or reading system. School librarians, whose role within the school organization is in flux right now, are facing competition from instructional coordinators, technology integrators, and other job titles that stress the need for proficiencies with technology rather than instructional design skills. Faculty usually view change as an administrative imposition upon tried-and-true methods of obtaining student achievement. They can view those who imposed it as the enemy. These effects of change make the idea of conflict and its pushback—resistance—totally understandable. They also present school librarians with an unprecedented opportunity to be of service to all members of our educational communities during a time of unprecedented change (Evans 1–3).

BUILDING UP CHIPS IN THE BANK

Empathizing with what faculty, administrators, and parents are experiencing with regard to accelerating change can help place school librarians in a leadership position in schools. Some actions are as easy as learning the names and responsibilities of everyone in the school. Knowing that someone is responsible for extended day care gives librarians the chance to provide and recommend appropriate videos right before vacation periods when students are too hyped up to complete homework.

Employing positive hearsay techniques is another way to build relationships. When you've heard something nice said about a colleague, pass it on. When change threatens, it affects morale. School librarians can be the bearers of positive news, help with on-demand reading tips and lists of the best education apps, and maintain a safe zone location for faculty to just come and chat about how their day is going (Hartzell 167).

As technology continues to make even greater inroads on faculty professional and personal lives, assess how school librarians can provide them with assistance. Use Survey Monkey or Google Forms and conduct a needs assessment to ascertain what new programs and services might be of help with their curriculum or the administrative side of teaching. Seek their advice about library policies affecting use of resources, collaborative units, or consumption of food in the library. Once you gain a seat on the technology, curriculum, and strategic planning committees, attend as a consultant in addition to a participant. Offer to obtain price quotes for new technologies, call peer schools about their decision to drop or retain AP classes, or provide research about the latest education trend for current awareness. Remain up to date regarding developments with state, Common Core, and other curriculum and assessment standards. When a new course has been approved, design and insert a new library resource–based unit into it. Testing and grading consume a significant amount of teachers' time. If you have space, set up a place for test make-up in the library to relieve teachers from proctoring them after or during preparation times (Hartzell 168).

The hallmark of all good teachers is the distribution of kudos to their students at appropriate times, but they rarely receive them in return. When they do win an award, receive special notice, or receive commendations for either an in-school or community event, publicize it. Other faculty as well as students will be interested and may connect more to a teacher who recently completed a marathon, raised funds for cancer research, or published an article in a physics education journal (Hartzell 170).

Providing teachers with personalized assistance and instruction with new technologies is probably one of the most valuable parts of a school librarian's job description. Usually after a new technology session, a significant number of faculty will have not received sufficient training to feel comfortable implementing it with their classes. Creating group, department-based, and individual sessions for them to simply practice using a new device or software with a nonjudgmental librarian will provide school librarians with a wealth of goodwill that can be used to further their influence within the school community.

BECOME AN INTRAPRENEUR WITHIN THE ORGANIZATION

Another way to view the organizational role of the school librarian is from an intrapreneurial perspective. This type of librarian is associated with the word *growth*. Many other types of librarians are already embracing the concept. In 2009 the first conference titled "Entrelib: The Conference for Entrepreneurial Librarians" was held, and the theme was promoting librarians as change agents. In 2016 the conference title was "Imagine the NEXT?" (Almquist and Almquist 24).

In a time of change, schools have a critical need for the library's programs and services. Always be thinking of ways to expand them, gain additional funding, and go beyond the status quo. If students are reluctant to visit the Study Skills, Reading, or Literacy Center because they believe it stigmatizes them, approach an administrator with a proposal to move it to the library, where the librarian can easily supply the students with additional resources. Investigate the opportunities for writing federal, state, and county grants to fund special library programs to purchase equipment or materials to enhance the collection. If the school cannot afford to fund a makerspace in the library, seek donated tools and a volunteer who is willing to teach students how to use them creatively and safely.

Intrapreneurial librarians are characterized by impatience. They do not wait for events to occur—they anticipate them. When they see the need for change in an organization, they devote time to developing an idea and then act. If they find research supporting that genrefying the collection seems to result in additional fiction reading by students, they initiate the steps to accomplish it. Their impatience with the status quo seems to imbue them with a sense of urgency, and they tend to set short timetables for achieving their goals. Intrapreneurial librarians are motivated by a need for personal success. They enjoy solving problems; selling new ideas to administrators, faculty, and students; and seeing them come to fruition. Acting in an intrapreneurial rather than reactive fashion earns them what all librarians want—power and influence in their organizations (Almquist and Almquist 14–15).

NAVIGATING THE ORGANIZATIONAL POWER STRUCTURE

Because schools are changing so rapidly, conflict is endemic to the culture. Hartzell gently warns us that when librarians are invited to be part of the change effort, the powers-that-be have really issued an invitation to a fight. Change involves the re-divvying up of resources, power, and influence. Moving a library item up to the top of the agenda indicates its degree of importance. Whether the issue is to seek more space, funding, furniture, or equipment, how an issue is framed is a definite factor in determining its outcome. Describing a desired goal as benefiting several departments or the entire school is essential to avoid loss aversion. If department chairs or members of a department believe that they will lose autonomy, equipment, or influence over a policy, it will probably jeopardize the library's chances of having any initiative achieved or adopted. Positioning agenda items as positively affecting the collective interest of the entire school makes the item more challenging for those who might oppose it. Framing an issue to reflect that it will help affect student achievement, enhance learning, or ease teachers' workloads may also well determine the goal's successful outcome (Arbuthnott and Scerbe 176–178).

When a school librarian gains a seat on the technology, curriculum, or strategic planning committee, polite listening is our overt role, but the covert one needs to be advocating for more of what will eventually be distributed (Hartzell 7). It can range from acquiring space for more comfortable seating to the acquisition of a 3D printer. Moving a library item to the top of the agenda provides time for more measured debate. Your role on the new course adoption committee, for example, is to ensure that every new course contains a librarian-designed resource-based unit. The overall objective of every meeting is to reduce the school library's dependency on others and increase their dependency on your department for programs and services. The more dependent other parts of the school become on the school library for information literacy skills, technology instruction, and reading guidance, the more power and influence the school librarian has amassed to effect change (Hartzell 7).

RESOURCES, RECIPROCITY, AND POWER

Many historians believe that a major contributing factor to winning World War II was the Allied Forces' control over the supply of oil. Oil was considered an indispensable resource for the waging of war, and preventing the enemy from accessing oil facilitated an end to a massive global conflict (Miller). Basic to exercising power and influence is controlling resources. Having a collection of print and nonprint materials available is essential to school librarians' successful functioning. Hartzell defines a resource as "anything you control that someone else wants" (Hartzell 77). For librarians, this resource is not necessarily a collection of materials—it can also be available space, personalized service, instructional design capabilities, technology assistance, or expertise. It is how visible we are at using, displaying, and teaching with these resources that can endow us with power and influence within the school community. Linking the success of the school's mission with these resources should be a major organizational priority.

Our print and nonprint collections are available to everyone in the school, not just students. Librarians curate online resources to accompany a presentation given by an administrator to parents about sleep-deprived adolescents. School librarians show the film *Screenagers: Growing Up in the Digital Age* to parents in the library and accompany it with group discussion questions afterwards. Purchasing books to support a new course being offered in "Literature of the Civil War" for an English department member is a daily task. Preparing database-use tip sheets for students during term paper season taps into a vast resource of information sources that literally contains something for every member of the school (Hartzell 77).

School librarians are members of the helping professions, which assist with the growth of or treat the problems of a person's intellectual and social well-being ("Helping-Profession . . ."). As such, we are accustomed to offering our programs and services gratis to our students and colleagues. Reciprocity, however, should not be considered a negative term in the give-and-take of our services. On the contrary, it should be invoked to enable us to gain the power and influence within our schools to ensure our students' academic success. Reciprocity implies some kind of obligation for provided assistance. Sociologists who have studied it believe that it saturates human exchanges of every type. The incurrence of obligation can make it challenging for a recipient to resist future requests for support of the library's programs and services (Cialdini 30).

Reciprocity does not confine itself just to assistance with the library's resources. It can include covering a colleague's classes in an emergency, helping an administrator who is taking an online course with research to write a paper, or providing a faculty member with a list of fun places to visit during a weekend with relatives. The size of the debt does not scale evenly. It is difficult to assess how deep of an obligation someone who uses the library's resources and a librarian's' expertise feels toward a school librarian. It may occur when you tell them that the database you ordered for their department may be on the chopping block because of possible budget cuts that will trigger a reciprocal action on their part in the form of a protest, memo of support, or appeal to an administrator. It may manifest itself with a yes vote to place some new technology in the library for all to use, rather than just the students who have access to the technology lab.

Reciprocity is constructed upon a foundation of expertise not only with our print collection but also with our unique talents to find information from a variety of online and print resources. The studies cited in Chapter 7 reveal that college students are unable to identify credible sources of information and are graduating from their respective institutions with a dismal level of information-seeking skills. Some are now our colleagues, and other faculty members are of the legacy media generation, and they also lack precise searching skills.

The online resources that we have at our command are available through state and school consortia, regardless of our level library. It is indeed a goldmine for helping us initiate reciprocity among all adult members of the school community. Our searching skills rival anyone's in the school. Professionally, we also practice the American Library Association's rules regarding client privacy so our colleagues know that we can be trusted to handle any information request with a high degree of sensitivity and professionalism. Becoming known as the person to go to with any information question places school librarians in a position of power and influence (Hartzell 56–57).

NAVIGATING SCHOOL CULTURE FOR SUCCESS

Herodotus is most frequently associated with the aphorism "Custom is king of all" (Kaplan). Every organization has unique customs or a culture that reveals itself in subtle ways to all employees. How a school responds to violations of the honor or dress codes, parent complaints, and student test score results are "tells" about its ethos and value system. Librarians must navigate this organizational culture to become powerful and influential members of it. Operating as an insurgent within it requires librarians to contribute to the teaching and learning in the school by constantly reading the cultural tea leaves. Understanding the school norms and being aware of the undercurrent of relationships among various faculty members and administrators are challenging. Oberg asserts that school culture is highly formed by the norms of "conservatism, individualism, and presentism" (Oberg 11). The first factor, conservatism, characterizes the education profession's traits that make it appealing to practice. The profession of teaching encompasses attainable post–high school education, interaction with a younger demographic, helping others, perpetuation of school life, remunerative work, and a quality of life that permits pursuit of other activities. Faculty members who experienced school as rewarding, for example, are less likely to seek changes in the school's structure or to commit the time and work to affecting significant changes in their delivery of instruction. The individualism of teachers is derived from their initiation into it. Teachers are given their own set of classes and learn how to manage them mainly without the opportunity to observe their peers' methods or techniques. Their skills are honed from personal experience, and they consider them indigenous to themselves. Presentism entails how their remuneration is determined. Although some school districts have tried to link salaries to student outcomes, the majority of teacher salaries are based on the amount of education they have attained and the years of experience they have within the school district. The latter norm has been a factor in K–12 education for decades and will probably continue in the future. It informs us that instituting major changes, including school-wide collaborative teaching and integrating resource-based units in every subject, represents a sea change for most faculty. The motivation for altering their teaching to accommodate a shared type of instruction is not particularly strong (Oberg 9–14).

Even though research shows that collaboration has excellent learning outcomes, teachers remain resistant to it for additional reasons that must be considered when navigating school culture. The element of time is a major factor. Teachers are always in short supply of it because of the bureaucratic necessities involving scheduled state assessments, daily grading, and progress reporting. Effort is another. Unless the librarian can shoulder the workload for designing the entire unit and seeking only minor adjustments from the teacher as a subject expert, the time and energy to integrate resource-based units into curricula can be viewed as just another unwanted burden. Collaborative teaching also entails some lifestyle changes, where teachers are serving in a consultant capacity rather than in an instructive position where they are facing or lecturing the class. Faculty members may be leery of their teaching style being exposed to others in the library, which consequently places their self-esteem at risk. It is also important to consider role reversal when a librarian may be instructing students in the first two days of a unit and teachers view themselves in a subsequently inferior position (Oberg 15).

OVERCOMING ORGANIZATIONAL RESISTANCE

Many of these correlative cultural factors are unspoken between teachers and librarians. They call for us to develop organizational acumen and expertise in how to overcome resistance and gain cooperation without having formal authority. Navigating the culture to achieve our instructional and organizational goals necessitates being truly attuned to the psychological reasons behind a teacher's reluctance to embrace collaborative instruction. Since resistance seems to center itself around the elements of time, effort, lifestyle, and self-esteem, school librarians need to be ingenious in discovering ways to maximize time by offering to co-evaluate units, preparing assessment rubrics, and posting assignment templates and other learning aids that will save time during a lesson. Keeping a teacher's effort in the unit's planning stage to a minimum can also be achieved by interviewing them about the unit's learning objectives, time frame, number of required sources, and other aspects in a short session so that the librarian can assume the sole design burden. Creating an orderly yet relaxed atmosphere to coteach the unit can do a great deal to ease the issues centered around different teaching styles and possible loss of self-esteem. Indicating a willingness to edit, add, or amend unit questions quickly at a teacher's request not only makes a teacher feel in control of the unit but also shows the librarian's deference to the teacher as subject expert (Oberg 9–20).

These steps can achieve a great deal to overcoming collaboration resistance and improve the instructional role of the school librarian within the school community. Time is not on our side when it comes to organizational change. Studies show that instructional innovative change even of the simplest type can take three to five years. Major change where resource-based units are present in all curricular areas takes ten years to see fruition (Fullan 210). In a time of accelerating changes, it remains to be seen whether school librarians can carve out a critical instructional role within our schools that makes us invaluable to our organizations and highly competitive in the educational marketplace.

ORGANIZING FUTURE-READY LIBRARIES

Librarians are facing the fiercest competition ever in the form of a highly addictive device that is claiming our students' attention during almost every waking moment. We need to contend with this technological incursion that is shortening our students' attention spans and lessening their desire for intellectual endeavors. We need to engage them in immersive activities with reading recommendations, differentiated instruction, programs, contests, and displays that are delivered as personally as possible (Middleton 45). According to Middleton, author, of *Yes! On Demand*, many of our users approach our library as they would a hardware store, intimidated by the number of shelves and their numerous contents. While our students receive instruction in how to find materials on our shelves, they usually forget how to navigate them and may be hesitant to seek librarian assistance in finding materials. Leading them to a resource or service they need rather than pointing to the direction where it lies can start creating a warm, welcoming environment that leads them to ask for further assistance or provides them with that home-run book that may hook them on reading for life. Personalized service and assistance also provide librarians with the opportunity to replicate students' favorite retail store experiences like Starbucks and the Apple Store, which they associate with comfort, care, and connection (Middleton 48).

Organizing our libraries to facilitate personalized service and to create an environment where students want to remain long after their classes are officially over should be uppermost during changing times. Schnapp of the Harvard University MetaLab proposes the design of a hybrid space where digital and analog coexist (Palfrey 63). A hybrid library of this type would feature comfortable reading and studying areas to encourage more face-to-face exchanges, active learning classrooms, media production facilities, makerspaces, and small rooms for group work (Sullivan vii–ix). Evolving into a hybrid library is making it future ready because parts of the print collection, especially in the sciences, will definitely be moving into digital format. The demand for different digital formats will also grow with more students accessing information through YouTube and video-streaming services rather than through online databases. This information format can be expected to increase in the physical sciences because of its high explanatory value when it is accompanied by movement and pictures of a scientific process or phenomenon.

Presently the learning commons design concept seems to capture the essence of a hybrid library, but there is no set type of design that should be imposed. Before reconfiguring a conventional library to render it future ready, school librarians need to read the technological and cultural tea leaves. Examine the school's mission statement and read between its lines. Try and determine the who, what, where, when, and how of technology use within the school. Conduct a needs assessment to discover how many teachers are using interactive whiteboards, software apps, online library databases, e-Textbooks, and the like. Is the curriculum totally devoted to preparing students for college, or does it also have a vocational component? Would students benefit from a makerspace, or would establishing a multipurpose room/area for collaborative purposes be a better use of the space? Collections of legacy media need to provide students with manga and graphic novels and popular fiction. Print materials should be available that support instructional units. The seating should be comfortable with space configured for immersive reading and just daydreaming. Consider having a cyber café for students to drink coffee and cocoa, check for texts, socialize, or read. Create a multipurpose hybrid presentation space where students might interact with authors on Skype or meet them in person, listen to stories read to them by a librarian, or listen to an audiobook or podcast. A librarian in McLean County, Illinois, used this type of hybrid space to set up a live interview with an astronaut on the International Space Station for a science class (Long).

If there is room, establish a technology petting zoo where students and faculty can experiment with any new equipment that has been purchased. This can provide some teachers with an opportunity to play around with it before they encounter it in their classroom. Set up a genius bar that can be staffed with student techies who receive community service credit. Assigned to the library for specific periods, they can assist students as well as faculty with installing apps on their smart devices and can troubleshoot pesky devices or software (King 55). The space also needs to be wired for students to employ a student-response app on their smart devices or watch a TED talk on an interactive whiteboard (Johnson 113–114).

Teaching spaces are critical. They need to be constructed so that the librarian or a teacher can impart information or knowledge to an entire class in the first ten minutes and then move them into collaborative areas of the library for small group work. Small rooms that are multipurpose need to be available for faculty as well. Teachers should be able to have a parent conference or have a department or team meeting in these rooms. If the library is not super busy, they should also be available to anyone who wants to use them (Johnson 114–115).

KEEP WATCHING THE SPACE

Observe how the library spaces are being used, and be willing to alter them depending on how the spaces are currently being employed. Do students prefer to stand while they are working? Are they moving around a great deal to get supplies from one area and then returning to their work spaces? When seated in chairs, how are they seated? What areas of the library seem to attract them the most? Are they moving to certain areas of the library because they need to charge their devices? If so, purchase a charging station or create one with chargers that can be glued to an immovable surface. Do students have easy access to printers, can they easily connect to the Internet, and can they upload or download content from smart devices to social media sites (King 55)? Is there sufficient space for all of the daily activities? How frequently do you have to turn classes away because you are oversubscribed (Sullivan 36–37)?

FUTURE SPACE SHARING

Consider the user population. While the main one during the day and school year are students and teachers, what spaces, equipment, and supplies might be needed if extended day programs are instituted in the school district? Does the school have a summer school, and would teachers and students benefit from using the space? The one-stop shopping concept can easily be transferred to a library setting and would also be embraced by administrators tasked with justifying reconfiguring the library space or building a new one. Study skills or learning centers marry well with libraries. Students encountering problems with research assignments can receive additional assistance from a librarian with a curated analog and digital collection of materials. Even though school librarians are adept at teaching and employing new technologies with classes, help from a resident member of the technology department can be a godsend. Placing a member of this department in a library-based multimedia lab or production studio can help with student presentations that are required to be in digital format. Consider developing co-expertise with a member of the technology department in using all or some of the following: Photoshop, Flash, Illustrator, Comic Life, GarageBand, iMovie, FlipShare, Prezi, Final Cut Express, and software programs and applications (Sullivan 19).

Palfrey urges school librarians to search for "that sweet spot where fun and learning" unite (Palfrey 81). For our types of libraries, we are serving a population demographic that we are charged to educate rather than entertain. While a hybrid library needs to reflect the academic mission of our schools, it can still be configured to reflect the different media formats students now use to acquire information and build knowledge. In the near future, neither analog nor digital will dominate our collections. Both types of information materials are essential for our students to experience an intellectual and cultural life. More importantly, however, will be the need for them to interact with each other in a setting conducive to debate, discussion, collaboration, and study that is filled with access to curated analog and digital materials (Palfrey 81).

BUILDING A DIGITAL LIBRARY

School librarians have to bridge the analog and digital worlds with a hybrid library. We need to and can make as much information available to our students online as is contained in our conventional libraries. Our students can access information from any place, anywhere, and at any time. Many of them are taking online classes and/or are required to take one before they graduate. Significant numbers of students attend online virtual schools. From previously cited research, most of them are unable to discern whether the online information they retrieve is valid, reliable, and credible. As more information of questionable quality continues to pour onto the Internet, students and faculty will be seeking curated places that contain credible sites for information pertaining to all subjects and disciplines. The school digital library should be their first stop in any school-related information search.

Develop a mission and collection development policy that reflects the school's educational mission and culture. In the future, this library may well rival the school's conventional library in size and scope (Craver 1). Think of it as possessing two types of content: internally and externally developed. Every link should contain a brief annotation to facilitate selection and should be relied upon to open. Their availability should be checked frequently.

Internally developed content should include general introductory information about the library, as well as policies and procedures pertaining to acquisitions, controversial materials, and the like. Furnish publicity descriptions for special programs such as reading contests, exhibits, and displays. Provide bibliographies and webographies for recreational and curriculum-based reading. Post resource-based library instructional units complete with assessment rubrics, syllabi, and sample finished products. Host online forms for eChat, homework help, reference assistance, and term paper counseling. Be sure to place links to the latest school library research findings concerning information literacy and reading and the correlation with schools having a certified librarian and positively affecting student achievement. Stay current with the latest research in this area and link to the results when they are published. If major suggestions are being proposed concerning the library's programs and services, having the latest research at your fingertips can be helpful in counteracting it (Craver 20).

Externally developed content should feature access to the online public access catalogs of the school library, all schools within the district, the local public library, and state and local college libraries. Links to the school library's online databases and ones accessible with a public library card at the local and state levels should also be made available. Include access to trial database subscriptions, the school portal, and curated websites that are credible and reliable (Scheeren 174).

It is with curated websites that school librarians' expertise and knowledge of the curriculum become invaluable during a time of change. When our students are citing advertisements thinking that they are valid news stories, the need for our services in selecting and providing curriculum-related websites is critical. Legacy materials in the form of books are expensive, and creating a balanced print collection is a budgetary challenge for many school librarians. Selecting materials for inclusion in a digital library, with the exception of purchasing subscription databases, is free. Materials no longer suitable for inclusion can be deleted with one click, and they are available to our students, administrators, and faculty on a 24/7 basis (Craver 19).

Unlike conventional libraries where the print collection needs to be housed within a designated footprint, thus limiting the number of volumes that can be acquired, the procurement of free websites has no limits. An important aspect of the collection development policy for the library's population demographic should be that the majority be full text and interactive whenever possible (Craver 19). While the former policy goal is more easily achievable, the latter may also be found at some outstanding humanities and physical sciences sites. Subscribing to LibGuides provides an easy-to-use format for presenting and annotating the sites and, more importantly, allows school librarians to provide course-specific lists of free and subscription-based sources on one or more easily accessible pages (Davidson-Heller). Pay a virtual visit to the Harker School Library Portal and the Wheeler School LibGuides for inspiration.

Reference books are being replaced in school libraries with eCollections and by students successfully performing Internet searches that provide answers to superficial specific queries. However, many free useful reference sources should be included in a digital library that will supplement the print collection and be available long after a conventional school library has closed for the day. Annually scan the list of Best Free Reference Websites for an annotated group of new ones. If constructing a digital library for the first time, browse through the site's combined index for additional ones. In 2017 this excellent resource included Data.gov, containing government statistics on subjects ranging from society, economics, science, and technology; Wonderpolis, featuring full-text articles and 1,800 questions traditionally posed by children; and The First Amendment Library complete with an interactive timeline, articles, and a searchable database of 900 First Amendment–related Supreme Court decisions ("2017 Annual List of . . .").

Since students will continue to initiate any information searches with Google, place links to Google Scholar, Trends, the advanced search option, searching tips, YouTube, Maps, and Earth in the online reference section. Instruct them in the additional features, and promote Google's time-saving applications. Collect full-text and, if possible, interactive websites in the arts. Photography, art, and crafts books are expensive to purchase and not as widely used as other parts of the collection. Museum sites regularly sponsor interactive tours of their latest exhibit and provide an opportunity for students to go on a virtual visit if they are unable to tour the conventional one. Collecting websites about the arts widens a user's vision of the world and can stimulate creativity. College information, particularly about financial aid, is of ever-growing importance, and providing links to financial aid resources, tips on interviewing, free College Board sample test sites, and tutoring assistance is essential at the secondary school library level. During application time, alert the college counseling department to these links. Plan to attend a College Night and publicize them to parents and students.

Just as school librarians need links to the latest research concerning school library science, so do administrators with education. Conduct a brief interview with administrators to determine what type of studies they deem helpful when meeting with a parent, board of education members, or a superintendent. Establish a monthly awareness service for them, and forward them relevant links and then maintain it within the digital library collection. As students advance in foreign language classes, they complete research assignments on the geography, culture, and history of foreign countries. Most of the information is required to be in the language they are studying. Finding valid and reliable sites in French, Spanish, and other foreign languages can be a challenge for foreign language instructors. Supplying ones that they can easily refer to in class and that their students can access 24/7 is providing an invaluable service.

One of the richest sources of free websites to mine exists in the social sciences and the humanities. Meeting Common Core Standards requires students to read deeply and think critically using evidence from original texts and primary sources to formulate their own questions about the material ("Common Core State Standards . . ."). Obtain a list of all the texts being taught from the curriculum director or manager of the school's book store and search for free, full-text websites that contain literary criticism, primary documents, and data that support the texts.

Publicize their presence on the school library's website at faculty and departmental meetings. Use the library's Twitter, Facebook, and other social media sites to publicize it to students (Craver 83).

Sites relating to science are also abundant on the Internet. Search for interactive ones in the sciences because they illustrate concepts more clearly than text. View HHMI Biointeractive for numerous sites related to teaching biology, and Bozeman Science Resources that furnish standards-aligned videos for teaching courses including AP chemistry, physics, earth science, and environmental science (Freeman).

Assistance with homework, especially after school hours, is readily available even if the school district does not subscribe to online tutoring services. It is usually securable by obtaining a card to the local public library. Students can log on during prescribed times and receive help from a local public librarian or be connected to an online tutoring service through the public library system. The Internet also contains some excellent homework help sites that bear inclusion in the school's digital library, such as Khan Academy, Study Geek, Fact Monster, P.J. Pinchbeck's Homework Helper, and Common Core Works (Dower).

While the sky is the only limit for creating the free section of an online library, school librarians will still need to create a collection development policy similar to the one that librarians presently use for print materials. As our students migrate from pages to pixels, it is critical that we supply them with quality resources that replicate the print ones that they formerly accessed in equal depth and scope. Choosing the correct medium to meet their information needs will be challenging for librarians since they already prefer digital formats. For specific courses, school librarians will need to instruct and demonstrate to students when analog materials are still the best resource to meet their information needs (Johnson 71–72).

In the conventional library print materials can be promoted and displayed easily on the tops of shelves, tables, and other areas as in a bookstore. The contents of a digital library also need to be marketed to students, faculty, administrators, and parents but in a different fashion. Building reliance on the school's digital library for librarian-designed, resource-based units creates repetitive opportunities for use of it and new electronic acquisitions to be highlighted. Our user population, however, is being bombarded with information at a rate that is stressing their tolerance levels for any more of it (Johnson 173).

Choosing specific means of delivery is probably better than sending out general announcements. Biology teachers are probably not interested in learning that the school library has just acquired the National Security Archive database as they are in receiving notice about the addition of the HHMI Biointeractive site. Delivering specific digital library information at the point of need will probably merit more attention and possible use than posting generic announcements (Lepczyk).

MANAGING IN A TIME OF CHANGE

Managing a school library has assumed another dimension in a period of change. It requires overseeing the successful operation of a reconfigured conventional library and growing digital library. Positioning the school library's programs and services at the center of the school community involves diplomatic negotiations among competing interests and departments. It means developing a management "can-do" style characterized by optimism and a sense of purpose that encourages users to constantly seek our assistance for their technological, intellectual, and instructional needs.

Creating cave spaces for immersive reading and quiet study and room for collaborative work that is sometimes noisy and physically active best suits a flexible administrative style. Students are so addicted to their smart devices that our libraries have to be bold in our management approaches to wean them to our credible resources and judicious expenditure of their time (Johnson 114). Whenever possible, develop a culture of "Yes" where all staff are trained to assist everyone in the school with their information needs. Empower staff members to be flexible when interpreting policies regarding noise, food in the library, or neglecting to sign up when bringing a class (Middleton 32). Manage to solve problems rather than cause them. If a faculty member has an emergency and moving classes temporarily to the library will alleviate the conflict, agree to it (Middleton 34).

Build a future-ready library by training staff to troubleshoot common technology problems such as logging on to printers, accessing the school network or portal, uploading and downloading software programs, and using makerspace tools. Charge them with watching for emerging technology trends and alerting others within the department. Introduce them to the American Library Association's Center for the Future of Libraries and The Digital Shift, a blog on new media. If there is sufficient funding, send a staff member to the annual Computers in Libraries Conference. It features an entire conference track devoted to school libraries and technology with expert, practitioner presenters (King 55). Produce some "stretch goals" for staff members that encourage them to move beyond their comfort zones. Their progress may be rewarding and energizing for the entire department. Just as librarians bestow kudos on students for excellent work, recognize staff and faculty members who have contributed to the library's programs and services. When credit is being given, accept it as a team. It will give staff members a buy-in for future projects because they know that their contributions will be recognized as well (Middleton 33).

Over the years our job description has evolved, and it will continue to do so as technology makes significant inroads into how we acquire, access, and deliver information to students, faculty, and administrators. By applying some of the trend analysis techniques referred to in Chapter 1, school librarians should be able to remain on top of many major technology trends. Maintaining control over legacy and digital resources provides the opportunity to achieve influence and power within our organizations. Curating information for our students and faculty regarding new technologies gives us new organization and management opportunities. Offering a webinar on how to incorporate student-response systems into lessons and demonstrating how they provide faster instructional feedback and reduce grading time is a means to manage an emerging technology and become the arbiter of knowledge about it. Designing an online course for faculty or interested students about how to use and implement a new technology or use the library's databases more effectively is another way to manage school libraries for power and influence (Hennig 85–87).

If there is one department where relations constantly need to be positively fostered, it is the technology department. Although school librarians hold all the cards with regard to information resources, the technology department controls the distribution of equipment, network bandwidth, data security, and the daily successful operation of technology within the school. Their cooperation and support for the school library's programs and services are essential to its success (Johnson 61). Although both departments may convene their own meetings, it is critical that the communication channels between members of this kingpin department and the school library be positively maintained. Placing a permanent member of the department at each other's meetings and planning sessions can ensure mutual progress and success for the entire school community. Each department has the opportunity to explain how students need to safely access and use online information on a 24/7 basis (Johnson 61). While a merger of these departments does not seem in the cards for school libraries at present, it may be in the future depending upon economic and employment trends.

In 2013 Hamilton College in New York merged its college library and technology service departments and formed a Library and Information Services Department. College administrators believed that it positioned the school to better support the growing digital library collection of subscription databases and free websites. In this merger's case, both departments were located in the same building and simply moved staffers with overlapping responsibilities closer to enable them to work together. Everyone retained their titles, but the group worked as one with two separate leaders. The plan to merge was based on the identification of synergies between both departments regarding teaching students' information literacy skills. College administrators believed that the two departments could be natural partners (Straumsheim).

The Meadows School serving pre-K–12 students in Las Vegas, Nevada, has also merged their library and technology departments and designed an integrated library and technology curriculum to teach the following: "creativity and innovation; communication and collaboration; research and information fluency; critical thinking, problem solving, and decision making; digital citizenship and technology operations concepts" ("The Meadows School . . .").

The opportunity for a merger or co-residence arrangement of these two departments in a reconfigured conventional library needs to be diplomatically explored for future organization and management purposes. The learning goals of both departments are similar in many respects. In the future, school librarians will manage a space that will be the center for information and knowledge, digital citizenship, resource-based learning, collaboration, and advanced literacy. It may contain a robot who is reading a story to a group of children, a place to experience diving to the depths of the sea within a virtual reality program, or a cave space for snuggling up with a book. Whether it is renamed a learning commons, information center, or library and technology commons, it will continue to be a space for students to create, perform, and share information with one another in a variety of media formats. Managing this type of space will be exciting because for students it will assume the role of a "third space"—neither home nor school. It will be a place where young people live and consider it their space (Loertscher and Koechlin E4).

> **Questions**
>
> 1. Should a school library reflect the school's culture? Why or Why not?
> 2. When schools undergo significant technological changes, how does it make various departments vulnerable?
> 3. Does a digital library require different marketing and promotion techniques?
> 4. Discuss the pros and cons for combining the school library and technology departments.
> 5. In the future, do you think school librarians can master all the new technologies that will reside in our libraries?

REFERENCES

Almquist, Arne J. and Sharon G. Almquist. 2017. *Intrapreneurship Handbook for Librarians: How to Be a Change Agent in Your Library*. Santa Barbara, CA: Libraries Unlimited.

Arbuthnott, Katherine D. and Andrea Scerbe. 2016. "Goal Framing in Public Issues and Action Decisions." *Analysis of Social Issues and Public Policy*. 16(1): 175–192.

Cialdini, Robert B. 1984. *Influence: Social Psychology in Action*. New York: William Morrow.

Collins, Jim. 2009. *How the Mighty Fall: And Why Some Companies Never Give In*. New York: Random House.

"Common Core Standards Initiative." 2010. Available at: http://www.corestandards.org.

Craver, Kathleen W. 2002. *Creating Cyber Libraries: An Instructional Guide for School Library Media Specialists*. Santa Barbara, CA: Libraries Unlimited.

Davidson-Heller, Karen. May 7, 2016. "LibGuides: A Compelling Tool for Learning." Massachusetts Library Association. Available at: https://www.maschoollibraries.org/newsletter/libguides-a-compelling-tool-for-learning.

Dower, Erin. 2018. "Top 10 Free Homework Help Websites." Familyeducation.com. Available at: https://www.familyeducation.com/school/top-10-free-homework-help-websites.

Evans, Robert. 2010. "Change Is What It Means." Available at: http://www.rodelfoundationde.org/wp-content/uploads/2014/03/Change-Is-What-It-Means_Dr-Robert-Evans.pdf.

Freeman, Brandie. March 19, 2018. "The 30 Best Science Websites for Grades K-12." Available at: https://www.weareteachers.com/best-science-websites.

Fullan, Michael. 1991. *The New Meaning of Educational Change*. New York: Teachers College Press.

Grimes, Andrew J. October 1978. "Authority, Power, Influence and Social Control: A Theoretical Synthesis." *Academy of Management Review*. 3(4): 724–735.

Hartzell, Gary N. 2003. *Building Influence for the School Librarian: Tenets, Targets, and Tactics*. 2nd ed. Santa Barbara, CA: Libraries Unlimited.

"Helping-Profession in English." Accessed October 25, 2018. Available at: https://glosbe.com/en/en/helping%20profession.

Hennig, Nicole. 2017. *Keeping Up with Emerging Technologies: Best Practices for Information Professionals*. Santa Barbara, CA: Libraries Unlimited.

Johnson, Doug A. 2013. *The Indispensable Librarian: Surviving and Thriving in School Libraries in the Information Age*. 2nd ed. Santa Barbara, CA: Linworth.

Kaplan, Robert D. January/February 2007. "A Historian for Our Time." *The Atlantic*. Available at: https://www.theatlantic.com/magazine/archive/2007/01/a-historian-for -our-time/305562.

King, David Lee. May 2018. "Future Proofing Your Library." *American Libraries*. Available at: https://americanlibrariesmagazine.org/2018/05/01/futureproofing-your -library-technology.

Klinger, Don A. et al. 2009. *Exemplary School Libraries in Ontario*. Ontario Library Association. Available at: https://www.accessola.org/web/Documents/OLA/Divisions /OSLA/Exemplary-School-Libraries-in-Ontario.pdf.

Lance, Keith Curry. March 2018. "School Librarian, Where Art Thou?" *School Library Journal*. Available at: https://www.slj.com/?detailStory=school-librarian-art-thou.

Lepczyk, Tim. 2013. "Marketing and Market Research for Digital Library Collections." Eduhacker.com. Available at: http://www.eduhacker.net/libraries/digital-library -marketing-market-research.html.

Loertscher, David V. and Carol Koechlin. March/April 2014. "Climbing to Excellence." *Knowledge Quest*. 42(4): E1–E10.

Long, Cindy. December 6, 2017. "Not Your Grandfather's School Library." *neaToday*. Available at: http://neatoday.org/2017/12/06/not-your-grandfathers-school-library.

"The Meadows School Library & Technology." n.d. Available at: https://www.themead owsschool.org/academics/library-technology.

Middleton, Kathy L. 2017. *Yes! On Demand: How to Create a Winning Customized Library Service*. Santa Barbara, CA: Libraries Unlimited.

Miller, Keith. 2019. "How Important Was Oil in World War II?" Available at: https:// historynewsnetwork.org/article/339.

Oberg, Dianne. Summer 2009. "Libraries in Schools: Essential Contexts for Studying Organizational Change and Culture." *Library Trends*. 58(1): 9–25.

Palfrey, John. 2015. *BiblioTech: Why Libraries Matter More Than Ever in the Age of Google*. New York: Basic Books.

Scheeren, William O. 2015. *Technology Handbook for School Librarians*. Santa Barbara, CA: Libraries Unlimited.

Straumsheim, Carl. December 4, 2015. "Library Bound." Inside Higher Education. Available at: https://www.insidehighered.com/news/2015/12/04/how-and-why-hamilton -college-merged-library-it.

Sullivan, Margaret. 2013. *Library Spaces for 21st-Century Learners*. Chicago: American Association of School Librarians.

"2017 Annual List of Best Free Reference Websites." 2017. Available at: https://www .rusaupdate.org.

Waters, Tony and Dagmar Waters. 2015. *Weber's Rationalism and Modern Society: New Translations on Politics, Bureaucracy, and Social Stratification*. New York: Palgrave MacMillan.

"Why Are Digital Research Skills So Important for College Students?" 2015. Available at: https://www.quora.com/why-are-digital-research-skills-so-important-for-college -students.

9

A Summons for Survival

With calls for closing libraries because the Internet is sufficient to satisfy all students' information needs, it is natural to pose some questions. Are school libraries on the brink of extinction? Will conventional libraries disappear to be replaced with remote access to eBooks and online databases administered by educational technologists or digital librarians? Will technology accelerate so quickly that answers to reference questions and other information needs can be responded to by a form of algorithmic-driven artificial intelligence? Is virtual reality going to become the main content delivery platform within the next five years? In a time of rapid change, these types of questions are not going to grant school librarians years to debate and respond with appropriate action. The future is now, and school librarians must prepare for it by anticipating the trends occurring with technology, the economy, employment, education, and instruction.

During the coming decade, conventional school libraries will appear very different from today's physical libraries and will be offering programs and services based on data, algorithms, and machine learning. The potential for school libraries is exciting, but to survive in this time of acceleration will require significant changes and adjustments. New instructional and organizational strategies must be developed if school librarians are to survive in the coming years. School librarians have outlasted many economic ups and downs in the previous decades, but the continued existence of our profession has never been as challenged as today. Americans are facing a technological revolution that is moving at an alarming pace. School administrators feel pressure to respond to it by replacing members of our profession with educators who can provide demonstrated expertise with technology and integrate it successfully into school curricula. Many administrators remain unaware of the essential role that our reading programs play with increasing school achievement and do not realize that educational technologists are not qualified to provide them.

Parents are rightfully concerned about the urgent need for their children to obtain education beyond high school and how the growing inequality among Americans is a threat to their children's economic and social welfare. They are also awakening to how technology is affecting their children's attention spans and ability to interact socially with one another and are becoming concerned about their compulsion to stay perpetually connected to their smart devices.

School librarians have been issued a summons for survival in a time of rapid change. Never before have we become so essential to our parent institutions. Our library programs and services are instructionally and democratically imperative if schools are to furnish students with the information literacy skills, training, and knowledge that they must acquire to gain remunerative employment and security in America.

My vision for school libraries is filled with hope and promise. Despite the significant changes already appearing with technology, the economy, education, and society, I believe that we have been granted a unique opportunity to survive and thrive in the coming decade. Our organizational charge is to position school libraries as absolutely fundamental to the goals and objectives of educational institutions. We must become the hubs for information access to legacy and digital media, dissemination, and instruction. Our educational mission is to design programs, project-based units, and services that assist faculty to instruct and help students to learn.

With change accelerating in all these areas, it is critical that school librarians gain power and influence within schools to redesign their libraries and to confront the challenges of this tumultuous time. School librarians who fail to anticipate their futures will probably have it shaped for them by stressed administrators, anxious parents, and insistent students. If school librarians do not address this exceptional mandate to change their libraries, they may well face extinction as a profession.

ACTION 1

School librarians must demonstrate competence and proficiency in employing all types of technology for instructional purposes with students, faculty, administrators, and parents to thrive in a time of change.

In a time of reduced budgets and staffing cuts, school librarians without demonstrable technology skills are vulnerable to administrators who need educators to explain, operate, and integrate various instructional technologies into the curriculum. More importantly, we must be able to show that new technologies enhance learning and frequently save faculty time as justification for future acquisitions. Developing full competency with various technologies may involve taking classes and attending workshops about new technologies and how to appropriately incorporate their use into the curriculum. School librarians should never miss an opportunity to attend new technology sessions. When members of the technology department are hosting trial demonstrations of new equipment or software, school librarians need to be the first to attend. If members of the technology department plan to visit sites to determine whether to purchase new hardware or software, school librarians should make sure that they are included.

Being competent with technology will entail showing teachers how to employ it in their classes by offering mini-workshops and demonstrations for specific departments. Even when schools have technology departments with members who can assist and instruct the school community, our skill level with current and new technologies must remain equal to that of technology department members. It is these departments that encroach on our perceived role in the school. Regardless of the courses school librarians have taken in children's and young adult literature, instructional design, and reference services, it will be the competence that we consistently demonstrate with various technologies that will endear us to administrators, faculty, parents, and students. Our technology competence will also attract faculty to the school library for assistance with project-based learning units, reading guidance, and information literacy skills. It will also invite consultation from students who require assistance for school assignments. Faculty members and students will develop a confidence concerning our ability to handle technology emergencies and show them the ins and outs of new software programs, including all of its bells and whistles.

Demonstrating competence with existing and new technologies creates inroads for school librarians to collaborate with faculty members and will dispel the associative reading stereotypes that many administrators have traditionally held of school librarians. It also boosts the reputation of school librarians with students who, more than other generations, respect expertise in this area. Knowing how to relevantly employ technology with classes, faculty, and parents creates an aura that the profession of school librarianship is contemporary and more than ready to meet all challenges during a time of change.

ACTION 2

School librarians need to serve and actively participate on committees that make decisions concerning future technology acquisitions and implementation.

Possessing competency with technology needs to be coupled with an expertise in anticipating trends to avoid making some of the costly business decisions of the past. Our access to online databases arms us with the ability to research trends, apply trend analysis techniques, and alert the powers-that-be of their pros and cons. Providing a consumer-type research service for committee members creates a dependency on our professional expertise for all types of information beyond just technology. It makes our participation at technology, curriculum, and strategic planning committees crucial.

Obtaining seats on these important committees is not guaranteed, but it can be a reciprocal placement for previous reference or instructional work performed on behalf of administrators, department chairs, and faculty members. When graciously accepting kudos for providing reference assistance or instructing a class, school librarians need to ask for seats on these committees if they are not already assigned. Having a role to play on these committees provides school librarians with the opportunity to widen their sphere of influence for future consultation and advice and place library goals and objectives at the forefront. It also gives us the chance to learn of future staffing and department changes before it is too late to respond to them.

ACTION 3

School librarians need to develop evidence-based instructional practices and programs that will enable them to justify future investment by schools and other government, corporate, and nonprofit institutions.

The economic tea leaves do not augur well for solutions to the fiscal problems plaguing most school libraries. Increasing debt, ranging from personal to national and corporate, will probably make it unlikely that school libraries are going to be the recipients of adequate funding within the coming years. To maintain many library programs and services will necessitate seeking funding from traditional and alternative sources. Obtaining a yearly budget increase for the library will need to be justified by data culled from local and national library research. School librarians will need to link project-based learning, voluntary reading programs, and information literacy instruction to increased student achievement. If we are to apply for additional funding in the form of grants, evidence will be requested that demonstrates that our instructional programs result in improved student abilities to (1) correctly identify information needs, (2) select relevant information from legacy and digital media, (3) confirm the credibility of sources, and (4) integrate and synthesize information into an accepted media format. Nationally conducted studies show the correlation of a qualified librarian in a school library positively relates to increased student achievement and will be useful in formulating proposals for continued and additional funding. Locally derived data revealing similar findings, however, will probably carry more weight with school superintendents and administrators.

School librarians need to collect relevant data and conduct similar studies with their student populations. Mining data from our online public access catalogs (OPACs) can provide us with local evidence to reinforce the results of national studies pertaining to the reading and school achievement connection in our specific schools. Local data showing a similar correlation between those students who read copiously and increased school achievement can be disseminated on students' progress reports. Connecting the quantity of material that a child is reading and their scores on national reading assessments provides an opportunity to communicate regularly with parents about a child's progress and encourages parents to not only monitor a child's reading at home but also promote it during library-sponsored sustained silent reading (SSR) periods.

ACTION 4

School librarians must use newly configured hybrid libraries to provide students and their parents with information concerning changes in employment opportunities and the need for perpetual retraining and education.

The employment picture for almost every occupation is not promising. Even those who obtain education beyond high school are predicted to experience job insecurities as machine learning and artificial intelligence encroach upon any aspect of job descriptions involving routinized work. Constantly emphasizing the need for lifelong learning in the form of reading, retraining, and enrolling in higher education is the responsibility of school librarians because of the evidence that we possess showing its correlation with economic viability. We need to furnish students with materials that assist them in preparing for entrance exams, such as the SAT or ACT. Sponsoring speakers who are willing to discuss the positive and negative aspects of their careers is not just the responsibility of the counseling department. It is an area where our libraries can be associated with lifelong learning, which is one of our profession's enduring values. Explaining to parents why students need to obtain education and occupational training beyond high school should be our responsibility. It provides us with the opportunity to justify our reading programs and the instructional role that we have with information literacy. Showing our students comparative data that reflect the relationship between obtaining education beyond high school and potential earnings may help motivate them.

ACTION 5

School librarians must develop programs, services, and hybrid libraries that are reflective of students' cultural, social, and behavioral needs.

Responding to the social, cultural, and behavioral trends that we are already observing in our students is going to be challenging in the years to come. Their decided preference for all things digital places many of them at risk for problems concerning distraction, social isolation, and a declining ability to empathize with others. Their constant need to be connected to social media makes them susceptible to filter bubbles, online harassment, and influence by companies that have neither their educational nor psychological well-being at heart.

One positive trend occurring with the social and cultural changes that school librarians are witnessing is a growing movement among the medical profession, school administrators, and parents that our students need age level–based, sustainable technology use guidelines. School librarians must be at the forefront of their development and implementation. We are perfectly positioned to provide school board members, administrators, and parents with not only the latest research concerning the use and abuse of various technologies but also examples of sustainable technology use policies that have been successfully enacted in other school districts.

As empathy continues to decline with the population demographic that we serve, school librarians need to respond by providing them with programs that help evoke it. With a hybrid library at the ready, our programs can include book talks, book trailers, book clubs, speakers, authors, movies, videos, discussion groups, role-playing activities, games, readers' theater, and mixed reality software.

While members of the iGeneration seem to exhibit a growing acceptance of differences regarding gender identities and sexual orientation and a need for inclusivity, school librarians must play a significant role in acquiring, promoting, and displaying digital and print materials that support students at risk for any type of discrimination. We can also be responsive to many of our students' need for a physical space that feels warm, welcoming, and safe for them.

Creating a hybrid library that allocates space for quiet study, reflection, and even daydreaming must be a component of any hybrid library design process. School libraries have always served as temporary havens for students with busy schedules, personal problems, and those simply seeking a place to dwell. School librarians must make certain that we have constructed similar spaces when contemplating any modifications to conventional school libraries.

ACTION 6

School librarians must take primary responsibility for designing project-based learning units that incorporate information literacy skills in all subject areas.

While collaboration with teachers has been advocated for the past twenty years in school libraries, it has usually been challenging to execute because of the characteristics exhibited by members of the teaching profession. They are reluctant to open their classroom doors to librarians and resistant to bringing their students to the library for instruction. Administrators are also uninformed about the instructional role of school librarians. With the loss of so many school librarian positions to digital librarians, instructional coordinators, and educational technologists, school librarians must assume the primary responsibility for designing, teaching, and assessing project-based learning units.

Obtaining teachers' consent to integrate project-based instructional units into their curricula is significant, but it is only the first step. Faced with inflexible teaching schedules, teachers are truly challenged to find the time to produce syllabi, formulate questions, create relevant subject-based activities, and decide how to assess the results. If school librarians are going to survive in a time of change, they must take responsibility for all aspects of instructional design. Consulting teachers for brief interviews regarding projects' learning objectives, duration, and learning modes should probably only take one planning period. From that point on, the school librarians need to employ the hybrid library's resources and appropriate technologies to create questions, choose relevant databases, design appropriate activities, and create evaluation tools. School librarians must learn to rely only briefly upon teachers as subject experts and consultants for sample questions and proposed activities.

A school librarian–designed unit provides us with the opportunity to integrate information literacy skills into all project-based instruction and other types of resource-based education. Within these units lies the ability to teach students how to determine the credibility of a source, its relevance to the topic, when print materials are more suitable, how to recognize information bias, and other important principles of information literacy. Integrating these skills into a subject-based unit makes them relevant to students and hopefully becomes part of their mental checklist when approaching any academic subject that requires information seeking.

Coteaching units is vitally important even though school librarians have been almost solely responsible for their design. Teachers must recognize that they are the subject experts and thus responsible for various decisions pertaining to students' specific questions. They must be helped to feel comfortable sharing the stage with school librarians in presenting the material. This phase of unit design may require additional tact and diplomacy on the part of school librarians, since research shows that some teachers can feel threatened stepping off the stage for even part of the class. Designing an acceptable assessment rubric will assist both parties to grade finished products more quickly, distribute the results, and if problems appear, readjust the unit accordingly.

Index

A/B testing, 17–18, 37, 52, 174
Aberystwyth University and A.I., 43
Achievement levels, 127–129
Active open-mindedness, 3
Addiction: attachment formation, 172–173; behavioral science, 171–172; future technologies, 173
Aging of the population, 70
ALA Center of the Future of Libraries, 216
Algorithms: abuse potential, 21–22, 31; educational use, 20; formation, 19–20; GAN (generative adversarial network), 44–45; Google types, 41; role of school librarians, 22
AlphaGo, ix, 2
Alternative Face, 44
Amazon: convenience factor, 172; earnings, 105; eBook sales, 55–56; employment role, 103, 133; factory robots, 31, 95; monopoly, 15, 49, 84–85, 104; search style, 25; taxes, 85; voice activated bots, 30
Amazon Mechanical Turk, 103
Anti-cyberbullying software, 170–171
API (application programming interface), 28–29
Artificial intelligence: area of development, 41; dangers, 43–44; diagnostic abilities, 42–43; education, 42; forms of learning, 41; GAN (generative adversarial network), 44–45; Khan Academy, 42; school libraries, 42–43
AT&T, xiv–xv, 28
Attention literacy, 174–175
Attention span, 162
Augmented reality, 45–46, 47–49, 173

Aural literacy, 190
Automation: effects on workers, xv; industrial robots, 95; jobs at risk, xv
Availability heuristic, 9
Awesome Box, 27

Belief bias, 9–10
Big data: benefits, 17–18; characteristics, 16; drawbacks, 16–18; school libraries, 19, 35; uses, 17–19, 28
Big Five: dominance, 84–85, 104–105; education role, 86–87; influence, 85; monopoly, 84–85; privacy, 85; taxes, 85; wealth, 84
Black Monday, 93
Blended learning, 143–144
Book industry: eBooks, 54–56, 214; future, 59; status, xi, 16; studies, 57–58
Bots, 29–30, 192
Bozeman Science Resources, 215
Broward County School District, 6
Bureaucratic dependency map, 202

Cambrian age, 1
Captology, 172
Castro Valley Unified College, 46
Cell phones. *See* Smartphones
CEO earnings, 77
Change effects of, 203–204
Charter schools: establishment of, 137–138; research studies, 139; virtual, 138–139
Child poverty, xiii–xvi, 76, 156, 158
Cincinnati Public Schools, 33
CIPHER, 6–7
Cloud computing, 22–23
Collaborative learning, 145–147

College costs, 81–82

College Preparatory School, 146

Committee membership, 223–224

Common Core Standards: adoption and repeal potential, 131, 137; content need, 126, 130; critical thinking skills, 192; implementation and school librarians, 6, 147, 181, 205, 214–215

Content creators, 164

Contingent labor force, 101–102

Council on Library and Information Sources, 26

Credential inflation, 110

Critical thinking skills, xii, 10, 88, 115–116, 142, 184–185, 192–193

Cushing Academy, 54–55

Cyberbullying, xiii, 169–170

Data literacy, 189

Deep learning, 142–143

Deficit, 71

Demographics, 121

Depression, xiii, 167–171

Deskilling, 108–109

Digital education, 134, 136–137

Digital library construction, 212–215

Digital Public Library of America, 26

Digital shift, 216

Digital use divide, 115–117, 159

Distraction reduction apps, 174

Dual enrollment programs, 140–141

Early College High School Initiative (ECHSI), 140

Early college programs, 139–140

Ebeling Elementary School, 51

Economic climate, 69

Economic mobility, 75–78

Economic phases, 94

Economic polls, 69

Economic progress, 69

Edpuzzle, 135

Education: dilemma, 133–134; funding, 72; income, 110–111

EduStar, 18

El Capitan High School, 36

Empathy, 165–166, 169–170, 225

Employment: counterintuitive trends, 108–109; future jobs, 113–115; future of, xv, 104–106; government responsibility, 114–115; impact of advanced technologies, 104–107; optimistic viewpoints, 107–108; robots, 96–96; routinized work, 96

Engage NY, 195

E-reading research, 57–58

Ethical literacy, 190–191

Explorez Project, 48

Evaluation of information skills, 187–188

Every Student Succeeds Act (ESSA), 72

Evidence-based practice: Common Core Standards, 129, 195; employment, 112; faculty, 38, 52; PISA tests, 130; school librarians, 73, 147, 224–225; technology, 132, 136

Facebook: addiction, 172; employment, xv; fake news, 191; monopoly, 18, 84–85, 88; research studies, 166–167, 171, 174; school librarians, 88, 133; screen time, 160–161; surveillance, 28

FearNot!, 170

Feedback, 27

Fox versus hedgehog, xii, xvi, 2

Fremont Rider's Law, 14–15

F.U.T.U.R.E., 8–9

Future: forecasting, xi, xii, xv, xvii; qualities of, 2, 3; rationale, 2; teachable skills, 4–5; techniques, 5

Future Shock (Alvin Toffler), ix–x

Future-ready school library, 210–211, 216

GAN (generative adversarial network), 45

GitHub, 7

Global education competition, 129

Globalization, 98–99

Go, ix, 27

Google: dominance, 86; influence, 86; trust in, 86

Google Cardboard Viewer, 50

Google Data Studio, 197

Google Expeditions, 50

Google Hummingbird, 41

Google NGram Viewer, 16

Google Pigeon, 41

Google Possum, 41

Google Prediction, 28

Google Scholar, 214

Google Translate, 40–41

Google Trends, 16

Great American Read, 194

Harvard University Library Innovation Lab, 26–27

Hempfield Area High School Library, 25
HHMI Biointeractive, 215
High tech versus high touch, 53, 135
High-achieving countries, 130
Hololens, 46
Horizon Report, xvii
Hotseat, 36
Hybrid library, 210–212, 224–226

iGeneration: allure of screen activities,
160–161; anxiety, 162, 167–168;
attention literacy, 174–175;
characteristics, 153–155; cyberbullying,
169; demographics, 156–157;
depression, 167–169; distraction, 162;
empathy, 165–166; inclusivity
conundrum, 155–156; information
literacy, 186–187; learning
characteristics, 184–185; loneliness,
161, 165–166; multitasking, 162–163;
platform preferences, 160; screen
activities, 158–160; sleep deprivation,
168; social media abuse, 161–162;
suicide, 168–169; unhappiness, 166
Illiteracy, xvi, 120, 122
Inclusivity conundrum, 155–156, 225
Inequality: income, xvi 15, 78, 124;
reactions to, 75–76; significance, 80;
students, 78
Information literacy skills, 186–188, 208,
224–225
Information-seeking skills, 191–194, 197
Instruction: collaboration work, 116;
information-seeking skills, 116–117;
resource-based units, 116
Instructional role, 182–188
Insurgents in bureaucracies, 201
International Children's Digital Library,
26
Internet of Things (IoT), 33–35
Intrapreneurship, 205–206

Jawbone, 6
Jeopardy!, ix, 28, 98
Jobs, Steve, 171

Khan Academy, 42, 215

Lateral searches, 193
Learner multimodal analytics (LMS),
135–136
Learning commons concept, 210–211

Lie detection experiments, 192
Lifelique, 46
Lifelong learning, xiv–xv, 84, 111–113,
116
Literacy: arresting decline, 125; data, 122;
democracy, 127; inequality, 123–124;
reading score, 123; reduced pleasure
reading, 123; test of, 122
Low achievement cost, 128–129
LSTA (Library and Services and
Technology Acts), 72
Lumos Labs, 32

Machine learning, 27–28, 108–109
Magic Leap, 45
Make It Rain, 49
Managing accelerating change, 215–217
Meadows School, 217
Memory reading experiment, 194
Mentira, 48
Microsoft's Academic, 43
Minority students, xiii–xvi
Mixed realities, 45–47, 173
M-learning (mobile learning), 35–39
Moore's Law, 13
Music industry, x
Mythical Maze app, 49

NASA and virtual reality, 51
National debt, 70–71
Navigating organizational culture,
206–208
Nearpod, 51
Neural networks, 40–41
News evaluation sites, 193–194
Newspaper industry, x, 16, 193

Off-shoring versus re-shoring, 99–100
Online: charter schools, 138–139; chat, 27;
databases, 43; education, 132–133, 144;
games, 173–174; reading, 124; virtual
charter schools, 138–139
OPACs, 25
Oregon House Bill 2220, 7
Organization: decline stages, 203;
resistance, 209–210; support, 204–205,
208–209
Overqualified workers, 109

Parent involvement, 224–225
Parenting styles, 79
Personal debt, 73

PISA, 127, 129–130

PISA test, 127–130

Platforms, 24–26

Pokémon Go, xvi, 47

Polanyi's paradox, 39

Popup Picks, 3–4

Poverty: child, xiii–xvi, 76, 156, 158; definition, 74; food stamps, 76; homelessness, 158; minority students, xiii–xvi; neighborhoods, 156–157; re-shoring, 100; unemployment, 158

Project-based learning units, 145, 184–185, 188–189, 222–227

Public libraries, 73

Reading: administrative unawareness, 221; decline, 128; guidance, 195–196; immersive reading, 131, 132, 188–189, 194–196, 216; knowledge acquisition, 194–195; motivation studies, 196–197; use of legacy media, 163

Reinforcement learning, 41

Renton Prep Christian School, 46

Robots, 31–33, 96–97

SAT scores, 128

SAT test, 126–129

School: choice, 137, 141–142; funding, 80

School librarians: administrative acceptance, 183; artificial intelligence, 43–44; attention literacy, 174–175; augmented reality, 49–50; bots, 30; bureaucracies, 201; change agents, 203; cloud, 23–25; collaboration, 226–227; committee membership, 223–224; decline of, xv, 181, 203; digital learning, 132–133, 135; digital versus print, 59; distraction, 163; evidence-based practices, 224–225; iGeneration, 157–158, 169–171, 225–226; information literacy, 184–188; instructional role, 182; insurgency role, 201, 206–207, 209–210; intrapreneurship, 205; IoT, 34; lateral searching, 193; literacy, 126–127; multitasking, 163; project-based learning, 226–227; school choice, 141–142; screen activities, 161–162, 164–165; space configuration, 211–212; survival challenges, 220–221; technology employment, 221–222

School libraries: data collection, 73, 75; future-ready, 210–211; government, 114–115; hybrid libraries, 210–212, 224–226; inequality, 80–81; learning commons, 210–211; national debt, 72, 86; staffing, 19, 72, 75, 202, 204, 222–223; stagnant income effect, 74; value, 75

Screen time: addiction, 171–173; anxiety, 167–168; depression, 167–168; envy, 167; homework, 163; loneliness, 165–166; monitoring apps, 162; peer surveillance, 167; platform preferences, 160; teens, 58, 15; tweens, 58, 159; unhappiness, 166; usage differences, 159–160

Screenagers: Growing Up in the Digital Age, 58

Semantic Scholar, 43

Sentiment analysis, 16

ShelvAR, 49

Skill requirements, 110–111

Smart ID cards, 33–35

Smartphones, xi, 27, 159

Social mobility, 76

Socrative, 17

Space sharing, 212, 217

Spending per child, 79

Spheros, 31

Stagnant incomes, 73–74

Stanford History Education Group, 193

Suicide, xiii, 168–171

Supervised learning, 41

Survival actions, 222–227

Sustainable technology guidelines, 225

TeachAssist robots, 31

Teaching profession, 106–107

TeachLivE, 48

Technology: addictive qualities, 173; at-risk occupations, 96; costs to schools, 133–134; department, 217; digital education, 132–133; elements of, 13; employment of, 222–223; incursions, 95; research studies, 133–134; sustainable use guidelines, 164

Technology petting zoo, 211

Telecommunications industry, x

Test scores, 42

Textual literacy, 188

Time Well Spent, 174

Timelooper, 51

Transliteracy instruction, 188–191

Trend analysis, xvii, 1–10

Trending pedagogies, 142–147
Truck driving, 105–106
Trust Project, 193
Tuition costs, 81

Uber, 9–10, 103–104
Unemployment rate, 100–101
United States: demographics, 70;
   household wealth, 76
University of Nebraska College of
   Education and Human Sciences, 36
Unsupervised learning, 41

Virtual reality, 47–53, 173
Visual literacy, 189

Wages and education, 74–75
Washington, D.C., Public Libraries, 25–26
Washington Leadership Academy, 51
Watson, ix, 28, 98, 109
What Works Clearinghouse, 134
Workers' earnings, 74
Workforce trends, 97–98

Youngstown, Ohio jobs disaster, 93

About the Author

Kathleen W. Craver, PhD, is a school library consultant and the former head librarian at National Cathedral School in Washington, DC. Dr. Craver is the author of *School Library Media Centers in the 21st Century* (Greenwood, 1994); *Teaching Electronic Literacy* (Greenwood, 1997); *Using Internet Primary Sources to Teach Critical Thinking Skills in History* (Greenwood, 1999); *Creating Cyber Libraries* (Greenwood, 2002); *Term Paper Resource Guide to Nineteenth-Century U.S. History* (Greenwood, 2008); and *Developing Quantitative Literacy Skills in History and the Social Sciences* (Rowman & Littlefield, 2014).